DETROIT

KiDS

CATALOG

GREAT LAKES BOOKS

A complete listing of the books in this series can
be found at the back of this volume.

Philip P. Mason, Editor
Department of History
Wayne State University

Dr. Charles K. Hyde, Associate Editor
Department of History
Wayne State University

DETROIT

KiDS

CATALOG

A Family Guide for the 21st Century

Ellyce Field

WAYNE STATE UNIVERSITY PRESS • DETROIT

Manufactured in the United States of America.
04 03 02 01 00   5 4 3 2 1

Library of Congress Cataloging-in-Publication Data

Field, Ellyce, 1951-
    Detroit kids catalog : a family guide for the 21st
        century / Ellyce Field.
        p. cm. -- (Great Lakes books)
    Includes index.
    ISBN 0-8143-2829-6 (alk. paper)
        1. Detroit Region (Mich.)--Guidebooks. 2.
    Children--Travel--Michigan--Detroit Region--
    Guidebooks. I. Title. II Series.

    F574.D43 F54 2000
    917.74'340443--dc21

                                        00-020681

Designer: Mary Primeau

Sites listed were chosen by the author. No one paid
to be included in this book. Every effort was made to
be sure all information in this book was correct when
we went to press. However, hours, exhibits, prices,
and even locations change from time to time. So,
please call ahead.

To my husband,
Steve, my best friend,
for his love and support.

To my three sons,
Jordan, Andrew, and Garrett,
for their ideas and enthusiasm.

To my parents,
Belle and Chuck Ruben,
for teaching me to reach for my goals.

To my editors,
Kathy Wildfong and Alice Nigoghosian,
for their hard work and attention to detail.

To my research assistant,
Marjie Friedman,
for her conscientious and careful work.

Contents

14. Michigan at Work — Tours 419

Animals • Arts & Crafts • Clothing • Cultural •
Ecology • Farming • Fire & Police • Food •
Government • History • Industry • Media • Medical
Research • Mining • Natural Wonders • Sports •
Toys • Transportation • Utilities

15. Programs for the Schools 459

Animals • Arts & Crafts • Creative Writing • Crime
Prevention • Dance • Drug Education • Ecology •
Fitness • History • Living History • Magic • Music •
Performing Arts • Puppets • Recycling • Science •
Space • Storytelling • Theater • Transportation •
Values • Ventriloquist

Preface

Detroit Kids Catalog: A Family Guide for the 21st Century is the tenth anniversary edition of the Kids Catalog series. With this new 21st century edition of our family travel book, we are going back to our roots. Our very first family tour book, published in 1990, was called *Detroit Kids Catalog*.

Detroit Kids Catalog: A Family Guide for the 21st Century salutes Detroit's 300th birthday in 2001 by placing the focus on Detroit and 78 surrounding cities, all within 11 Michigan counties and the greater Windsor area. Most sites are approximately 120 miles, or a two-hour drive, from Detroit.

As we go to press, the landscape of downtown Detroit is changing dramatically. We watch in anticipation and amazement as Fox Town and the Woodward–Grand Circus corridor become home to the Tigers, and in 2002 the Lions, as well as a theater district boasting over seven venues and a new crop of restaurants. While casinos will also shape our city in the 21st century, the emphasis on family remains strong. Detroit's Cultural Center museums are thriving. The Detroit Institute of Arts and Detroit Science Center have instituted new, year-round family programming, and are now bringing in more traveling exhibits, including a line-up of just-released IMAX movies playing at the Detroit Science Center's IMAX Theatre. The Detroit Historical Museum has reinvented itself with high-tech, family-friendly exhibits and a hands-on history room just for children.

In Dearborn, three new sites have opened on the Henry Ford Museum/Greenfield Village campus. The Automotive Hall of Fame and Spirit of Ford celebrate the automobile industry's spirit of innovation with hands-on, audio-visual displays and demonstrations. At Henry Ford Museum's new IMAX Theatre, families can enjoy 3-D movies and IMAX films.

The new 12,000-square-foot indoor National Amphibian Conservation Center and the "Arctic Ring of Life," a new polar bear environment, have opened at the Detroit Zoo in Royal Oak. Cranbrook Institute of Science in Bloomfield Hills has expanded its exhibit space with a brand new addition that boasts both a giant mastodon and full-size Tyrannosaurus Rex skeleton. The popular Ann Arbor Hands-On Museum has also doubled its size.

Since the publication of the first *Detroit Kids Catalog,* a lot has happened in our family as well. The three little boys who used to accompany me on all my outings have grown up. Our oldest son, Jordan, is now in the middle of law school, and our twin sons, Andrew and Garrett, are sophomores at the University of Michigan.

I'm still writing about families for *The Detroit News,* contributing a weekly parenting feature and calendar of parenting events, in addition to my weekly family entertainment column and calendar, which has been running since 1987.

It's now time for your family to become Hometown Tourists as you explore new sites and revisit old favorites. I hope you use *Detroit Kids Catalog: A Family Guide for the 21st Century* often.

1
First Things First

TIP

Too much sibling fighting every time you get in the car? Try rotating older children to the front seat as one adult takes a turn in the back seat. And bring along a ton of toys, snacks, books, CDs, and tapes.

Things to Know

The secret to successful family outings is to PLAN AHEAD. Be sure to CALL AHEAD to verify times, prices, directions, and special events whenever you go anywhere with your kids. This way, you'll minimize disappointment and unnecessary frustration.

This chapter is designed to help you plan ahead and learn how to best use *Detroit Kids Catalog*. Listed are: publications that offer calendars of kids' events; telephone information numbers; emergency resources; information about transportation and tours; Canada and customs; Metro Detroit's best kid stuff; family memberships; birthday party sites; free sites; scout badge opportunities; and at the malls.

WEATHER AND CLOTHES

Detroit is famous for its changeable weather, its extremes and its surprises. When it isn't doing any of the above, it's safe to say: summer is hot; autumn is cool; winter is snowy cold, and spring is wet. So dress the kids in layers and throw an extra jacket or sweatshirt in the backseat. Take along a sun hat or visor in the summer and carry boots, hats, and mittens in the winter. I always used to carry a large shopping bag or a backpack to hold the layers as they were peeled off.

PUBLICATIONS

My family columns and calendars in *The Detroit News* highlight family entertainment and parenting events for the coming weekend and week. 313-222-2300. www.detnews.com

metroPARENT, a monthly parenting newspaper available by subscription, offers a monthly calendar of kids' events. 248-352-0990.

How to Use This Book

I wrote this book for busy parents who enjoy traveling around town with their kids, but have very little time to plan out a detailed adventure and would rather have all the information at their fingertips, with all the suggestions and pitfalls mentioned.

Chapters are arranged around a specific theme, for example, museums or parks. Sites are listed in alphabetical order. The most important information (address, phone, location, hours, admission, ages, plan, parking, lunch, and facilities) is listed. A short annotation describes the site and gives you its flavor.

Here are some important facts to remember:

Age designation of a particular site is based on my experience with my children, who when they were small, were some times very mature, cooperative travelers, but at other times very reluctant, irritable travelers! No one knows your children's needs, interests, and attention span better than you do, so use the age designation as a suggested guideline. However, please respect a specific age requirement for admittance to a site or performance.

Plan refers to how long you should plan on the visit taking. I've indicated *approximate* amounts of time by: "all day visit" (6+ hours), "half day visit" (4+ hours), "short visit" (2+ hours) and "under one hour." Keep in mind that the best laid plans often go awry. If your baby needs a nap, your guest has to get to the airport, or your children become cranky and hungry, your half day visit could turn into a short visit. Come back on a more relaxing day.

Lunch tells you where you can find food on the premises or nearby. If you're going out for the day, it doesn't hurt to pack a snack or a picnic lunch just in case the kids get hungry, which they always do, when you're lost or driving on the expressway.

Facilities includes information about stroller rental, bathrooms, and gift shops.

Chapters 8, 9, and 13 group sites by type or location. Because the sites in chapters 5, 6, 7, 10, 11, 12, 14, and 15 are so various, a brief description of the site or its activities—for instance, "Petting Farm" or "Music & Dance"—appears above the entry in these chapters.

Detroiters love their cars. Most of us have sturdy wheels and are not afraid to drive from here to there. For this reason, the chapters include sites in Southeastern Michigan, plus cities that are within a 2-hour drive (approximately 120 miles) from Detroit, such as Ann Arbor, Ypsilanti, East Lansing, Lansing, Jackson, Flint, and Port Huron.

Enjoy traveling with your kids. With each excursion, you'll develop a core of family memories and a love for Metro Detroit.

Telephone Information

GENERAL INFORMATION

Metropolitan Detroit Convention and Visitors Bureau Information Center: 313-202-1813
Metropolitan Detroit Convention and Visitors
    Bureau Main Office: 313-202-1800
    (open Monday–Friday)

Michigan Regional Tourist Associations:

Upper Peninsula: 906-774-5480, 1-800-562-7134, www.uptravel.com

West Michigan: 616-456-8557, 1-800-442-2084, www.wmta.org

Sunrise Side: 1-800-424-3022

Michigan Travel Bureau: 1-888-784-7328, www.michigan.org

Michigan Travel Bureau: TDD 1-800-722-8191 (for the hearing impaired)

Michigan State Chamber of Commerce: 517-371-2100 (for the name, address, and phone of a specific city's chamber of commerce), www.michamber.com

Sterling Heights Special Recreation Services (programs for children with disabilities): 810-977-6123, ext. 200

Sell Ticket Service (Ticket Broker): 248-262-1555

Time: 248-472-1212

Ticketmaster: 248-645-6666,
www.ticketmaster.com

Windsor Convention and Visitors Bureau:
519-255-6530, www.city.windsor.on.ca/cvb

EMERGENCY NUMBERS

Babysitting—Hourly Drop-Off:

My Place Just For Kids:
248-540-5702 (Birmingham)
810-247-KIDS (Sterling Heights)
248-737-5437 (West Bloomfield)

Dental:

District Dental Center: 313-871-3500

Tri-County Dental Health Council: 248-559-7767

Wayne County Medical Society: 313-567-1640,
wcns/@msms.org

Hospitals:

Beaumont Hospital, Royal Oak: 1-800-633-7377,
Emergency 248-551-2000

Bon Secours of Michigan, Grosse Pointe:
313-343-1000, Emergency 313-343-1605

Botsford General Hospital, Farmington Hills:
248-471-8000, Emergency 248-471-8556

Children's Hospital of Michigan, Detroit:
313-745-5437, Emergency 313-745-0113

Henry Ford Hospital, Detroit: 313-876-2600,
Emergency 313-916-1545

North Oakland Medical Center, Pontiac:
248-857-7200, Emergency 248-857-7257

Oakland General Hospital, Madison Heights:
248-967-7000, Emergency 967-967-7670

Providence Hospital, Southfield: 248-424-3000,
Emergency 248-424-3331

St. John Hospital, Detroit: Pediatric ER
313-343-3400

St. Joseph Mercy Hospital, Ann Arbor:
734-572-3456, Emergency 734-572-3000

St. Joseph Mercy Hospital, Pontiac:
248-858-3000, Emergency 248-858-3100,
Pediatric After Hours Center 248-858-3493

University of Michigan Medical Health Centers,
Ann Arbor: 734-936-4000,

Emergency 734-936-6662,
Pediatric Walk-In Clinic 734-936-4230

Medical Societies:

Oakland County Medical Society: 248-646-5400,
www.ocms-mi.org

Macomb County Medical Society: 810-790-3090,
www.mcms@msms.org

Wayne County Medical Society: 313-567-1640,
www.wcms/@msms.org

Police, Fire, EMS:

911 in Wayne, Oakland, Macomb, Washtenaw,
and Livingston Counties.

BOX OFFICE NUMBERS

The Ark, Ann Arbor: 734-761-1451

Boarshead Theatre, Lansing: 517-484-7805

Bonstelle Theatre, Detroit: 313-577-2960

Century Theatre, Detroit: 313-963-9800

Chrysler Theatre, Windsor: 1-800-387-9181

Cobo Arena, Detroit: 313-983-6616

Detroit Opera House, Detroit: 313-874-SING

Detroit Repertory Theatre, Detroit: 313-868-1347

Detroit Symphony Orchestra, Detroit:
313-576-5111

Fisher Theatre, Detroit: 313-872-1000

Fox Theatre, Detroit: 313-983-6611

Gem Theatre, Detroit: 313-963-9800

Hilberry Theatre, Detroit: 313-577-2972

JET, West Bloomfield: 248-788-2900

Joe Louis Arena, Detroit: 313-983-6606

Lydia Mendelssohn Theatre, Ann Arbor:
734-763-1085

McMorran Place, Port Huron: 810-985-6166

Macomb Center for the Performing Arts,
Mount Clemens: 810-286-2222

Marquis Theatre, Northville: 248-349-8110

Masonic Temple, Detroit: 313-832-7100

Meadow Brook Theatre, Rochester:
248-377-3300

Meadow Brook Music Festival, Rochester:
248-377-0100

Michigan Opera Theatre, Detroit: 313-237-SING

Michigan Theater, Ann Arbor: 734-668-8397

Michigan Union Ticket Office, Ann Arbor:
    734-763-TKTS

Music Hall, Detroit: 313-963-7622

Orchestra Hall, Detroit: 313-576-5111

The Palace, Auburn Hills: 248-377-0100

Pine Knob, Clarkston: 248-377-0100

Pontiac Silverdome, Pontiac: 248-456-1600

Power Center, Ann Arbor: 734-763-3333

Second City, Detroit: 313-965-2222

Ticketmaster (Order tickets by phone using credit
    card): 248-645-6666

University Musical Society, Ann Arbor:
    734-764-2538

Wharton Center, East Lansing: 517-432-2000,
    1-800-WHARTON

Youtheatre, Southfield: 248-557-PLAY (7529)

Transportation and Tours

Unlike other major cities, Detroit is an automobile town. It is almost impossible to get around town without a car, unless you are staying downtown and visiting only downtown, uptown, and Cultural Center sites. Then you can hop on the People Mover, trolley, and a Woodward bus.

Driving is easy around Metro Detroit. We are a town with well-marked, easy-to-follow freeways. I-75, I-275, and US-10 are the major north-south highways. I-94, I-696, and I-96 are the east-west highways.

Traffic tends to be heavy going downtown during morning rush hour, generally 7:30–9 a.m., and leaving downtown in afternoon rush hour, 4:30–6 p.m. On Friday afternoon during the summer, northbound I-75 is quite dense. Ditto Sunday evening on southbound I-75. This is "Up North" traffic. Be sure to buckle up!

BUS LINES

Detroit People Mover: 313-962-7245

50 cents a ride. Token machines selling 50-cent coupons for dollar bills are in all stations. Monthly, semi-annual, and annual passes are available. Hours are 7 a.m.–11 p.m., Monday–Thursday. 7 a.m.–midnight, Friday. 9 a.m.–midnight, Saturday. Noon–8 p.m., Sunday.

SMART: 313-962-5515

The Suburban Mobility Authority for Regional Transportation provides commuter service between Detroit and the suburbs and between suburbs. There are also "connector" buses that provide curb-to-curb service and are useful for the handicapped. Fares vary with routes.

D-Dot: 313-933-1300

Detroit Department of Transportation has many bus routes throughout the city. Fare is $1.25, 75 cents with bus card for students, plus 25 cents for a transfer.

A mini-bus service connecting major downtown hotels with the business district costs 50 cents.

A doubledecker red trolley operates daily from Grand Circus Park to the Mariners Church on Jefferson. 7 a.m.–8 p.m. daily during the winter. 7 a.m.–midnight daily during the summer. It doesn't run Thanksgiving Day, Christmas Day, and New Year's Day. Fare is 50 cents. Trolley drivers do not give change. 313-933-1300.

Greyhound Lines: 1-800-231-2222

Detroit-Canada Tunnel Bus: 519-944-4111

Taxis

You'll have the best luck with cabs if you call for one and wait. Some cabs hang around the major downtown hotels, but rarely cruise near attractions. Cabs operate on a meter system. Basic charge is approximately $1.40 per mile. Meters start at $1.40.

The city's major cab companies are City Cab 313-833-7060, Checker Cab 313-963-7000, and Detroit Cab 313-841-6000.

RAILROADS

Amtrak: 1-800-872-7245

Service from Detroit to Chicago is offered from five Metro Detroit Stations: 11 West Baltimore in Detroit's Cultural Center; 16121 Michigan Avenue, Dearborn; 449 South Eaton, Birmingham; 1600 Wide Track Drive, Pontiac; 201 South Sherman, Royal Oak. Amtrak stations are also located in Ann Arbor, Jackson, Battle Creek, Kalamazoo and Niles.

The one-hour train ride to Ann Arbor from Metro Detroit is a great way to introduce the kids to rail travel. Have a family member drive the family car to Ann Arbor and meet you at the station so you can explore Ann Arbor by car.

Via Rail-Canada: 519-256-5511

AIR TRAVEL

Detroit City Airport: 313-852-6400

Detroit Metropolitan Airport: 734-942-3685 (airport operations), 734-942-3669 (lost and found). Call individual airlines for departure and arrival information.

Windsor Airport: 519-969-2430

Northwest Airlines: Detroit's largest carrier 1-800-225-2525 (reservations), 1-800-441-1818 (arrival, departure information).

Limousine Service: Commuter Transportation Co. 734-941-3252. This is the major shuttle service between the airport and area hotels. A booth is located in the airport baggage claim area. The service also schedules pickups from hotel to airport.

Rental Car Agencies

Detroit's largest and best-known national
    companies are

Avis 1-800-331-1212

Hertz 1-800-654-3131

National 1-800-328-4567

ORGANIZED TOURS

Classic Trolley: 313-274-6300

Detroit Department of Transportation:
    313-935-3808

Detroit Historical Museum: 313-833-9721

Detroit Historical Society: 313-833-7934

D-Tours: 248-647-6022

Great Adventure Tours: 1-800-638-3945

Kirby Tours: 313-278-2224

Canada and Customs

For a quick trip abroad, take the Detroit-Windsor
Tunnel or the Ambassador Bridge into Canada.
Traveling through the tunnel and across the bridge
will be a great adventure for children. There's plenty to do across the border, and the kids will marvel
at the colorful Canadian currency.

You can also drive into Canada across the Blue
Water Bridge that connects Port Huron to Sarnia,
Ontario. Lake Huron is on one side of the bridge;
the St. Clair River is on the other.

U.S. citizens should carry with them a driver's
license or proof of car ownership, personal identification, and birth certificate or naturalization
papers. Landed immigrants should carry their
passport. Foreign nationals should consult immigration officials for details on border crossing.

There is a toll collected at each side of the
Detroit River. It is $2.25 U.S. and $2.75 Canadian
for passenger cars at the Detroit-Windsor Tunnel;
$2.25 U.S. and $2.75 Canadian for passenger cars
at the Ambassador Bridge. The Blue Water Bridge
toll is $1.50 U.S. and $2 Canadian.

U.S. Customs: 313-226-3138

U.S. Immigration: 313-568-6020

Canadian Customs: 519-257-6473
Canadian Immigration: 519-257-7780

Be sure the kids are buckled up. Both Michigan and Ontario have a seatbelt law.

Metro Detroit's Best Kid Stuff

No guidebook is complete without a list of the area's best attractions. These sites have a proven track record and have been family favorites for many years. I offer this list knowing full well that when my children were small, they sometimes enjoyed the neighborhood playground more than a visit to Detroit's best children's sites. Apply your discretion in using this list. As your children grow, your family favorites will change. Check the index for a more complete listing.

Alfred P. Sloan Museum, Flint
Ann Arbor Hands-On Museum, Ann Arbor
Belle Isle Aquarium, Detroit
Cranbrook Institute of Science, Bloomfield Hills
Detroit Historical Museum, Detroit
Detroit Institute of Arts, Detroit
Detroit People Mover, Detroit
Detroit Science Center, Detroit
Detroit Symphony Orchestra Tiny Tots Series,
Farmington Hills
Detroit Symphony Orchestra Young People's
Concerts, Detroit

Detroit Zoological Park, Royal Oak
Ella Sharp Museum, Jackson
Flint Children's Museum
Fort Malden National Historic Park, Amherstburg
Greenfield Village and Henry Ford Museum,
Dearborn
Impression 5 Science Center, Lansing
Michigan Historical Museum, Lansing
Michigan Space Center, Jackson
University of Michigan Exhibit Museum, Ann Arbor
Youtheatre, Southfield
During the summer:
Crossroads Village/Huckleberry Railroad, Flint
Four Bears Water Park, Utica
Meadow Brook Music Festival, Rochester
Penny Whistle Place, Flint
Pine Knob Music Theatre, Clarkston
Waterford Oaks Water Park, Waterford

JUST FOR TODDLERS

The following sites are geared for preschoolers through first grade. For maximum enjoyment, be sure to visit while the kids are still small. Check the index for a more complete listing.

Ann Arbor Hands-On Museum
Belle Isle Zoo, Detroit
Bumper bowling
Children's Museum, Flint
Detroit Symphony Orchestra Tiny Tots Series,
Farmington Hills
Discovery Room, Jewish Community Center,
West Bloomfield
Domino's Farms, Ann Arbor
Huron-Clinton Metroparks Tot Lots
Indoor Playgrounds
Maybury State Park Petting Farm, Northville
Meadow Brook Music Festival Children's Series,
Rochester
Neighborhood Playscapes
Penny Whistle Place, Flint
Prehistoric Forest, Irish Hills
Youtheatre's Wiggle Club, Southfield

JUST FOR TEENS

For a family outing with teens, take my foolproof advice: have your teenager invite along a friend, then the two can pretend they aren't really with you. Most teens won't even mind having the family tag along to the following sites. Check the index for a more complete listing.

Basketball centers, batting cages, disc golf, go-carts, horseback riding, laser tag, miniature golf, skiing, snowshoeing, wall climbing

Concerts at Joe Louis Arena, The Palace, or Pine Knob (you can wait for them in the "Parent Holding Area," known as the Quiet Room)

Cranbrook Institute of Science laser shows, Bloomfield Hills

Detroit Science Center IMAX Theatre, Detroit

"The Fridge," Waterford Oaks, Waterford

Henry Ford IMAX Theatre, Dearborn

Longway Planetarium's laser shows, Flint

Red Oaks Golf Dome and Sports Village, Madison Heights

Sporting Events

Tours

The "Turbo Tour" at Spirit of Ford

U-pick berries, apples, pumpkins, and Christmas trees

Wave pools/waterslides

Whirly Ball, Ann Arbor, Flint, Clinton Township, West Bloomfield

Family Memberships

Many Michigan institutions offer yearly family memberships ranging from $25–$75. Here's your chance to support your favorite museum and become a V.I.P. at the same time. Family members enjoy free admission, newsletters, special parties, activities, and gift shop discounts. With a Family Membership, you'll be able to drop in on an institution for a short visit and not worry about staying long enough to "get your money's worth." Think of these institutions when holidays and birthdays roll around. Here's a sampling:

Alfred P. Sloan Museum, Flint: 810-760-1169

Ann Arbor Hands-On Museum: 734-995-5439

Charles H. Wright Museum of African American History, Detroit: 313-494-5800

Children's Museum, Flint: 810-767-5437

Cranbrook Academy of Art Museum: 248-645-3312

Cranbrook Institute of Science: 248-645-3245

Detroit Historical Society: 313-833-7934

Detroit Institute of Arts: 313-833-7971

Detroit Science Center: 313-577-840

Detroit Zoological Society: 248-541-5505

Henry Ford Museum/Greenfield Village, Dearborn: 313-271-1620

Impression 5 Science Center, Lansing: 517-485-8115

Birthday Parties

Unless you're a camp counselor at heart and don't mind messy faces and gooey hands, not to mention post-party clean-up, you'll want to find a special site to hold your party—preferably one that will engage your gang of party animals for several hours of supervised activities, entertainment or sports. Browse through Chapters 5–14. Your favorite museum, historic site, nature center, indoor playground, children's theater, rink, bowling alley and tour are usually happy to accommodate a group. And don't forget to try your local YMCA, city recreation department and fire station. A few on the list will actually bring their special activity party to you. These are noted with an asterisk.

Here's a sampling of Metro Detroit party sites to get you started:

Adray Sports Arena, Dearborn: 313-943-4098

Ann Arbor Hands-On Museum: 734-995-5439

Arts & Scraps, Detroit: 313-640-4411

ArtVentures, Ann Arbor: 734-994-8004, ext. 116

Basketron, Dearborn Heights: 313-563-8766

Beverly Hills Racquet and Health Club,
    Southfield: 248-642-8500

Birmingham Bloomfield Art Center, Birmingham:
    248-644-0866

Bonaventure Roller Skating Center, Farmington
    Hills: 248-476-2201

Caesarland (5 locations),
    Clawson: 248-435-3770;
    Southgate: 734-285-5545;
    Warren: 810-754-8888;
    Waterford: 248-674-7408;
    Westland: 734-729-5100

*Carousel Acres, South Lyon: 248-437-PONY

Charles L. Bowers School Farm, Bloomfield Hills:
    248-645-4830

The Children's Museum, Detroit: 313-873-8100

Chuck E. Cheese (8 locations),
    Canton: 734-981-0333;
    Dearborn: 313-274-5310;
    Flint: 810-733-7404;
    Lansing: 517-321-1233;
    Pontiac: 248-338-4857;
    Rochester Hills: 248-299-4540;
    Roseville: 810-293-0808;
    Southgate: 734-283-6513

Classic Trolley Company: 313-274-6300

Coe Rail, Walled Lake: 248-960-9440

Cranbrook Institute of Science: 248-645-3200

Crown Coach Carriage Rides, Birmingham:
    248-360-1373

Detroit Historical Museum: 313-833-1805

Detroit Science Center: 313-577-8400

Detroit Tigers: 313-471-BALL

Dinosaur Hill Nature Preserve, Rochester:
    248-656-0999

Discovery Zone (4 locations),
    Flint: 810-230-6800;
    Madison Heights: 248-585-7942;

Sterling Heights: 810-566-6801;
West Bloomfield: 248-788-9393

Drayton Plains Nature Center, Drayton Plains:
248-674-2119

E. L. Johnson Nature Center, Bloomfield Hills
Recreation, Bloomfield Hills: 248-433-0885

*Fit-N-Fun Tumblebus, 810-329-3391

Flint Children's Museum, Flint: 810-767-5437

*Flower Gallery, Orchard Lake: 248-706-1370

Fun with Plaster (2 locations):
Farmington: 248-442-2690;
West Bloomfield: 248-932-5210

The Groove Gallery, Royal Oak: 248-398-8162

The Ground Round, Livonia: 734-462-1735

Gymboree, Birmingham 248-646-2350

Gymnastic Training Center of Rochester:
248-852-7950

*Haverhill Farms, White Lake Township:
248-887-2027

Hess-Hathaway Petting Farm, Waterford
Township: 248-674-5441

Jeepers! (4 locations),
Auburn Hills: 248-972-3200;
Livonia: 734-762-5118;
Roseville: 810-296-6569;
Southfield: 248-557-5500

Jewish Community Center (two locations),
Oak Park: 248-967-4030;
West Bloomfield: 248-661-1000

Kid Kingdom, Canton: 734-981-0711

Kids Koncerts, Southfield: 248-424-9022

Kidsports, Southfield: 248-352-5437

Laser Quest, Madison Heights: 810-616-9292

Magic Club McDonald's, Allen Park:
313-386-9401

Major Magic's All Star Pizza Review (2 locations),
Clinton Township: 810-790-6080;
Madison Heights: 248-541-6110

Marvin's Marvelous Mechanical Museum,
Farmington Hills: 248-626-5020

Metro Hoops, Sterling Heights: 810-731-HOOP

*Miniature Motorways, 734-261-6169

My Jewish Discovery Place, West Bloomfield:
248-661-7682

My Place Just For Kids, (2 locations),

Birmingham: 248-540-5702;
West Bloomfield: 248-737-5437

The Nature Center at Friendship Woods,
Madison Heights: 248-585-0100

*Oakland County Parks Mobile Recreation,
Waterford, 248-858-0916

*Party Pop-Ins, 734-528-0879

Pewabic Pottery, Detroit: 313-822-0954

Phazer Land, Farmington: 248-442-7880

Plaster Playhouse, Sterling Heights:
810-566-0666

*Plasterworks, (2 locations), Canton:
734-981-3930; Union Lake: 248-360-9920

*Rushlow's Arabians, Huron Township:
734-782-1171

Skateland Fun Zone: 734-671-0220

Sparky's, Livonia: 248-477-3333

The Sports Academy, Novi: 248-380-0800

Sugarbush Farms, Chesterfield Township:
810-778-6361

Thing-a-Majig, Franklin: 248-851-3805

Townsend Hotel Tea, Birmingham: 248-642-7900

U.S. Blades and Laser World, West Bloomfield:
248-661-4200

William Costicks Activity Center Pool,
Farmington Hills: 248-473-1834

YMCA of Metropolitan Detroit, Birmingham:
248-644-9036

Youtheatre, Southfield: 248-557-7529

Youtheatre Presents Not Just For Kids at the
Michigan Theater, Ann Arbor: 734-668-8397,
ext.30

Free Sites

If you're looking for a low-cost way to entertain
the kids, here's a sampling of free Metro Detroit sites:

African Heritage Cultural Center
Art Gallery of Windsor
Drayton Plains Nature Center
Eastern Market
E.L. Johnson Nature Center

Fisher Building

For-Mar Nature Preserve

Fort Gratiot Light House

Fort Malden National Historic Park

Kensington Metropark petting farm

Kresge Art Museum

Library puppet shows, storytelling, summer reading programs

Madison Heights Nature Center

Maybury State Park petting farm and park

Michigan Historical Museum

MSU Museum

Michigan State University Horticultural Gardens

My Discovery Room, Jewish Community Center

Nature Centers at Huron-Clinton Metroparks

Neighborhood parks and playscapes

Summer outdoor music concerts

Starr-Jaycee Park train

Sterling Heights Nature Center movies

Story hour, almost every Saturday morning at these area book shops: Borders, Barnes and Noble, Ann Arbor's Little Professor, Rochester's Halfway Down the Stairs

Tot lots at Huron-Clinton Metroparks

Tours

Underground Railroad-Second Baptist Church

University of Michigan Museum of Art

Wolcott Mill

Scout Badge Opportunities

Scout troupes and 4-H clubs can learn skills required for badges and fair competition at many area museums and nature centers.

Ann Arbor Hands-On Museum, Ann Arbor:
734-995-5439

Carl F. Fenner Nature Center,
Lansing: 517-483-4277

Detroit Science Center, Detroit: 313-577-8400,
ext. 417

Henry Ford Museum, Dearborn: 313-271-1620,
ext. 382

Indian Springs Metropark, Clarkston:
1-800-477-3192

Nankin Mills Interpretive Center, Westland:
734-261-1990

The Nature Center at Friendship Woods, Madison
Heights: 248-585-0100

Potter Park Zoo, Lansing: 517-483-4221

St. Clair County Farm Museum, Armada:
810-325-1737

Stony Creek Metropark, Washington:
1-800-477-7756

Troy Museum and Historic Village, Troy:
248-524-3570

Turner-Dodge House, Lansing: 517-483-7660

University of Michigan Matthaei Botanical
Gardens, Ann Arbor: 734-998-7061

Wolcott Mill Metropark, Ray Township:
1-800-477-3175

Woolly Country Classroom, Mt. Bruce Station,
Romeo: 810-798-2568

At the Malls

Metro Detroit malls offer more than just shopping. Many feature indoor playscapes, family entertainment series and storytimes, discount clubs for children, and special holiday events at Easter, Christmas, and during school vacations
The Alley–Trapper's Alley, Detroit, 313-963-5445

Briarwood Mall, Ann Arbor, 734-769-9610

Eastland Center, Harper Woods, 313-371-1500

Fairlane Town Center, Dearborn, 313-593-1370

Frandor Mall, Lansing, 517-333-5300

Genesee Mall, Flint, 810-732-4000

Great Lakes Crossing, Auburn Hills,
   248-454-5000

Lakeside Shopping Center, Sterling Heights,
   810-247-4131

Lansing Mall, Lansing, 517-321-3534

Laurel Park Place, Livonia, 734-462-1100

Livonia Mall, Livonia, 248-476-1160

Macomb Mall, Roseville, 810-293-7800

Meadowbrook Village Mall, Rochester Hills,
   248-375-9451

Meridian Mall, Okemos, 517-349-2030

Northland Center, Southfield, 248-557-8874

Oakland Mall, Troy, 248-585-6000

Somerset Collection, Troy, 248-643-6360

Southland Center, Taylor, 734-374-2800

Summit Place, Waterford, 248-682-0123

Tel-Twelve Mall, Southfield, 248-353-4111

Twelve Oaks Mall, Novi, 248-348-9438

Universal Mall, Warren, 810-751-3161

Westland Shopping Center, Westland,
   734- 425-5001

Wonderland Mall, Livonia, 734-522-4100

2
A City Listing of Sites

TIP

Develop your children's sense of adventure. Let them help plan short family excursions by going through this book and choosing sites that sound exciting to them.

Here is a listing of all the sites and tours described in this book, arranged by the city in which they are located. Plan on browsing through this chapter often to plan your family adventures. You might even be surprised to find what's available in your own hometown.

Michigan Cities

Ada
Amway Corporation

Allen Park
Allen Park Civic Arena
Cabrini Catholic Church Playscape
Magic Club McDonalds

Almont
Blake's Almont Farm
Brookwood Fruit Farm

Alpena
Besser Company

Ann Arbor
Ann Arbor Climbing Gym
Ann Arbor Farmers' Market
Ann Arbor Hands-On Museum
Ann Arbor Junior Theatre
Ann Arbor Symphony Orchestra
Ann Arbor Young Actors Guild
Argo Park Livery
The Ark
ArtVentures
Brown Park
Buhr Park Ice Rink
Buhr Park Pool
Cobblestone Farm
Colonial Lanes
Delhi Metropark
Dixboro General Store
Domino's Farm

Ecology Center
Feat of Clay
Fuller Pool
Furstenberg Park
Gallup Canoe Livery
Gordon H. Sindecuse Museum of Dentistry
Huron Hills Ski Center
Junior Theatre
Kelsey Museum of Archeology
Kerrytown Plaza
Kid Kingdom
Leslie Science Center
Little Dipper Candle Shoppe
Lurie Bell Tower
Michigan Theater
Mixer Playground
Museum of Art
Performance Network
Phoenix Memorial Laboratory
Power Center
Project Grow
Scrap Box
Shameless Rainbow Youth Theater
Stearns Collection of Musical Instruments
University of Michigan Exhibit Museum of Natural
History
University of Michigan Exhibit Museum of Natural
History Planetarium
University of Michigan Matthaei Botanical
Gardens
University of Michigan Wolverines
Veterans Park
Whirly Ball Ann Arbor
Wide World Sports Center
Wild Swan Theatre
Yost Ice Arena
Young People's Theater
Youtheatre at Michigan Theater

Armada

Blake's Big Apple Orchard
Blake's Orchard and Cider Mill

Coon Creek Orchard
G.B.'s Fishin' Hole
St. Clair County Farm Museum
Sundown Riding Stables

Auburn Hills

Detroit Pistons Basketball
Detroit Rockers
Detroit Shock
Detroit Vipers
Jeepers!
Mulligan's Golf Center
Oakland County Animal Control
The Palace
Walter P. Chrysler Museum

Augusta

W.K. Kellogg Experimental Forest

Augusta Township

Wasem Fruit Farm

Avoca

Jeffrey's Blueberries

Belleville

Boughan's Tree Farm
Lower Huron Metropark
Pumpkin Factory
Thornhollow Tree Farm

Berkley

Berkley Ice Arena
Hartfield Lanes

Beulah

Homestead Sugar House Candies

Beverly Hills

Beverly Hills Village Park

Birmingham

Baldwin Public Library
Birmingham-Bloomfield Symphony Orchestra

Birmingham Ice Sports Arena
Birmingham YMCA
The Community House
Crown Coach, Inc.
Gymboree
Kaput Kapot
Popcorn Players
Shain Park
Springdale Park Playscape
The Townsend Hotel

Bloomfield Hills
Bloomfield Youth Theatre
Charles L. Bowers School Farm
Cranbrook Academy of Art Museum
Cranbrook House and Garden
Cranbrook Institute of Science
Cranbrook Institute of Science Planetarium
Detroit Country Day Lower School Playscape
E.L. Johnson Nature Center
Saarinen House
Temple Beth El
Wallace Ice Arena

Bridgman
Cook Energy Information Center

Brighton
Brighton Farmer's Market
Golf-O-Rama
Huron Meadows Metropark
Island Lake Recreation Area
Mt. Brighton Ski Area
Warren's Tree Farm

Brooklyn
Arend Tree Farms
Michigan International Speedway
Walker Tavern Historic Complex

Brown City
Frank Industries, Inc.

Buchanan

Bear Cave Resort
Tabor Hill Winery

Burton

For-Mar Nature Preserve and Arboretum
Michigan Human Society-Genesee County

Cadillac

Four Winns Boat Company

Canton

Canton Softball Center Complex
Kid Kingdom
Lower Rouge Parkway
Plasterworks
Real Life Farm
Skatin' Station
The Summit on the Park

Canton Township

Mary's Farm Market

Carleton

Calder Brothers Dairy Farm

Casco

Pankiewicz Farms Cider Mill

Chelsea

Gerald E. Eddy Geology Center
Jiffy Baking Mixes
Purple Rose Theatre
Stoney Ridge Farm

Chesterfield Township

Lionel Trains Visitor Center

Clarkston

Bellair's Hillside Fiber Farm and the Sheep Shed
Cherry Hill Lane
Cohn Amphitheatre at Independence Oaks
County Park
Independence Oaks County Park
Indian Springs Metropark

Lewis E. Wint Nature Center at Independence
Oaks County Park
Pine Knob Music Theatre
Pine Knob Ski Resort
Starlab at Independence Oaks County Park

Clawson
Ambassador Skating Rink
Clawson Parks & Recreation Children's Series

Clinton
Southern Michigan Railroad

Clinton Township
C.J. Barrymore's Sports and Entertainment
Clinton Historical Commission   ⌡
Frontier Lanes
Macomb Center for the Performing Arts
Macomb Junior Players
Morley Candy Makers, Inc.
Shores Skateland
Whirly Ball of Michigan
Windemere Equestrian Center
Youtheatre at Macomb Center for the
Performing Arts

Clio
Runyan's Country Tree Farm

Cohoctah
Cohoctah Tree Works

Commerce Township
Long Family Orchard and Farm

Concord
Sweet Seasons Orchards

Copper Harbor
Delaware Copper Mine

Croswell
Croswell Berry Farm and Restaurant

Davisburg
Davisburg Candle Factory
Springfield Oaks

Dearborn
Adray Sports Arena
Automotive Hall of Fame
Cherry Hill Lanes
Classic Trolley Company
Dearborn Historical Museum: McFadden Ross
House and Exhibit Annex
Ford Discovery Trail
Greenfield Village
Henry Ford Community College Children's
Theatre
Henry Ford Estate–Fair Lane
Henry Ford Museum
Henry Ford Museum IMAX Theatre
Lower Rouge Parkway
Middle Rouge Parkway
Museum of Arab Culture(ACCESS)
Plowshares Theatre Company
The Ritz-Carlton Hotel
Spirit of Ford
University of Michigan-Dearborn Ice Arena
University of Michigan-Dearborn Environmental
Study Area

Dearborn Heights
Basketron
Canfield Ice Arena
Warren Valley Golf Course

Detroit
African Heritage Cultural Center
Agnes' Bike Rental
Ambassador Bridge
Anna Scripps Whitcomb Conservatory
Art and Scraps
Belle Isle
Belle Isle Aquarium
Belle Isle Nature Center
Belle Isle Zoo
Bonstelle Theatre

Brunch with Bach
Century Theatre
Chandler Park Family Aquatic Center
Charles H. Wright Museum of African American
History
Chene Park
Children's Museum
Children's Museum Planetarium
Clark Park
Cobo Arena
Cobo Conference and Exhibition Center
Detroit Historical Museum
Detroit Institute of Arts
Detroit Opera House
Detroit People Mover
Detroit Public Library-Children's Library
Detroit Puppet Theater
Detroit Red Wings
Detroit Repertory Theatre
Detroit Science Center
Detroit Science Center IMAX Dome Theatre
Detroit Symphony Orchestra
Detroit Tigers-Comerica Park
Detroit Trolley
Detroit-Windsor Tunnel
Diamond Jack's River Tours
Dossin Great Lakes Museum
Eastern Market
Eastside YMCA
Fiona's Tea House
Fisher Building
Fisher Mansion/Bhaktivedanta Center
Fisher Theatre
Fox Theatre
Garden Bowl
Gem Theatre
Greektown
Hart Plaza
Heritage Museum of Fine Arts for Youth
Hilberry Theatre
Historic Fort Wayne
International Institute

Jack Adams Ice Arena
Joe Louis Arena
Masonic Temple
Michigan Humane Society-Central Shelter
Michigan Opera Theatre
Michigan Sports Hall of Fame
Mosaic Youth Theatre of Detroit
Motown Historical Museum
Music Hall
Northeast Water Treatment Plant
Northland Roller Rink
Northside YMCA
Northwestern YMCA
Nsoroma Institute
Oakwood Blue Jackets Bowl
Orchestra Hall
Palmer Park
Peddy Players Theatre Company Youth Theatre
Pewabic Pottery
Redford Bowl
Renaissance Center
Roller-Cade
St. Aubin Park
The Second City
Splat Ball City Playing Field
State Fairgrounds
Trapper's Alley
Tuskegee Airmen National Museum
Underground Railroad-Second Baptist Church
United States Post Office—George W. Young
Facility
University of Detroit Titans
Wayne State University Tartars
Western YMCA

Dexter

Coldsprings Farm
Dexter Area Museum
Dexter Blueberry Farm
Dexter Cider Mill
Dexter-Huron Metropark
Hudson Mills Metropark

Mosher Tree Farm
Spring Valley Trout Farm

Dowagiac
Wicks' Apple House

Drayton Plains
Drayton Plains Nature Center

Dryden
Seven Ponds Nature Center

East Lansing
Abrams Planetarium

Jack Breslin Student Events Center
Kresge Art Museum
Laser Storm
Michigan State University Barns
Michigan State University Botany Greenhouse
and Butterfly House
Michigan State University Dairy Plant
Michigan State University Farm Tours
Michigan State University Horticultural
Demonstration Gardens
Michigan State University Museum
Michigan State University Spartans
Pro Bowl-East
Vertical Ventures Rock Climbing and Wilderness
Program
Wharton Center for the Performing Arts

Elsie
Green Meadow Farm

Erie
Erie Orchards and Cider Mill
Trabbic Farms Pumpkin Patch

Fair Haven
The Cooperage

Farmington
Bel Aire Lanes
Farmington Farmers' Market
Farmington YMCA
Fun With Plaster
Phazer Land

Farmington Hills
Bonaventure Roller Skating Center
Drake Sports Park
Drakeshire Lanes
Farmington Hills Ice Arena
Gill Elementary Playscape
Glen Oaks
Longacre House
Marvin's Marvelous Mechanical Museum and Emporium
Mercy High School Auditorium
Sport and Fun
William Costicks Activity Center Pool

Fenton
Capt. Phogg
Parshallville Cider Mill
Spicer Orchards Farm Market and Cider Mill

Ferndale
Luxury Lanes

Flat Rock
Flat Rock Speedway
Oakwoods Metropark

Flint
Alfred P. Sloan Museum

Crossroads Village Cider Mill
Crossroads Village/Huckleberry Railroad
Discovery Zone
Flint Children's Museum
Flint City Market
Flint Institute of Arts
Flint Youth Theatre
Genesee Belle at Crossroads Village
GM Truck Group
Longway Planetarium
Michigan Labor Museum and Learning Center
Mott Farm
Penny Whistle Place
Whirlyball Fun Center

Flushing

Almar Orchards
Chaprnka Tree Farm
Koan's Orchards
King Park Golf
McCarron's Orchard

Frankenmuth

Frankenmuth Brewery, Inc.

Franklin

Franklin Cider Mill

Fraser

Great Lakes Sport City
Liberty Bowl
Total Soccer

Garden City

Ford Road Miniature Golf
Garden City Ice Arena
Maplewood Family Theatre

Gladstone

Hoegh Pet Casket Company

Goodrich

Porters Orchard and Cider Mill

Grand Blanc
Galaxy Lanes
Trim Pines Farm

Grand Ledge
Fitzgerald Park
FunTyme Adventure Park
Grand Ledge Outcroppings
Sundance Riding Stables

Grand Rapids
Bissel, Inc.
Gypsum Mine Tour

Grass Lake
Arend Tree Farms
Fodor's Christmas Tree Farm

Gregory
DeGroot's Strawberries

Grosse Ile
Adventure Island

Grosse Pointe Farms
Grosse Pointe Children's Theatre
Grosse Pointe War Memorial

Grosse Pointe Shores
Edsel and Eleanor Ford House

Hamtramck
Veterans Memorial Park

Hanover
Childs Place Buffalo Ranch

Haslett
Lake Lansing Park

Hazel Park
Hazel Park Raceway
Mauro's Miniature Golf

Hickory Corners
Kellogg Farm

Highland
Broadview Christmas Tree Farm
Huff Tree Farm

Holland
Wooden Shoe Factory

Holly
Diehl's Orchard and Cider Mill
Groveland Oaks Waterslide
Holly Recreation Area
Michigan Balloon Corporation
Mt. Holly, Inc.
Seven Lakes State Park

Holt
William M. Burchfield Park

Howell
Howell Nature and Conference Center
Pleasant Knoll Tree Farm
Waldock Tree Farm

Huntington Woods
Burton Elementary Playscape

Huron Township
Rushlow's Arabians
Willow Metropark

Ida
Marlin Bliss Tree Farm
Matthes Evergreen Farm

Independence Township
Waterford Hills Road Racing

Inkster
Inkster Civic Arena

Jackson
Dahlem Center
Ella Sharp Museum
Illuminated Cascades
Jackson Harness Raceway

Michigan Space and Science Center

Kearsage

Delaware Copper Mine

Lake Orion

Bald Mountain Recreation Area
Basketball America
Willow Creek Miniature Golf

Lakeport

Lakeport State Park

Lansing

All of Us Express
Apple SportPlex Family Entertainment Center
BoarsHead Theatre
Carl F. Fenner Arboretum
GM Lansing Car Assembly Plants
Holiday Lanes
Impression 5 Science Center
Lansing Ice Arena
Lansing Lugnuts
Louis F. Adado Riverfront Park and
River Trail
Metro Bowl
Michigan Historical Museum
Michigan Women's Historical Center and
Hall of Fame
Michigan State Capitol
Potter Park Zoo
Pro-Bowl West
Quality Dairy Cider Mill
R.E. Olds Transportation Museum
Riverfront Cycle
Riverwalk Theatre
Royal Scot Golf and Bowl
Turner-Dodge House
Washington Park
Woldumar Nature Center

Lapeer

Candy Cane Christmas Tree Farm

Leonard
Addison Oaks
Rochester Hills Stables

Lincoln Park
Lincoln Park Community Center

Livonia
Devon-Aire Ice Arena
Eddie Edgar Ice Arena
Family Entertainment Series
Friendly Merri-Bowl Lanes
Greenmead Museum and Historical Village
Jeepers!
Livonia YMCA
Observer and Eccentric Newspapers
Riverside Roller Arena
Sparky's
Wilson Barn
Woodland Lanes

Macomb Township
Denewith's Pick Your Own Strawberry Farm

Madison Heights
Astro Lanes
Discovery Zone
Double Action Indoor Shooting Center
Laser Quest
Madison Heights Civic Center
The Nature Center at Friendship Woods
Red Oaks Golf Dome and Sports Village
Red Oaks Waterpark

Manchester
Alber Orchard and Cider Mill

Marquette
United States Olympic Education Center

Mason
Adventures Aloft

FunTyme Adventure Park

Melvindale
Melvindale Ice Arena

Midland
Dow Visitor's Center

Milford
Alpine Valley
Heavner's Canoe and Cross Country Ski Rentals
Highland Recreation Area
Kensington Metropark
Kensington Nature Center and Farm Center
Proud Lake Recreation Area

Monroe
Monroe County Historical Museum
Navarre-Anderson Trading Post and Country
Store Museum
Navarre Farms
River Raisin Battlefield Visitor's Center
Sterling State Park
Weier's Cider Mill

Montrose
Montrose Historical and Telephone Pioneer
Museum
Montrose Orchards

Mount Clemens
Crocker House
Great Western Riding Stable Company
Macomb YMCA
Marino Sports Center, Inc.
Metro Beach Metropark
Shipwreck Lagoon at Metro Beach Metropark
Michigan Transit Museum
Mount Clemens Farmers' Market
Mount Clemens Ice Arena and Fitness Center
Recreation Bowl
Selfridge Military Air Museum

Mount Morris
Wolcott Orchards

Napoleon
Makielski Berry Farm

New Baltimore
Stahl's Bakery

New Boston
Apple Charlie's and South Huron Orchard and
Cider Mill
Davies Orchard
Green Tee
Huron Christmas Farm
Pumpkin Patch

New Haven
Opper-Land Pines

Newport
Fermi 2 Power Plant

Northville
Cotton Candy Players
Genitti's Hole-in-the-Wall
Guernsey Farm Dairy
Marquis Theatre
Maybury State Park Petting Farm
Meyer's Farm
Middle Rouge Parkway (Edward Hines Park)
Mill Race Historical Village
Northville Downs
Northville Farmers' Market
Parmenter's Northville Cider Mill
REI
Showcase Stables

Novi
Motorsports Museum and Hall of Fame
Novi Bowl
Novi Expo Center
Novi Ice Arena
Novi Youth Theatre
Soccer Zone
Sports Academy

Oakland Township
Middleton Berry Farm

Oak Park
Compuware-Oak Park Arena
David Shepherd Park
Jewish Community Center
Oak Park Mini-Golf
Oak Park Municipal Pool

Okemos
FunTyme Adventure Park
Meridian Historical Village
Meridian Township Farmer's Market
Nokomis Learning Center

Onsted (Irish Hills)
Eisenhower Presidential Car
Prehistoric Forest
Stagecoach Stop, U.S.A.

Orchard Lake
Flower Gallery
Pine Lake Marina

Orion Township
Orion Oaks

Ortonville
Ashton Orchards and Cider Mill
Cook's Farm Dairy

Hadley Hill Farm
Ortonville Recreation Area
Oak Haven Farm
Oakwood Riding Stables

Otisville

Smiths Farm

Oxford

Candy Cane Christmas Tree Farm
Just A Folly Farm
Sky Adventures
Upland Hills Ecological Awareness Center
Upland Hills Farm

Paw Paw

St. Julian Winery
Warner Vineyards

Petoskey

Kilwins Quality Confections, Inc.

Pinckney

Hell Creek Ranch
Hell Survivors, Inc.

Plymouth

Compuware Sports Arena
Oasis Golf/Tru-Pitch Batting Cages
Plymouth Community Family YMCA
Plymouth Cultural Center
Plymouth Farmer's Market
Plymouth Historical Museum
Plymouth Orchards and Cider Mill
Plymouth Whalers

Pontiac

Detroit Lions, Inc.
Paintball Arena
Pine Grove Historical Museum
Pontiac Farmers' Market
Pontiac Lake Recreation Area
Pontiac Silverdome

Port Huron

Blue Water International Bridge
Blue Water Trolley
Fort Gratiot Lighthouse
Huron Lightship Museum
Knowlton Ice Museum
London Farm Dairy Bar
McMorran Place Complex
Mary Maxim, Inc.
Museum of Art and History
Port Huron Border Cats
Tollander Tree Farm

Ray Township

Wolcott Mill Farm Learning Center
Wolcott Mill Metropark

Redford

The Arc Lekotek
Bell Creek Park and Lola Valley Park
Historic Redford Theatre
Mayflower Lanes
Redford Ice Arena

Richfield Township

Richfield Park BMX Track

River Rouge

River Rouge Arena

Riverview

Riverview Highlands Ski Area

Rochester

Avon Players
Bloomer Park
Dinosaur Hill Nature Preserve
Leader Dog for the Blind
Meadow Brook Hall and Knole Cottage
Meadow Brook Music Festival
Meadow Brook Theatre
Meadowbrook Village Mall Puppet Theatre
North Oakland County YMCA

Oakland University Department of Music,
Theater and Dance
O'Neill Pottery
Paint Creek Cider Mill and Restaurant
The Painted Pot
Rochester Cider Mill
Stoney Creek Farm
Wright and Filippis, Inc.
Yates Cider Mill

Rochester Hills

Michigan Humane Society-North
Rochester Bloomer Park
Rochester Hills Museum at Van Hoosen Farm

Rockford

Wolverine World Wide, Inc.

Rockwood

Lake Erie Metropark Wave Pool
Marshlands Museum and Nature Center at Lake
Erie Metropark

Romeo

Frontier Town
Hy's Cider Mill
Miller's Big Red
Mt. Bruce Station
Rapp Orchard
Stony Creek Orchard and Cider Mill
Summer Gardens
Verellen Orchards
Westview Orchards and Cider Mill of Romeo

Roseville

Basketball City
The Great Skate
Jawor's Golf
Jeepers!
Rose Bowl Lanes

Royal Oak

Bluewater Michigan Chapter—National Railway
Historical Society
Detroit Dance Collective

Detroit Zoological Park
Golden Bear Golf Center
Grand Slam Baseball Training Center
Groove Gallery
Historic Baldwin Theatre
John Lindell Ice Arena
Royal Oak Farmers' Market
Royal Trolley
South Oakland YMCA
Stagecrafters Youth Theatre
Starr-Jaycee Park Train
Target Sports
Total Soccer
Upstairs Magic Theatre at The Wunderground
Wagner Park

Ruby

Ruby Farms of Michigan
Ruby Tree Farm

Saginaw

Japanese Cultural Center and Tea House
Saginaw Water Works

St. Clair Shores

Great Lakes Yachts
Harbor Lanes
Home Plate Sports Center
Lakeshore Family YMCA
St. Clair Shores Civic Center

St. Johns

Beck's Cider Mill
Uncle John's Cider Mill

Salem Township

Obstbaum Orchards and Cider Mill

Saline

Battlegrounds Paintball
Sun Tree Farms
William Lutz
Windy Ridge Orchard and Cider Mill

Shelby
ICT Shelby (Man-Made Gemstones)

Shelby Township
Joe Dumars Field House
River Bends Park

Shingleton
Iverson Snowshoe Company

Southfield
Alex and Marie Manoogian Museum
Beech Woods Recreation Center
Beverly Hills Racquet and Health Club
Jeepers!
Kids Koncerts, Southfield Parks and Recreation
Plum Hollow Lanes
Southfield Civic Center-Evergreen Hills
Southfield Sports Arena
Total Soccer
Youtheatre at the Millennium Centre
WKBD UPN 50

Southgate
Basketball City
Southgate Ice Arena
Ted's Southgate Golf Center

South Lyon
Carousel Acres
Driver's Berry Farm
Erwin Orchards
Mulligan's Golf Center
Washburn One-room Schoolhouse
Wildwood Equestrian Center
Witch's Hat Depot Museum

Sterling Heights
Bakers Delight
Breakfast Playground at Lakeside Mall
DeKrieser Elementary Playscape
Discovery Zone
Five Star Lanes

Freedom Hill
Friendly Ark Sterling Lanes
Metro Hoops
My Place Just For Kids
Plaster Playhouse
Soccer Zone
Sterling Heights Nature Center
Spring Brook Stables

Stockbridge
Dewey School
Skyhorse Station Evergreen Plantation
Waterloo Area Farm Museum

Sumpter Township
Crosswinds Marsh

Swartz Creek
Sports Creek Raceway

Sylvan Lake
Sylvan Lanes

Taylor
Midway Golf Range
M.V. Trampoline Center

Tipton
Hidden Lake Gardens
Hillside Farm

Traverse City
Amon Orchard Tours
Candle Factory

Trenton
Belmar II
Elizabeth Park
Kennedy Ice Arena
Trenton Historical Museum

Troy
Art Castle
Boulan Park Playscape

Bowl One
Firefighters' Park
Lloyd A. Stage Natural Heritage Park-Troy Nature
Center
Raintree Park
Skateworld of Troy
Thunderbird lanes
Troy Lanes
Troy Museum and Historic Village Green

Union Lake
Plasterworks

Utica
Four Bears Water Park
Middleton Cider Mill
The Rink, Inc.

Vulcan
Iron Mountain Iron Mine

Walled Lake
Coe Rail

Warren
Friendly Bronco Lanes
Pampa Lanes
Regal Lanes
Starlight Archery Co.
Universal Lanes
Van Dyke Sport Center
Warren Area Family YMCA

Washington
Stony Creek Metropark
Washington Scouting Museum

Waterford
Dodge No. 4 State Park
Lakeland Ice Arena
Rolladium
Waterford Hills Road Racing
Waterford Oaks County Park
Waterford Oaks Wave Pool and Waterslide

Waterford Township
Hess-Hathaway Petting Farm

Watertown Township
MiniBeast Zooseum and Education Center

Wayne
State Wayne Theatre
Wayne Aquatic Center
Wayne Community Center

West Bloomfield
Detroit Archers
Discovery Zone
Fun with Plaster
Holocaust Memorial Museum
Jewish Community Center
Jewish Ensemble Theatre (JET)
My Jewish Discovery Room
U S Blades
West Bloomfield Trail Network
West Bloomfield Woods Nature Preserve
Whirly Ball West
You're Fired

Westland
Michigan Humane Society-West
Nankin Mills Interpretive Center
Skateland West
Sport-Way
Wayne/Westland YMCA
Westland Sports Arena
William P. Holliday Forest and Wildlife Preserve

White Lake Township
Bridlewood Farms Equestrian Center
Haverhill Farms
Highland Recreation Area Riding Stables
Pontiac Lake Riding Stable
Kelley's Frosty Pines
White Lake Oaks

Willis
Potter Farm

Wixom

Ford Motor Company Wixom Assembly Plant
Total Soccer

Woodhaven

Skateland Fun Zone

Wyandotte

Downriver YMCA
Ford-MacNichol Home
Marx Home
Yack Arena

Ypsilanti

Depot Town Caboose
Makielski Berry Farm
Quirk Theatre
Rolling Hills County Park
Rolling Hills Family Water Park
Rowe's Produce Farm
Wiard's Orchards and Country Fair
Yankee Air Force Museum
Ypsi-Arbor Lanes
Ypsilanti Farmers' Market
Ypsilanti Historical Society and Museum
Ypsilanti Putt-Putt

Southern Ontario Cities

Amherstburg

Fort Malden National Historic Park
Navy Yard Park
North American Black Historical Museum
Park House Museum

Essex

John R. Park Homestead
Southwestern Ontario Heritage Village

Kingsville

Jack Miner Bird Sanctuary

Pelee Island Cruises
Pelee Island Winery

Leamington

Pelee Island Transportation
Point Pelee National Park

Maidstone Township

John Freeman Walls Historic Site and
Underground Railroad Museum

Ruthven

Colasanti's Tropical Gardens

Sarnia

Canatara Children's Farm

Windsor

Art Gallery of Windsor
Chrysler Theatre at Cleary International Centre
Coventry Gardens and Peace Fountain
François Baby House
Gibraltar Climbing Company
Hiram Walker and Sons, Unlimited
Ojibway Park and Nature Center
Parkview Lanes
Playdium Recreation
Queen Elizabeth II Gardens
Walker's Candies
Willistead Manor
Windsor Raceway
Windsor Symphony Orchestra

3
Maps

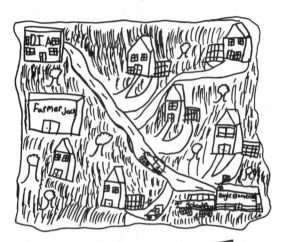

Teach map skills by giving your
kids a map and markers. They
can trace your route and circle
every city you visit.

The maps in this chapter are intended as general guides to the area. Maps of the cities of Detroit, Windsor, Ann Arbor, Flint, and Lansing show the location of some of the highlights of these cities. For more city and site information, check Chapter 2—A City Listing of Sites—and the index.

State of Michigan

Southeastern Lower Michigan

Downtown Detroit

1. Bonstelle Theatre
2. Cobo Conference Center
3. Detroit News and Free Press
4. Detroit Opera House
5. Detroit-Windsor Tunnel
6. Eastern Market
7. Fox Theatre
8. Gem and Century Theatres
9. Greektown
10. Hart Plaza
11. Joe Lewis Arena
12. Masonic Temple
13. Music Hall
14. Renaissance Center
15. Second City
16. Tiger Stadium
17. Trappers Alley
18. Trolley
19. Underground Railroad-Second Baptist Church
20. Puppet Art Theatre

Cultural Center/New Center

1. Children's Museum
2. Detroit Historical Museum
3. Detroit Institute of Arts
4. Detroit Police Horse Stables
5. Detroit Public Library
6. Detroit Science Center
7. Fisher Building
8. Orchestra Hall
9. Hilberry Theatre
10. International Institute
11. Motown Museum
12. Museum of African American History
13. Wayne State University
14. Your Heritage House

Oakland County

1. Cranbrook Educational Community
      House and Gardens
      Institute of Science
      Art Museum
      Saarinen House
2. Detroit Zoological Park
3. Holocaust Memorial Center
4. Independence Oaks County Park
5. Kensington Metropark
6. Madison Heights Nature Center
7. Meadow Brook Music Festival
8. Meadow Brook Hall
9. Meadow Brook Theatre
10. The Palace
11. Pine Knob Music Theatre
12. Red Oaks Waterpark
13. Rochester Hills Museum at the Van Hoosen Farm
14. Troy Museum and Village Green
15. Walter P. Chrysler Museum
16. Waterford Oaks County Park
17. Youtheatre at the Millennium Theatre

Macomb County

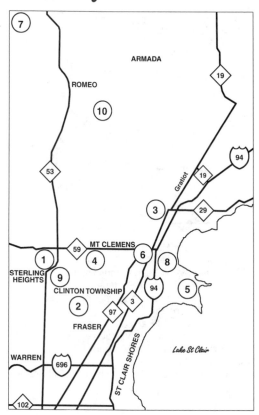

1. Four Bears Water Park
2. Freedom Hill
3. Lionel Trains Visitor Center
4. Macomb Center for the Performing Arts
5. Metro Beach Metropark
6. Morley Candy Makers
7. Mt. Bruce Station
8. Selfridge Military Air Museum
9. Sterling Heights Nature Center
10. Wolcott Mill Metropark

Dearborn / Western Wayne County

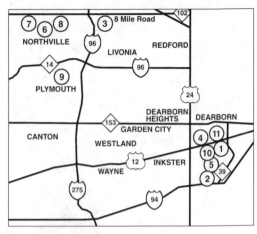

1. Automotive Hall of Fame
2. Greenfield Village
3. Greenmead Museum and Historic Village
4. Henry Ford Estate-Fairlane
5. Henry Ford Museum and IMAX Theatre
6. Marquis Theatre
7. Maybury State Park
8. Mill Race Historical Village
9. Plymouth Historical Museum
10. Spirit of Ford
11. U of M Dearborn Environmental Study Area

Southern Ontario

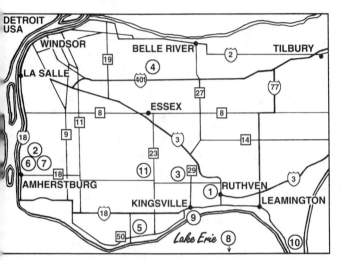

1. Colasanti's Gadens
2. Fort Malden National Historic Park
3. Jack Miner Bird Sanctuary
4. John Freeman Walls Historic Site
5. John R. Park Homestead
6. North American Black Historical Museum
7. Park House Museum
8. Pelee Island
9. Pelee Island Winery
10. Point Pelee
11. Southwestern Ontario Heritage Village

Windsor

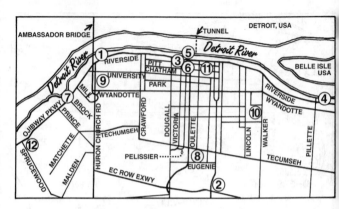

1. Ambassador Park
2. Art Gallery of Windsor
3. Chrysler Theatre at Cleary International Centre
4. Coventry Gardens/Peace Fountain
5. Dieppe Gardens
6. François Baby House
7. MacKensie Hall
8. Queen Elizabeth Gardens
9. University of Windsor
10. Willistead Manor
11. Windsor City Market
12. Windsor Raceway

Ann Arbor

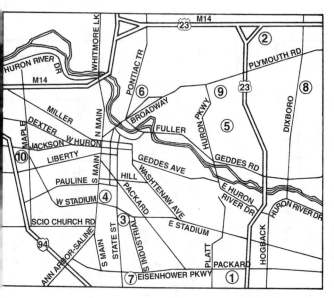

1. Cobblestone Farm
2. Domino's Farms
3. Ecology Center
4. Michigan Stadium
5. Phoenix Memorial Lab
6. Project Grow—Leslie Science Center
7. Scrap Box
8. U of M Matthei Botanical Gardens
9. U of M Music School—Stearns Collection of Musical Instruments
10. Veterans Park

Downtown Ann Arbor/ U of M Campus

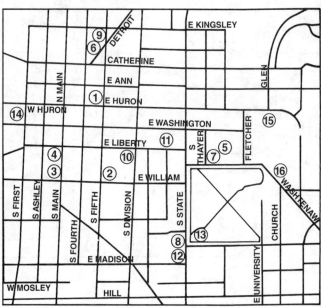

1. Ann Arbor Hands-On Museum
2. Ann Arbor Public Library
3. Ark
4. ArtVentures
5. Burton Memorial Tower
6. Farmer's Market
7. Hill Auditorium
8. Kelsey Museum
9. Kerrytown Plaza
10. Liberty Plaza
11. Michigan Theater
12. Michigan Union
13. Museum of Art
14. Performance Network
15. Power Center
16. U of M Exhibit Museum

Greater Flint Area

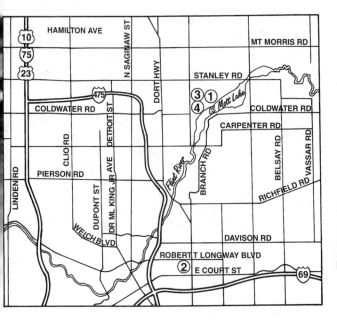

1. Crossroads Village/Huckleberry Railroad
2. Cultural Center
3. Mott Farm
4. Penny Whistle Place

Downtown Flint

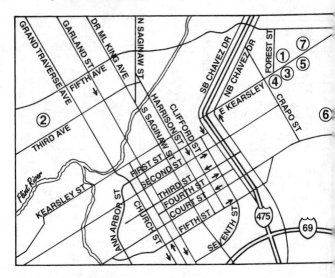

1. Alfred P. Sloan Museum
2. Children's Museum
3. Flint Institute of Art
4. Library
5. Longway Planetarium
6. Mott Community College
7. Whiting Auditorium—Youth Theatre

Greater Lansing Area

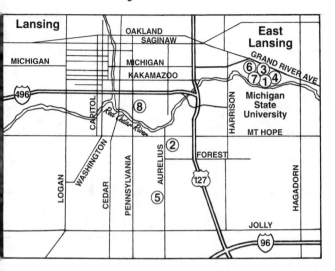

1. Abrams Planetarium
2. Carl E. Fenner Arboretum
3. Horticultural Gardens
4. Kresge Art Museum
5. Lorann Oils
6. Michigan Union
7. MSU Museum of Natural History
8. Potter Park Zoo

Downtown Lansing

1. Impression 5 Museum
2. Michigan Historical Museum
3. Michigan Women's Historical Center and
       Hall of Fame
4. Oldsmobile Park
5. R. E. Olds Transportation Museum
6. State Capitol
7. Turner-Dodge House

4
Monthly Calendar of Special Events

Keep track of your kids at a crowded festival by dressing them in the same color T-shirt. Free up your arms and hands by carrying all the essentials in a backpack, and be sure to attach a big bag — for stowing more essentials — on the back of your stroller.

We Michiganians love to celebrate our seasons, our ethnicity, our children, our products, our arts. Throughout the year, we hold hundreds of festivals and special events just perfect for family outings. Here is a monthly list of the area's best family-oriented annual events. If I missed your favorite festival, please send me the information and we'll try to include it in this book's next edition.

Be sure to check *The Detroit News* for my weekly Kids' Calendar for more up-to-the-minute information. And keep a watchful eye on this calendar so you won't miss something special and have to wait an entire year for it to come around again.

January

Chilly Willy Winter Festival

Novi Parks and Recreation sponsors a day of activities including a snow sculpture contest and winter activities, kids' imagination station, and chili cookoff. 248-347-0400.

Christmas Tree Recycling

Drop off your Christmas tree during the first weekends in January at selected Oakland County Parks for use in park recycling projects. Call 248-858-0906 for locations.

Festival of Bands

Community bands from the Metro Detroit area join together for several sound-spectacular shows in Novi's Twelve Oaks Mall. 248-348-9438.

Harlem Globetrotters

With their famous theme song "Sweet Georgia Brown" playing in the background, the Globetrotters skip around the Joe Louis Arena and the Palace, showing off fancy footwork and basketball tricks. Kids love the teasing banter and the surprises. If you sit up close, you might get a free treat . . . or quite wet. 248-377-0100 (The Palace).

Kids Fair

Children create science and art projects and participate in a host of hands-on activities sponsored by the people in their neighborhood—hospitals, pharmacies, police, merchants, television and radio stations, newspapers, and museums. Held at the Palace, the last Sunday in January. Coordinated by the Jewish Community Center, 248-661-1000.

Martin Luther King, Jr. Day

Marches, plays, musical presentations, and storytelling commemorate the birthday of slain Civil Rights leader Martin Luther King, Jr. Celebrated the third Monday of January. Call AAA Michigan for their calendar of commemorative events. 313-336-1500.

North American International Auto Show

Cobo Center is transformed into a glitzy automobile heaven for nine days, beginning the first or second weekend in January. The kids will enjoy the excitement, the shiny new cars, trucks, and vans, and the fun promotions and giveaways. 248-643-0250.

Plymouth Ice Sculpture Spectacular

Professional chefs and ice carvers from around the world work in frigid temperatures, wielding chisels and chain saws to create over 200 larger-than-life sculptures. Their ice art lines the streets of Plymouth's shopping district and fills Kresge Park. In order to see everything, dress warmly and put little ones in strollers. The Masonic Temple on Penniman, across from the park, sells hot chocolate and cookies. 734-453-1540 or 734-459-6969.

Sesame Street Live!

Fox Theatre hosts the 90-minute show of fast-paced song, dance, and vaudevillian routines performed by larger-than-life Sesame Street characters. Kids preschool to fourth grade will enjoy the heartwarming songs, colorful costumes, and silly shticks. 313-983-6611. For charging tickets by phone, Ticketmaster, 248-645-6666.

Toy Soldier and Figure Show

Young and old collectors won't want to miss this trade show of over 60 dealers selling toy soldiers and figures. Usually the third Sunday in January. 248-586-1022.

February

Black History Month

Many cultural institutions hold special children's events, workshops, and activities to highlight black history. Of great interest: films, performances, exhibits, and living history at the Museum of African American History, 313-494-5800. The Youtheatre's Saturday performances by nationally known African American theater troupes, 248-557-7529. African American Family Day at the Detroit Historical Museum, 313-833-1805. Henry Ford Museum's special weekends throughout February offer music, storytelling, dramatic performances, cooking demonstrations, games, and tours to illustrate important events in African American history, 313-271-1620. Music, storytelling and activities at the Detroit Public Library and branches, 313-833-4042, and at the Ann Arbor District Library, 734-327-4200. Black History Month Blues Series at the Monroe County Library and branches, 734-241-5277. Children's Museum Saturday workshops, 313-873-8100. Special exhibits at Flint's Sloan Museum, 810-760-1169. "Out of Africa" program at the University of Michigan Matthaei Botanical Gardens, 734-998-7061.

Daddy-Daughter Valentine's Day Dances

During the first two weeks of February, more than two dozen local communities offer daddies and their daughters a 90-minute to two-hour deejay dance complete with punch and cookies, corsages or flowers, prizes, and a photo momento to take home. Sign up early—spots fill up fast.

A sampling: Allen Park, 313-928-0770. Bloomfield Hills, 248-433-0885. Brighton, 810-229-1419. Clawson, 248-435-4500. Dearborn Heights, 313-277-7900. Eastpointe, 810-445-5080. Farmington Hills, 248-473-9570. Ferndale, 248-546-2380. Fraser, 810-294-0450. Grosse Pointe, 313-885-4600. Hazel Park, 248-547-5535. Livonia, 734-466-2410. Madison Heights, 248-589-2294. Mt. Clemens/Chesterfield Township, 810-949-0400. Northville, 248-349-0203. Novi, 248-347-0400. Oak Park, 248-691-7555. Pontiac, 248-332-5977. Rochester, 248-656-8308. Southfield, 248-354-9603. Troy, 248-524-3484. Warren,

810-268-8400. Waterford, 248-674-5441. West Bloomfield, 248-334-5660. Westland, 734-722-7620.

Longhorn World Championship Rodeo

Watch nationally ranked cowboys and cowgirls rope and ride. Usually the third week in February, at the Palace. 248-377-0100. Ticketmaster, 248-645-6666.

Outdoorama

Displays of outdoor equipment, wildlife exhibits, and live entertainment help families get in the mood for camping and outdoor adventures. Novi Expo Center, 1-800-777-6720.

Paczki Day

In other cities, the day before Lent might be called Shrove Tuesday or Fat Tuesday, but in Hamtramck the last day to indulge in goodies is called Paczki Day, so named for paczkis (pronounced poonsh-keys), delicious fruit-filled pastries. Bring home a dozen. Hamtramck Chamber of Commerce, 313-875-7877.

Super Summers for Kids

Meet with representatives from Michigan summer camps, enrichment programs, student tours, and teen summer employment. Held the last Sunday in February. 248-851-7342.

Valentine's Day

Check your local library for a Valentine's story hour or craft program. Also many community parks and recreation programs hold Valentine's Day dances.

Winterfest

Downtown Birmingham and Shain Park offer an ice fantasy—ice carving demonstrations and illuminated evening display. Usually the first weekend in February. 248-644-1800.

The World Famous
Royal Lipizzaner Stallions

Regal white Andalusians and their riders offer a razzle-dazzle show of stylized pageantry, focusing on the centuries-old art of dressage. The Palace, 248-377-0100. Ticketmaster, 248-645-6666.

March

Ann Arbor Pow Wow

One of the top Native American celebrations in North America takes place annually at Chrysler Arena in Ann Arbor and features songs, dances, and arts and crafts. 734-763-9044.

Detroit Kennel Club Dog Show

North America's largest one-day, all-breed, benched dog show comes to Cobo Exhibition Center. A great opportunity to take the kids dog shopping. 313-877-8111.

Don't Miss the Easter Bunny

The Easter Bunny's March/April calendar (depending on when Easter falls) is packed with special bunny breakfasts, candy egg hunts, story-telling, and songs. Sure, he's at every mall, but you might want to sign the kids up for some of the area's very special Easter Bunny events.

A sampling: "Bunny Breakfast," Schoolcraft College, Livonia, 734-462-4422. "Brunch with the Bunnies," Crossroads Village, Flint, 1-800-648-7275. "Bunnyville, U.S.A.," Detroit Zoo, 248-399-7001. "Easter Bunny Breakfasts," Hudson's Restaurants, 248-443-6247. "Easter Bunny Brunch," Grosse Pointe War Memorial, 313-881-7511. "Easter Egg Hunt," Domino's Petting Farm, 734-930-5032. "Easter Egg Hunt," Eastern Market, 313-833-1560. "Easter Egg Hunt," Melvindale Parks and Recreation, 313-928-1201. "Easter Egg Hunt," Olde World Canterbury Village, Lake Orion, 248-391-5700. "Easter Egg Hunt," Southwest Detroit Parks and Recreation, 313-297-9337. "Easter Carnival," Warren Parks and Recreation, 810-751-8080. "Eastertime Fun," Edsel and Eleanor Ford House, 313-884-4222. "Easter play," Junior Actors of Ridgedale, Troy, 248-689-6240. "Easter train," Macomb Mall, 810-293-7800. "Egg Walk," E. L. Johnson Nature Center, Bloomfield Hills, 248-433-0885. "Great Marshmallow Drop," Belle Isle, 313-877-8077. "Great Marshmallow Drop," Elizabeth Park, Trenton, 734-261-1990. "Great Easter Egg Hunt," Centerline Recreation Center, 810-757-1610. "Jelly Bean Express Train and Activity Center," Universal Mall, Warren, 810-751-3161. "Mr. Bunny Egg Hunt," West Bloomfield Parks and Recreation, 248-738-2500.

"Parkey's Easter Egg Hunt," Farmington Hills, 248-474-6115. The Easter Bunny's Mother usually visits the Youtheatre during its Easter-week performances, 248-557-7529.

Family Fun Month

Hands-on activities for all ages salute innovation and creativity. Every weekend in March. Henry Ford Museum, 313-271-1620.

Guernsey Farm Dairy

The dairy in Northville offers a free St. Paddy's Day party, 11 a.m.–3 p.m., the Sunday before St. Pat's Day, every other year. 248-349-1466.

Ice Shows–A March Sampling

The ice shows cometh in March and continue through May at area ice arenas. Here's a chance to see earnest local skaters strut their stuff in creative and colorful numbers. Your kids will adore seeing other children perform. Call for dates and times. Birmingham Ice Arena, 248-645-0730. St. Clair Shores Civic Arena, 810-774-7530. Trenton's Kennedy Ice Arena, 734-676-7172. Westland Sports Arena, 734-729-4560. Wyandotte's Yack Arena, 734-324-7265.

Indoor Super Fair

The Pontiac Silverdome offers a taste of summer in late March or early April with carnival rides, kiddie rides, games arcade, and fair food—all in the snow- and rain-free indoors. 248-456-1600.

Maple's Sweet Story

Area nature centers, farms, and metroparks offer maple sugar demonstrations and walks through sugar bush country, with hands-on tastes. Selected weekends, throughout March. Carl F. Fenner Arboretum, Lansing, 517-483-4224. Ella Sharp Museum, Jackson, 517-787-2320. Firestone Farm at Greenfield Village, 313-271-1620. Gerald E. Eddy Geology Center, Chelsea, 734-475-3170. Kensington Farm Center, 248-685-1561; or Indian Springs Nature Center, 248-625-7280, or call toll-free, 1-800-47-PARKS. Lloyd A. Stage Outdoor Education Center, 248-524-3567. Michigan State University's Kellogg Experimental Forest, 616-671-2356. Seven Ponds Nature Center, Dryden, 810-796-3200. U of M Dearborn Environmental Study Area, 313-593-5338.

Maple Syrup Festival

Step up close to the big maples and snitch a taste of the running sap, then walk over to the Sugar House and watch the sap being processed into maple syrup. Cranbrook Institute of Science offers children a look behind the grocery store shelves. Several weekends in March. 248-645-3200.

The Matzah Factory

See how matzah (unleavened bread used during the Jewish holiday of Passover) is made. Kids wear baker's caps and are offered hands-on experience, plus a sample to take home. Jewish Community Center, West Bloomfield, 248-661-1000.

Motor City Comic Con

Three days of comics heaven for collectors. Buy and sell comics and meet the industry's best know publishers, artists, and writers. Novi Expo Center, 248-426-8059.

Purim Carnival

The ancient Jewish holiday is celebrated with a costume parade, food, carnival games, storytelling, and hamantaschen baking. Hamantaschen are traditional three-cornered, fruit-filled pastries. Designed for kids preschool to early elementary. Jewish Community Center, West Bloomfield, 248-661-1000.

St. Patrick's Day

One of Detroit's liveliest parades takes place the Sunday before St. Patrick's Day with lots of green hoopla and a stroll down Michigan Avenue in Corktown. Check newspaper listings for a full schedule of events, including Irish folksinging and ethnic dancing at local halls. Or call the Irish-American Club, 313-964-8700.

The Shrine Circus

Wild animals, cavorting clowns, prancing horses, daring trapeze artists—everything you always wanted in a circus and more. The kids can see from almost every seat in the State Fair Coliseum, 313-369-8250.

Spring Vacation Programs

A variety of community institutions, parks and recreation programs, and area libraries offer programs for children during spring break. A sampling: "Children's Easter Vacation Festival"—free movies, mime, puppets, magic, and stories at the Detroit Public Library, 313-833-1490. "School Break Specials"—free puppets, storytelling, music, and theater at Birmingham's Baldwin Public Library, 248-647-1700. "Spring Pioneer Living Day Camp," Cobblestone Farm, 734-994-2928. "Spring Science Day Camp," Leslie Science Center, 734-662-7802. "Spring Vacation Program"—daily swim, field trip, games, and crafts at the Farmington YMCA, 248-553-4020. Hands-on experiments and demonstrations, Cranbrook Institute of Science, 248-645-3200.

Disney on Ice

The latest Disney animated movie comes to three-dimensional life with extravagant costumes, sets, lights, and music. Joe Louis Arena, Detroit. 313-983-6606. Ticketmaster, 248-645-6666.

April

Baby Animal Day

Upland Hills Farms brings the farm animals to the city, at the Birmingham Community House. 248-644-5832.

Bloomfest

Celebrate spring at the area's largest garden show. Over four acres of gardens, floral art, flower marketplace, and hands-on gardening activities for children at Cobo Center. Usually the second weekend in April. 248-646-2990.

Day of Puppetry

The Detroit Puppeteers Guild presents a day of puppet-making workshops and fine puppet performances. 810-463-0480.

Detroit Public Schools Student Exhibition

Detroit school children share their dreams and visions in this joyous annual show (now more than half a century old), which fills the Detroit Institute of Arts with puppets, drawings, sculpture, paintings, textiles, mixed media, and photography. Your kids will become inspired to run home and create. 313-833-7900.

Ice Shows—An April Sampling

Dearborn's Adray Arena, 313-943-4098. Melvindale Ice Arena, 313-928-1200. Southfield Sports Arena, 248-354-9357.

Law Day

The police and fire departments of Allen Park and Melvindale team up to demonstrate their wares and their capabilities. Kids are encouraged to touch and try. 313-928-0535.

Law Fair

Oakland County Bar Association offers a day of legal merrymaking and information with Officer Mac, the State Police remote control robot; demonstrations of lie-detectors, breathalyzers, and police cars, plus balloons and coloring books. Held at rotating Oakland County sites the last Sunday in April. 248-334-3400.

Royal Hanneford Circus

In addition to clowns, trapeze artists, and jugglers, this circus is famous for wonderful animal acts. See trained tigers, ponies, sea lions, dogs, and bears. The Palace, 248-377-0100.

Sheepshearing Day

It's a Scottish Spring Festival at the Rochester Hills Museum complete with sheepshearing, old-fashioned craft demonstrations, bagpipes, highland dancing, and authentic food. 248-656-4663.

Spring Farm Days

Join the 19th-century Firestone Farm family as they get ready for spring. Help with the chores, clear and plant the fields, welcome spring lambs, and watch demonstrations of soap making and sheep shearing. Held the end of April. Greenfield Village, 313-271-1620.

Vetavisit

Michigan State University's College of Veterinary Medicine holds an annual open house the second or third Saturday of April. Children are invited to look through microscopes, milk cows or goats, watch demonstrations of drug-sniffing dogs and sheep shearing, and meet llamas, horses, and snakes. 517-355-5165.

May

Civil War Remembrance

The Civil War comes to life with reenactment groups portraying both military and civilian life. Memorial Day Weekend at Greenfield Village. 313-271-1620.

Cinco de Mayo

Celebrate May 5th with children's activities, food, and folk art. Mexicantown, 313-842-0450.

Detroit Mini Grand Prix

The New Center Area hosts a mini grand prix for the entire family. While 50 three-horsepower go-carts race in seven heats, Kids Korner offers children's activities; clowns, jugglers, balloon animals, free ice cream, storytelling, crafts, video games, and more. Usually mid-May. West Grand Boulevard and Second, Detroit, 313-875-MINI.

Eastern Market Flower Day

Pile the kids in the little red wagon, stroll around Eastern Market, and buy your spring flowers at bargain prices. The day gets bigger every year, and features food, entertainment, clowns, and artists. Park at the Detroit Institute of Arts or the Charles H. Wright Museum of African American History and hop on a shuttle to the market. Always held the Sunday following Mother's Day. 313- 833-1560.

East Lansing Art Festival

Downtown East Lansing hosts several hundred artists selling their wares, three stages offering continuous performances, international food booths, and children's activities. 517-337-1731.

Feast of Sainte Claire

Costumed reenactors recreate colonial American daily life, reenact Revolutionary War battles, and offer fife and drum corps entertainment. Pine Grove Park, along the St. Clair River, Port Huron. Memorial Day weekend. 810-982-0891.

The First People's International Fair and Pow Wow

Native American dancers, storytellers, food, and crafts. Gibraltar Trade Center, Mount Clemens. 810-756-1350.

Gem and Mineral Show

Exhibits, demonstrations, and free mineral kits for children. Usually the second weekend in May. Dearborn Civic Center. 313-943-2350.

Heritage Festival

Rochester Municipal Park is the site of old-fashioned family fun, including a pioneer homestead, encampments, petting farm, craft booths, demonstrations, and pony rides. Usually Memorial Day weekend. Coordinated by Dinosaur Hill Nature Center, 248-656-0999.

Ice Shows—A May Sampling

Great Lakes Sport City, 810-294-2400. Berkley Ice Arena, 248-546-2460. Garden City Ice Arena, 734-261-3491.

Incredible Israel Fest

Celebrate Israel Independence Day with a 3.5 mile walk, family concerts, hands-on activities, rides, food, and fireworks. Usually Sunday at the end of May. Jewish Community Center, West Bloomfield. 248-645-7878.

It's All Happening at the Zoo

Belle Isle Zoo, Detroit Zoo Train, and Log Cabin Learning Center open for the season May 1. 248-398-0900.

Memorial Day Parades

Check your local city office for Memorial Day parade activities. These cities generally offer parades: Beverly Hills, Brighton, Ferndale, Grosse Pointe Shores, Milford, Pleasant Ridge, Pontiac, Royal Oak, St. Clair Shores, Sterling Heights, Utica, Walled Lake, Warren, Wayne/Westland, and Wyandotte.

Mount Clemens Art Fair and Tastefest

Over 100 juried artists, music, kids' art projects and face painting, food samplings from area restaurants, and family entertainment. Held downtown Friday and Saturday of Mother's Day weekend. 810-469-8666.

Renaissance City Storyfest

A Wayne State University conference that offers evening and matinee storytelling concerts, perfect for family entertainment. 313-577-5342.

Samantha at Greenfield Village

Step back into the 19th century and enjoy a Suffragette march, hands-on projects, manners lesson, and ride in a Model T, in a two-hour program based on the life of American Girls character Samantha Parkington. For girls nine years and older and their moms, grandmas, and women friends. Offered throughout May-October, Greenfield Village. 313-271-1620.

Spring Festival

Spring has sprung at the Kensington Farm and Nature Centers. There are lots of baby animals, sheep-shearing and wood-carving demonstrations, hayrides, and wildflower walks. 248-685-1561.

Very Special Arts Festival

Over 100 artists and 150 performing artists celebrate the power of artistic creativity over physical and mental challenges. Two days of theater, dances, and music showcasing the talents of students with disabilities. Usually held the middle of May at a mall in Southeastern Michigan. 313-892-1750.

June

Civil War Muster

Canons roar and war cries echo as reenactors create a taste of military and civilian life during the 1860's. A special evening candlelight tour is scheduled on Saturday night. Kensington Metropark, Milford. 248-685-1561.

Carrousel of Nations

Windsor's many ethnic and cultural communities sponsor two weekends of multi-cultural experiences, including foods, dances, and music. 519-255-1127.

Colonial Life Festival

18th-century America comes to life with Revolutionary War reenactments, fife and drum music, and fashions from the 1700's. Usually held the last weekend of June. Greenfield Village, 313-271-1620.

East Dearborn International Festival

Live stage performances, multi-cultural dance groups, pop and traditional Arab music, magicians, carnival rides, and lots of Mideastern food. Usually held mid-June. 313-842-7010.

HAP Family Fair

Free arts and crafts, environmental activities, children's entertainment, science demonstrations, and parenting, health, and recycling information. Held inside and on the grounds of the Southfield Civic Center. 248-552-6420.

Heritage Day

The Troy Historical Museum sponsors a day of ethnic celebration and musical entertainment. Usually the fourth Sunday in June. 248-524-3570.

International Freedom Festival

Beginning mid-June through July 4, over 100 events celebrate the friendship between Canada and the United States, including parades, music,

fireworks, and boat races. Windsor's Children's Day is held along the riverfront mid-June with a big wheel grand prix and teddy bear picnic. 313-923-7400 (Detroit), 519-252-7264 (Windsor).

Log Cabin Day

Visit a Michigan log cabin and join in hands-on pioneer crafts and games during the last Sunday in June.

Michigan Challenge Balloonfest

There's something for every member of the family at Howell's annual three-day weekend event: more than 80 colorful hot-air balloons, sky-divers, acrobatic stunt kites, antique cars, medieval village, entertainment, arts and crafts, and a midway. Usually the third or fourth weekkend in June. 517-546-3920.

Motor Muster

Greenfield Village hosts a classic car show featuring cars, trucks, bicycles, and other nostalgic vehicles from 1933–1969. Held the third weekend in June. 313-271-1620.

National Strawberry Festival

Strawberry lovers, rejoice! Belleville ushers in the strawberry season with a weekend celebration of games, parades, children's entertainment, and berry delights. 734-697-3137.

Oak Park Funfest

Ten days of special activities celebrating Independence Day, including a parade, concerts, fireworks, and children's fun day. 248-691-7555.

Rendezvous on the Rouge

Life in Detroit during the French and Indian War, 1754–1763, is recreated with costumed reenactors, portraying French and British militia and Great Lakes Indians. The colonial-era encampment is held at Dearborn's Ford Field. 313-565-3000.

Summer Festival

Greenfield Village comes to life with an expanded menu of daily hands-on activities, demonstrations, musical and dramatic performances, storytelling, games, and a chance to "meet" famous inventors from the past. Mid-June through August, 313-271-1620.

July

Ann Arbor Art Fair

Besides the displays by fine artists, there's enough food, street musicians, and stage entertainers to turn any child on to art. Your budding artists can exercise their imagination and create make and take crafts at two hands-on activity sites found at Liberty and Fifth Avenue, and Church Street, south of South University. Both run daily. The fair is always Wednesday–Saturday, the third full week in July. 734-994-5260.

Children's Celebration

Flint's Cultural Center sets the stage for a day of hands-on activities and children's shows. Usually held mid-July. 810-234-1695.

Civil War Re-Creation

Relive the Civil War with costumed reenactors, artillery demonstrations, and military ball. The second weekend in July. Nike County Park, Newport. 734-243-7118.

Family Fun at the Ann Arbor Summer Festival

Free children's entertainment, dance, demonstrations, hands-on activities, and arts and crafts held at the Top of the Park, mid-June to mid-July. Also, several unique family shows are scheduled throughout the month-long arts festival. 734-647-2278.

Hot Air Jubilee

Over 60 hot-air balloon launches each sunrise and sundown, arts and crafts, bands, entertainment, children's activities, and food. Jackson. 517-782-1515.

Huron River Day

Learn about ecology and celebrate water sports at Ann Arbor's Gallup Park. The day's activities include canoe races, youth fishing derby, nature walk, children's games, crafts and entertainment, bicycle maintenance clinic, and windsurf sailing demonstrations. 734-994-2778.

July Fourth Festivities and Parades

Check your local city for parade and fireworks schedules. Area historic villages also offer special July Fourth activities. A sampling: Cobblestone Farm, Ann Arbor, 734-994-2928; Crossroads Village, Flint, 810-736-7100; Greenfield Village, Dearborn, 313-271-1620.

July Fourth Concerts

Bring a picnic supper and enjoy Greenfield Village's old-fashioned Fourth. The evening includes the Detroit Symphony Orchestra playing traditional patriotic music, and a fireworks display. July 2–4. 313-271-1620.

Michigan 50's Festival

Time for rockin' and rollin' to continuous live entertainment. The festival also features arts and crafts, children's activities, fireworks, and an oldies car show. Usually the last weekend in July. Novi Expo Center, 248-348-5600.

Michigan Taste Fest

Celebrate the Fourth of July weekend in Detroit's New Center Area with continuous children's entertainment, hands-on crafts and activities, samples of made-in-Michigan products and specialties of Michigan chefs, plus evening concerts by nationally known musicians. 313-872-0188.

Port Huron's Blue Water Festival

Port Huron comes to life with family fun, including a carnival, midway, parade, and entertainment. 810-985-9623.

Spirit of Detroit Thunderfest

The Detroit River is the course for the annual hydroplane races. School groups are also invited to tour the race pits as part of "New Kids on the Course." Watch the races from general admission and reserved seating available along the river, or free viewing from Belle Isle. Thursday–Sunday during the second weekend in July. To charge tickets by phone, Ticketmaster 248-645-6666. For information, 313-331-7770.

Waterford Summer Festival

Continuous entertainment, ice cream social, car show and cruise, children's arts and crafts, pony rides. Third or fourth weekend in July. 248- 623-9389.

August

African World Festival

Live entertainment, children's programs, art workshops, an artists market, and food booths celebrate the music, dance, arts, and food of Africa. Sponsored by the Charles H. Wright Museum of African American History and held along the river at Detroit's Hart Plaza. 313-494-5800.

Cascades Civil War Muster

The bluster and glory of the Civil War come to life as hundreds of authentically costumed reenactors bring their encampments to Jackson's Cascade Falls Park for a weekend of mock battles and military demonstrations. Usually held the weekend before Labor Day. 517-788-4320.

Celebration of Emancipation

Greenfield Village focuses on African American traditions, customs, and contributions during this weekend celebration of the Emancipation Proclamation. Usually the first weekend in August. 313-271-1620.

Franklin Village Roundup

Celebrate Labor Day Monday with an old-fashioned village parade, car display, horse show, and art fair. Held in old Franklin. 248-626-9666.

Highland Games

Watch Scottish athletes compete in traditional games including the Stone Put, Farmer's Walk, and Caber Toss—the tossing of a 15-foot pole resembling a modern-day telephone pole. The day also includes bagpipe and drum concerts, Scottish dancing, food, and children's games. Usually held on Saturday in early August at Livonia's Greenmead Historical Village. St. Andrew's Society, 313-832-1849.

Michigan State Fair

The Michigan farmer is still at the heart of this granddaddy of all Michigan fairs. Kids will love viewing the award-winning animals, collecting free made-in-Michigan samples in the coliseum, feeding the animals at the petting farm, cheering for the little porkers in the Racing Pigs, learning to fish at the DNR Pocket Park, and watching animals give birth at the Birthing Center. Every day offers a full variety of children's performers and nationally known entertainers. I recommend taking advantage of all the fair freebies, contests, and concerts. Plan on spending a lot of money on midway rides. Held the last weekend in August through the first weekend in September. 313-369-8250. Reserved concert tickets are available through Ticketmaster, 248-645-6666.

Oakland County 4-H Fair

Springfield Oaks in Davisburg hosts livestock exhibits, demolition derby, monster trucks, petting zoos, racing pigs, and carnival rides. Usually opens the fifth Monday prior to Labor Day. 248-634-8830.

Old French Town Days

With period music, battlefield drills, children's games and arts and crafts, costumed reenactors recreate French civilian and military life in 18th-century Michigan. The last weekend in August. Hellenberg Park, Monroe. 734-243-7137.

Renaissance Festival

The 16th century comes to vivid life with authentically costumed roving players, jugglers, and jousters, wenches and knaves, a village marketplace, plus Renaissance-flavored games, rides, and food. The kids will enjoy the continuous merriment and ribald entertainment. Held weekends in the Holly area from mid-August through the end of September. 248-634-5552 or 1-800-601-4848.

Royal Oak Grand National

Kids thrill to the sights and sounds of over 30 remote control, quarter-scale cars vrooming around a 150-lap race course. Music, mimes, clowns, food, and face painting turn downtown Royal Oak into a large street fair. Usually held on a Saturday late in August. 248-547-4000.

Saline World Championship Rodeo

Rodeo champions from around the country compete in six events, including bareback riding, saddle bronc riding, and cowgirl barrel racing. Washtenaw Farm Council Grounds. Usually end of August. 734-429-4835.

Tenneco Automotive Grand Prix of Detroit

Belle Isle hosts the Indy cars, their drivers, and the fans. The island glitters in the sun and offers everyone a great view. Fans can take continuous bus, trolley, or boat shuttles to the island. The first weekend in August. 313-393-7749.

Tin Cups and Hard Tack

Reenactors relive the days of the Civil War with an encampment, music, hands-on activities, and special exhibits. Saturday, mid-August. On the grounds and inside the Michigan Historical Museum, Lansing. 517-373-3559.

War of 1812 Battle Reenactments

The War of 1812 comes to life with two days of battle reenactments, complete with soldiers, Indians, and early Michigan settlers. Usually held the third weekend in August. Lake Erie Metropark, Rockwood. 734-379-5020

Woodward Dream Cruise

All-day classic car parade along Woodward Avenue, plus live entertainment, children's rides, games, and activities in communities along the Woodward corridor, from the State Fairgrounds to Pontiac. Held the second weekend in August. 1-888-493-2196.

Ypsilanti Heritage Festival

Parades, concerts, living history encampment, old-fashioned circus, and antique car shows highlight Ypsilanti's historical past. Usually held at the end of August. Riverside Park, 734-483-4444.

September

Apples and Honey

Celebrate the Jewish New Year with storytelling, hands-on activities, holiday cooking, and entertainment. Jewish Community Center, West Bloomfield, 248-661-7649.

Art in the Park

While Mom and Dad browse through the art fair, children can create at the art station and have their faces painted. Usually held the second weekend in September. Shain Park, Birmingham. 248-456-8150.

Art 'n Apples

Enjoy autumn's warm weather at an outdoor art fair, featuring a juried show, children's hands-on crafts, and entertainment. Rochester's Municipal Park, 248-651-6700.

Autumnfest

The city of Southfield celebrates its pioneer history with a day full of butter churning, rug weaving, farm animals, dancing, singing, and touring the old Mary Thompson home, built in 1831. Usually the second Sunday of the month. 248-424-9022.

Best of Our Town

Historic Crossroads Village presents an old time fair with craft demonstrations, backwoods skills, and harvesting demonstrations. Two weekends in September. 1-800-648-7275.

Children's Fair at the Detroit Festival of the Arts

Join Detroit's biggest street party and celebrate the arts. At the Children's Fair on Wayne State University's Gullen Mall, there are more than 70 free activities, including face painting, puppet making, chalk drawing, musical performances, and storytelling. Throughout the Cultural Center, you'll find a juried art show of adult artists and an art show of young artists, street performers, live music, food, poetry readings and more. Held inside and outside all the Cultural Center institutions, mid-September. 313-577-5088.

Depot Days

South Lyon's McHattie Park complex, which includes Witch's Hat Depot Museum, Washburn one-room schoolhouse, and a red caboose, set the stage for a weekend of old-fashioned activities, including entertainment, hands-on crafts, a Native American encampment, and a celebrated frog jumping contest. Held the first weekend after Labor Day. 248-437-9929.

Fall Festival

Ann Arbor's Cobblestone Farm sponsors a traditional 19th-century harvest festival featuring cooking, crafts, outdoor games, and a corn husking bee. 734-994-2928.

Fall Festival

Kensington Metropark celebrates the season with family activities: hay rides, puppet shows, woodcraft demonstrations, nature crafts, clowns, candle dipping, and apple cider making. Usually a mid-September weekend. 248-685-1561.

Fall Harvest Days

It's autumn at Greenfield Village in Dearborn. Celebrate the changing season with harvest activities, cider making, and entertainment. Held the first two weekends in October. 313-271-1620

Hawk Fest

The annual fall migration of thousands of birds of prey is the focus of this festival featuring hawk identification workshops, kids' crafts, photo display, educational speakers, live birds of prey, and hawk-watch wares. The third weekend in September. Lake Erie Metropark. 734-379-5020.

Heritage Festival

Celebrate Wyandotte's history with a weekend of battle reenactments, arts and crafts fair, entertainment, harvest activities and house tours. Usually held the first weekend after Labor Day. 734-246-4520.

Heritage Harvest Day

Seven Ponds Nature Center celebrates autumn with colonial crafts, sheep-to-shawl and pioneer skill demonstrations, antique steam engines, old-time tools and equipment, traditional music, children's games, and petting farm. Usually held in early September. 810-796-3200.

Honey and Apples Festival

Press your own apple cider, learn how bees make honey, and walk along the nature trails at Cranbrook Institute of Science, Bloomfield Hills. The last weekend in September and first weekend in October. 248-645-3200.

Michigan Indian Days

The public is invited to experience Native American dancers, crafts, and traditional foods at an authentic gathering of tribes and nations from across the United States and Canada. Hart Plaza. 313-535-2966.

Montreux/Detroit Jazz Festival

The nation's leading jazz musicians play non-stop during the four-day Labor Day weekend. And just for kids—listen as Michigan high school and college bands jazz it up and get into the action. Hart Plaza, Detroit. 313-963-7622.

Old Car Festival

Learn how to crank start a car and enjoy a parade of antique cars from 1932 and earlier. Mid-September at Greenfield Village. 313-271-1620.

Railroad Days

Visit a Hobo's Camp, enjoy a Railroader's lunch and watch vintage train cars chug around the village. End of September at Greenfield Village. 313-271-1620.

Rendezvous on the Huron

Travel back to the days when huge birch bark canoes ruled the Great Lakes waterways. Paddle the 34-foot voyageur canoe, wander through a trapper's camp, try your hand at ax throwing and skillet tossing, and watch live period entertainment. First weekend in September. Kensington Metropark Farm Center, 248-685-1561.

Revolutionary War Encampment

Watch tactical demonstrations with muskets and cannons; visit the soldiers' encampment; shop through the row of historical merchants. The first weekend in September at Fort Malden National Historic Site. 519-736-5416.

Riverfest

Celebrate Labor Day weekend along the Grand

River in Lansing's Riverfront Park. The three-day festival offers music, performing arts, children's activities, carnival rides, Sunday night Electric Float Parade (on the river), and Monday night fireworks. 517-483-4499.

Sheep and Wool Festival

Children's lamb parade, farm games, hayrides, fiber workshop, and demonstrations of shearing, spinning, dyeing, felting, and weaving. Last weekend in September. Mt. Bruce Station, Romeo. 810-798-2660.

Somewhere in Time

Journey back to the 19th century and enjoy old-fashioned pleasures—a ride along the Detroit River on the Diamond Belle Riverboat, historic trolley tours of Old Trenton, antique car display, arts and crafts, entertainment, and horseshoe tournament. Usually mid-September. Elizabeth Park, Trenton. 734-261-1990.

UniverSoul Circus

The nation's only all-black circus pulls into town at the end of September and offers aerialists, unicyclists, equestrians, clowns, elephants and tigers, plus a look at African American history. Chene Park, Detroit. 313-393-7827, Ticketmaster 248-645-6666.

Victorian Festival

Northville Chamber of Commerce hosts a variety of turn-of-the-century activities including horse-drawn carriage rides, family contests and games, strolling musicians, mimes, and entertainment. Usually held the second or third weekend in September. 248-349-7640.

Wiard's Orchards Country Fair

It's a country fair every weekend, mid-September through October, at Wiard's Orchards in Ypsilanti. You can pick apples and pumpkins, take a pony or miniature train ride, play games, watch craft demonstrations, listen to country music, explore a haunted house, and eat harvest foods. 734-482-7744.

October

Autumn Harvest Indian Festival

Join dancers in full regalia as they perform traditional dances, and enjoy movies, storytelling, demonstrations of native crafts, children's activities, arts and crafts, and Native American–style foods. Novi Expo Center, 248-348-5600.

Children's Halloween Ball

For a donation to the Children's Leukemia Foundation of Michigan, your little urchin gets a pizza dinner, beverage, goody bag, and entertainment. 248-353-8222.

Dearborn Civil War Days

Learn about Dearborn's role in the Civil War with costumed reenactors, Civil War–era music, and hands-on activities. The first weekend in October. Commandant's Quarters, 313-565-3000.

Fall Festival: A Blast to the Past

Travel back to Michigan's pioneer days and meet costumed reenactors in a wilderness camp setting, take part in pioneer and Native American crafts, and enjoy music and an evening Contra Dance. First Saturday in October. University of Michigan Matthaei Botanical Gardens, 734-998-7061.

Fall Fun Days at Symanzik's Berry Farm

Walk through a corn stock forest into a pumpkin patch bathed in sunlight. Children can pick their own pumpkins and gourds, play in a mock barn, visit farm animals, and take a ride on "space trollies." Weekends during October. 810-636-7714.

Fall Harvest Days

Help the 19th-century Firestone Farm family get ready for winter with fall home and harvesting chores. Create corn husk dolls and wheat ornaments. The first two weekends in October. Greenfield Village, 313-271-1620.

Fiber Faire

Sheep shearing demonstrations, spinning, felting, dyeing and quilting workshops. Hand-crafted items for sale. Armada Fairgrounds, the first weekend in October. 810-727-9083.

Halloween Parties

During the last two weeks of October, little ghosts and goblins are invited to costume parties and haunting nature walks at area institutions. A Sampling: "Ancestor's Night," Charles H. Wright Museum of African American History, 313- 494-5800. "Bloomer Haunted Forest," West Bloomfield, 248-738-2500. "Friendly Forest," Clintonwood Park, Clarkston, 248-625-8223. "Halloween Camp-In," Ann Arbor Hands-On Museum, 734-995-5439. "Halloween Activities," Detroit Recreation Centers, 313-224-4367. "Halloween Celebration," Cobblestone Farm, Ann Arbor, 734-994-2928. "Halloween Ghosts and Goodies," Flint's Crossroads Village, 1-800-648-7275. "Halloween Happenings," a story walk through the woods, Independence Oaks, 248-625-6473. "Halloween Hoot," a walk through a haunted forest, Rochester's Dinosaur Hill, 248-656-0999. Halloween play and trick-or-treating, Edsel and Eleanor Ford House in Grosse Pointe Shores, 313-884-4222. "Halloween Zoobilee," Belle Isle Zoo, 248-398-0900. "Haunted Forest," Belle Isle Nature Center, 313-852-4056. "Haunted Hollow," Troy Parks and Recreation nature walk, 248-524-3484. "Haunted Stroll," Wilson Barn, Livonia, 734-427-4311. "Historical Haunts," Detroit's Historical Museum, 313-833-1805. "Lansing Zoo Boo," Potter Park Zoo, 517-371-3926. "Maybury Madness," Maybury State Park forest walk, Northville, 248-349-0203. "Mother Goose Halloween Walk," Greenmead Historical Village, Livonia, 248-477-7375. "The Past of Halloween," Wolcott Mill Metropark, 810-749-5997,

"Safety Street," University of Detroit-Mercy, 313-993-1254. "Spooky Saturday," Flint's Sloan Museum, 810-760-1169. "Tales From the Cranbrook Crypt," Cranbrook Institute of Science, 248-645-3200. "Zoo Boo," Detroit Zoo, 248-398-0900.

Halloween Trick-or-Treat

Many area malls offer children a safe and warm alternative to traditional house-to-house trick-or-treating, along with entertainment and storytelling. Here's a sampling: Fairlane Town Center, Dearborn, 313-593-1370. Lakeside Mall, Sterling Heights, 810-247-1744. Livonia Mall, Livonia, 248-476-1160. Macomb Mall, Roseville, 810-293-7800. Oakland Mall, Troy, 248-585-6000. Summit Place, Waterford, (248) 682-0123. Tel-Twelve Mall, Southfield, 248-353-4111. Twelve Oaks, Novi, 1-800-362-1211.

Harvest Festival

Hayrides, demonstrations of blacksmithing, basket weaving, corn harvesting, rope making, wool spinning and weaving, old-fashioned children's games and activities. Maybury State Park, Northville. 248-349-8390.

Harvest Home Festival

The Troy Historical Museum sponsors 19th-century fall harvest activities for the entire family. Bob for apples, design your own scarecrow, participate in a hay bale toss or corn husk and shelling contest, and enjoy 19th-century music. Usually early October. 248-524-3570.

Haunted Houses

For some families, Halloween isn't Halloween without blood curdling screams and gruesome tableaux. Many area haunted houses are run by community groups and your entrance fee helps raise money for worthwhile programs. Since most haunted houses are not suitable for the very young or the faint-hearted, many houses offer special not-so-scary children's afternoons.

Here is a sampling of rooms with a boo: Blake's Big Apple Orchard Haunted Barn, Armada, 810-784-9710. Detroit Sportsmen's Congress Haunted Forest, Utica, 810-739-3500. Dungeon of the Dead, Warren, 810-751-8080. Greenville's Haunted Mill of Greenville, 616-754-0044. Haunted Hayride, Miller's Big Red, Romeo, 810-752-7888. House of Nightmares, Warren, 810-445-6730. Howling Hayrides, Romeo, 810-752-6328. Silo X,

Clinton Township, 1-888-222-4088. Suicide Saloon, Wyandotte, 734-284-3861. Troy Haunted Hollow, 248-524-3484. Warren Goodfellows Haunted Gallery, 248-524-4964. Wiard's Orchards Haunted House, Ypsilanti, 313-482-7744. Wilson Barn, Livonia, 313-427-4311. YMCA Camp Cavell haunted weekend, 1-800-354-9922. The following area Jaycees also offer well-attended haunted houses (phone numbers change from year-to-year with each new chairperson, so call information or your local Chamber of Commerce for the Jaycee chapter in your city): Allen Park, Dearborn Heights/Garden City, Farmington, Flat Rock, Flushing, Howell, Livonia, Madison Heights (Mutiliation Mansion), Monroe, Milford, Novi, Oxford, Pontiac, Plymouth/Canton, Redford, Riverview, Rochester, Salem, South Lyon, Taylor, Trenton, Union Lake, Warren, Waterford, Wayne/Westland, Woodhaven, Wyandotte.

Motor City Comic Con

Comic collectors won't want to miss this annual gathering of comic dealers, publishers, artists, and writers. Southfield Civic Center, 248-426-8059.

Old World Market

Southfield Civic Center Pavilion houses Detroit's largest ethnic festival, full of food, music, dances, and crafts of over 50 nationalities. Usually mid-October. Sponsored by the International Institute, 313-871-8600.

Pioneer Days

The Waterloo Farm in Stockbridge comes to life with demonstrations of 19th-century fall harvest crafts, food, and music. Usually the second Sunday in October. 517-596-2254.

Ringling Brothers and Barnum & Bailey Circus

The circus comes to Joe Louis Arena with ferocious tigers, majestic elephants, silly clowns, and daring trapeze artists. Did you expect anything less? Usually early October. 313-983-6606 or for charging tickets by phone, Ticketmaster 248-645-6666.

South Lyon Pumpkinfest

Parade, carnival rides, and pumpkin contests. First weekend in October. 248-437-8703.

Upland Hills Pumpkin Festival

Upland Hills Farms in Oxford turns your pumpkin picking into a Halloween experience. Meet Farmer Webster, enjoy hay and pony rides, a petting farm, play area, haunted house, and concessions. Weekends during October. 248-628-1611.

Youtheatre

Youtheatre kicks off its season at the beginning of October offering performances of puppetry, mime, music, drama, and children's entertainers. Almost every Saturday through May, 248-557-7529.

November

Annual Dance Concert Series

Wayne State University Dance Company presents an annual dance concert for children. School groups are welcome during the week; the public is invited to weekend performances. Usually held mid-November. 313-577-4273.

Children's Only Shops

Children can shop 'til they drop at these cute shops stocked with inexpensive gifts for family and friends. They usually open Thanksgiving weekend and run through mid-December. "Elves Shelves," Detroit's Renaissance Center, 313-568-5600. "Children's Only Shop," Detroit Historical Museum, 313-833-1805. "Children's Only Holiday Shop," The Community House, Birmingham, 248-644-5832. "Little Door Store," Hudson's Somerset North, 248-816-4000. "Shopping for Kids Only," Southfield Parks and Recreation, 248-354-9603.

Detroit A Glow/Community Sing-along

Crowds gather after work on the Monday before Thanksgiving to watch as the Hart Plaza Christmas tree lights are turned on. A community sing-along is held in Cobo Center following the lighting ceremony. 313-961-1403

Detroit Thanksgiving Festival

Floating bumblebees, the seven dwarfs, dinosaurs, and Santa himself. Detroit's answer to the Macy's Parade takes place along Woodward Avenue on Thanksgiving Day morning. Dress warmly and arrive early for a good view. America's Thanksgiving Parade kicks off a weekend Thanksgiving celebration, including the Little

Gobbler's Race (the morning of the parade), and A Parade of Rides and Games, an indoor carnival held at Cobo Center, beginning Thanksgiving Day and running through early December. 313-923-8259.

Disney on Ice

The latest Disney animated movie comes to three-dimensional life with extravagant costumes, sets, lights, and music. Joe Louis Arena, Detroit. Usually in early November, and also again in March. 313-983-6606. Ticketmaster 248-645-6666.

Fantasy of Lights

Howell's downtown historic district sparkles with lights and features a craft and holiday bazaar, free carriage rides, music, holiday activities, refreshments, Victorian characters, and visits with Santa. Opens with a parade Thanksgiving weekend and then runs the first three Sundays in December. 517-546-3920.

Festival of Trees

Cobo Center is transformed by 100 professionally decorated trees, a gingerbread village, and an aisle of wreaths. Begins just before Thanksgiving and runs through Thanksgiving weekend. 313-877-8111.

Festival of Trees

Over 100 professionally decorated trees, a gingerbread village, yuletide entertainment, and weekend Teddy Bear Teas for youngsters. Begins the Wednesday before Thanksgiving and runs through Thanksgiving weekend. Lansing Center, downtown Lansing. 517-367-TREE.

Festivals of Light

Many communities are dressed in twinkling lights for the holidays and offer festivities and walk- or drive-through tours. Most begin Thanksgiving weekend and run through New Year's Eve. Here's a sampling: "Celebration of Lights," Sarnia's Centennial Park, 519-336-3232. "Christmas at Crossroads," Flint, 810-736-7100. "Fantasy of Lights Parade," downtown Howell, 517-546-3920. "Festival of Light," Ypsilanti's Riverside Park, 734-483-4444. "Freedom Hill Aglow," Sterling Heights, 810-979-7010. "Lightfest Celebration in Lights," Wyandotte's BASF Waterfront Park, 734-324-7290. "Lights Before Christmas," Toledo Zoo, 419-385-5721. "Nautical Mile Night of Lights,"

St. Clair Shore's Blossom Heath Park, 810-445-5350. "Silver Bells in the City," downtown Lansing, 517-372-4636. "Spirit of Christmas," Ann Arbor, 734-930-5032. "'Tis the Season," Flint Cultural Center, 810-760-1087. "Wayne County LightFest," Hines Drive, Middle Rouge Parkway, 734-261-1990. "Wild Lights," Detroit Zoo, 248-398-0900. "Wonderland of Lights," Lansing's Potter Park Zoo, 517-371-3926.

Gingerbread Houses

Learn how to assemble a gingerbread or graham cracker house and build a sweet family tradition. The following sites offer classes for parents and children: Purchase children's gingerbread house kits at Arts and Scraps, Detroit, 313-640-4411. Bakers Delight, Sterling Heights, 810-268-8000 (for groups only). Children's Museum, Detroit, 313-873-8100. The Community House, Birmingham, 248-644-5832. Grosse Pointe War Memorial, Grosse Pointe Farms, 313-881-7511. Henry Ford Estate–Fairlane, Dearborn, 313-593-5590. Kitchen Glamour, Novi, Redford, and Rochester locations, 313-537-1300. Longacre House, Farmington Hills, 248-477-8404.

North American Horse Spectacular

Live horse demonstrations, trade show. First weekend in November. Novi Expo Center. 517-485-2309.

Santa Parades

Small towns throughout Michigan usher in the holiday season with bands, floats, costumed characters and, of course, Santa. Call for dates and times. Grosse Pointe, 313-886-7474. Howell, 517-546-3920. Sarnia, Canada, 1-800-265-0316. Wyandotte, 734-246-4505.

Silver Bells in the City

Celebrate the holidays in downtown Lansing with the lighting of the State Tree, electric light parade, ice sculptures, community sing, free carriage rides, free treats, and entertainment. The Friday before Thanksgiving. 517-372-4636.

Spirit of Christmas

Drive through Domino's Farms, ablaze with over 500,000 lights and holiday displays that retell the story of Christmas. Indoor activities include a festival of trees, pictures with St. Nicholas,

Christmas gift shop, and pizza store. Thanksgiving weekend through December 31. Ann Arbor. 734-930-5032.

Thanksgiving Weekend Specials

Hands-on activities and demonstrations specially designed for family outings on Thanksgiving weekend. Cranbrook Institute of Science, 248-645-3200.

December

Detroit's holiday season officially opens with Santa's grand arrival during the Thanksgiving Parade. From November 24 through December 31, the city is a child's paradise, decorated in tinsel and lights, full of jolly St. Nicks at every mall. Families have their pick of puppets, plays, concerts, caroling, parades, festivals, workshops, and breakfasts with Santa. Here is a sampling of the city's very special holiday events. Keep an eye on my *Detroit News* calendars for specific times and dates.

PUPPETS, PLAYS, SHOWS, AND CONCERTS

Children's Classics

The following theaters and troupes have fine productions of children's classics during December: Avon Players, Rochester Hills, 248-608-9077. Bonstelle Theatre, Detroit, 313-577-2960 (every other year they perform "A Christmas Carol"). Bower Theatre, Flint, 810-760-1018. Detroit Puppet Theater, 313-961-7777. Flint Youth Theatre, Flint, 810-760-1018. Genitti's Hole in the Wall, Northville. 248-349-0522. Grosse Pointe Children's Theatre, Grosse Pointe, 313-881-7511. Macomb Center for the Performing Arts, Mount Clemens, 810-286-2222. Marquis Theatre, Northville, 248-349-8110. Stagecrafters Youth Theatre at the Baldwin Theatre, Royal Oak, 248-541-6430. Wild Swan Theater, 734-995-0530. Youtheatre, Southfield, 248-557-7529.

A Christmas Carol

Don't forget to treat the kids to their annual dose of Scrooge and Bob Cratchit. Three theaters annually perform the classic tale: Macomb Center for the Performing Arts, Mount Clemens, 810-286-2222. Meadow Brook Theater, Rochester, 248-377-3300. Michigan Theater, Ann Arbor, 734-668-8463.

Holiday Planetarium and Lasera Shows

Cranbrook Institute of Science offers "Ornaments," a 3-D holiday lasera show, 248-645-3236. The Children's Museum in Detroit offers two holiday planetarium shows, 313-873-8100. Holiday planetarium shows are also offered at Flint's Longway Planetarium, 810-760-1181, and MSU's Abrams Planetarium, 517-355-4672. University of Michigan Exhibit Museum Planetarium, offers two holiday planetarium shows, 734-763-6385.

Nutcracker Suite

There will be many performances of the Nutcracker this month. Each triumphs the season with vibrant and magical costumes, scenery, music, and dance. The Ann Arbor Chamber Music Orchestra and the Ann Arbor Civic Ballet at Michigan Theater, Ann Arbor, 734-668-8397. The Birmingham-Bloomfield Symphony with the Michigan Ballet Theater at West Bloomfield High School, West Bloomfield, 248-645-2276. The Detroit Symphony Orchestra at the Detroit Opera House, Detroit, 313-576-5111. Eric Johnston's Detroit Ballet at Farmington High School, Farmington. 248-473-9570. Harlem Nutcracker, a contemporary take on the classic holiday ballet, using Duke Ellington's arrangement of Tchaikovsky's Nutcracker Suite, Detroit Opera House, 734-763-3100. Midwest Dance Theater at Mercy High School, Farmington Hills, 248-669-9444. The Plymouth-Canton Ballet Co. at Plymouth-Salem High School, Plymouth, 734-451-2112.

Radio City Christmas Spectacular

The high-kicking Radio City Rockettes share the stage with dancing teddy bears, wooden soldiers, Santa, and a living Nativity Scene. Fox Theatre, Detroit. Tickets by phone, 248-433-1515. Information and group sales, 313-983-6611.

Sing-Along with Santa

The Ann Arbor Symphony Orchestra joins Santa for an annual family concert. Ann Arbor. 434-994-4801.

OLD-FASHIONED VILLAGES AND
OUT-OF-THE-ORDINARY VISITS WITH SANTA

Breakfast with Santa

Dress up the kids in their holiday finery for a fancy breakfast buffet with Santa which includes songs, stories, cookie making, and a complimentary portrait with Santa. The Ritz-Carlton, Dearborn. 313-441-2000.

Brunch with Santa

After a child-pleasing brunch, Santa arrives by helicopter and visits with the children. The day ends with gifts and caroling. Grosse Pointe War Memorial, Grosse Pointe Farms. Early December. Call for reservations. 313-881-7511.

Chelsea's Festival of Lights

Old-fashioned weekend includes hayrides, visits with Santa, cookie decorating, caroling, and craft sales. 1-800-265-9045.

Christmas at Crossroads

Flint's Victorian village is decked out in holiday cheer, with over 400,000 lights, caroling, special Christmas shows, traditional crafts, and rides in horse-drawn wagons, sleighs, or on the Huckleberry Railroad. From Thanksgiving weekend through the end of December. 810-736-7100.

Christmas at the Detroit Historical Museum

Don't miss the annual old-fashioned holiday fun: the decorated Old Detroit Streets, the miniature Glancy train chugging around an antique village, and the exhibit of antique children's toys. 313-833-1805.

Christmas Past

Travel back to the 1800's and celebrate Christmas with hand-made decorations, hot spiced cider and cookies, music, and crafts. First weekend in December. Waterloo Farm, Stockbridge. 734-426-4980.

Christmas Past In Greenfield Village

The village is decked out in holiday finery. Costumed staff demonstrate old-fashioned crafts, food preparation, and decorating. Plus holiday music, sleigh rides, shopping, and an 1850's holiday meal in the Eagle Tavern. The Saturday after Thanksgiving through early January. 313-271-1620.

Country Christmas

Ann Arbor's Cobblestone Farm, a 19th-century historic farmstead, offers traditional craft and holiday baking demonstrations, caroling, Santa, and children's games. Usually held the last Sunday in November and first Sunday in December. 734-994-2928.

Country Christmas

An old-fashioned Christmas celebration with storytellers, musicians, crafts for sale, fresh cookies, farm animals, Santa, and model trains. Weekends through December. Bridge Cultural Center, Trenton. 734-675-7300.

Dexter's Victorian Christmas

The village is decorated in Victorian cheer, with carolers, street performers, and sleigh rides. First two Saturdays in December. 734-426-5514.

Fantasyland

Visit with Santa and enjoy the many life-size nativity scenes and elaborate, electrical winter and holiday scenes. Lincoln Park. Opens Saturday after Thanksgiving and runs through Christmas Eve. 313-386-1817.

Hanging of the Greens

Create holiday ornaments, listen to holiday music, and stroll through the decorated historic village at the Troy Historical Museum. First Sunday in December. 248-524-3570.

Heritage Holidays

Explore winter traditions of the past with crafts and displays. Wolcott Mill Metropark, Ray Township. 1-800-477-3175 or 810-749-5997.

Holly Day Festival

Historic Franklin village revives the spirit of a small town Christmas with carriage rides, home tours, craft and food demonstrations, Santa, and carolers. Usually the first Saturday in December. 248-626-9666.

Holly's Olde-Fashioned Christmas Festival

Quaint shops, seasonal decorations, entertainment, and strolling characters from *A Christmas*

Carol create a festive mood in downtown Holly's Battle Alley. Thanksgiving weekend and first three weekends in December. 248-634-1900.

Letters to Santa

Pull out the crayons and have the little ones write a note to Santa. Include your name and address so Santa can send a personal, handwritten reply. Mail your letters to Santa Claus, c/o Troy Post Office, North Pole, 48099. Or to the Royal Oak Post Office: Santa Claus, 1 Candy Cane Lane, North Pole, MI 48068-1234. Or hand mail the letters at Lakeside Mall's North Polestal System.

Lunch with Santa

Visit with Santa and enjoy a hotdog lunch and horse-drawn hayride through the park. Lake Erie Metropark, Rockwood. 734-379-5020.

Meadow Brook Hall Holiday Tours

Knole Cottage, a six-room children's playhouse on the grounds of Meadow Brook Hall, becomes Santa's home for approximately two weeks after Thanksgiving. Older children will appreciate the decorations and floral displays in Meadow Brook Hall, the 120-room mansion. 248-370-3140.

Noel Night

The University Cultural Center is aglow with lights, music, and choirs, plus activities, entertainment, food, and shopping for families, inside and outside all the institutions. The first Saturday in December. 313-577-5088.

Nutcracker Teas

Enjoy afternoon tea, then meet with Santa in the miniature playhouse. Edsel and Eleanor Ford House, Grosse Pointe Shores. 313-884-4222.

Santa Lunch

Lunch, puppet show, holiday sing-along, and complimentary photo. The Art Center, Mount Clemens. 810-469-8666.

Santa's at the Whitney

Enjoy an elegant, four-course, waiter-served meal and meet with Santa on the restaurant's second floor. Detroit. 313-832-5700.

Santa's Workshop

Take a trail through the snowy woods to Santa's

workshop, meet with him, enjoy a bowl of oyster stew, and receive a small present. Henry Ford Estate–Fair Lane, Dearborn. Early December. Call for reservations, 313-593-5590.

Snacks with Santa

Kensington Metropark Farm Center sets the pastoral stage for a chat with Santa, sleigh ride, and snack. Usually held the first and second weekend in December. 1-800-47-PARKS.

Traditions of the Season

Dearborn's Henry Ford Museum relives Christmas traditions from past generations. There's a towering tree decorated with cookies, candy, and small toys; an animated Lionel train layout; and gingerbread village. Santa presides over all the merriment. Saturday after Thanksgiving through early January. 313-271-1620.

Victorian Christmas Celebration

Enjoy sights, sounds and smells of Christmas past and a visit from Santa and Mrs. Claus at Wyandotte's historic homes, the Ford-MacNichol Home, Marx Home, and Bishop Park Log Cabin. 734-246-4520.

Visit with Santa and Mrs. Claus

Time to see if you were naughty or nice: give your wish list to Santa and his wife and enjoy old-fashioned treats and activities. Rochester Hills Museum, Rochester. 248-656-4663.

OTHER DECEMBER HAPPENINGS

Chanukah Celebrations

Celebrate the Jewish Festival of Lights with special puppet shows or children's theater at the Jewish Community Center, in West Bloomfield, 248-661-1000 or Oak Park, 248-967-4030.

Dreidel House

Walk inside a giant wooden dreidel house and have a hands-on Chanukah experience—play dreidel and create holiday arts and crafts. Jewish Community Center, West Bloomfield, 248-661-1000.

Kwanzaa Celebrations

During the seven days of Kwanzaa, celebrate

African American values, customs, and heritage with family activities, storytelling, concerts, and workshops at the Charles H. Wright Museum of African American History, 313-494-5800; Children's Museum, 313-873-8100.

New Year's Eve Family Festivals

Many communities offer a wholesome, non-alcoholic family New Year's celebration with continuous entertainment, including puppets, music, dance, theater, mime, storytelling, juggling, craft workshops, teen dance, and— as a grand finale—a midnight laser or fireworks show and sing-along. "Fest Eve," Lansing, 517-483-9222. "First Night," Birmingham, 248-540-6688. "New Year Jubilee," Ypsilanti, 313-483-4444. "Northville Night," 248-349-0203. "Times Square," Pontiac, 248-857-5603.

New Year's Eve Overnights

Bring sleeping bags and pillows an get ready for an evening of games, goodies, and movies and an early morning breakfast. Here's a sampling of sites offering children's overnights: Jewish Community Center, West Bloomfield, 248-661-1000. My Place, 3610 West Maple, Birmingham, 248-540-5702. Warren Family YMCA, 810-751-1050.

Vacation Camps

If you're a parent who must work during winter vacation, take heart. The following places offer children ages 6–12 special programming—arts and crafts, sports, movies, and field trips—all week long. Academy of Sacred Heart, Bloomfield Hills, 248-646-8900. Beverly Hills Racquet and Health Club, Southfield, 248-642-8500. Birmingham YMCA, 248-644-9036. Dinosaur Hill Nature Preserve, Rochester, 248-656-0999. Fit and Fun for Kids, Southfield. 1-800-474-2244. Franklin Fitness and Racquet Club, Southfield, 248-352-8000. Jewish Community Center, West Bloomfield, 248-661-1000. Kidsports, Southfield, 810-352-KIDS. Warren Family YMCA, 810-751-1050.

Vacation Day Specials

For families looking for special vacation activities, Detroit's Children's Museum offers a week's worth of daily planetarium shows and workshops, 313-873-8100. Detroit Institute of Arts offers a week of puppet shows, art workshops, and storytelling, 313-833-4249. Cranbrook Academy of Art Museum offers storytelling concerts, 248-645-3312.

5
Museums

TIP

Become a family member of your favorite museum. You'll have the pleasure of many short—and free—visits, without the pressure of having to see it all.

There's nothing like a museum to awaken children's creativity and curiosity about the world. Yet even a museum full of dinosaur bones, space suits, African masks, or Van Goghs can be a formidable place for a young child. Try to make the museum outing match your child's temperament and interests. Never try to see everything. Just spend a brief time (no more than two hours at a time) visiting several exhibits. Take a break to have a snack—kids will remember giant cookies, space ice cream, or peppermint sticks—and be sure to visit the gift shop. Most area museums have a wide variety of children's toys, books, and trinkets, many for under $3. Leave before everyone is exhausted, let your children take home a special gift, and they'll be eager to return.

African History
African Heritage Cultural Center

21511 West McNichols, Detroit
313-494-7452

Location: In the old Redford Public Library, on the corner of McNichols and Burgess
Hours: 10 a.m.–4 p.m., Monday–Saturday. Call ahead to schedule school tours.
Admission: Free
Ages: 4 and up
Plan: Under one hour
Parking: Free in lots to the west and south of building
Lunch: You'll find a variety of fast food restaurants on McNichols
Facilities: Bathrooms

Created from the 1990 State Fair exhibit "African Origins," the African Heritage Cultural Center traces man's beginning in Africa and his spread throughout the ancient world. Exhibits range from a model of the three-million-year-old Australopithecine, Lucy, to a scale model of a temple in the city of Timbuktu.

Armenian History
Alex and Marie Manoogian Museum

Adjacent to St. John's Armenian Church
22001 Northwestern Highway, Southfield
248-557-5977

Location: Between 8 and 9 Mile Road
Hours: 1–5 p.m., Tuesday–Friday. 1–4 p.m., Saturday and Sunday. Closed Monday and holidays.
Admission: $3 adults, $1 students. Group tours available; call ahead.
Ages: 5 and up
Plan: Under one hour
Parking: Free on site
Lunch: Nearby Northland Shopping Center offers many restaurant choices
Facilities: Bathrooms

Within Southfield's landmark gold-domed church, artifacts of Armenian religious and cultural history are displayed in a 12,000-square-foot museum. Paintings, sculpture, carpets, religious objects, manuscripts, household, and personal objects—some dating back nearly 3,000 years—trace the precious and tragic history of the Armenian people. Don't leave without entering the beautiful main sanctuary.

Natural History

Alfred P. Sloan Museum

1221 East Kearsley Street, Flint
810-760-1169

Location: Flint's Cultural Center, off of I-475 and I-69 in downtown Flint
Hours: 10 a.m.–5 p.m., Monday–Friday. Noon–5 p.m., Saturday and Sunday. Closed major holidays.
Admission: $4 adults, $3.50 seniors, $3 children 5 to 12, under 5 free. Group rates and family memberships available.
Ages: 3 and up
Plan: Half day visit
Parking: Free on site
Lunch: Picnic area on front lawn. Halo Burger, Flint's fast-food burger, on South Saginaw between Court and Fourth Streets.
Facilities: Bathrooms, drinking fountain. The museum store has a large collection of dinosaur gifts.

The Sloan is primarily known for its large collection of antique and experimental cars tracing the city's love affair with the automobile. Michigan natives will enjoy the Sloan's state-of-the-art permanent exhibit, "Flint and the American Dream," chronicling Flint's development as a car town in the

20th century. The museum is also full of engaging exhibits covering the spectrum of natural history. Meet Sheriff Tuffy Tooth, play hands-on games in a Health Education gallery, and step back into Genesee County history in the recreated fur trader's cabin, lumber camp, and pioneer log cabin. Small children will marvel at the history discovery center.

Hands-On Science

Ann Arbor Hands-On Museum

220 East Ann Street, Ann Arbor
734-995-5439

Website: www.aahom.org
Location: Downtown Ann Arbor, on Ann Street, between Fourth and Fifth Streets.
Hours: 10 a.m.–5 p.m., Tuesday–Saturday. 1–5 p.m., Sunday. Groups can make special arrangements for morning visits. Children's classes are held on Saturday mornings.
Admission: $6 adults, $4 children, students, and seniors, and under 3 free. Family memberships available.
Ages: All ages
Plan: Half day visit. Once the kids get busy, they won't want to leave.
Parking: Structures on adjacent streets, or use metered street parking
Lunch: There are many restaurants on State Street and South University, on the U of M campus. Or try one of the giant combo sandwiches at Zingerman's Deli, 422 Detroit Street, 734-663-3354.
Facilities: Bathrooms, elevator, and imaginatively stocked gift shop

The Ann Arbor Hands-On Museum is one of the area's most ambitious and successful "please-touch" museums, and recent expansion has enlarged the museum to four times its original size. Future scientists have a variety of sensory experiences to choose from. On your first visit, it takes a few minutes to get accustomed to the activity. If you're visiting with preschoolers, start with the preschool gallery's water tables, large colorful climber, and puzzles. Fool around in the giant bubble capsule and visit the Discovery Room. Older elementary children enjoy the darkened optics and light gallery, computers, and games.

Art Gallery of Windsor

3100 Howard Avenue, Windsor
Ontario, Canada
519-969-4494

Website: www.mnsi.net/adw
Location: In the Devonshire Mall, Howard and E.C. Row
Hours: 10 a.m.–7 p.m., Tuesday–Friday. 10 a.m.–5 p.m., Saturday. Noon–5 p.m., Sunday. Closed Monday.
Admission: Free
Ages: All ages
Plan: Short visit
Parking: Free in mall parking lot
Lunch: Restaurants and food court in mall
Facilities: Bathrooms. Gift shop offers children's items.

The Art Gallery of Windsor features two centuries of Canadian art and is the area's most child-friendly art museum. Children can relax on bean bag chairs and read, draw, or play with puzzles in a corner playspace. The Children's Gallery exhibits art of interest to children, hung low enough for a child's viewing. The Devonshire Mall also offers children many diversions, including kiddie rides, movie complex, food court, and toy stores.

Transportation

Automotive Hall of Fame

21400 Oakwood Boulevard, Dearborn
(313) 240-4000

Location: On the Henry Ford Museum campus, just off the southwest corner of the Henry Ford Museum parking lot

Hours: 10 a.m.–5 p.m. daily through October 31. 10 a.m.–5 p.m. Tuesday–Sunday November–Memorial Day. Demonstrations are offered daily as needed.

Admission: $6 adults, $5.50 seniors, $3 children ages 5–12. Field trips for 15 or more children, $2.25/child, one adult goes free with every five children. Pre- and post-visit activity kit are available.

Ages: 7 and up

Plan: Short visit

Parking: Free on site

Lunch: The lobby café offers reasonably priced drinks, sandwiches, soup, and baked goods, plus five tables

Facilities: Bathrooms, gift shop with unusual souvenirs for automobile lovers including puzzles, books, posters, key chains, model cars, and animal cracker knock-offs in the shape of your favorite classic cars

At the new Automotive Hall of Fame, both children and adults gain a better understanding of the risks and accomplishments of many of the automobile industry's giants. In an engaging seven-minute introductory film, we meet "The Driving Spirit," a delightful turn-of-the-century lad, who becomes our tour guide through the state-of-the-art multi-media and hands-on displays. In addition to watching lively demonstrations, kids will enjoy climbing into a 1923 trucker's sleeping loft, cranking up a Model-T, and drawing futuristic cars. By personalizing the celebration of innovation and creativity, children leave with a can-do attitude.

African American History

Charles H. Wright Museum of African American History

315 East Warren, Detroit
313-494-5800

Website: www.maah-detroit.org
Location: In the Cultural Center, on the corner of East Warren and Brush
Hours: 9:30 a.m.–5 p.m., Tuesday–Sunday. Closed Monday.
Admission: $5 adults, $3 children, group admission rates available
Ages: All ages
Plan: Half day
Parking: Use lot behind the museum off Brush
Lunch: Sit-down restaurant with patio seating in warm weather
Facilities: Museum store with many African American heritage gifts, including books, art, clothing, greeting cards, commemorative stamps, and coloring books. Student amphitheater, classrooms, 341-seat theater, bathrooms.

The 120,000-square-foot museum is the largest African American History museum in the world. Visitors will marvel at the beautiful domed rotunda, lit up at night as a beacon in the sky. Three exhibition galleries offer the history and accomplishments of a diverse people. Using high tech, multimedia displays, the permanent gallery highlights the contributions and stories of the African American experience by tracing African Americans from their homeland in Africa through voyage to America, slavery, the Abolitionist period, and the tumultuous 20th century. A 70-foot replica of a slave ship with 50 life-size figures offers visitors a dramatic history lesson. Additional gallery space shows traveling exhibits. The museum offers family and youth programming year-round, with a special lineup during February's Black History Month and during Kwanzaa in December.

Culture & Arts

Children's Museum

67 East Kirby, Detroit
313-873-8100

Location: In the Cultural Center, just north of the Detroit Institute of Arts. A prancing silver horse sculpture made of chrome car bumpers sits on the front lawn.
Hours: October–May: 1–4 p.m., Monday–Friday. 9 a.m.–4 p.m., Saturday. Workshops noon and 2 p.m. Saturday. Planetarium shows, 11 a.m. and 1 p.m., Saturday. July–August: 1 p.m. planetarium

shows, 2 p.m. workshops, Monday–Friday.
Admission: Free for museum, $2 for workshops
Ages: 4–12
Plan: Half day, including workshop and planetarium show
Parking: Use metered parking along Kirby or park in the Science Center lot on John R ($3) and walk a block to the museum
Lunch: The DIA Kresge Court Cafe is across the street
Facilities: Bathrooms, drinking fountain. Gift shop with lots of handmade and educational toys and gifts.

The Children's Museum is one of Detroit's best kept secrets. Its Saturday morning and summer afternoon workshops are consistently well-organized, creative explorations of the arts, taught by Detroit Public School teachers. Throughout the house are displays of stuffed and live animals, musical instruments, puppets, old-fashioned toys, boats, and ethnic crafts. Be sure to notice the large, elaborately furnished Jeremiah Hudson dollhouse. The Planetarium shows, held in a small, intimate room, and offered with a sense of humor and wonder, are comfortable first-time stargazing experiences for young children.

Military History

The Cooperage

8832 Dixie, Fair Haven
810-725-2484

Location: Six miles east of I-94, off of 23 Mile Road (M-29)
Hours: 5:30–7:30 p.m., Monday–Friday. 12:30–5 p.m., Saturday. Call for information on Civil War reenactments.
Admission: Free. Civil War living history lectures available for scout troops and school groups for a fee; call to schedule.
Ages: 5 and up
Plan: Under one hour
Parking: Free on site
Lunch: There are restaurants along M-29
Facilities: Bathrooms. Gift shop doubles as a general store for reenactors, selling authentic reproductions of Civil War–era uniforms, dresses, hats, and children's clothing, antique glasses, pipes, jewelry, and watches.

Civil War buffs will admire The Cooperage's wealth of neatly displayed artifacts—mess kits, hardtacks, rifles, bayonets, pistols, cartridge pouches, pipes, tintypes, letters, uniforms, and Confederate money. They will also enjoy chatting with owner Richard Glaz, an enthusiastic Civil War reenactor, who often comes to work dressed as a sutler, a savvy Civil War–era merchant.

Cranbrook Academy of Art Museum

1221 North Woodward, Bloomfield Hills
248-645-3312
1-877-GO-CRANB (taped information)
248-645-3323(group tour information)

Website: www.cranbrook.edu/museum
Location: Enter off Woodward Avenue, just north of Cranbrook Road
Hours: 11 a.m.–5 p.m., Tuesday–Sunday. 11 a.m.–9 p.m., Thursday. Closed Monday. June–mid-August: Extended Friday hours and special programming, 11 a.m.–10 p.m. Tours for school groups are available.
Admission: $5 adults, $3 children, students and seniors. Under 7 free. Family membership available. Discounted joint membership with Cranbrook Institute of Science available on Friday evenings in the summer.
Ages: 5 and up. Please be sure to hold onto your children since many of the exhibits are three-dimensional and easy to bump into.
Plan: Under one hour
Parking: Park along the semi-circle in front or in the lot on the east side of the museum
Lunch: Picnicking on Cranbrook grounds is strictly forbidden. You'll find fast food and family restaurants along Woodward Avenue.
Facilities: Bathrooms on lower level. Gift shop has a great selection of children's art books, beautifully illustrated picture books, art supplies, and artsy toys.

A shift in programming in the past few years now welcomes children and families to this haven for avant-garde and contemporary art. Connected to the Cranbrook Academy of Art, the museum displays unusual and witty art, plus the renowned Cranbrook Collection. The museum also offers family events emphasizing bizzaro fun and the notion that art has endless possibilities and its definition is ever-expanding.

Hands-On Science
Cranbrook Institute of Science

1221 North Woodward, Bloomfield Hills
248-645-3209
1-877-GO-CRANB (taped information)

Website: www.cranbrook.edu
Location: Enter off Woodward, just north of Cranbrook Road. You'll know you're there when you see the stegosaurus.
Hours: 10 a.m.–5 p.m., daily. Additional hours, 6–10 p.m. Friday. Closed on major holidays. Nature Place: 1–5 p.m., Saturday and Sunday. Lasera and planetarium shows Friday evenings and weekends.
Admission: $7 adults, $4 children ages 3–17 and seniors, under 3 free. $2 adults, $1.50 children ages 3–17 and seniors, $1 members additional for planetarium shows. $2.50 additional for lasera shows, under 3 are free. Family membership and group rates available.
Ages: All ages for the museum, 5 and up for most lasera and planetarium shows
Plan: Half day visit
Parking: Lot south of and in front of building
Lunch: Planet Café offers upscale meals, Starbucks coffee, and snacks
Facilities: Bathrooms, drinking fountain, and Science Store on lower level. The extensive Science Store specializes in children's science toys, kits, and creative gifts.

Cranbrook Institute of Science, almost doubled in size since its 1999 renovation and addition, is the all-purpose science museum for children of all ages. Interactive exhibits, a Nature Place full of touch-me displays, lasera and planetarium shows, science demonstrations, and seasonal family events encourage science creativity and exploration. A giant fleshed-out wooly mammoth and t-rex skeleton welcome visitors to the new galleries.

Family membership is well worth its price. The membership allows you free entrance into the Detroit Science Center, Ann Arbor's Hands-On Museum, and Lansing's Impression 5 Science Center, as well as the Institute's spring Maple Syrup Festival and Honey and Apples Festival, perfectly choreographed sensory events celebrating the seasons. For a fee, your children can also take classes at the Institute throughout the year.

Fire-Fighting Equipment

Presently closed during renovation; hopes to reopen and move to new location in the Cultural Center.

Detroit Fire Department Historical Museum

2737 Gratiot Avenue, Detroit
313-596-2956

The red brick building with the large yellow doors, Detroit's oldest standing Engine House, is full of beautifully restored fire rigs, fire-fighting clothing, and artifacts. It offers children a glimpse into the exciting and dangerous history of Detroit fire fighting.

 History

Detroit Historical Museum

5401 Woodward Avenue, Detroit
313-833-1805

Website: www.detroithistorical.org
Location: In the Cultural Center, across from the Detroit Institute of Arts, on Woodward Avenue
Hours: 9:30 a.m.–5 p.m., Tuesday–Friday. 10 a.m.–5 p.m., Saturday and Sunday. Closed major holidays.

Admission: $4.50 adults, $2.25 children ages 12–18 and seniors, under 11 free. Free admission on Wednesday.
Ages: All ages
Plan: Short visit
Parking: Use street meters or free lot on west side of building
Lunch: Go across the street to the Detroit Institute of Art's Kresge Court Café or enjoy luncheonette fare at Cappy's Fine Foods, on the northeast side of Woodward and Kirby, 313-871-9820
Facilities: Bathrooms on lower level. Beautifully appointed gift shop with many old-fashioned replicas and hand-made toys.

If you grew up in Detroit, you will hardly recognize the newly refurbished historical museum. The old favorites are still as wonderful as ever and new high-tech exhibits round out the museum space. Introduce your children to the basement level's "Streets of Old Detroit," the hauntingly authentic cobblestone streets full of old shop windows. Adjacent to the "Streets" is the elaborate Lionel Train Village.

On the main floor, the new, state-of-the-art "Frontiers to Factories" exhibit tells the story of Detroiters at work from 1701 to the early 1900's. The "Motor City Exhibition" picks up the story and tells of the automobile's impact on Detroit's history with video screens, a mini-theater, and a working assembly line rescued from the now defunct Cadillac Clark Avenue Plant. Kids can walk up on the catwalk and look down on a car being born. Preschoolers will adore "I Discover," a living history exhibit that lets kids learn about history by trying on clothes and role playing. The museum also features a costume gallery and furnished doll houses on the first floor.

Saturday Wiggle Giggle Studios, held monthly, engage children in current exhibits with hands-on art projects.

Art

Detroit Institute of Arts (DIA)

5200 Woodward Avenue, Detroit
313-833-7900
313-833-7981 (student tour information)

Website: www.dia.org
Location: In the heart of the Cultural Center, on the east side of Woodward Avenue, just south of Kirby
Hours: 11 a.m.–4 p.m., Wednesday–Friday. 11 a.m.–5 p.m., Saturday and Sunday. Closed Monday, Tuesday, and major holidays.
Admission: Suggested fee: $4 adults, $1 children. Founders members free.
Ages: All ages
Plan: Half day visit
Parking: Use the Detroit Science Center lot east of the DIA on John R, $3 for all day parking. Available meter parking on street is difficult to find.
Lunch: The Kresge Court Café is a pleasant cafeteria offering a wide selection of hot and cold meals, plus snacks. Be sure to show your kids the faces and gargoyles in stone along the walls of the dining room. You could bring your lunch and augment it with a snack or drink. The dining room has open access; it isn't necessary to go through the food line. Hours: 11:30 a.m.–3 p.m., Wednesday–Friday. 11:30 a.m.–3:30 p.m., Saturday and Sunday. The American Grille Restaurant offers more elegant fare. 11:30 a.m.–2:15 p.m., Wednesday–Saturday. 11 a.m.–2:45 p.m., Sunday Brunch. Reservations are suggested, 313-833-1857.
Facilities: Bathrooms and drinking fountain near the café. The gift shop, located at the Farnsworth entrance, has a children's section full of beautifully illustrated picture books, books about artists, T-shirts, art kits and supplies.

The DIA has wonderful secrets and visual delights for children of all ages. Begin your visit walking through the rainbow hallway to the Kresge Court Café and up the hidden, winding wrought iron staircase to the Great Hall's showcases of knights' armor and swords. The Rivera Court, with the famous Diego Rivera murals, is straight ahead. Be sure to visit the mummies, African masks, and Impressionist and Modern galleries. Get the kids involved by asking them to mimic a gesture or expression they see in a painting or sculpture.

Bring along sketching paper and pencils and encourage them to draw their favorite artwork. The kids will enjoy fooling around with CHIP, the multi-media interactive computer program, located at kiosks throughout the museum. "The Mystery of the Five Fragments," a one-hour creative treasure hunt for ages 8–12, can be checked out at the Rivera Court information desk. Many galleries and special exhibits offer children's guides, located in wall holders near the gallery entrance. The DIA is home to Brunch with Bach and offers year-round family and youth art classes. "First Fridays," an evening of music, art demonstrations, and drop-in workshops, is held the first Friday of each month, 6–9 p.m.

Hands-On Science
Detroit Science Center

5020 John R, Detroit
313-577-8400
313-SCIENCE (information line)

Website: www.sciencedetroit.org
Location: One block east of Woodward on the corner of Warren and John R, behind the DIA
Hours: 9:30 a.m.–2 p.m., Monday–Friday. 11:30–5 p.m., Saturday. 12:30–5 p.m. Sunday. Extended hours during summer and throughout the year for IMAX viewing on Friday and Saturday evenings. Closed major holidays. The IMAX Dome Theatre shows IMAX movies throughout the day. (Preschoolers might be uncomfortable with the IMAX movie's motion and speed.)
Admission: $3 adults and children 13 and up, $2 children 3–12 and seniors, under 3 are free. Admission includes exhibit hall, laser show, and demonstrations. $4 additional for IMAX movie ticket. Family membership gives you free admission to Cranbrook Institute of Science and Lansing's Impression 5 Science Center except for special events.
Ages: All ages
Plan: Half day visit
Parking: Lot adjacent to entrance, off John R, $3 all day parking
Lunch: Vending machines on Exhibit level (third floor)
Facilities: Bathrooms and drinking fountain on

Exhibit level. Gift shop near entrance has great science and space items.

The Detroit Science Center boasts the Midwest's oldest IMAX dome and dozens of hands-on science and technology exhibits, including "Cyberspace Safari," state-of-the-art computer terminals for children to explore the World Wide Web and play science-oriented computer games. Short laser shows and science demonstrations are offered each day. IMAX movie schedules generally include three or four film offerings each week.The center is currently undergoing a renovation and building project which should be completed by spring 2001.

History

Dexter Area Museum

3443 Inverness, Dexter
734-426-2519

Website: www.hvcn.org/info/
Location: At Inverness and Fourth Street
Hours: 1–3 p.m., Friday and Saturday, May 1–Christmas. Tours by appointment only.
Admission: Free. Family membership available.
Ages: 5 and up
Plan: Under one hour
Parking: Free on site
Lunch: Three restaurants are located in downtown Dexter on Main Street or drive to Ann Arbor, 20 minutes east off I-94
Facilities: Bathrooms. Gift shop offers toys and craft and hobby books.

This 1883 church built by early German settlers showcases local history items. Children will enjoy the early dentist's office, printing equipment, antique toys and dolls, model train layout, telephone switch board, and old household appliances and farm tools.

Marine History

Dossin Great Lakes Museum

100 Strand
Belle Isle Park, Detroit
313-852-4051

Location: Cross the Belle Isle Bridge and go southeast to Strand Road on the south shore of Belle Isle

Hours: 10 a.m.–5 p.m., Wednesday–Sunday. Closed major holidays.

Admission: $2 adults, $1 seniors and children ages 12–18, under 12 free. Free admission on Wednesday.

Ages: All ages

Plan: Short visit

Parking: Free on site

Lunch: Belle Isle is full of picnic tables

Facilities: Bathrooms, drinking fountain. Gift shop has nautical items.

You won't get seasick at the Dossin Museum, but you will come away with a better understanding of ships, their innards, and perils at sea. There's a large collection of scale-model Great Lakes ships, a spectacular carved oak Gothic Room, once a smoking lounge on a 1912 steamer, and a room full of recreational sailing exhibits spanning two centuries. Kids can view Detroit and Windsor through the periscope that goes up through the roof, practice navigating in an authentic freighter pilothouse that extends over the Detroit River, and pose next to the War of 1812 cannon on the museum lawn.

Hands-On Creative Play

Flint Children's Museum

1602 West Third Avenue, Flint
810-767-5437

Location: One mile west of downtown, between Chevrolet and Cadillac

Hours: 10 a.m.–5 p.m., Monday–Saturday. Noon–5 p.m., Sunday.

Admission: $11 family, $3 adult, $2.50 children, 2

and under free. Group rates and family member-
ships available.
Ages: 2–13
Plan: Half day
Parking: Free parking behind museum
Lunch: Pop machine. You'll find fast food restau-
rants on Ballanger Highway.
Facilities: Bathrooms, drinking fountains. Gift
shop with lots of inexpensive items.

With carefully planned true-to-life displays, Flint
Children's Museum invites children to role-play
various occupations and hobbies, providing them
with the props and costumes for pretending.
Children become firefighters, clowns, musicians, or
weather forecasters and talk-show hosts at a child-
sized TV studio. There's a Cinderella Coach, grocery store, stress bridge to jump on, Glow Room,
and tile maze, plus a collection of bones, stones,
and insects. Groups can make an appointment to
play with "Stuffee," a five-foot-tall stuffed character
who comes complete with removable lungs, heart,
appendix, stomach, and other organs. Your kids
won't want to leave.

Flint Institute of Arts

1120 East Kearsley Street, Flint
810-234-1695

Location: Flint's Cultural Center, off of I-475 and I-
69 in downtown Flint
Hours: 10 a.m.–5 p.m., Tuesday–Saturday. 1–5
p.m., Sunday.
Admission: Free, donations accepted
Ages: All ages
Plan: Short visit
Parking: Use lot adjacent to Sloan Museum
Lunch: Try Halo Burger, Flint's famous fast food
burger, on South Saginaw between Court and
Fourth Streets
Facilities: Bathrooms, drinking fountain, gift shop

Flint's art museum offers children a sampling of
art from every period of history. Children will enjoy
the collection of paperweights displayed in lighted
tables, the modern sculpture gallery, and the exte-
rior court sculpture that moves with the wind.

History

François Baby House: Windsor's Community Museum

254 Pitt Street West
Windsor, Ontario, Canada
519-253-1812

Website: www.city.windsor.on.ca/wpl/museum
Location: Pitt Street West and Ferry Street
Hours: 10 a.m.–5 p.m., Tuesday–Saturday. 2–5 p.m., Sunday during May–September only. Closed Monday.
Admission: Free
Ages: 6 and up
Plan: Less than an hour
Parking: Use metered street parking and parking garage
Lunch: Restaurants and riverside picnic areas nearby
Facilities: Bathrooms

A Windsor history exhibit and two changing exhibits are on display in this very small museum, once the home of François Baby. Kids will enjoy calling the house the "BAH-bee" house and playing with hands-on activities in the lower level's children's history room.

Dental History

Gordon H. Sindecuse Museum of Dentistry

Kellogg Building, U of M School of Dentistry
Fletcher Street, Ann Arbor
313-763-0767

Location: On Fletcher Street, near the corner of North University, in the Kellogg Building.
Hours: When the Dental School is open, generally 7 a.m.–5:30 p.m., Monday–Friday.
Admission: Free
Ages: 3 and up
Plan: Under one hour
Parking: Use Fletcher Street parking lot or find metered street parking
Lunch: Many restaurants are located two blocks away on State Street
Facilities: Bathrooms

A visit to the dentist will be a breeze after seeing what would have been in store for you before the age of electricity. On display are fully furnished, antique dental operating rooms and dental equipment, and whimsical displays of international toothpaste containers and postcards with a dental theme.313-297-9360

Transportation and History
Henry Ford Museum

20900 Oakwood Boulevard, Dearborn
313-271-1620
313-982-6150 (24-hour information line)
313-271-1570 (IMAX Theatre)

Website: www.hfmgv.org
Location: Michigan Avenue and Southfield Freeway
Hours: 9 a.m.–5 p.m., daily. Closed Thanksgiving Day and Christmas Day.
Admission: $12.50 adults, $11.50 seniors, $7.50 children 5 to 12, under 5 free. IMAX Theatre: $7.50 adults, $6.50 children 5 to 12 and seniors, $6 children 4 and under and members. Combination tickets: Henry Ford Museum or Greenfield Village and IMAX: $17.50 adults, $16 seniors, $12.50 children 5 to 12, $6 children 4 and under. Henry Ford Museum and Greenfield Village and IMAX: $28 adults, $27 seniors, $19 Children 5 to 12, $6 children 4 and under. Group rates and family memberships available.
Ages: All ages
Plan: Half day or full day. With small children, it's impossible to comfortably visit both the museum and adjacent Greenfield Village in one day, but you can easily fit an IMAX movie into your museum visit.
Parking: Use free lots adjacent to the museum and village
Lunch: American Café or Wiener Mobile Café
Facilities: Bathrooms and drinking fountains in many locations. The two gift shops near the museum entrance are well stocked with old-fashioned coloring books, model cars and trains, books, candies, and toys.

Henry Ford Museum is the repository of automobile and aviation history, American furnishings, social history, and other collections begun by its founder, Henry Ford. Its 12 acres of memorabilia and artifacts have been successfully repackaged into wonderful, state-of-the-art, user-friendly, interactive exhibits.

Try to visit the highlights. Children will enjoy the permanent exhibits, "The Automobile in American Life," and "Made in America," plus the presidential assassination artifacts — Abraham Lincoln's shawl, theater program, and rocking chair, the car John F. Kennedy was riding when assassinated and the car Ronald Reagan and James Brady were riding during the attempted assassination. The entire family will enjoy playing on "The Innovation Station," a Willy Wonka-like gizmo powered entirely by human energy, creative thought, and cooperation. Pick up your play time tickets at the entrance for one of the daily 20-minute games. A perennial favorite is also the Alleghany, a 1940's locomotive—one of the world's largest steam engines. In addition, a hands-on craft area encourages kids to use their creativity. A carpeted area offers toddlers a chance to role play and crawl around. Children will also enjoy watching 3-D movies in the brand new IMAX Theatre.

One recommended strategy for enjoying the museum and village—become a family member or buy a seasonal pass. Then you will feel comfortable making many short visits throughout the year.

African American Heritage, Art

Heritage Museum of Fine Arts For Youth

110 East Ferry, Detroit
313-871-1667

Location: One block north of DIA, corner of Ferry and John R

Hours: 10 a.m.–5 p.m., daily. 10 a.m.–3 p.m., Saturday. Call to schedule a tour
Admission: Tours, $3 adults, $1 children. Fee for classes
Ages: Preschool and up
Plan: Under one hour
Parking: Metered parking along John R
Lunch: Go to the DIA Kresge Court Café
Facilities: Bathrooms

The Heritage Museum of Fine Arts for Youth offers children programs in fine arts instruction throughout the year. The beautifully restored pre-World War I home also offers a wide selection of black heritage materials including folk tales, field recordings, and African and rural South handicrafts and household implements. Children are allowed to play with the doll, puppet, and musical instrument collection. There are also changing fine arts exhibits.

Jewish History

Holocaust Memorial Museum

6602 West Maple Road, West Bloomfield
248-661-0840

Location: On the Jewish Community Center Campus, west of Drake Road. Adjacent to the Jewish Community Center.
Hours: 10 a.m.–3:30 p.m., Sunday–Thursday. 9 a.m.–12:30 p.m., Friday. Free public tour, 1 p.m., Sunday. School group tours are encouraged; educational materials are available for pre-visit preparation.
Admission: Free, donations welcome
Ages: Not recommended for children under sixth grade
Plan: Short visit
Parking: Two lots adjacent to building
Lunch: Cafeteria on main floor of adjacent Jewish Community Center
Facilities: Bathrooms. Archives and library.

Children need preparation before visiting the Holocaust Memorial Museum. The museum's explicit displays, videos, and photos offer an insightful and emotional look at the destruction of European Jewry during the Holocaust. Guided group tours are highly recommended.

Hands-On Science

Impression 5 Science Center

200 Museum Drive, Lansing
517-485-8116
517-485-8115 (recorded information)

Website: www.impression5
Location: Between Grand and Cedar Avenues, three blocks east of the Capitol
Hours: 10 a.m.–5 p.m., Monday–Saturday. Noon–5 p.m., Sunday. Closed holidays.
Admission: $4.50 adults, $3 children 3 to 18 and seniors, under 3 are free. Group rates and family memberships available.
Ages: All ages
Plan: Half day. The kids won't want to leave.
Parking: Lot in front of building
Lunch: A café on the first level closes one hour before museum closing
Facilities: Bathrooms, drinking fountain, coat check. Gift shop with extensive selection of science items.

Children and adults skip from exhibit to exhibit, playing, touching, building, and experimenting in this giant science playground. There's something for every age. Break into a jazzy tune on a giant cello in the Music Room; walk through a human heart maze; try a handicapped obstacle course; create undulating bubbles at the Bubble Table and make slime in the Chemistry Lab. A special play area is designed for children under 3.

Multi-Ethnic

International Institute

111 Kirby, Detroit
313-871-8600

Location: Just east of the Children's Museum, north of the DIA
Hours: 8:30 a.m.–5 p.m., Monday–Friday. Call to arrange school or group tours.
Admission: Free. Nominal fee for school tours.
Ages: Elementary school children and up
Plan: Under one hour
Parking: Meters across the street or use Detroit Science Center Parking Lot on John R

Lunch: Small World Café, featuring ethnic food, 11 a.m.–2 p.m., Monday–Friday.

Facilities: Bathrooms. The "Tiny Shop" offers international toys and greeting cards in many languages, plus UNICEF gift shop with cards and books.

The "Hall of Nations" exhibit showcases thousands of colorful dolls from countries around the world. Since school programs are held in this room, call ahead to be sure the exhibit room will be free during your visit.

Archeology

Kelsey Museum of Archeology

434 South State Street, Ann Arbor
734-647-0441
734-764-9304 (recorded information)

Website: www.umich.edu/~kelseymuseum

Location: On the University of Michigan campus, just north of the Student Union, on the west side of State Street and south of William Street.

Hours: 11 a.m.–4 p.m. Tuesday–Friday. 1–4 p.m. Saturday and Sunday. Closed Monday. Call to reserve group tours.

Admission: Free. Donations are welcome. $1/person for group tours.

Ages: All ages

Plan: Under one hour

Parking: Street meters or the Borders parking structure on Maynard, just north of William.

Lunch: Walk north along State Street where espresso drinks, sandwiches, ice cream, and bagels abound. The Student Union, just south of the museum, also offers a variety of food choices.

Facilities: Bathrooms

Long a repository of ancient Egyptian, Greek, and Roman artifacts, the Kelsey is well known in scholarly circles. But budding archeologists will want to visit the three well-lit, refurbished galleries to see mummies, sarcophagi, canopic jars, and tomb artifacts. During family days, held on Saturdays throughout the year, children prepare a doll for mummification and burial, listen to Egyptian folktales, create jewelry, have their faces painted, and go on a mock dig.

History

Knowlton Ice Museum

1665 Yeager Street, Port Huron
810-987-7100

Location: I-94 and Water Street
Hours: By appointment
Admission: Free, contributions welcome
Ages: 7 and up
Plan: Under one hour
Parking: Free parking in front lot
Lunch: Surrounding restaurants
Facilities: Bathrooms. Antiques for sale.

There was a time when ice was harvested from the nearest frozen lake and river, stored in shoreside icehouses, and delivered house to house by an iceman in horse and wagon. Mickey and Agnes Knowlton have preserved a slice of this icy past. Museum displays include ice memorabilia—picks, scrapers, plows, signs, wooden ice boxes, toys, and a turn-of-the-century ice wagon.

Art

Kresge Art Museum

Michigan State University, East Lansing
517-355-7631 (information tape)
517-353-9834

Website: www.msu.edu/unit/kamuseum
Location: On Auditorium Road, MSU campus
Hours: Labor Day–mid-May: 9:30 a.m.–4:30 p.m. Monday, Tuesday, Wednesday, Friday. Noon–8 p.m. Thursday. 1–4 p.m. Saturday and Sunday. Mid-May–July 31: 11 a.m.–4 p.m., Monday–Friday. 1–4 p.m., Saturday and Sunday. Closed August and between Christmas and New Year's Day.
Admission: Free. Family memberships available.
Ages: All ages
Plan: Short visit
Parking: Meters in front of building. $1 parking permits for two hours are available at the front desk.
Lunch: Fast food and vending machines are located in the Student Union, corner of Abbott and Grand River. Many other restaurants are located on Grand River, across from campus.

Facilities: Bathrooms. Small gift cart with inexpensive items.

Small museums of art are always fun for children; they can digest the art experience. The Kresge Art Museum offers changing exhibits of art from prehistoric to contemporary, in an uncluttered, relaxing environment.

Michigan History

Michigan Historical Museum

717 West Allegan, Lansing
517-373-3559, 517-373-2353 (tours)

Website: www.sos.state.mi.us/history/html
Location: Several blocks west of the Capitol, on Allegan between Butler and Sycamore Streets
Hours: 9 a.m.–4:30 p.m., Monday–Friday. 10 a.m.–4 p.m., Saturday. 1–5 p.m., Sunday. Call to arrange group or school tours. Special events throughout the year offer hands-on activities, craft demonstrations, arts and crafts, and family entertainment.
Admission: Free
Ages: All ages
Plan: Half day
Parking: Large parking lot adjacent to the museum charges 25 cents per hour, Monday–Friday. Free parking on weekends.
Lunch: Vending machines
Facilities: Bathrooms. Museum shop with Michigan souvenirs, history books, and Made-in-Michigan products.

This imposing, 315,000-square-foot facility offers both children and adults a multi-sensory,

hands-on vision of Michigan's past, from prehistoric times to the 20th century, told through the eyes of Michigan's people. Kids will enjoy walking into a mine shaft, the facade of a lumber baron's home, a replica Ford factory line, union hall, and Willow Run Bomber Plant workers' locker room, watching a short film in an opulent 1920's theater, and fooling around in a Motown recording booth.

Space

Michigan Space and Science Center

2111 Emmons Road, Jackson
517-787-4425

Location: Jackson Community College campus
Hours: November–April: 10 a.m.–5 p.m., Tuesday–Saturday. May–October: 10 a.m.-5 p.m., Tuesday–Saturday. Noon–5 p.m., Sunday.
Admission: $4 adults, $2.75 students and seniors, 5 and under free. Group rates available.
Ages: All ages
Plan: Short visit
Parking: Lot adjacent to museum
Lunch: Snacks and pop vending machines, and tables in lobby. Picnic tables on grounds.
Facilities: Outdoor play area, bathrooms, drinking fountain. Gift shop with a variety of low-cost items. Be sure to try the astronaut ice cream (for maximum enjoyment, let the freeze-dried bits melt in your mouth; don't chew them).

The Michigan Space Center brings space travel down to earth. Hands-on experiences, true-to-life displays, and National Aeronautics and Space Administration artifacts help kids understand life in space from the astronaut's point of view. The museum even attempts to answer those nitty-gritty questions kids always ask, such as: How do astronauts go to the bathroom? Take a shower? Eat? There are space suits worn by the first astronauts, a sky lab shower, space food, moon rocks, and Apollo space capsule. Be sure to check with the gift shop for the movie schedule.

Sports History

Michigan Sports Hall of Fame

Cobo Center, One Washington Boulevard, Detroit
313-877-8111

Website: www.cobocenter.com
Location: Washington Boulevard at Jefferson. Gallery is hanging on the walls, main floor, south end of Cobo Center.
Hours: 6 a.m.-midnight, daily
Admission: Free
Ages: All ages
Plan: Less than an hour
Parking: Use Cobo Arena garage
Lunch: Several restaurants within Cobo Center
Facilities: Bathrooms, drinking fountain on each floor of Cobo Center

Children with a love of sports will enjoy a stroll through these hallways, where Michigan sports heroes have been immortalized.

Michigan & Natural History
Michigan State University (MSU) Museum

West Circle Drive
Michigan State University Campus
East Lansing
517-355-7474 (taped recording)
517-355-2370

Website: www.museum.msu.edu
Location: West Circle Drive, on the MSU campus
Hours: 9 a.m.–5 p.m., Monday–Friday. 10 a.m.–5 p.m., Saturday. 1–5 p.m., Sunday. Group tours available.
Admission: Free, donations welcome
Ages: All ages
Plan: Short visit
Parking: Metered parking in front. $1 parking permits for two hours can be purchased in museum office.
Lunch: Fast food and vending machines are located in the Student Union, corner of Abbott and Grand River. Many other restaurants are located on Grand River Avenue, across from campus.
Facilities: Bathrooms. General store/gift shop with a variety of inexpensive gifts.

The MSU museum is small enough for kids to comfortably see almost every display. There are dramatic dioramas of cave people, an old-fashioned city street, a full-sized, hungry-looking bear, stuffed animals, authentic fur trader's cabin, dinosaur bones, and a lower level full of evocative masks.

In the Family Room, a relaxing corner of the lower level set aside for hands-on exploration and quiet activity, kids can read, play a computer game, or draw.

Women's History

Michigan Women's Historical Center and Hall of Fame

213 West Main Street, Lansing
517-484-1880

Website: www.leslie.k12.mi.us/~mwhfame
Location: Off I-96, Main Street exit, six blocks south of the State Capitol building, adjacent to Cooley Gardens
Hours: Noon–5 p.m., Wednesday–Friday. Noon–4 p.m., Saturday. 2–4 p.m., Sunday.
Admission: $2.50 adults, $2 seniors, $1 students 5 to 18. Group rates available.
Ages: Third grade to adult
Plan: Short visit
Parking: Free parking at Cooley Garden entrance off Capitol Avenue
Lunch: Picnic area in Cooley Garden
Facilities: Bathrooms. Gift shop selling books, notecards, posters, and American women paper doll cutouts.

From abolitionist Sojourner Truth to former First Lady Betty Ford, the Women's Center offers a picture of the lives, achievements, and history of Michigan women. Children old enough to appreciate historical exhibits will enjoy learning about famous Michigan women. The center also features original artwork by Michigan women.

History

Monroe County Historical Museum

126 South Monroe Street, Monroe
734-243-7137

Location: South Monroe Street (M-125) and Second Street
Hours: 10 a.m.–5 p.m., daily, May 1–September 30. 10 a.m.–5 p.m., Wednesday–Sunday, October 1–April 30.
Admission: Free

Ages: All ages
Plan: Under one hour
Parking: Free on site
Lunch: Restaurants available in town
Facilities: Bathrooms. Gift shop with early history, Woodland Indian, and General Custer items.

This small museum, housed in a 1910 post office building, offers Woodland Indian displays, military items, and General George Custer memorabilia.

History

Montrose Historical and Telephone Pioneer Museum

144 East Hickory Street, Montrose
810-639-6644

Website: www.telemusm6fm.org
Location: One block off M-57 in downtown Montrose
Hours: 1–5 p.m., Saturday and Sunday; closed major holidays. Tours are offered daily; call ahead. Special Christmas exhibits run November–end of January; a Blueberry exhibit corresponds to Montrose's Blueberry Festival, held the third week in August.
Admission: Free museum admission, donations accepted. Tours, $2.
Ages: 3 and up
Plan: Under one hour
Parking: Free on site
Lunch: Restaurants along M-57 (Vienna Road)
Facilities: Bathrooms, a gift counter selling new and antique phones

Give the kids a glimpse into the past before cell phones. Hands-on displays let children operate a switch board, crank up a battery operated phone to talk to one another, and listen in on a party line. The historical section of the museum includes a furnished, turn-of-the-century barbershop, bank, schoolhouse, leather shop, and operating weaving loom. Historical exhibits feature antique clothing, kitchen implements, and dolls.

Transportation

Motorsports Museum and Hall of Fame

Novi Expo Center
43700 Expo Center Drive, Novi
248-349-RACE

Website: www.mshf.com
Location: Southwest corner of I-96 and Novi Road
Hours: 10 a.m.–5 p.m., daily.
Admission: $5 adults, $3 children under 12 and seniors. Group tours available.
Ages: 5 and up
Plan: Under one hour
Parking: Usually free; minimal charge during Expo Center shows.
Lunch: Pizza concession during Expo Center shows
Facilities: Bathrooms, gift shop

Immerse yourself in fast car heaven. Watch clips of racing highlights and roam through the maze of motor sports legends. Over 40 sports cars, stock cars, drag racers, hydroplanes, airplanes, and motorcycles are on display. For a nominal fee, root for your car on a four-lane slot racing track. A move to the Michigan State Fairgrounds in Detroit is anticipated by fall 2000.

African American History, Music

Motown Historical Museum

2648 West Grand Boulevard, Detroit
313-875-2264

Location: Off Lodge Freeway, West Grand Boulevard exit, west one block
Hours: Noon–5 p.m., Monday and Sunday. 10 a.m.–5 p.m., Tuesday–Saturday.
Admission: $6 adults, $3 children 11 and under
Ages: 6 and up
Plan: Short visit
Parking: Free parking on street
Lunch: Eat in the nearby New Center Area's Fisher Building, or New Center One
Facilities: Bathrooms, gift shop

Enter the modest white stucco house with its "Hitsville, USA" sign and be transported back to the 1960's and the birthplace of the Motown sound. A nine-minute video traces Motown's history and

Berry Gordy Jr.'s dream. Walk into Studio A and hear a recording session in progress. Motown hits play softly in the background and bring to life the displays of Motown memorabilia: gold and platinum records, sequin-covered costumes worn by the stars, colorful album covers, and priceless photos. Barry Gordy Jr.'s upstairs apartment has been lovingly and authentically restored to the early Motown era. This is Detroit's answer to Nashville, Tennessee. A move to an enlarged space with a restaurant, on Woodward, is anticipated by fall 2001.

Arab Culture

Museum of Arab Culture (ACCESS)

Arab Community Center
2651 Saulino Court, Dearborn
313-842-7010

Location: Off Vernor and Dix Roads
Hours: 9 a.m.–5 p.m., Monday–Friday
Admission: Free. Minimal feel for school groups.
Ages: All ages
Plan: Under one hour
Parking: Use lot in front of the center
Lunch: Many Middle Eastern restaurants nearby
Facilities: Bathrooms, library, lounge

Winding through the hallways of the community center and in a large exhibit room are wall-mounted display cases of Arab heirlooms and treasures as well as artifacts demonstrating Arab culture, history, religion, and lifestyle. Included are Saudi Arabian rugs, pots, and baskets, and scale models of Middle Eastern architecture. An archival exhibit documenting 100 years of Arab American life in Dearborn can be found in the Conference Room. The center also houses a lending library with audio-visual educational tools available for teachers and will arrange school group visits to a local mosque and Middle Eastern restaurant.

Museum of Art

525 State Street, Ann Arbor
734-764-0395

Website: www.umich.edu/~umma

Location: In the heart of The University of Michigan's Central Campus, across from the Michigan Union
Hours: Memorial Day–Labor Day: 11 a.m.–5 p.m., Tuesday–Saturday. 11 a.m.–9 p.m. Thursday. Noon–5 p.m., Sunday. During school year: 10 a.m.–5 p.m., Tuesday–Saturday. 10 a.m.–9 p.m., Thursday. Noon–5 p.m., Sunday.
Admission: Free
Ages: Older children, or young children who enjoy art
Plan: Less than an hour
Parking: Use metered parking on the street
Lunch: Many restaurants nearby
Facilities: Bathrooms, drinking fountain, gift shop with a variety of imported gifts for children, plus books and many art-inspired items

The Museum of Art is a small building with just enough art for a quick visit and introduction to art. The museum gift shop sells an inexpensive treasure-hunt coloring book that offers families a self-guided tour of the art collection. During summer hours, young artists will enjoy fooling around at the hands-on arts and crafts activities table.

Michigan & Natural History
Museum of Art and History

1115 Sixth Street, Port Huron
810-982-0891

Location: 1/2 mile off US-25, corner of Wall and Sixth Streets
Hours: 1–4:30 p.m., Wednesday–Sunday
Admission: $2 adults, $1 seniors and students, under 7 free. Paid admission allows entrance to Huron Lightship Museum.
Ages: All ages
Plan: Short visit
Parking: Adjacent to museum on street
Lunch: Drive into town for an authentic 1920's dining experience at Diana's Sweet Shop, 307 Huron. 810-985-6933.
Facilities: Bathrooms, gift shop

Three hundred years of local history are displayed in the restored, three-story, former Carnegie library. Children will enjoy the Indian artifacts, pioneer log home, artifacts from Thomas Edison's boyhood home, and playing captain as they pilot the ship in the third floor's marine gallery.

Jewish Culture, Hands-on Creative Play
My Jewish Discovery Room

Jewish Community Center
6600 West Maple Road, West Bloomfield
248-661-7634
248-661-7634 (birthday parties)

Location: On the Jewish Community Center's second floor
Hours: 10 a.m.–2 p.m., Sunday. Birthday parties and groups by appointment only.
Admission: Free
Ages: 3–7
Plan: Short visit
Parking: Free parking in two lots adjacent to Center
Lunch: Kosher cafeteria on the Center's main floor
Facilities: Bathrooms, drinking fountains, elevator. Small gift counter on main floor with Jewish holiday items, candy, and gum.

Discovery Room is a well-planned and creatively executed hands-on Jewish museum, designed to let young children explore, create, and role-play while learning about the Detroit Jewish community, Israel, the Bible, and Jewish holidays. There are many self-contained thematic environments, each with a variety of sensory activities, educational toys, and take-home resource materials for parents. While lively music plays overhead, children can search for artifacts in an archeological dig; fax a message to Jerusalem's Wailing Wall; play wedding with Ken and Barbie dolls in a miniature synagogue; and take a trip aboard an El Al jet. Attention all Jewish grandparents: This is a perfect grandparent-grandchild outing.

Michigan, Native American History
Nokomis Learning Center

5153 Marsh Road, Okemos
517-349-5777

Website: www.nokomis.org
Location: 1 mile north of Meridian Mall, along Marsh Road
Hours: 10 a.m.–5 p.m., Tuesday–Friday. Noon–5 p.m., Saturday. Closed Sunday and Monday. Tours for 15 or more include lecture, demonstration, game, and craft. Call ahead to schedule tours.

Admission: $2 adults, $1 children. $2 for tour.
Ages: All ages. For tour, kindergarten and up.
Plan: Under one hour
Parking: Free on site
Lunch: Restaurants and fast foods located on Grand River and Marsh Roads. Central Park offers picnic tables and covered picnic shelter.
Facilities: Bathrooms. Small gift shop features Native American handicrafts, books, and music tapes.

Displays of art, crafts, and artifacts preserve the heritage and tell the story of the Woodland Indians of the Great Lakes—the Ojibway, Ottawa, and Potowatomi tribes, known as "The People of the Three Fires."

African American History

North American Black Historical Museum

277 King Street
Amherstburg, Ontario, Canada
519-736-5433

Location: From the tunnel, take Riverside Drive (Highway 18) into Amherstburg
Hours: Open mid-April–October 30: 10 a.m.–5 p.m., Wednesday–Friday. 1–5 p.m.. Saturday and Sunday. Also open February weekends.
Admission: $4.50 adults, $3.50 seniors, $2 students, 14 and under. $10 single family unit.
Ages: All ages
Plan: Short visit
Parking: Adjacent to museum
Lunch: Eat in Amherstburg or nearby city of Sandwich
Facilities: Bathrooms, gift shop

The Windsor area meant freedom for runaway slaves on the Underground Railroad as they moved through Detroit. The North American Black Historical Museum preserves the heritage of Essex County's black community, which had its beginnings during this turbulent era. The museum, 1855 log house, and Nazarene A.M.E. Church depict black origins from Africa through slavery, followed by freedom and development.

History

Plymouth Historical Museum

155 South Main Street, Plymouth
734-455-8940

Location: Main and Church Streets, two blocks north of downtown Plymouth
Hours: 1–4 p.m., Wednesday, Thursday, Saturday. 2–5 p.m. Sunday. Open any time by appointment for groups of 20 or more.
Admission: $5 family, $2 adults, 50 cents children 5–17, under 5 free. Family membership available.
Ages: 5 and up
Plan: Short visit
Parking: Use lot on south side of building
Lunch: Drive back to downtown Plymouth
Facilities: Bathrooms. Gift shop with many folk toys, Indian items, and handcrafted dolls.

This is an engaging historical museum set up with kids in mind. On "Main Street Plymouth," kids can peek into storefronts representing trades and professions of the early 1900's. Downstairs is a hands-on area that helps children understand the olden days through make-believe. They can try on clothes from grandma's trunk, play with old-fashioned foods from a general store bin, and use McGuffey's Primers and slates to play school.

Transportation History

R.E. Olds Transportation Museum

240 Museum Drive, Lansing
517-372-0422

Location: Off Michigan Avenue, three blocks east of the Capitol
Hours: 10 a.m.–5 p.m., Monday–Saturday. Noon–5 p.m., Sunday. November–April: Closed on Sunday.
Admission: $8 family, $4 adults, $2 seniors and children, under 5 free. Group rates and family membership available.
Ages: 5 and up
Plan: Under one hour
Parking: Free lot on site
Lunch: Café across the parking lot in Lansing's Impression 5 Museum
Facilities: Bathrooms. Gift shop with model car kits, car posters, pictures.

R.E. Olds Transportation Museum, with its extensive collection of antique cars, posters, pictures, advertisements, and old motoring clothing, is a must for children with a passion for cars. The museum's two special events, Riverfest on Labor Day weekend, and August's Car Capital Event, feature antique vehicles and entertainment.

History

River Raisin Battlefield Visitor's Center

1403 East Elm Street, Monroe
734-243-7136

Location: 1 mile west of I-75, on Elm and Detroit Avenue
Hours: 10 a.m.–5 p.m. daily, Memorial Day–Labor Day. 10 a.m.–5 p.m., Saturday and Sunday, rest of year.
Admission: Free
Ages: All ages
Plan: Under one hour
Parking: Free on site
Lunch: Restaurants available in town
Facilities: Bathrooms

"Remember the Raisin!" Monroe's fiery role in the War of 1812 comes to life in this museum. A fiber optic map of the battle is projected onto a wall and details the movement and fighting of the British, American, and Native American forces.

Military History

Selfridge Military Air Museum

Selfridge Air Base, Mount Clemens
810-307-5035

Location: Take I-94 east to exit 240 (Hall Road), then two miles east on Hall Road to the Air Base
Hours: 1–5 p.m., Sunday, April 14–November 1
Admission: $3.50, children under 12 and military are free. Tours available.
Ages: 5 and up
Plan: Under one hour
Parking: Free, on site
Lunch: Picnic tables
Facilities: Bathrooms. Gift shop features model airplanes, aviation toys and aviation history items.

Most children will be able to see the Air Force, Air Reserve, and National Guard exhibits in several minutes, but they will want to spend a lot of time outdoors playing in the field of once-heroic, now-grounded Navy and Air Force planes. Sunday airplane maneuvers will also keep the kids entertained. They will hear and see the planes zooming across the sky.

Transportation

Spirit of Ford

1151 Village Road, Dearborn
313-31-SPIRIT

Location: On the campus of Henry Ford Museum/Greenfield Village and the Automotive Hall of Fame
Hours: 9 a.m.–5 p.m., daily. Special evening hours during the summer. Closed Thanksgiving Day, December 24 and 25, and New Year's Day.
Admission: $9 adults, $8 seniors, $7 children ages 5–12, $6 children ages 3–4. Group discounts available.
Ages: 4 and up
Plan: Short visit
Parking: Free lots
Lunch: Henry Ford Museum offers lunch options
Facilities: Bathrooms, drinking fountains. Gift shop with many Ford-logo items, model car kits, and car travel games.

The new, 50,000-square-foot center showcases shiny new Fords and offers hands-on exhibits, a virtual reality ride, and many clever audio-visual displays. For adults and children over 42 inches tall, the highlight is definitely "Turbo Tour," a virtual reality ride that turns you into a car on the assembly line as it is stamped, welded, painted, dunked into water, and then test-driven by a maniac. Two spray sensors provide the accompanying factory scents of sparks, heat, paint, and new leather. Children will also enjoy creating their own cars at the K'NEX Station and testing them on several ramps. Like salads at upscale museum cafeterias, cars can be purchased according to their weight.

Music

Stearns Collection of Musical Instruments

1100 Baits Drive, Ann Arbor
734-763-4389

Location: School of Music Galleries, University of Michigan North Campus
Hours: 10 a.m.–4:30 p.m., Wednesday–Saturday. 1–5 p.m., Sunday. Guided tours are available by appointment. Call Around Town Tours, 734-994-5192.
Admission: Free. Minimal fee for tours.
Ages: 5 and older
Plan: Under one hour
Parking: Metered lot in back of building
Lunch: Snack bar open daily. For lots of restaurants, drive onto the main U of M campus.
Facilities: Bathrooms

For children fascinated by music and instruments, here's an opportunity to see unusual instruments both old and new. Among the many fascinating examples, kids are sure to notice the Damaru, a Tibetan drum made from a human skull, African thumb pianos, and the very modern Moog synthesizer.

African American History

Tuskegee Airmen National Museum

Historic Fort Wayne
6325 West Jefferson, Detroit
313-843-8849

Location: Near the entrance of Historic Fort Wayne
Hours: April 1–September 31: 10 a.m.–3 p.m., daily. November 1–March 31: By appointment only, for groups of five or more.
Admission: No charge, donations welcome
Ages: All ages
Plan: Under one hour
Parking: Visitor parking lots near Fort entrance
Lunch: Have an authentic Mexican meal in Mexicantown, located west of I-96, between 23 Street and Scotten, and Vernor and Bagley. Try Evie's Tamales, (313) 843-5056 or Xochimilco, (313) 843-0179.
Facilities: Bathrooms

Photographs, uniforms, and memorabilia tell the story of the Tuskegee Airmen, the country's first Black Army Air Force Battalion.

Natural History
University of Michigan Exhibit Museum of Natural History

1109 Geddes Avenue, Ann Arbor
734-763-6085 (taped information)
734-764-0478 (reservations)

Website: www.exhibits.lsa.umich.edu/
Location: Geddes Avenue near Washtenaw Avenue, on the U of M Central Campus
Hours: 9 a.m.–5 p.m., Monday–Saturday. Noon–5 p.m., Sunday. Planetarium shows: 10:30 and 11:30 a.m., 12:30, 1:30, 2:30, and 3:30 p.m., Saturday. 1:30, 2:30, 3:30 p.m. Sunday. 1, 2, and 3 p.m., Monday–Friday, during July and August.
Admission: Museum, free to families, fee for group tours. Planetarium show, $3.25 adults, $3 seniors and children 12 and under.
Ages: All ages
Plan: Half day including planetarium show
Parking: Use the public structure on Fletcher Street
Lunch: Walk into campus. There are many restaurants on South University and State Street.
Facilities: Bathrooms and drinking fountain. Gift shop with variety of inexpensive dinosaur and science items.

The University of Michigan Exhibit Museum is a great destination for the dinophile in your family. Its second floor is full of dinosaur fossils. You'll find skeletons of an allosaurus, a duck-billed anatosaurus, and the "Jurassic Park" raptor, Deinonychus, plus the giant leg of a brontosaurus, and the extinct elephant bird's tremendous egg. Kids walk through and can't believe their eyes. For a bird's eye view, walk up to the third floor and peek over the balcony onto the backs of the prehistoric monsters. The museum's extensive stuffed wildlife collection will also delight younger children.

Transportation

Walter P. Chrysler Museum

One Chrysler Drive, Auburn Hills
1-888-456-1924

Location: From I-75, take Exit 78—Chrysler Drive and follow signs to Daimler-Chrysler World Headquarters
Hours: 10 a.m.–6 p.m., Tuesday–Saturday. Noon–6 p.m., Sunday. School groups can call to schedule tours.
Admission: $6 adults, $3 children under age 12 and seniors, Chrysler employees free.
Ages: Recommended ages 10 and older
Plan: Short visit
Parking: Free on site
Lunch: Vending machines. Opdyke and Squirrel Roads have a variety of fast food restaurants.
Facilities: Bathrooms. Gift shop with Chrysler brand clothes and Chrysler-related videos, books, kits, and collectibles.

The new 60,000-square-foot museum tells the story of Daimler-Chrysler's American heritage. The emphasis is on Chrysler history, personalities, and innovations. Seventy-five historic vehicles from 1902 through the mid-1990's take center stage, along with interactive displays, dioramas, and video presentations.

Scouting History

Washington Scouting Museum

Old Van Dyke Road, Washington
810-781-4703

Location: In the former Washington High School, fi mile north of 26 Mile Road.
Hours: Tours available to scouting groups with up to 30 people maximum.
Admission: Free, donations are welcome. School groups are also welcome
Ages: Tiger Cubs and Brownies and up
Plan: Under one hour
Parking: Free on site
Lunch: Nearby McDonald's
Facilities: Bathrooms

No, you can't earn a badge by visiting the museum, but you can see how uniforms have changed in over half a century. On display at the Washington Scouting Museum are medals, uniforms, scouting equipment, and manuals, including books once owned by Boy Scouts' founder Sir Robert Baden-Powell. Learn about scouting from a 57-year expert on the subject. Included in the tour is a walk through the historical section.

History

Witch's Hat Depot Museum

300 Dorothy Street, South Lyon
248-437-9929

Location: Just south of downtown South Lyon, in McHattie Park
Hours: 1–4 p.m., Thursday. 1–5 p.m., Sunday. April–early November. Call to arrange school and group tours.
Admission: Free
Ages: Elementary school and up
Plan: Under one hour
Parking: Free parking in lot adjacent to museum
Lunch: Family-owned restaurants and fast-food franchises are located in town, on Lafayette and Lake Streets
Facilities: Bathrooms, gift counter
    The Witch's Hat Depot Museum, so named for its unique roof, offers artifacts of everyday life from the 1860's to the 1940's, including children's clothing, dolls and toys, farm and kitchen implements, Civil War and World War I uniforms, and photographs. McHattie Park also includes the Washburn one-room schoolhouse and an authentic red caboose. Children can climb up onto the caboose and play engineer and sit at small wooden desks in the restored schoolhouse and practice their lessons on slates. Depot Days, scheduled on the first September weekend after Labor Day, features old-fashioned, small town activities, entertainment, and children's games.

Military History

Yankee Air Force Museum

Willow Run Airport, Ypsilanti
734-483-4030

Website: www.yankeeairmuseum.org
Location: Willow Run Airport, Hangar 2041, east side of field
Hours: 10 a.m.–4 p.m., Tuesday–Saturday. Noon–4 p.m., Sunday.
Admission: $5 adults, $4 seniors, $3 children 5–12. Under 5 are free. Group rates available.
Ages: 6 and up
Plan: Under one hour
Parking: Free, on site
Lunch: Drive into Ypsilanti or Belleville
Facilities: Bathrooms. Gift shop with aviation pins, patches, books, models and posters.

For children with a passion for airplanes, a visit to the Yankee Air Force Museum is a must. Housed in a tremendous hangar are colorful examples of World War II and Korean War era airplanes. Aviation history exhibits are on the second level. Feel free to engage the volunteers in discussion; they will gladly give you an informal tour of the aircraft. Special Air Shows are offered on Memorial Day and Founders' Day, September 22.

History

Ypsilanti Historical Society and Museum

220 North Huron Street, Ypsilanti
734-482-4990

Location: Off I-94, exit 183, follow Huron Street to Cross Street. On the east side of Huron Street.
Hours: 2–4 p.m., Thursday, Saturday, and Sunday
Admission: Free
Ages: 6 and up
Plan: Under one hour
Parking: Metered parking on street. City lots nearby.
Lunch: Depot Town offers several restaurants
Facilities: Bathrooms, drinking fountain. Gift shop has old-fashioned toys.

The restored Victorian home offers authentic furnishings, period clothing, home and farm tools and implements, plus changing exhibits from the 1800's. Children who are interested in history and old enough to understand "look but don't touch" will especially enjoy the winding staircase, Scottish Drum and Bugle Corps uniform, dollhouse, and old toys.

6
Historic Sites

TIP

Make it a point to visit historic villages and museums during a special living history event. Kids learn history best when they are dipping candles, playing old-fashioned games, or watching costumed interpreters demonstrate old-time crafts and chores.

Listed in this chapter are a diverse assortment of 19th-century restored homes, villages, and farmsteads, forts, auto baron mansions, lighthouses, and landmarks. Michigan's historic sites often reveal its communal pioneer history and the important role it played in the automobile industry. Many sites have a commitment to living history, offering demonstrations and costumed guides that are quite appealing to children five and older. While the auto baron homes tours are not geared specifically to children, each home has aspects that children will find interesting. After accompanying me on many homes tours, my children became quite adept at staying near the guide and asking questions. They now see history as an accumulation of many personal stories.

U.S. - Canada Bridge
Ambassador Bridge

Juncture of I-75 and I-96, Detroit
313-849-5244

For children, a drive across this bridge is high adventure. Peeking out the window, they can see both the Detroit and Windsor skylines, as well as the Detroit River and its barge traffic. When we visit Windsor, we always try to use both the bridge and tunnel in our coming and going. Open 24 hours, daily. A toll fee ($2.25 U.S., $2.75 Canadian) is collected before entering on both sides of the Detroit River.

U.S. - Canada Bridge
Blue Water International Bridge

At end of I-94 going east, Port Huron
810-984-3131

We like to take this less-trafficked bridge into Canada when we are going to Eastern Ontario. Toll fees are $1.50 U.S., $2 Canadian. On the way back to the U.S., we always stop for an ice cream cone at the London Farm Dairy Bar (2136 Pine Grove Avenue, 810-984-5111), just south of the foot of the bridge. Above the dairy sign, a giant cow with horns looks out at the traffic.

Carillon Tower

Burton Memorial Tower

300 block of South Thayer Street, Ann Arbor
734-764-2539

Visitors can climb to the top floor of the carillon tower, one of the landmarks on the University of Michigan campus, during concerts from 12–12:30 p.m. weekdays and 10:15–10:45 a.m. Saturdays, when school is in session. Way up there you'll have a bird's-eye view of Ann Arbor and will also see and hear 55 bells, the world's third heaviest carillon instrument.

Farmhouse

Cobblestone Farm

2781 Packard, Ann Arbor
734-994-2928

Website: www.ci.ann-arbor.mi.us
Location: On Packard Road, between Platt and Stone School Roads
Hours: 1–4 p.m., Friday and Sunday, May–September. Groups can call to schedule tours.
Admission: $5 family rate, $2 adults, $1.50 children 3–17 and seniors, under 3 free
Ages: 5 and up
Plan: Short visit
Parking: Free, behind the barn
Lunch: Picnic area near playground. Many restaurants in nearby Briarwood Mall or on U of M campus.
Facilities: Bathrooms. Gift shop with handcrafted toys and concession, located in Cobblestone Farm Center. Playground on grounds of Buhr Park.

Cobblestone Farm is a living farm museum that tells the story of 19th-century Michigan farm life through a variety of restored, authentically furnished buildings: the elegant Ticknor-Campbell house, a pioneer log cabin, and a replica of an 1880's barn, full of animals. Costumed guides lead public tours through the house; the other buildings are open for browsing. Children will benefit most from a pre-arranged group tour. Throughout spring, summer, and fall, there are weekend festivals and Living History programs which offer demonstrations of 19th-century crafts and chores.

Historic Home

Cranbrook House and Gardens

380 Lone Pine Road, Bloomfield Hills
810-645-3149

Website: www.cranbrook.edu
Location: On Cranbrook Educational Campus
Hours: Home tour: June–September: 11 a.m. and
1:15 p.m., Thursday. 1:30 and 3 p.m., Sunday.
Groups of 15 or more can schedule special tours.
Garden tour: June–September: 2 p.m., Thursday.
1:30 p.m., Sunday. Self-guided Garden Walk:
May–August: 10 a.m.–5 p.m., Monday–Saturday.
11 a.m.–5 p.m., Sunday. September: 11 a.m.–3
p.m., daily. October: 11 a.m.–3 p.m., weekends.
Admission: Home tour: $10 adults, $9 seniors.
Garden tour: $5 adults, $4 children and seniors,
under 3 free. Self-guided Walk: $5 adults, $4 children and seniors, under 3 free.
Ages: Home tour: older children. Garden walk: all
ages.
Plans: Home tour is one hour; Garden tour is 90
minutes.
Parking: Along Lone Pine Road or across the
street in Christ Church parking lot
Lunch: You'll find restaurants in nearby Birmingham or along Woodward Avenue or Telegraph Road
Facilities: Bathrooms in house

Cranbrook House is an English manor house
designed by Albert Kahn and built in the early
1900's for *The Detroit News* publisher and
Cranbrook founders, George Booth and his wife,
Ellen Scripps Booth. Older children will enjoy learning about the life of these two influential people.
The gardens surrounding the home offer 40 acres
of formal plantings, woods, pine forest walks, and
two lakes. The gardens are a perfect way to experience seasonal changes. Kids love scampering
along the paths and ducking into the pine forest.

Historic Home

Crocker House

15 Union Street, Mount Clemens
810-465-2488

Location: Cass Avenue and Gratiot
Hours: 10 a.m.–4 p.m., Tuesday–Thursday; 1–4
p.m., first Sunday of each month. Closed in

January and February. Increased hours during December. Group tours available.
Admission: $2 adults, 50 cents children
Ages: 8 and up
Plan: Under one hour
Parking: Lot or street
Lunch: Restaurants in town
Facilities: Bathrooms. Small gift shop with Victorian replica toys and other inexpensive items.

Older children with an interest in the Victorian age will enjoy Crocker House's authentically furnished rooms and costumed mannequins. They will also enjoy the home's special Christmas exhibits, including a decorated Victorian dollhouse, and decorations.

Historic Village & Train
Crossroads Village/Huckleberry Railroad

6140 Bray Road, Flint
810-736-7100
1-800-648-7275

Website: www.geneseecountyparks.org
Location: Just north of Flint. Follow I-475 off either I-75 or I-69 to Saginaw Street (Exit 13). Go north to Stanley Road. Go east to Bray Road. Go south to Village.
Hours: End of May–Labor Day: 10 a.m.–5:30 p.m., Tuesday–Friday. 11 a.m.–6:30 p.m., weekends and holidays. Train departs hourly 11 a.m.–4p.m., weekdays. Noon–5 p.m., weekends and holidays. Genesee Belle cruises begin at 12:30 p.m., daily at the village. 7 and 8:30 p.m., Sunday, June–Labor Day at Stepping Stone Falls. Village/train weekends only through September. Halloween programs in October. Christmas at Crossroads: 3:30–9:30 p.m., Fridays, Saturdays, Sundays, and selected weekdays, beginning the last weekend in November–end of December. Bunny Train prior to Easter.
Admission: Village and train ride: $9.25 adult, $6.25 children 4–12, $8.25 seniors, 3 and under free. Genesee Belle: $3.75 adults, $2 children ages 1–12, 12 months and under are free. Evening cruise, $4.50 adults, $3.50 children 1–12, 12 months and under are free. Group rates and family membership available.
Ages: 3 and up
Plan: Full day visit

Parking: Free lot adjacent to village
Lunch: Small cafe, ice cream parlor, picnic area, cider mill
Facilities: Bathrooms. General store features country and handcrafted items, dolls, and candy. Depot Souvenir Shop offers train memorabilia and novelty items.

Crossroads Village and Huckleberry Railroad offer families a perfect summer outing. Take a 45-minute ride on the full-size steam train and enjoy a 45-minute scenic cruise aboard the Genesee Belle, a paddle wheel riverboat. Walk the 19th-century village streets and explore 30 beautifully restored buildings, including three working mills, a toy maker's barn, one-room schoolhouse, and general store. Duck into the Opera House for a 20-minute live show. Costumed guides, hands-on experiences, craft demonstrations, a ride on a restored ferris wheel, carousel, miniature train and pony carts, and special encampment and craft weekends add to children's enjoyment. Celebrate Halloween with a ride aboard a spooky train and trick-or-treating in the village. Christmas at Crossroads Village is a festive time with over 400,000 sparkling lights, Santa's workshop, and holiday entertainment.

Historic Buildings

Dearborn Historical Museum: McFadden Ross House, Exhibit Annex, Commandant's Quarters, and Gardner House

915 South Brady, Dearborn
313-565-3000

Location: Just north of Michigan Avenue
Hours: 9 a.m.–5 p.m., Monday–Saturday, May–October. 1–5 p.m., Monday–Saturday, November–April.
Admission: Free
Ages: All ages
Plan: Short visit
Parking: Use lot adjacent to buildings
Lunch: Nearby Fairlane Town Center has a wide variety of restaurants both inside the mall and on the grounds
Facilities: Bathrooms, gift shop

The 1800's come to life in four buildings. The first two are located on Brady Street. The McFadden-

Ross House contains domestic and period exhibits; the Exhibit Annex has craft shops, wagons, and buggies. The Commandant's Quarters, located at the corner of Michigan and Monroe, houses military exhibits and period rooms. Gardner House, an old, 1831 homestead, is located behind McFadden Ross House.

Caboose

Depot Town Caboose

23fi Cross Street, Ypsilanti
734-482-4920

While shopping or browsing in Ypsilanti's restored Depot Town shops, be sure to let the kids climb on board the shiny red caboose and play "engineer."

Detroit-Windsor Tunnel

Detroit-Windsor Tunnel

100 East Jefferson, Detroit
313-567-4422

Young children won't believe you at first when you tell them they are driving under the Detroit River. Older children will be amazed that such a tunnel could ever be built. It's a Detroit landmark that makes your trip to Windsor begin as an adventure. The tunnel is located at the foot of Randolph and Jefferson. Open 24 hours, daily. A toll fee ($2.25 American, $2.75 Canadian) is collected before entering on both sides of the Detroit River.

One-Room Schoolhouse

Dewey School

11501 Territorial Road, Stockbridge
517-851-8247

Location: Mayer and Territorial Roads, just off M-106, south of Stockbridge. Located close to the Waterloo Area Farm Museum.
Hours: 1–4 p.m., Sunday, June–first weekend in October. Special "Rural Schooldays" tour available during May and September.
Admission: Minimal donation per person, children

under 5 free. $1.50 for half-day tour, $3 for full day tour.
Ages: First grade and up for school tours.
Plan: Under one hour
Parking: Free lots adjacent to schoolhouse
Lunch: Picnic area in nearby Waterloo Recreation Area
Facilities: Gift counter with old-fashioned school supplies

Children can become 19th-century schoolchildren in this one-room historic schoolhouse.

Historic General Store

Dixboro General Store

5206 Plymouth Road, Ann Arbor
734-663-5558

Location: The village of Dixboro is just east of Ann Arbor
Hours: 10 a.m.–6 p.m., Monday–Thursday, and Saturday. 10 a.m.–8 p.m., Friday. 11 a.m.–5 p.m., Sunday.
Admission: Free
Ages: All ages
Plan: Under one hour
Parking: Free lot behind store
Lunch: Restaurants in town

The Dixboro General Store defines the small, quaint village of Dixboro, along with an old schoolhouse, church, and popular Lord Fox Restaurant (734-662-1647). The store, which has been in operation since 1839, sells reproduction items, candles, hand-crafted furniture, antiques, toys, gifts, and collectibles. Visit on a U of M football Saturday.

Auto Baron Home

Edsel and Eleanor Ford House

100 Lake Shore Road, Grosse Pointe Shores
313-884-4222
313-884-3400 (recorded information)
Website: www.fordhouse.org
Location: Off I-94, Vernier Road Exit. Go east to Lake Shore Drive (Jefferson).
Hours: One-hour tours are offered every hour on the hour, 10 a.m.–4 p.m., Tuesday–Saturday. Noon–4 p.m., Sunday. Group tours by appointment. Grounds are open May–October: 10 a.m.–4 p.m., Tuesday–Saturday. Noon–4 p.m., Sunday.

Admission: $6 adults, $5 seniors, $4 children.
May–October: Grounds only, $4 per person.
Ages: 7 and up
Plan: Short visit
Parking: Free, on site
Lunch: The Tea Room serves a light lunch, 11:30
a.m.–2:30 p.m., Tuesday–Sunday, April–December.
Facilities: Bathrooms and gift shop in Activity
Center. The gift shop sells a selection of gardening
and art appreciation gifts, children's toys and
crafts, and Ford House memorabilia.

Friendly, engaging tour guides help children
find many things of interest in the Edsel and
Eleanor Ford home, such as the ever-present view
of Lake St. Clair, curious and beautiful decorative
pieces, and a many-sided mirror in the Art Deco
study that gives off infinite images. Best of all, the
tour offers an inside look into one of Detroit's first
families. After the 50-minute tour, walk or drive
over to the Play House. For most children, this will
be the highlight of the visit. Built to resemble the
mansion, this playhouse is created in three-quarter
size with furnishings to match. Adults will feel like
Alice in Wonderland. The House and Activity
Center offer special art exhibits, teas, and holiday
children's shows.

Railcar

Eisenhower Presidential Car

7203 US-12, Onsted (Irish Hills)
517-467-2300

Location: In front of Stagecoach Stop, U.S.A., off
US-12
Hours: June–August: 10:30 a.m.–5:30 p.m.,
Saturday and Sunday. Self-guided tours or group
tours available.
Admission: $1.50/person. Group rates available.
Ages: 5 and up
Plan: Under one hour. With Stagecoach Stop, plan
on a half day visit.
Parking: Free on site
Lunch: Restaurant in Stagecoach Stop, fudge
shop adjacent to railroad car, picnic areas
Facilities: Bathrooms. Gift Shop in Stagecoach
Stop.

Once known as the "White House on Wheels,"
this railroad car was used by President Eisenhower
from 1952 to 1960. Today it houses Eisenhower

memorabilia and offers children a look at the conditions of coach travel. Kids will especially enjoy seeing where Eisenhower slept and ate.

Historic Farmstead

Ella Sharp Museum

3225 Fourth Street, Jackson
517-787-2320

Location: 4 miles south of I-94 and US-127 intersection
Hours: 10 a.m.–4 p.m., Tuesday–Friday. 11 a.m.–4 p.m., Saturday and Sundays. Closed Mondays, and holidays.
Admission: $5 family, $2.50 adults, $2 seniors, $1 children 5–15, under 5 are free. Family membership available.
Ages: 2 and up
Plan: Half day visit
Parking: Free on site
Lunch: Granary Restaurant: 11 a.m.–2:30 p.m., Tuesday–Saturday. Adjacent Ella Sharp Park has picnic area and playground.
Facilities: Bathrooms, drinking fountain. Gift shop full of kids' toys, games, books, tapes, jewelry, and science items.

The Ella Sharp Museum is a historic complex with a vision of the future. The cornerstone of the complex is the beautifully restored 19th-century Merriman-Sharp family farmhouse. 25-minute tours are scheduled on the hour and half hour, daily, 11 a.m.–3:30 p.m. Children will enjoy learning about the life of Jackson's most famous lady, and seeing the toys and dolls in the children's room. There are many other authentically furnished, restored buildings along Farm Lane: the Eli Stilson log house, country store, print shop, schoolhouse, barn, and woodworking and broom-making shops.

The modern galleries include three changing art and history galleries and the Discovery Gallery with hands-on exhibits that will delight children.

Detroit Landmark

Fisher Building

3011 West Grand Boulevard, Detroit
313-874-4444

Point out the Fisher Building's green tiled roof to the kids, and it will always be a point of reference for them. Once in the lobby, crane your necks upwards to see the impressive mosaic, marble, and tiled ceiling; shop and browse, but don't forget the fun stuff. Take the kids through the skywalks and tunnels (the Fisher Building is connected to New Center One and Hotel St. Regis) and up and down New Center One's glass elevators. The Fisher Building is home to the Fisher Theatre. Park in Crowley's lot.

Auto Baron Home

Fisher Mansion/Bhaktivedanta Center

383 Lenox, Detroit
313-331-6740

Location: This site is off the beaten track. Take I-94 east to Cadieux exit. Go south to East Jefferson, then west to Dickerson. Follow Dickerson south. Dickerson becomes Lenox Avenue at Essex Street. After one block on Lenox, look for the Fisher Mansion on your right.
Hours: One-hour tours: 12:30, 2, 3:30, and 6 p.m., Friday–Sunday. Group tours for 20 or more people available during the week.
Admission: $6 adults, $5 seniors and students, $4 children, children 10 and under free when accompanied by adult
Ages: 8 and older
Plan: Short visit
Parking: Free, use second gate
Lunch: Govinda's, located in the elegant dining room, offers gourmet vegetarian cuisine as well as kid-pleasing desserts. Noon–9 p.m., Friday and Saturday. Noon–7 p.m. Sunday. Last seating 1/2 hour before closing. Open Mother's Day–Labor Day.
Facilities: Bathrooms. East Indian grocery and gift shop with made-in-India items, books, snacks, and incense.

Children with a vivid imagination will love this home, built by Auto Baron Lawrence Fisher in the 1920's, in a highly opulent and decorative style. Everywhere there are carved wooden faces, painted ceilings, gold inlaid patterns, and detailed tiles. Children will enjoy the indoor boatwells, the secret doors, and haunting mirrors.

The mansion, now cultural center for Krishna Consciousness followers, also has a remarkable collection of Indian paintings, tapestries, masks, and sculptures. Children are welcomed on the tours and encouraged to ask questions. There are two optional audio-visual presentations, one 10 minutes, the other 20 minutes, both with Krishna religious content. The theme and message of both go over the heads of children, but they might enjoy the colorful costumes and images.

Fort Gratiot Lighthouse

2800 Omar Street, Port Huron
810-984-2602

Location: I-94 and Hancock Street
Hours: Tours by appointment only, 810-385-7387.
Admission: Free
Ages: 6 and up
Plan: Under one hour
Parking: Free lot to the right of lighthouse
Lunch: Picnic area behind lighthouse
Facilities: Bathrooms
Kids will enjoy climbing up the spiral staircase and romping around the outside picnic area of the oldest lighthouse in operation in the United States.

Fort Malden National Historic Park

100 Laird Avenue
Amherstburg, Ontario, Canada
519-736-5416

Location: From the tunnel, take Riverside Drive (Highway 18) to Amherstburg. Turn right at Alma Street, left at Laird Street. Approximately 25 minutes from tunnel.
Hours: May–October: 10 a.m.–5 p.m., daily. Rest of year: 1–5 p.m., Sunday–Friday, closed Saturday.
Admission: $2.50 adults, $2 seniors, $1.50 children 12 and under. 5 and under free.
Ages: All ages
Plan: Short visit
Parking: Free lot in front of fort
Lunch: Picnic areas along fort's grassy avenues
Facilities: Visitor center, bathrooms, benches along Detroit River

Built in 1796 by the British, Fort Malden saw action during the War of 1812. Today, her four remaining buildings sit among rolling hills and grassy avenues. Kids will enjoy almost everything about this fort. The video is only six minutes long, and costumed guides demonstrate musket firing and other 19th-century military routines. Children are allowed to try on military costumes. Best of all, the hills and avenues are perfect for running and rolling. After your visit, drive down a block to Austin "Toddy" Jones Park, located at the corner of Laird Avenue South and North Street. Here you'll find creative slides and swings, plus a wooden fort climber.

Detroit Landmark
Fox Theatre
2211 Woodward, Detroit
313-396-7600

Website: www.olympiaentertainment.com
Golden ornaments, red marble pillars, sculptured animals with jeweled eyes, glittering chandeliers— these are only a few of the details that make the Fox a majestically exotic former movie palace. Try to catch a family show, which will have more modestly priced tickets than the major attractions.

Historic Theme Mall
Frontier Town
67300 Van Dyke, Romeo
810-752-6260

Location: On Van Dyke, between 31 and 32 Mile Road
Hours: 10 a.m.–6 p.m., daily
Admission: Free
Ages: All ages
Plan: Under one hour
Parking: Free parking lots
Lunch: Ice cream parlor serving ice cream as well as sandwiches, soups, and chili
Facilities: Bathroom
Set on ten and a half acres, Frontier Town is an old-fashioned Western town with many unique retail stores, including toy and doll shops, chocolate and country stores. Children will enjoy the petting farm and working water wheel.

Historic Theater

Gem and Century Theatres

333 Madison Avenue, Detroit
313-963-9800

These small, intimate theaters have been authentically restored to their former 1920's glory days. Come in and take a peek and stay for a cabaret-style musical revue.

Detroit Landmark

Greektown

Monroe Street near Beaubien, Detroit

Come to Greektown hungry and sample baklava, shish kabob, and flaming cheese. Monroe Street is lined with Greek bakeries, restaurants, ice cream parlors, and fudge shops. Trappers Alley, a festival marketplace opening onto Monroe Street, has a People Mover station on the third level. A temporary casino is located adjacent to Trappers Alley, with an entrance off East Lafayette.

Historic Village

Greenfield Village

20900 Oakwood Boulevard, Dearborn
313-271-1620
313-271-1976 (24-hour information)
313-271-1570 (IMAX Theatre)

Website: www.hfmgv.org
Location: Michigan Avenue and Southfield Freeway
Hours: 9 a.m.–5 p.m., daily, mid-March–first week in January. Closed Thanksgiving Day and Christmas Day.
Admission: $12.50 adults, $11.50 seniors, $7.50 children 5 to 12, under 5 free. IMAX Theatre: $7.50 adults, $6.50 children 5 to 12 and seniors, $6 children 4 and under and members. Combination tickets: Henry Ford Museum or Greenfield Village and IMAX: $17.50 adults, $16 seniors, $12.50 children 5 to 12, $6 children 4 and under. Henry Ford Museum and Greenfield Village and IMAX: $28 adults, $27 seniors, $19 children 5 to 12, $6 chil-

dren 4 and under. Group rates and family memberships available. Additional fees for Steam Train Ride, Suwanee Steamboat, Carousel, and Carriage Tours

Ages: All ages

Plan: Full day

Parking: Free, adjacent to museum and village

Lunch: The Eagle Tavern for full dinners, A Taste of History Restaurant—a cafeteria on the Village Green—for an edible history lesson, Suwanee Restaurant at Suwanee Park for cafeteria selection, Main Street Lunch Stand for light refreshments, Covered Bridge Lunch Stand for snacks. Picnicking is allowed throughout the village. I recommend bringing a picnic lunch and adding snacks as the day wears on.

Facilities: Bathrooms, drinking fountains, stroller rental. Three gift shops. The well-stocked Village Store, located at the entrance, has many reproductions of old-fashioned children's toys, books, and craft items.

Greenfield Village is one of the Detroit area's best-known sites. Its restored homes, workshops, and stores offer a glimpse into America's past and a look at inventors Thomas Edison, George Washington Carver, the Wright Brothers, and Henry Ford, men who revolutionized our world. The restored Hermitage Plantation Slave Houses and the 1879 Mattox Home, owned by former slaves, depict how African Americans lived before and after slavery was abolished. The village is too large to see everything on one visit with small children. Your best bet is to concentrate on the sure-fire child-pleasers. Take the 30-minute round-trip train ride and visit the Firestone Farm, a working farm where costumed interpretive guides live and work according to a 19th-century schedule. The nearby demonstration barns, particularly glass blowing and printing, appeal to children and offer vivid memories. Ride the Suwanee Steamboat and the restored carousel, then buy an ice cream, and call it a day. You can always come again. Enjoy hands-on activities, costumed characters, roving players, playlets, old-fashioned "Base Ball," and crafts during Summer Festival, mid-June–August. There are many theme weekends throughout the summer and fall, and Christmas festivities in December.

Historic Village

Greenmead Museum and Historical Village

20501 Newburgh Road, Livonia
248-477-7375

Location: Newburgh and Eight Mile Roads
Hours: Village hours: 9 a.m.–5 p.m., Monday–Friday, May–October. Drop-in tours: 1–4 p.m., Sunday, May–October. Group tours available by appointment. Sunday concerts during December.
Admission: $2 adults, $1 children.
Ages: 5 and up
Plan: Short visit
Parking: Free on site
Lunch: Picnic tables in park
Facilities: Outhouses available during spring. Gift shop with variety of old-fashioned toys and trinkets.

This small historic 19th-century village includes Shaw House, Kingsley House, the Hill farmstead, Newburg School, a church, general store, and interpretive center. Kids will enjoy the interpretive center's ten-minute slide show, the general store's penny candy, and the restored buildings' furnishings and costumed mannequins. The on-site park has a small playground. There are special programs and decorations at Christmas.

Auto Baron Home

Henry Ford Estate–Fair Lane

4901 Evergreen
University of Michigan-Dearborn
313-593-5590

Location: Michigan Avenue and Evergreen Road
Hours: Home tours: 1–4:30 p.m., Sunday year-round. On the hour 10 a.m.–3 p.m., except at noon, Monday–Saturday, April–December. Guided nature tour of grounds: year-round, call for reservations. Self-guided nature tour: year-round, maps available in the Visitor Center. Breakfast with Santa is held in December.
Admission: Home tour: $7 adults, $6 children and seniors, children under 5 are free
Ages: Suggested 8 and up for home tour, 2–10 for Breakfast with Santa.
Plan: Home tour: 1 1/2 hours
Parking: Free lot across from estate

Lunch: Pool restaurant: 11 a.m.–2 p.m., Monday–Friday, year-round; picnic areas

Facilities: Bathrooms. Gift shop with Ford-related items, old-fashioned toys, and books.

The 1½-hour tour of Henry and Clara Ford's mansion might be too much for little children, but older children will enjoy walking single file through a 300-foot-deep underground tunnel connecting the main house with the electric power house, peeking into the indoor bowling alley, being allowed to sit on the inauthentic furniture as the tour guide speaks, and seeing how one of the 20th century's most famous couples lived.

For small children, the main attraction on this estate is the white clapboard miniature farmhouse, full of hands-on, 19th-century clothes, games, toys, and miniature farm and household implements. Parents need to duck while entering the farmhouse; children fit perfectly.

Fort

Historic Fort Wayne

6325 West Jefferson, Detroit
313-833-1805

Presently closed due to budget cuts; hopes to re-open soon. Call to schedule tours of Tuskegee Airmen National Museum.

The 83-acre fort includes the Tuskegee Airmen National Museum, a restored 1880 Victorian Commanding Officer's House, visitor center, and the Spanish-American War Guardhouse.

Lightship

Huron Lightship Museum

Pine Grove Park, Port Huron
810-982-0891

Location: Pine Grove Avenue, just north of downtown business district

Hours: Summer: 1–4:30 p.m., Wednesday–Sunday. September, April, and May: 1–4:30 p.m. Saturday and Sunday. Additional hours are available by appointment only.

Admission: $2 adults, $1 seniors, 50 cents students, 6 and under free. Admission allows entrance to Museum of Art and History.

Ages: All ages. Main deck is stroller accessible.
Plan: Under one hour
Parking: On site
Lunch: Concessions available during the summer; downtown Port Huron offers a variety of restaurants. For ice cream, visit the London Farm Dairy Bar (2136 Pine Grove Avenue, 810-984-5111).
Facilities: Public restrooms in the park.

Before the days of electrically lighted buoys, lightships were used to warn ships of shallow water and help them steer their course. The Huron Lightship, built in 1920, was anchored six miles north of the Blue Water Bridge and retired from active duty in 1971. It is the last lightship to operate on the Great Lakes. Two decks (levels) are open to the public in a self-guiding tour.

Historic Farmstead, African American History

John Freeman Walls Historic Site and Underground Railroad Museum

Puce Road, Maidstone Township
Ontario, Canada
519-258-6253 (office, not site)

Location: Take Highway 401 east, exit Puce Road north. The site is approximately one mile north on Puce Road, 20 minutes from Windsor-Detroit border.
Hours: July 1–Labor Day: 10 a.m.–4 p.m., daily. May 15–October 15: School and group tours available by appointment.
Admission: $3 per person.
Ages: All ages
Plan: Short visit
Parking: Free on site
Lunch: Picnic area
Facilities: Bathrooms. Gift shop with Canadian and Underground Railroad crafts and souvenirs.

Former slave John Freeman Walls and his wife escaped to freedom and settled in Maidstone Township in 1846. Their farmstead became an important terminal on the Underground Railroad. This historic site features a train caboose museum of Underground Railroad history and African art, a 1798 log cabin, and 1846 log cabin. A movie about the museum is also shown. The site makes history vividly come to life.

Historic Village
John R. Park Homestead

360 Fairview Avenue, Essex
Ontario, Canada
519-738-2029

Location: Essex County Road 50 between Kingsville and Colchester. From Windsor, take Highway 18 southeast through Harrow and watch for white sign. Turn onto Road 50 (45 minutes southeast of Windsor).

Hours: 11 a.m.–4 p.m., Sunday–Thursday, year-round. Group tours available, call at least two weeks in advance.

Admission: $10 family, $3 adults, $2 children 4 to 16, 3 and under free

Ages: 5 and up

Plan: Short visit

Parking: Free, on site

Lunch: Picnic area, cold drinks and snack foods for sale

Facilities: Bathrooms. Gift shop with wooden toys and candy sticks.

The John R. Park Homestead, including Park's 1842 home and several restored buildings—shed, smoke house, ice house, outhouse, blacksmith shop, sawmill, and livestock stable—offer children a hands-on look into 19th-century life. Costumed guides demonstrate and involve children in seasonal crafts such as candle dipping, spinning, and butter churning, and 19th-century games. Children will also enjoy the short introductory video presentation, nature trail, and swimming in Lake Erie from the homestead's small beachfront. Many special seasonal events celebrate maple syrup, fall harvest, and Christmas. Also, there are special events each weekend in July and August.

Restored Shopping Plaza
Kerrytown Plaza

407 North Fifth Avenue, Ann Arbor
734-662-5008

Specialty shops and restaurants are located in this charming setting of restored 19th-century buildings. Kids will love the aromas coming from the specialty foods shops and market. Little Dipper Candle Shop lets children dip their own candles

($1.50/pair; daily. Groups should call for reservation, 734-994-3912). On Wednesday and Saturday mornings, the adjacent Farmers' Market is bustling with activity.

Carillon Tower

Lurie Bell Tower

Next to Pierpont Commons
On U of M's North Campus, Ann Arbor
734-764-2539

Visitors can climb to the top floor of the carillon tower, which houses a 60-bell carillon, during concerts from 1–1:30 p.m. weekdays, 5–5:30 p.m. Thursdays, and 1:15-2 p.m. Sundays, when school is in session. Summer carillon concerts are also held at 7 p.m. seven selected Mondays, beginning mid-June. Bring a picnic and enjoy the outdoor concert.

Auto Baron Home

Meadow Brook Hall and Knole Cottage

Oakland University, Rochester
248-370-3140

Location: On Adams Road, five miles north of I-75
Hours: Tours offered: July 1–August 31: 10:30 a.m.–3 p.m., Monday–Saturday and 1–3:45 p.m., Sunday. Rest of year: 1:30 p.m., daily. Holiday walk: 10 a.m.–5 p.m. or 10 a.m.– 8 p.m., depending on the day, late November–Christmas.
Admission: $8 adults, $4 children 5–12, 4 and under are free. Knole Cottage tour, $1 adults and children. Holiday walk: $12 adults. $6 children.
Ages: 8 and up
Plan: Short visit (indoor tour takes approximately 1 1/2 hours)
Parking: Free lot adjacent to mansion
Lunch: Summer Tea Room open 11:30 a.m.–3 p.m., Monday–Friday, July 1–August 31. Available for groups at other times by prior reservations.
Facilities: Bathrooms. Gift shop with Meadow Brook Hall memorabilia and stationery.

Matilda Dodge Wilson, widow of auto baron John Dodge, built her 100-room Tudor mansion in the 1920's for approximately $4 million. Meadow Brook Hall is Michigan's Biltmore, a magnificent tribute to a bygone era, decorated richly with authentic furnishings. The 1½-hour tour is not appropriate for small children, but patient older children will be rewarded with visual architectural delights and interesting anecdotes. Meadow Brook Hall's grounds are lovely at every season, and children will want to walk into the woods to explore the Knole Cottage, a six-room playhouse built to three-quarter size for Matilda and John Wilson's daughter. During the Christmas walk, Santa presides over Knole Cottage, and children are encouraged to visit during daylight hours. Car buffs won't want to miss "Concours d'Elegance," the classic, antique, and sports car show, the first Sunday in August.

Historic Village

Meridian Historical Village

5151 Marsh Road, Central Park, Okemos
517-347-7300

Location: In Central Park, behind the Meridian Township Hall
Hours: November–May: 2–5 p.m., Saturday. June–October: 10 a.m.–1 p.m., Saturday. Guided tours and school programs by appointment only. Special seasonal programs include summer day camp; Music in the Park, 6:30–8:30 p.m. selected Wednesdays in June and July; Christmas in the Village, 10 a.m.–6 p.m., the first Sunday in December.
Admission: $1 adults, 12 and under are free. $1.50/person for guided tours
Ages: All ages
Plan: Short visit
Parking: Free at park
Lunch: Bring your picnic suppers to the outdoor music concerts
Facilities: Bathrooms in village buildings, at township hall, and in the covered park pavilion. Gift shop in Heathman house features stick candy, handcrafted wooden toys, and pioneer-themed gifts

Located in the scenic Central Park on the banks of Lake Catherine, the village features the furnished Grettenburger farmhouse and Unruh barn, Randall one-room schoolhouse, Heathman house, Proctor tollhouse, and gazebo. Changing exhibits tell the story of Michigan's pioneers.

Historic Village
Mill Race Historical Village

Griswold, north of Main Street, Northville
248-348-1845

Location: 4 miles west of I-275
Hours: 1–4 p.m., Sundays, June–October.
Grounds open unless there is a wedding on site.
Pre-arranged tours available all year. School
groups can spend a day in the Wash Oak School,
April–June, or September–November.
Admission: Donation, fee for tours
Ages: 8 and up
Plan: Short visit
Parking: Free on site
Lunch: Picnicking is allowed on grounds
Facilities: Bathrooms in main house, small gift shop
This historic village includes a restored 19th-
century home with exhibits of local history, plus
several other restored homes and buildings—
church, inn, school, and blacksmith shop—all on a
seven-acre site along Mill Pond. Children will enjoy
the one-room schoolhouse and gazebo.

Historic Buildings
Navarre-Anderson Trading Post and Country Store Museum

North Custer Road at Raisinville Road, Monroe
734-243-7137

Location: Four miles west of Monroe on North
Custer at the Raisinville Bridge
Hours: 1–5 p.m., Wednesday–Sunday, Memorial
Day–Labor Day. Group tours available.
Admission: Free
Ages: All ages
Plan: Under one hour
Parking: Free adjacent to Country Store Museum
Lunch: Restaurants in town
Facilities: Bathrooms. Country store offers penny
candy and souvenirs.
The restored and furnished trading post, built in
1789, is the oldest residence in Michigan. The
Country store is typical of the early 1900's general
store. Children will enjoy choosing penny candy.

Historic Home

Park House Museum

214 Dalhousie Street, Amherstburg
Ontario, Canada
519-736-2511

Location: Highway 18 and Rankin Avenue
Hours: Summer: 11 a.m.–5 p.m., daily. Winter: 11 a.m.–5 p.m., Tuesday–Friday, and Sunday. Closed Monday and Saturday. Call to schedule group tours.
Admission: $7 family, $2 adults, $1.50 seniors, $1 children 6 to 16, under 6 free. Family membership available. Group rates available.
Ages: 7 and up
Plan: Short visit
Parking: Free on street
Lunch: Picnic area, restaurants, bakery, and ice cream parlor on Dalhousie Street
Facilities: Gift shop with books and tin ware.

Park House, the oldest house within a 250-mile radius of downtown Detroit, was built in Detroit in 1796 and later moved across the river. The first floor has been restored to show what life was like in the 1850's. Costumed guides demonstrate early domestic life, including tinsmithing, candle making, and cooking. Children will be interested in the changing displays of artifacts in the merchant's office, children's nursery, and sewing room. Upstairs, there are pioneer and local history exhibits. Best of all, Park House is located in the Navy Yard, along the Detroit River, a wonderful place to picnic and boat watch in the summer.

Historic Home

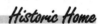

Pine Grove Historical Museum

405 Oakland, Pontiac
248-338-6732

Location: 1/2 mile north of Y-Track Drive
Hours: Research library, 9 a.m.–3 p.m., Thursday and Friday. Group tours available by appointment only.
Admission: Group tours, $4 adults, $2 children 16 and younger and seniors. One-room schoolhouse can be rented for 50 students at a time, $25/day.
Ages: 6 and up
Plan: Short visit
Parking: Free on site

Lunch: Carriage house doubles as a lunchroom. Picnicking is allowed on the museum's four acres.
Facilities: Bathrooms. Gift shop with old-fashioned, hand-made toys and items, ranging in price from 25 cents to $20.

At Pine Grove, the home of former Michigan Governor Moses Wisner, children are encouraged to step back into the past. The Greek Revival home is chock full of authentic furnishings, clothing, and home implements. The 4 1/2-acre estate also includes a fully equipped summer kitchen, smoke house, root cellar, and one-room schoolhouse. Costumed guides lead group tours and offer children hands-on experiences.

Detroit Landmark
Renaissance Center

Jefferson Avenue, Detroit
313-568-5600

Kids will marvel at the four futuristic office towers surrounding the world's tallest hotel at the Renaissance Center, which has come to symbolize Detroit. Purchased by General Motors as its global headquarters, the Renaissance Center has been undergoing renovations. Kids will love the old favorites, like riding the People Mover to the RenCen station and the rotating restaurant at the top of the 73-story Marriott hotel. GM World, a new interactive exhibit space, features current and concept vehicles. Future improvements include the GM Heritage Museum and the five-story, glass-enclosed Wintergarden opening in 2001.

Historic Farmhouse
Rochester Hills Museum at
Van Hoosen Farm

1005 Van Hoosen Road, Rochester
248-656-4663

Location: One mile east of Rochester Road off Tienken Road, four miles north of M-59
Hours: 1–4 p.m., Wednesday–Saturday
Admission: $3 adults, $2 seniors and students grades 3–12, grades 2 and under free
Ages: 8 and up

Plan: Short visit, includes walking tour of Stoney Creek Village
Parking: Free on site
Lunch: Picnic area along Stoney Creek
Facilities: Bathrooms. Gift shop with local history books, stationery, craft items.

The Sarah Van Hoosen Jones homestead is a low, rambling estate nestled in the middle of historic Stoney Creek Village. Authentic furnishings and household implements make 19th-century rural Michigan come to life. Children will especially enjoy the doctor's office and farm office, and the kitchen with its 1902 washing machine and old-fashioned ice box. The grounds and gazebo are ideal for an afternoon walk. There are special annual events, including Christmas activities and summer camp. Archaeological digs are in progress on the site.

Historic Home

Saarinen House

1221 North Woodward, Bloomfield Hills
248-645-3323

Location: All tours begin at the Cranbrook Academy of Art Museum
Hours: May–October: Public docent-guided tours 1 p.m., Tuesday–Saturday. 1 and 3 p.m., Sunday. Private group tours, call two weeks in advance to schedule, $10/person.
Admission: $7 adults, $5 students and seniors, $3 members
Ages: Minimum age 7 years
Plan: 90-minute tour
Parking: Free in lots adjacent to art museum
Lunch: You'll find a variety of fast food restaurants going south along Woodward.
Facilities: Bathrooms and book shop are located in art museum.

Eliel Saarinen, the guiding artistic soul of the Cranbrook Educational Community, was both resident architect from 1925–1950 and President of the Academy of Art from 1932–1946. Saarinen designed Cranbrook's layout, buildings, grounds, and sculpture gardens. Saarinen House, his home and studio, has been restored to its original 1930's splendor, using many original furnishings, including his wife Loja's weavings. Children will enjoy the vistas of the museum grounds, the sculpture gardens, and Saarinen's use of natural details—particularly the peacock—for adornment.

Historic Village & Car Museum
Southwestern Ontario Heritage Village

Essex County Road 23, Essex
Ontario, Canada
519-776-6909

Location: From Detroit-Windsor bridge, take Highway 3 east to 23 south. The village is approximately 6 miles south of Highway 3 and 23 juncture.
Hours: 10 a.m.–5 p.m., Wednesday–Sunday, year-round. Last tour leaves at 4 p.m. Group tours available; call in advance to schedule. Special times available for school groups.
Admission: $10 family, $3.50 adults, $2.50 seniors and youth ages 13–17, $2 children ages 5–12, under 5 are free. Special events, $4.
Ages: All ages
Plan: Short visit
Parking: Free on site
Lunch: Picnic tables in village park. Refreshment stand available during special events.
Facilities: Bathrooms in car museum and village. Souvenirs and candy in general store.

Southwestern Ontario Heritage Village's 12 turn-of-the-century buildings—a railway station, schoolhouse, church, general store, shoe repair–barber shop, home, three log cabins, and barnyard buildings—are located in the midst of 54 wooded acres. A transportation museum documents the early settlers' travel from snowshoes and wagons to modern automobiles. The buildings, artifacts, and museum make history come to life for children. Special events include summer's Antique Farm and Factory Show; May and Labor Day Weekend's vintage car shows; April and September's antique car shows; and October's Murder Mystery weekend and arts and crafts show.

Restored Shopping Plaza
Trappers Alley

Monroe and Beaubien, Greektown, Detroit

Location: Corner of Monroe and Beaubien, five blocks north of the Renaissance Center, in the

heart of Greektown
Hours: 11 a.m.–9 p.m., Monday–Thursday. 11 a.m.–
11 p.m., Friday and Saturday. Noon–7 p.m.,
Sunday. Restaurants stay open later. Historic
group tours available; call ahead.
Admission: Free
Ages: All ages
Plan: Short visit
Parking: Street parking is very difficult to find. Use
surrounding lots.
Lunch: Fast-food booths with tables and chairs,
plus sit-down restaurants
Facilities: Bathrooms. People Mover Station locat-
ed on third level.

A fur tannery in the 1850's, Trapper's Alley is
now three levels of aromatic food booths, ethnic
restaurants, and colorful gift shops. Children will
enjoy the carnival atmosphere. Trappers Alley is
also a convenient People Mover station and is
adjacent to a temporary casino.

Historic Farmhouse

Trenton Historical Museum

306 St. Joseph, Trenton
734-675-2130

Location: Corner of Third and St. Joseph
Hours: 1–4 p.m. Saturday, year-round. Closed
January and August. Groups should call to sched-
ule tours.
Admission: Free
Ages: School age and up
Plan: Under one hour
Parking: Free on street
Lunch: Full selection of fast food restaurants
located one block away on West Jefferson
Facilities: Bathrooms. Some gift items for sale.

Visit the two-story Victorian home, built in 1881
and authentically furnished to illustrate the times.
Children will enjoy the home's children's toys, old
music box and phonograph, cannonball, and
kitchen implements, as well as the carriage shed's
old hearse, carriage, arrowheads, and tools.

Historic Village
Troy Museum and Historic Village Green

60 West Wattles, Troy
248-524-3570

Location: Corner of Wattles (Seventeen Mile Road) and Livernois
Hours: 9 a.m.–5:30 p.m., Tuesday–Saturday. 1–5 p.m., Sunday.
Admission: Free
Ages: 6 and up
Plan: Under one hour
Parking: Lot west of the museum
Lunch: Lots of restaurants in the area
Facilities: Bathrooms. Gift shop with old-fashioned toys, candy sticks, coloring books.

The Troy Museum offers several special exhibits each year of curious local artifacts. While young children might find these static exhibits boring, they will enjoy the village green's restored and furnished buildings. Buy each of the little historians a candy stick and roam around out back. You'll find a gazebo, pioneer log cabin, one-room school house, wagon shop, print shop, old township hall, and the Greek Revival home of early pioneer Solomon Casewell. Children will also enjoy the hands-on activities during December's Hanging of the Greens holiday program.

Historic Home
Turner-Dodge House

100 East North Street, Lansing
517-483-4220

Location: 2 miles north of the Capitol, on the corner of James and North Streets
Hours: 9 a.m.–5 p.m., Monday–Friday, by appointment only, for tours. Call ahead for reservations at least two weeks in advance.
Admission: Nominal fee for group tour
Ages: 4 and up
Plan: Youth tours are 1 hour and 15 minutes; adult tours are 45 minutes
Parking: Free in lot on east side of house
Lunch: Relax with a snack at the picnic tables or under the large Beech tree. Adult tour groups may request tea, coffee, and cookies. A variety of restaurants are located downtown on Cedar and

Saginaw Streets and Washington Square.

Facilities: Bathrooms, small gift shop selling period toys and gifts

Tour the lovely three-story Greek Revival home, originally built in 1853 and enlarged to 8,600 square feet in 1903. Youth tours engage children in old-fashioned dances, games, and chores. Children are also invited to attend summer craft workshops, scout troupe badge workshops and history camp. Enjoy old-fashioned Christmas activities at the house during December.

African American History
Underground Railroad–
Second Baptist Church

441 Monroe Avenue, Detroit
313-961-0920

Location: Monroe at Beaubien in Greektown
Hours: Pre-arranged tours by appointment only.
Admission: Small fee, donations accepted
Ages: 8 and older
Plan: Short visit. Tour lasts approximately one hour.
Parking: Use lot on Brush and Monroe; the church will validate the parking ticket.
Lunch: Nearby Greektown
Facilities: Bathrooms, drinking fountain

The Second Baptist Church was one of several Detroit stations on the famous Underground Railroad. Between 1836 and 1865, more than 5,000 fugitive slaves passed through the 12-by-13-foot windowless cellar room. For many, it was their last stop on the road to Canada and to freedom. The tour begins with an introduction in the chapel and then continues down a narrow staircase into the once-barren room. Colorful murals depict freedom routes and famous abolitionists. Church historian/tour guide Nathaniel Leach makes the era come to life. Sitting in the actual hiding room is quite an emotional experience.

African American History
Underground Railroad Heritage Sites

Metro Detroit was an important stop along the Underground Railroad, the series of safe houses and churches that sheltered runaway slaves during their journey to freedom in Canada. Check the index for tours of the following sites: Detroit's Second Baptist Church, and Windsor's John Freeman Walls Historic Site and Underground Railroad Museum. In addition, historic markers commemorate the site of the now-demolished home of Seymour Finney, known as the superintendent of the railroad, whose barn at the corner of Griswold and State was a major station, and the intersection of West Jefferson and Sixth, where escaped slaves prepared to make their way across the Detroit River into Canada.

Historic Inn & Barn

Walker Tavern Historic Complex

US-12, Brooklyn
517-467-4414

Location: Just north of US-12 on M-50, across the street from the Brick Walter Tavern, now an antique mart. Continue west on US-12 to antique store and flea market territory.
Hours: 11:30 a.m.–4 p.m., Wednesday–Sunday, Memorial Day–Labor Day. Closed Monday and Tuesday.
Admission: Free
Ages: 8 and older
Plan: Under one hour
Parking: Free lot
Lunch: Picnic tables and grills
Facilities: Port-a-johns

You can learn some interesting facts at the Walker Tavern Visitor Center. Built in the 1830's, the Walker Tavern was a regular stop on the Great Sauk Trail, the stagecoach route traveling between Detroit and Chicago. One hundred years ago, it took five days to get to Chicago from Detroit; it cost 25 cents a night and 25 cents for a meal at the tavern. Although the Visitor Center's exhibits are colorful and easy-to-read, they will only interest older children with a yen for history. Children of all ages will find the site's other two buildings very interesting. There's a blacksmith shop in the reconstructed barn and the Walker Tavern has been restored to look like an authentic 1840's inn, with furnished barroom, parlor, and dining room-kitchen. Hands-on children's workshops are offered on Wednesdays during the summer.

One-Room Schoolhouse

Washburn Schoolhouse

300 Dorothy Street, South Lyon
248-437-9929

Location: Just south of downtown South Lyon, in McHattie Park
Hours: 1–4 p.m., Thursday. 1–5 p.m., Sunday, April–November. Groups and schools can call to arrange tours at mutually convenient times.
Admission: Free
Ages: Elementary school children and up
Plan: Under one hour
Parking: Free parking in lot adjacent to museum
Lunch: Family-owned restaurants and fast-food franchises are located in town, on Lafayette and Lake Streets
Facilities: Bathrooms, gift counter in the Witch's Hat Depot Museum

Children get a taste of the 19th century as they sit at small wooden desks in the restored schoolhouse, practicing their lessons on slates.

Historic Farmstead

Waterloo Area Farm Museum

9998 Waterloo-Munith Road, Waterloo Township
734-426-4980

Location: I-94 west to exit 153. Take Clear Lake Road to Waterloo, then follow signs three miles to farm.
Hours: 1–4 p.m., Tuesday–Sunday, June–August. 1–4 p.m., Saturday and Sunday, September–early October. Last tour at 3:30 p.m.
Admission: $3 adults, $2.50 seniors, $1 students and children 5 to 11, under 5 free. Family memberships available. Ticket allows entrance to Dewey School.
Ages: 6 and up
Plan: Short visit
Parking: Free lot adjacent to farmhouse
Lunch: Picnic area on grounds and in nearby Waterloo Recreation Area
Facilities: Outhouses. Gift shop with lots of crafts and made-in-Michigan items and toys.

The Waterloo Museum consists of an 1850's farmhouse, log cabin, and outbuildings—ice house, barn, bake house, windmill, milk cellar, and farm repair shop—that were once part of the homestead of German immigrant Jacob Ruehle. Like many families of the time, the Ruehles were industrious, thrifty, and imaginative. Their personalities live on in the homestead, furnished in detail with authentic clothing, furniture, tools, and implements. Kids will enjoy the 150-year-old gadgets, including a sausage stuffer, honey extractor, rug beater, and copper boiler. There's even a dog treadmill attached to a churn so the family pet could help make butter. Tour guides encourage young visitors to polish silver with white ash and try on the child-sized yoke with hanging buckets used to carry water up to the house from the stream. Educational programs and tours are available to area school children. Special living history programs are offered during summer and fall.

Historic Home

Willistead Manor

1899 Niagara Street, Windsor
Ontario, Canada
519-253-2365

Location: Niagara Street at Kildare Road
Hours: 1–4 p.m., first and third Sunday of each month, January–June and September–November. 1–4 p.m., Sunday and Wednesday, July–August. 1–4 p.m., Sunday, and 7–9 p.m., Wednesday, December. No tours December 24–26, 31. Last tour begins a half hour before closing.
Admission: $3.75 adults, $3.50 seniors, $2 children under 13.
Ages: 6 and up
Plan: Short visit
Parking: Free on site
Lunch: Many restaurants along Riverside Drive in downtown Windsor
Facilities: Bathrooms. Christmas Shoppe in the Coach House during Christmas touring schedule.

Willistead Manor will fuel imaginative children with the stuff of great stories. The elaborately furnished home of Edward Chandler Walker, son of distillery founder Hiram Walker, spares no expense in details and materials. There are elaborate hand-carved wooden mantels, colorful furnishings, draperies, and an impressive staircase. Children will love the home's secret doorways and walk-in safe. Fifteen acres of park land offer families a wonderful place to explore.

Historic Building — Event Barn
Wilson Barn

29350 West Chicago, Livonia
734-427-4311

Location: West Chicago and Middlebelt
Hours: Farmer's Market: 8 a.m.–3 p.m., Saturday, July–last week of September.
Admission: Free except for Mustang Car Show and Antique and Hot Rod Show. Barn is available for family and group rental.
Ages: All ages
Plan: Short visit
Parking: Free in Emerson Middle School parking lot, adjacent to barn
Lunch: Picnic tables on grounds
Facilities: Restroom in barn, portable toilets on property

Visit the historic barn and shady park for these annual events: Pre-Easter flower sale; Mother's Day weekend flower sale; Antique and Hot Rod Show in June; "Music Under the Stars" in July and August; Mustang Car Show in August; Pumpkin Festival in October; and Christmas Sing-Along. Pumpkin fest features pony rides and petting zoo.

Grist Mill
Wolcott Mill Metropark

Kunstman Road, Ray Township
810-749-5997

Location: Kunstman Road, north of Twenty-Nine Mile Road, between Van Dyke and North Avenue in Ray Township, just outside of Romeo.
Hours: May–October: 10 a.m.–5 p.m., Monday–Friday. 10 a.m.–7 p.m., Saturday and Sunday. April and November: 10 a.m.–5 p.m., daily. December–February: 10 a.m.–5 p.m., Wednesday–Sunday. Groups may also schedule tours by advance appointment.
Admission: Free
Ages: School age
Plan: Short visit; 1 1/2-hour tour
Parking: Vehicle entry fee: $3 daily, $8 senior

annual, $15 annual. Wednesdays are free.
Lunch: Picnic tables
Facilities: Bathrooms

The restored, over 150-year-old Wolcott Mill offers imaginative displays on the milling industry, pioneer life, and farming, and many children's pioneer workshops throughout the year.

Historic Homes

Wyandotte Museums:
Ford-MacNichol Home

2610 Biddle Avenue, Wyandotte

and Marx Home

2630 Biddle Avenue, Wyandotte
734-324-7297

Location: Downtown Wyandotte
Hours: Tours of the Ford-MacNichol Home are offered noon–4 p.m., Monday–Friday and 2–5 p.m. the first Sunday of each month. Tours of the Marx home are available upon request.
Admission: $1 adults, 50 cents children
Ages: All ages
Plan: Tours are approximately 45 minutes to 1 hour
Parking: Free on site
Lunch: Drive south on Biddle Avenue to downtown restaurants
Facilities: Bathrooms. Gift shop selling Victorian gifts and history of Wyandotte books and souvenirs.

Visitors learn about Wyandotte history and the stories of its famous residents when they tour the restored 1896 Queen Anne Victorian Ford-MacNichol home. Period furnishings and wall treatments adorn the four levels. A basement exhibit chronicles Wyandotte history with artifacts from the Wyandotte Indians to the turn of the century. Children will especially enjoy the home's special living history events—September's Heritage Days and December's Victorian Christmas Celebration.

7
Science and Nature

TIP

Looking for rocks, bugs, or dinosaurs? Gift shops at science museums, zoos, and nature centers are the perfect place to jump-start your children's science or nature hobbies and find books, puzzles, and all the paraphernalia central to their collections.

This chapter helps you cater to your children's innate curiosity about the world. Watch them soar through space at area planetariums and explore science and their environment with hands-on exhibits and activities at area science museums and nature centers. Take a family stroll through the seasons along marked trails; visit eternal summer in area conservatories lush with tropical ferns and arid cacti. Feed corn kernels to a hungry goat; watch a baby calf suckle; witness electric eels at feeding time. It's all happening at area zoos, nature centers, and petting farms.

Planetarium

Abrams Planetarium

Michigan State University, East Lansing
517-355-4676,
517-332-STAR (current sky information)

Website: www.pa.msu.edu/abrams/
Skywatchers' Diary:
www.pa.msu.edu/abrams/diary.html
Location: Corner of Shaw Lane and Science Road, MSU campus
Hours: Building: 8:30 a.m.–Noon, 1–4:30 p.m., Monday–Friday. Planetarium shows: 8 p.m., Friday and Saturday, 2:30 and 4 p.m., Sunday. Closed August–mid-October. Weekday shows for groups by appointment, during the school year. Christmas show during December.
Admission: $3 adults, $2.50 students and seniors, $2 ages 12 and under. Group rates and family memberships available.
Ages: All ages
Plan: Short visit
Parking: In front of building. Free on weekends. $1 weekdays.
Lunch: Fast food and vending machines located in the Student Union, corner of Abbott and Grand River. Many other restaurants on Grand River Avenue, across from campus.
Facilities: Bathrooms. Gift shop with astronomy-related novelties, books, star maps.

The Abrams Planetarium's 360° domed sky theater, post-show sky talks, and blacklight space art gallery will introduce children to the wonders of the universe.

Greenhouses

Anna Scripps Whitcomb Conservatory

Belle Isle Park, Detroit
313-852-4064

Location: On Belle Isle
Hours: 10 a.m.–5 p.m., daily, year-round.
Admission: $2 adults and children 13 and up, $1 children ages 2–12 and seniors. Children under 2 are free.
Ages: All ages
Plan: Under one hour
Parking: Free on site
Lunch: Picnic area
Facilities: Bathrooms

Each room offers children a temperate climate with lush tropical flowers, greens, and unusual cacti. Point out the orange and banana trees; listen for chirping birds. The conservatory is a particularly nice place to visit during the winter. Kids can skip from room to room, soaking in the warmth.

Working Farm

Bellairs Hillside Fiber Farm and the Sheep Shed

8351 Big Lake Road, Clarkston
248-625-1181
1-888-887-6345

Location: Just off Dixie Highway and I-75
Hours: Noon–5:30 p.m. Tuesday–Saturday. Groups of six or more by appointment only.
Admission: $2.50 tour information packet per family
Ages: 5 and up
Plan: Short visit
Parking: Free, near farmhouse
Lunch: Picnic tables
Facilities: Bathrooms. Gift shop with wool and sheepskin clothing items, plus spinning craft supplies and novelty sheep gifts.

In season, kids can pet the lambs and watch sheep being sheared and goats milked at this family-run working farm. On special days there are also spinning demonstrations. The Bellairs family enjoys introducing children to sheep and their products. Sheepshearing Days are held in March and October. Lamb Walks during April/May. Barn

Walks and Christmas Shopping Open House November/December. School groups and tours should call ahead.

Aquarium

Belle Isle Aquarium

Belle Isle Park, Detroit
313-852-4141
248-398-0900 (information tape)

Website: www.detroitzoo.org
Location: On Belle Isle
Hours: 10 a.m.–5 p.m., daily. Electric eel feeding shows: 10:30 a.m., 12:30, and 2:30 p.m. daily. Additional 4:30 p.m. feeding on Sunday.
Admission: $2 adults and children 13 and up, $1 children ages 2–12 and seniors. Children under 2 are free.
Ages: All ages
Plan: Short visit
Parking: Free on site
Lunch: Picnic area
Facilities: Bathrooms located in nearby building. Gift shop with shells and other marine items.

The green-tiled, domed building is the nation's oldest aquarium, built in 1904. Murky and still, it echoes with an underwater sensation and houses more than 140 species of fish, reptiles, and amphibians, including a new shark exhibit. Kids become transfixed by the exotic and the frightening aquatic creatures gliding about in 50 well-labeled tanks. Electric eel feeding shows are worth seeing. As the eels are fed, their current turns on a light-bulb and sounds a horn.

Wildlife & Plants, Trails

Belle Isle Nature Center

Belle Isle Park, Detroit
313-852-4056

Location: On east end of Belle Isle
Hours: 10 a.m.–4 p.m., Tuesday–Sunday. Closed Mondays.
Admission: Free. Donations welcome.
Ages: 5 and up
Plan: Under one hour
Parking: Free, adjacent to center
Lunch: Picnic area across the street

Facilities: Bathrooms, nature trails

Nature Center displays, exhibits, films, slide programs, live native animals, wildlife habitat garden, and nature trails help children better understand their environment.

Zoo

Belle Isle Zoo

Belle Isle Park, Detroit
313-852-4083
248-398-0900 (information tape)

Website: www.detroitzoo.org
Location: On Belle Isle
Hours: 10 a.m.–5 p.m., daily, May 1–October 31.
Admission: $3 adults and ages 13 and up, $2 seniors, $1 children ages 2–12, under 2 are free
Ages: All ages
Plan: Short visit
Parking: Free on site
Lunch: Snack stands
Facilities: Bathrooms, souvenir stand

Belle Isle Zoo's elevated boardwalk is 3/4 mile long with a refreshment stand mid-way. It offers families with small children a wonderfully unique way to view over 130 animals, take a walk, and have a snack, all at the same time. Kids will love the exotic animals: pink flamingoes, kangaroos, zebras, lions, tigers, bears, and the siamangs—unusual, hooting apes. Children also have an up-close look at giant tarantulas and other creepy-crawlies at one of the nation's largest spider exhibits.

Working Dairy Farm

Calder Brothers Dairy Farm

9334 Finzel Road, Carleton
734-654-2622

Location: South Stoney Creek and Finzel Roads. Carleton is about 50 minutes south of downtown Detroit, off I-75 south.
Hours: 10 a.m.-8 p.m., daily, year-round. 4 p.m. milking demonstrations daily. Call ahead to schedule tours.
Admission: Free for farm visit. $4.75 per person for pre-arranged tour. $5.75 tour and ice cream treat.
Ages: All ages

Plan: Short visit
Parking: Free on site
Lunch: Picnic tables. A full-service ice cream parlor featuring Calder Brothers ice cream, plus a farm store selling Calder Brothers dairy products: milk bottled in glass, chocolate milk, buttermilk, sour cream, butter, eggs, and seasonally, eggnog.
Facilities: Bathrooms. Farm store also sells jellies, jams, and carmel corn.

Visit a true working dairy farm. The kids will enjoy petting and watching the animals—lots of cows, plus peacocks, dogs, burros, geese, deer, llamas, pot belly pigs, and chickens. Buy milk in bottles and enjoy delicious handmade ice cream. Prearranged tours include milking a cow by hand, bottle feeding a calf, watching a cow being machine-milked, and watching how milk is stored for transport to the Calder Brothers processing plant.

Petting Farm
Canatara Children's Farm

Lake Chipican Drive, off Christina Street
Sarnia, Ontario, Canada
519-337-4387

Location: Christina Street and Cathcart Boulevard, one mile north of Highway 402
Hours: Farm: 8 a.m.–8 p.m. daily, end of May–Labor Day. 8 a.m.–4 p.m. daily, September–May. Log Cabin: Noon–7 p.m. daily, end of May–Labor Day. 1–4 p.m. Sunday, September–May.
Admission: Free
Ages: All ages
Plan: Short visit
Parking: Free on site

Lunch: Picnic areas, concessions
Facilities: Bathrooms, playground

Within Canatara Park along Lake Huron is the small petting farm, perfect for young children. The farm has both domestic animals and poultry. Adjacent to the farm are two historic buildings: a pioneer log cabin, and carriage house. A new log cabin houses a small interpretive center with natural history displays.

Nature Center, Trails

Carl F. Fenner Arboretum

2020 East Mt. Hope Avenue, Lansing
517-483-4224

Location: Trowbridge Road exit off I-496, south on Harrison Road, west on Mt. Hope Avenue
Hours: Grounds: 8 a.m.–dusk, daily. Nature Center Building: December–March: 9 a.m.–4 p.m., Tuesday–Friday. 10 a.m.-4 p.m., Saturday and Sunday. Rest of year: 9 a.m.–4 p.m., Tuesday–Friday. 10 a.m.–5 p.m., Saturday. 11 a.m.–5 p.m., Sunday.
Admission: Free
Ages: All ages
Plan: Short visit
Parking: Free on site
Lunch: Picnic area
Facilities: Bathrooms. Nature center gift shop (open on the weekends) sells nature-oriented coloring books, story books, magnifying glasses, and polished stones.

For a 25-cent donation, children can buy packets of crackers to throw to the birds, geese, and squirrels living within the Fenner Arboretum's 120 acres. Walking along the easy trails you'll also find an herb garden, waterfowl pond, replica of a pioneer cabin, and if you're lucky, you'll catch a glimpse of the arboretum's American bison. The nature center houses displays, hands-on exhibits, and live Michigan animals. Seasonal events are the Maple Syrup Festival in March and the Apple Butter Festival in October.

Petting Farm
Charles L. Bowers Farm

1219 East Square Lake Road, Bloomfield Hills
248-433-0885

Location: Off I-75 between Adams and Squirrel Roads
Hours: Pre-arranged tours available 10 a.m.–3 p.m., weekdays. Open Barn Days, free to the public, 1–4 p.m. several Saturdays during spring and fall.
Admission: $2.50 per person for tour
Ages: Preschool–12th grade
Plan: Short visit
Parking: Free on site
Lunch: Lots of restaurants located on Telegraph Road
Facilities: Bathrooms

Children will enjoy the Charles L. Bowers School Farm experience, offered as part of a group tour or during the several Open Barn Days throughout the year. During a tour, children take a hayride, milk a cow, and see the animals. On Open Barn Days, children observe and participate in many rural activities—milking cows, churning butter, harvesting crops, spinning wool, feeding barnyard animals, preserving food, making cheese, and going on a hayride.

Planetarium
Children's Museum Planetarium

67 East Kirby, Detroit
313-873-8100

Location: In the Cultural Center, just north of the Detroit Institute of Arts. A prancing silver horse sculpture made of chrome car bumpers sits on the front lawn.
Hours: October–May: 11 a.m. and 1 p.m., Saturday. Afternoons only during the summer.
Admission: Free
Ages: Geared to elementary school children
Plan: Under one hour
Parking: Use metered parking along Kirby or park in the Science Center lot on John R ($3) and walk a block to the museum
Lunch: Eat across the street in the DIA Kresge Court Café
Facilities: Bathrooms, drinking fountain. Gift shop

with lots of handmade and unique toys and gifts.

Planetarium shows are held in a small, intimate, second-story room. With a sense of humor, they offer explanations of seasonal wonders, folk tales, and legends relating to the night sky. They are excellent first-time star-gazing experiences for young children.

Greenhouses, Petting Farm
Colasanti's Tropical Gardens

Ruthven, Ontario, Canada
519-326-3287

Website: www.colasanti.com
Location: Off Highway 3, approximately 25 miles from the Ambassador Bridge
Hours: 8 a.m.–5 p.m., Monday–Thursday. 8 a.m.–7 p.m., Friday–Sunday.
Admission: Free
Ages: All ages
Plan: Short visit
Parking: Free on site
Lunch: Picnic table area and snack bar with hot dogs, soft drinks, ice cream, and snacks
Facilities: Bathrooms. Almost all of the hundreds of species of tropical plants and cacti are for sale.

Enter a tropical rain forest or warming desert, and see 15 greenhouses full of brilliant tropical flowers and unusual cacti. Mixed in with these fragrant and colorful plants are exotic birds and a petting zoo that includes sheep, goats, ostrich, and bison. On the weekends, pony rides for children are available for $1. Or test your skill on an indoor miniature golf course.

Working Dairy Farm
Cook's Farm Dairy

2950 Seymour Lake Road, Ortonville
248-627-3329

Location: Take I-75 north to M-15 north. Go east on Seymour Lake Road one mile.
Hours: Summer: 9 a.m.–10 p.m., Monday–Saturday. Noon–10 p.m., Sunday. Winter: 9 a.m.–8 p.m., Monday–Saturday. Noon–8 p.m., Sunday. Call to schedule tours for groups of ten or more.
Admission: Free for grounds and farm store. $3 per person for tour, includes a complimentary ice

cream cone and glass of Cook's chocolate milk.
Ages: All ages
Plan: Short visit. Tour takes approximately one hour.
Parking: Free on site
Lunch: Picnic tables. Ice cream parlor with Cook's ice cream, farm store with Cook's dairy products—all made on premises.
Facilities: Outhouses. Farm store also sells seasonal items such as honey and pumpkins.

After visiting Cook's Farm Dairy, toddlers will have no problem telling you what a cow says. Cows are everywhere, lounging on the grass, nosing up against the fence. You can visit the cows in the barn and treat the family to an ice cream cone, or call ahead and schedule a tour. The informal tours start in the cow barn. After meeting newborn calves, you are taken into the production plant for a dry run of the process that turns cows' milk into ice cream and chocolate milk. The tour ends in the ice cream parlor/farm store with a complimentary cone and glass of chocolate milk.

Planetarium

Cranbrook Institute of Science Planetarium

1221 North Woodward, Bloomfield Hills
248-645-3209
1-877-GO-CRANB (taped information)

Website: www.cranbrook.edu
Location: Enter off Woodward, just north of Cranbrook Road. You'll know you're there when you see the stegosaurus.
Hours: Lasera and planetarium shows Friday evenings and weekends. Check the posted times when you arrive. Call ahead to order evening rock music lasera shows, as they fill up quickly. Additional shows are added during holidays and school vacations.
Admission: Museum: $7 adults, $4 children ages 3–17 and seniors, children under 3 free. Family membership available. Group rates available on weekdays. Planetarium shows: $2 adults, $1.50 children ages 3–17 and seniors, $1 members, plus museum admission. Lasera shows: $2.50 plus museum admission.
Ages: 5 and up for most lasera and planetarium

shows; 3 and up are admitted to the holiday show, "Ornaments."

Plan: Shows are approximately one hour
Parking: Free on site
Lunch: The Planet Café offers light meals and snacks
Facilities: Bathrooms, drinking fountain on lower level. The extensive Science Store specializes in children's science toys, kits, and creative gifts.

Cranbrook Institute of Science offers creative, colorful, and educational stargazing shows, and sound and light lasera shows in a state-of-the-art planetarium. Older children and teens will especially enjoy the lasera shows set to rock music.

Nature Preserve

Crosswinds Marsh

Haggerty and Will Carlton, Sumpter Township
734-261-1990

Location: South of Metro Airport, at Haggerty and Oakville-Waltz Road, west of the Will Carlton exit off I-275.
Hours: Dawn to dusk, daily
Admission: Free. Canoe rental, $10 for 2 hours; binocular rental
Ages: All ages
Plan: Half day
Parking: Lot nearby
Lunch: Picnic area available
Facilities: Nature trails, horse-back riding trails and cross-country skiing

One of the largest man-made wetlands in North America, this 1,050-acre nature preserve is home to more than 100 types of birds, 1000 species of plants and 40 types of mammals including muskrats, fox, coyotes and deer. Rent binoculars and view the wildlife as you walk along five miles of hiking trails or 1.4 miles of elevated boardwalks, or rent a canoe and paddle around marked trails.

Nature Center, Trails

Dahlem Center

7117 South Jackson Road, Jackson
517-782-3453

Location: One mile west of Jackson Community College, at the intersection of Kimmel and South Jackson Road
Hours: Office exhibits: 9 a.m.–5 p.m. Tuesday–Friday. Noon–5 p.m. Saturday and Sunday. Grounds: 8 a.m.–8 p.m. daily. School and group visits available upon request. Day camp programs during the summer.
Admission: Free
Ages: All ages
Plan: Short visit
Parking: Free on site
Lunch: Burger King is open weekdays inside Jackson Community College. You'll find more restaurant choices three miles north on South Jackson Road in Summit Oaks Shopping Center.
Facilities: Restrooms have outside access. Gift shop sells bird houses and building kits, feed, rocks and minerals, inexpensive jewelry, and children's science toys like telescopes.

At Dahlem Center's small exhibit area, kids get up-close-and-personal with turtles and a snake, explore a hands-on table full of skins, bones, and fur, and learn about environmental concerns. An inside observation window looks out onto a bird feeding station. The center also has a photography blind for bird photographers, five miles of hiking trails, and sponsors the Bluebird Recovery Program, which tracks endangered bluebirds. Bird watchers will find a lot of avian movement mid-April to end of May. The annual Bluebird Festival, held mid-March, offers a juried wildlife art show, plus educational presentations and displays.

IMAX Theater

Detroit Science Center IMAX Dome Theatre

5020 John R, Detroit
313-577-8400

Website: www.sciencedetroit.org

Location: One mile east of Woodward on the corner of Warren and John R

Hours: The Theater shows IMAX movies 10 and 11a.m., noon and 1 p.m., Monday—Thursday. 10 and 11a.m., noon, 1, 7, and 8 p.m., Friday. 11a.m., noon, 1, 2, 3, 4, 7, and 8 p.m., Saturday. 1, 2, 3, and 4 p.m. , Sunday. Closed major holidays.

Admission: $7 adults and children 18 and up, $6 children 3–17 and seniors, 2 and under free. Admission includes exhibit hall, IMAX movie, laser show and demonstrations. Family membership gives you free admission to Ann Arbor Hands-on Museum, Cranbrook Institute of Science, and Lansing's Impression 5 Museum except for special events.

Ages: All ages, but preschoolers might be uncomfortable with the IMAX movie's motion and speed

Plan: Movies vary from 40 minutes to one hour

Parking: Lot adjacent to entrance, off John R, $3 all day parking

Lunch: Eat in the DIA's Kresge Court Café Wednesday–Sunday.

Facilities: Bathrooms and drinking fountain on exhibit floor. Gift shop near entrance has great science, dino, and space items.

The IMAX's 360º domed screen will fill your senses and immerse you in the middle of the action. You might be soaring above the earth, climbing to the top of a mountain, or rushing down a waterfall. Nature's most beautiful images are caught in vivid breadth and color. The center is currently undergoing a renovation and building project which will add a planetarium and laser shows in spring 2001.

Zoo

Detroit Zoological Park

8450 West Ten Mile Road, Royal Oak
248-398-0900 (taped message)
248-399-7001 (zoo services)

Website: www.detroitzoo.org

Location: I-696 and Woodward Avenue. Entrance off Woodward, north of Ten Mile.

Hours: 10 a.m.–5 p.m., daily, May–October. 10 a.m.–8 p.m. Wednesday, June–August. 10 a.m.–4 p.m., daily, November–April. Daily Feeding Schedule: Penguins: 10:30 and 11:30 a.m.; Polar Bears: 2 p.m.; Sea Lions: 11 a.m. and 3 p.m.

Admission: $7.50 adults, $5.50 students 13 to 18

with school I.D. and seniors, $4.50 children 2 to 12, under 2 free. Minimal fee for zoo train (train operates daily May 1 through October 1, weekends through November 1, then shuts down until May 1). Family membership and group rates available.

Ages: All ages

Plan: Half day visit

Parking: $3 cars, $6 buses. Use parking garage across from entrance

Lunch: Picnic areas, tables, food concessions

Facilities: Bathrooms, drinking fountains. The Zootique offers a wide variety of animal-themed souvenirs, T-shirts, and educational gifts. Kids Kabs (strollers) $5/day+$1 deposit. Roller Chairs (fits an adult or 3 kids) $6/day+$1 deposit.

The Detroit Zoo offers families many attractions all rolled into one admission. The new National Amphibian Conservation Center boasts 12,000 square feet of indoor exhibits surrounded by wetlands. The Arctic Ring of Life, a new polar bear environment, features an underwater tunnel for visitors and an Inuit art gallery. The Wildlife Interpretive Gallery or WIG features a 2,000-gallon coral reef aquarium, small theater, hands-on exhibit space, art gallery, and computer information games. The WIG is attached to the Hummingbird Garden, where kids can commune with singing hummingbirds and brightly colored, free-flying butterflies. In the connected Free Flight Aviary, children witness giant nests and exotic birds. There are wonderful outdoor animal exhibits, including the "Great Apes of Harambee," a four-acre African rain forest environment. In the past few years, mandrills, anteaters, otters, and aardvarks have joined the zoo's menagerie. For younger children, there's a barnyard full of farm animals and the train to ride from one end of the zoo to the other. The Log Cabin Learning Center (located near the train station on the far end of the zoo) offers lots of hands-on experiences. Small children will also enjoy playing on the two creative outdoor playscapes and following an underground tunnel path in the prairie dog exhibit. Special events occur throughout the year, including the "Zoo Boo" at Halloween and "Wild Lights" in December.

Buried Dinosaur Bones

Dino Dig

Bloomer Park
Avon Road at John R, Rochester Hills
248-656-4753 (for groups up to 15)

Location: On the park's north side, adjacent to the colorful plastic playscape
Hours: 8 a.m.–dusk, daily year-round
Admission: $5 vehicle entry fee
Ages: Preschool–10
Plan: Short visit
Parking: Lot next to playscape area
Lunch: Bring a picnic; there are tables and shelters
Facilities: Bathrooms, playscape, ball field

Calling all elementary-school paleontologists. Rochester Hills parks ranger Al Brown has sculpted an 18-foot-long skeleton of a tyrannosaurus rex and buried it on its side in a sand pit, with just a few ribs provocatively showing. Children are encouraged to unearth the skeleton with a variety of plastic sand shovels and brushes. The play area also boasts several dinosaur bouncy rides.

Nature Center, Trails

Dinosaur Hill Nature Preserve

333 North Hill Circle, Rochester
248-656-0999

Location: Tienken and Rochester Roads
Hours: Nature center: Summer: 9 a.m.–3 p.m., Monday–Friday. 10 a.m.–noon Saturday. Winter: 9 a.m.–5 p.m., Tuesday–Friday. Closed Saturday. Trails: Dawn to dusk. There are trail maps in the center's mailbox.
Admission: Free. A fee is charged for group tours, classes, and special events.
Ages: All ages
Plan: Short visit
Parking: Free on street
Lunch: Picnic area
Facilities: Bathrooms. Squirrel Corner Gift Shop offers many inexpensive nature and dinosaur related items.

This gem of a city park sits quietly in the corner of a tidy neighborhood. In spite of its name, Dinosaur Hill is not a repository of dinosaur bones, but 16 heavily wooded acres full of trails and a combination nature center-library-classroom-gift shop. The center is full of nests, eggs, stuffed birds, small forest animals, butterflies, aquariums, and fossils. There are lots of hands-on artifacts and small eye lenses to encourage a closer look. Classes, field trips, summer camp, birthday parties, and special seasonal events are offered.

Petting Farm

Domino's Farms

Earhart Road, Ann Arbor
734-930-5032

Location: Off US-23, exit 41, at Earhart and Plymouth Roads
Hours: 10:30 a.m.–5 p.m., Monday–Friday. 11 a.m.–4 p.m., Saturday and Sunday, April–October 31. Animal shows and hayrides offered. Call ahead to schedule group hayrides and visits.
Admission: $3 adults. $2.50 children ages 2–12. Children 2 and under are free.
Ages: All ages
Plan: Short visit
Parking: Free on site
Lunch: Have a pizza at the world's only eat-on-the-premises Domino's Pizza restaurant in the World Headquarters building, open during Petting Farm hours. Or order a pizza from the farm phone and eat at picnic tables on the grounds.
Facilities: Bathrooms. Gift shop with animal mugs, pencils, T-shirts, magnets, and stuffed animals.

Sit on haystacks and meet the animals in an educational show that relies on children's participation. Wander through the barn, meet a llama and his friends, and take a short hayride—you just might see the buffalo herd at work.

Nature Center, Trails

Drayton Plains Nature Center

2125 Denby Drive, Waterford
248-674-2119

Location: 1/4 mile west off Dixie Highway, on Hatchery Road
Hours: Grounds only: 8 a.m.–9 p.m., spring and summer. 8 a.m.–6 p.m., after Daylight Savings. Interpretive Center: 11 a.m.–2 p.m., Tuesday–

Friday. 10 a.m.–4 p.m., Saturday. Noon–4 p.m., Sunday, spring and summer. 11 a.m.–2 p.m., Tuesday–Friday. Noon–4 p.m., Saturday, 1–4 p.m., Sunday, after daylight savings. Group programs available for minimum of 10 people; call ahead.
Admission: Grounds and interpretive center free. Minimum fee for group program.
Ages: School age children and up
Plan: Short visit. Tours are approximately 1 1/2 hours.
Parking: Free on site
Lunch: Picnic tables on site
Facilities: Bathrooms. Nature store with field guides, books, and coloring books for children.

Once the old state fish hatchery, Drayton Plains Nature Center sits on 137 acres on the banks of the Clinton River. Prairie, woods, and wetland make up its varied topography. Enjoy the outdoors year-round on 4 1/2 miles of marked nature trails. Inside the Interpretive Center, you'll find a variety of touch-and-see nature exhibits, including large fish tanks displaying local fish, such as blue gill and bass. Group programs include a visit to two pioneer log cabins on the grounds. Birthday parties and seasonal events, such as September's Pioneer Day, are also offered.

 Trails

E.L. Johnson Nature Center

3325 Franklin Road, Bloomfield Hills
248-339-3497

Location: On Franklin Road, south of Hickory Grove, north of Long Lake Road
Hours: 8 a.m.–dusk, Monday–Friday. 10 a.m.–4 p.m., most weekends. Children and families can sign up for classes run by the Bloomfield Hills Parks and Recreation. Special pre-arranged tours are also available.
Admission: Free for trails, minimum fee for programs
Ages: All ages
Plan: Under one hour
Parking: Free on site
Lunch: Telegraph Road offers a variety of fast food restaurants
Facilities: Bathroom in visitor center

This 32-acre site offers families a quiet trail through wooded terrain, dappled with wild flowers and a meandering stream. There are also wild animals—foxes, ducks, deer, and owls—that make their home in the woods.

Trail

Ford Discovery Trail

Henry Ford Estate–Fair Lane
On the U of M-Dearborn campus
4901 Evergreen, Dearborn
313-593-5590

Website: ww.umd.umich.edu/fairlane
Location: On the grounds of Henry Ford Estate–Fair Lane. Tours begin at the Potting Shed ticket booth, next to the Powerhouse.
Hours: 9 a.m.–3 p.m., Monday–Saturday. 1–4:30 p.m., Sunday.
Admission: $2 for self-guiding map and game sheets
Ages: Preschool and up
Plan: Under one hour
Parking: Free on site
Lunch: Picnic on the grounds or eat at the Pool Restaurant, 11 a.m.–2 p.m., Monday–Friday.
Facilities: Bathrooms in the Powerhouse and Potting Shed

Use the map and fill in the treasure hunt sheets as you walk along the 45-minute, self-guided walking loop. Children will enjoy seeing Henry Ford's root cellar, a 300-year-old Oak, underground boathouse, and miniature playhouse. After the hike, play bocce ball, Italian lawn bowling, on the estate lawn.

Education Center, Trails

For-Mar Nature Preserve and Aboretum and De Waters Education Center

5360 East Potter Road, Burton
810-789-8567
810-736-7100 (Genesee Parks)

Location: Northeast of downtown Flint in Burton
Hours: Education Center: Hours vary; call for an appointment. Nature Preserve and Arboretum: 8 a.m.–sunset, daily. For a guided hike, call for an appointment.
Admission: Free. Guided nature hikes, minimal fee.
Ages: All ages
Plan: Short visit
Parking: Free
Lunch: Picnicking on grounds is prohibited.
Facilities: Bathroom inside education center

For a first-hand look at nature, take a guided naturalist walk through the nature preserve's 380 acres; a handicapped-accessible trail is also available. The De Waters Education Center offers a demonstration beehive and hands-on nature games, exhibits, and displays.

Furstenberg Park

Fuller Road, Ann Arbor
734-994-2780

Location: Directly across from the entrance to Huron High School
Hours: 8 a.m.–10 p.m., daily
Admission: Free
Ages: All ages
Plan: Short visit
Parking: Free on site
Lunch: Picnic tables
Facilities: No bathrooms

This 38-acre nature area features a created prairie, restored woodland, Huron River edge lookouts, fishing deck, canoe landing, barrier-free trails, and picnic area.

G.B.'s Fishin' Hole

71201 Coon Creek, Armada
810-784-8354

Location: Northwest corner of 33 Mile and Coon Creek, approximately four miles east of M-53.
Hours: May 1–September 30: 11 a.m.–7 p.m., Wednesday–Friday. 10 a.m.–5 p.m., Saturday and Sunday. October 1-November 14: 11 a.m.–6 p.m., Wednesday–Friday. 1 a.m.–5 p.m., Saturday and Sunday. November 15–April 30: 10 a.m.–3 p.m., Saturday. Indoor fishing during inclement weather.
Admission: Free. You pay for whatever fish you catch. Fish are cleaned and iced for free.
Ages: 2 and up
Plan: Short visit
Parking: Free on site
Lunch: Picnic tables, barbecue grills, pop machines
Facilities: Outhouses

Spend the day relaxing in the country, fishing for farm-raised trout, catfish, perch, and bluegill. The farm supplies fishing poles, bait, and life jackets—a requirement for all children under 10. A barn with an indoor pool offers indoor fishing during summer's inclement weather and during the winter months.

Nature Center

Gerald E. Eddy Geology Center

Waterloo Recreation Area, McClure Road, Chelsea
734-475-3170

Location: Off Bush Road in the Waterloo Recreation Area
Hours: 9 a.m.–5 p.m., daily. Closed major holidays.
Admission: Parking permits, $4 daily, $20 annual, $5 senior annual
Ages: All ages
Plan: Short visit. The nature trails have walking times of 20 minutes to one hour.
Parking: Free on site
Lunch: Picnicking sites are located on the far east side of the recreation area
Facilities: Bathrooms. Gift shop with rock specimens, T-shirts and books.

While the emphasis is on rocks, the center also offers children a chance to see honeybee hives. There are 17 miles of hiking trails and a 22-mile backpacking trail.

Natural Phenomenon

Grand Ledge Outcroppings

Fitzgerald Park
133 Fitzgerald Park Drive, Grand Ledge
517-627-2149 or 517-627-7351

Just 12 miles west of Michigan State University, you can witness the 300-million-year-old sandstone cliff outcroppings that jut majestically from the shore of the Grand River. 60-foot sandstone ledges provide brave rock climbers a chance to try the sport. Fitzgerald Park also offers picnicking, fishing, canoeing and canoe rentals, cross-country skiing, recreation game area and naturalist services.

IMAX Theater

Henry Ford Museum IMAX Theatre

20900 Oakwood Boulevard, Dearborn
313-271-1570
1-800-747-IMAX

Website: www.hfmgv.org
Location: Southfield Freeway and Oakwood Boulevard
Hours: Every hour on the hour. 10 a.m.–5:30 p.m., Sunday–Thursday. 9 a.m.–8:30 p.m., Friday. 9 a.m.–9:30 p.m., Saturday.
Admission: $7.50 adults, $6.50 children ages 5–12 and seniors, $6 children 4 and under. Ticket prices are separate from museum or village admission. Combination tickets are available. Henry Ford Museum or Greenfield Village and IMAX: $17.50 adults, $16 seniors, $12.50 children ages 5–12, $6 children 4 and under. Henry Ford Museum and Greenfield Village and IMAX: $28 adults, $27 seniors, $19 children ages 5–12, $6 children 4 and under.
Ages: Kindergarten and up
Plan: Each movie is 35–45 minutes, but plan on a whole-day visit and enjoy the other museums and historic village on site
Parking: Free lot
Lunch: Café, snack bar, concession stand
Facilities: Bathrooms, drinking fountain, coat check, stroller availability

Henry Ford Museum's new 420-seat theater shows both two- and three-dimensional IMAX movies on its huge, 62x80-foot flat screen, with six-track digital surround sound. The movies tie into the programming at the village and include educational and unique subjects. Be sure to call ahead to reserve your tickets.

Petting Farm

Hess-Hathaway Petting Farm

825 South Williams Lake Road,
Waterford Township
248-360-3814
248-674-5441 (group tours)
Location: Just north of Cooley Lake Road
Hours: 10 a.m.–8 p.m., daily summer. 10 a.m.–5 p.m., daily winter. Call to reserve petting farm and

historic farmhouse tours, birthday parties, and scout badge opportunities.

Admission: $1/person animal visit and tour, $3/person for hayrides

Ages: Preschool–elementary

Plan: Short visit

Parking: Lot on site

Lunch: Picnic tables

Facilities: Preschool playground, walking trails, horseshoes, volleyball courts

Young children will enjoy a tour of this compact little farm with its red barns and white clapboard houses for hens and rabbits. The shepherd on duty encourages kids to feed the ducks and goats, hunt for eggs, and sit astride a friendly pony. The park also offers summer outdoor concerts and an antique car show/ice cream social.

Conservatory and Trails
Hidden Lake Gardens

M-50, Tipton
517-431-2060

Website: www.hlg.msu.edu

Location: On M-50, five miles west of junction of M-50 and M-52

Hours: 8 a.m.–dusk, daily April–October. 8 a.m.–4 p.m., daily November–March.

Admission: $3 weekends and holidays, $1 weekdays. Family memberships available.

Ages: All ages

Plan: Short visit

Parking: Free on site

Lunch: Picnic tables

Facilities: Bathrooms. Gift shop in visitor center has science items, "Hidden Lake" and Michigan State T-shirts and sweatshirts.

Walk the scented trails, feed swans, picnic amid tall pine trees, drive through six miles of winding roads, and wander through the conservatory's unique tropical and arid plants. Hidden Lake Gardens, owned by Michigan State University and full of Spartan spirit, is a peaceful place to stop on your way west across the state.

Trails

Howell Nature and Conference Center

1005 Triangle Lake Road, Howell
517-546-0249

Website: www.ismi.net/howellnature

Howell Nature Center is primarily a wildlife rehabilitation center, housing injured wildlife. While the center does not offer public hours, it does offer some scheduled school or group tours, school outreach programs, nature trails, and cross-country ski trails in the winter. Call ahead to schedule tours, school programs, and use of trails.

Nature Interpretive Centers

Huron-Clinton Metroparks Nature Centers

The following metroparks have nature centers with hands-on exhibits for children, live Michigan animals, nature trails, and year-round programs. Vehicle permits $2 weekdays (Wednesdays are free), $3 weekends, $15 annual, $8 seniors annual. General hours: 6 a.m.–dusk, daily, year-round. School groups should call for appointment. Call 1-800-47-PARKS or the individual nature center for more information. Website: www.metroparks.com

Hudson Mills Visitor Center

8801 North Territorial Road, Dexter
734-426-8211
(No nature center; naturalist will accommodate pre-arranged school and scout groups)

Indian Springs Nature Center

5200 Indian Trail, Clarkston
248-625-7280

Kensington Nature Center and Farm Center

2240 West Buno Road, Milford
248-685-0603

Lake Erie Marshlands Museum and Nature Center

32481 West Jefferson, Rockwood
734-379-5020

Metro Beach Nature Center

Metropolitan Parkway, Mt. Clemens
810-463-4332

Oakwoods Nature Center

Huron River Drive, Flat Rock
734-782-3956

Stony Creek Nature Center

4300 Main Park Road, Washington
810-781-4621

Wolcott Mills Farm Learning Center

65775 Wolcott, Ray Township
810-752-5932

Bird Sanctuary

Jack Miner Bird Sanctuary

Kingsville, Ontario, Canada
519-733-4034

Website: www.jackminer.com
Location: Three miles north of Kingsville, off Division Road (Road #29), on Road 3 West
Hours: Museum: 9 a.m.–5 p.m., Monday–Saturday, March–November, closed December–February. Grounds are open 9 a.m.–5:30 p.m., Monday–Saturday. Both museum and grounds are closed Sunday. October and November are peak migration months.
Admission: Free
Ages: All ages

Plan: Short visit
Parking: Free on site
Lunch: Picnic area
Facilities: Bathrooms, playground

Thousands of Canadian geese stop off at the Jack Miner Sanctuary during October and November on their way south. Children are encouraged to feed the waterfowl with handfuls of grain from the barley bucket located near the sanctuary's pond. Try to plan your trip for early morning or late afternoon. The geese come in for "breakfast" between 7 and 8 a.m. At 4 p.m., the geese put on an "airshow." They take off and land when an all-terrain vehicle drives through the flocks.

Conservation, Nature Center

Leslie Science Center and Project Grow

1831 Traver Road, Ann Arbor
734-662-7802

Location: Traver Road and Barton Drive, east of Plymouth Road
Hours: Grounds open sunrise–dusk, daily. Call two weeks ahead for tours of display area.
Admission: Free for park; tours and programs have minimal fee.
Ages: 3 and up
Plan: Under one hour
Parking: Free on site
Lunch: Restaurants are located nearby on U of M campus.
Facilities: Bathrooms in main residence. Project Grow office sells T-shirts.

Leslie Science Center is a site for conservation-related experiences, training, and education. Children will enjoy the indoor observation beehive and worm box. The center holds spring and fall festivals as well as classes, workshops, birthday parties, and summer camp. Project Grow sponsors area community gardens.

Nature Center

Lewis E. Wint Nature Center

Independence Oaks County Park
9501 Sashabaw Road, Clarkston
248-625-6473

Website: www.co.oakland.mi.us
Location: 2½ miles north of I-75 on Sashabaw Road
Hours: 10 a.m.–6 p.m., daily, Memorial Day–Labor Day. 10 a.m.–5 p.m., Tuesday–Sunday, school year. Summer Trail hours: 7 a.m.–dusk. Winter Trail hours: 8 a.m.–dusk. Family classes, scout badges, and programs are offered year round. Call ahead to book group tours.
Admission: Park entry fee during the summer, free admission to nature center
Ages: All ages
Plan: Short visit
Parking: On site
Lunch: Picnic areas available on rental basis, 248-625-0877.
Facilities: Bathrooms. Amphitheater located adjacent to nature center.

Children will enjoy the discovery area's miniaturized exhibits and life-size dioramas designed especially for hands-on learning. They will also enjoy looking through the windows and observing wildlife in the center's outdoor feeding station and exploring the constellations in Starlab, a portable planetarium. A 200-seat amphitheatre offers many year-round family programs. During the summer, visit the outdoor sensory and water gardens and spend a quiet moment in the gazebo.

Nature Center, Trails

Lloyd A. Stage Natural Heritage Park–Troy Nature Center
6685 Coolidge Highway, Troy

248-524-3567

Location: ¾ mile north of Square Lake Road, on Coolidge Highway
Hours: 8:30 a.m.–4:30 p.m., Wednesday, Friday, and Saturday. 8:30 a.m.–9 p.m., Tuesday and Thursday. Noon–9 p.m., Sunday, Memorial Day–Labor Day. 8:30 a.m.–4:30 p.m., Tuesday–Saturday. Noon–5 p.m., Sunday, rest of year. Scout and school groups are encouraged to call to arrange programs and tours.
Admission: Free. Fee for classes.
Ages: All ages
Plan: Short visit. Tours are approximately 1½ hours.

Parking: Free on site
Lunch: Picnic area
Facilities: Bathrooms. Gift shop with bird books, feeders, T-shirts, and notecards.

Lloyd A. Stage Natural Heritage Park–Troy Nature Center includes 99 acres of rolling meadow, forest, and stream, plus a farm site and Nature Center. The Nature Center houses exhibits, dioramas, hands-on displays, library, and gift shop. Self-guided nature trails are well marked and maps are available. The center also offers year-round family classes and outings. A Junior Naturalist Club is available for children. Maple Sugar Festival and Rent-a-Maple program in March.

Planetarium

Longway Planetarium

1310 East Kearsley Street, Flint
810-760-1181

Website: www.flint.org/longway
Location: Flint's Cultural Center, exit Longway Boulevard off I-475
Hours: Office: 8 a.m.–5 p.m., Monday–Friday. Planetarium shows: 1 and 2:30 p.m., Tuesday and Thursday, early July–Labor Day. 1 and 2:30 p.m., Saturday and Sunday, year-round. Lasera: 8, 9:15, and 10:30 p.m., Friday and Saturday, year-round.
Admission: Planetarium shows: $4 adults, $3 children 12 and under. Lasera shows: $5 adults, $4 children 12 and under.
Ages: All ages, but age requirements vary with show; call ahead
Plan: Short visit
Parking: Free on site
Lunch: Picnicking on planetarium lawn is permitted in warm weather
Facilities: Bathrooms. Gift shop with space, hologram, and star gazing gifts like gyroscopes, prisms, star explorers.

The Longway Planetarium is a treat for children of all ages. Be sure to call ahead to time your visit to one of their planetarium shows or laser shows set to rock music. Kids will also like the two 55-foot space murals lining the circular outer wall of the planetarium. Created with luminescent paint on black canvas, the murals make you feel as if you are looking out into space.

Nature Center, Trail

Marshlands Museum and Nature Center

Lake Erie Metropark
32481 West Jefferson, Rockwood
734-379-5020, ext. 379

Website: www.metroparks.com
Location: Lake Erie Metropark, along the coastal marsh of Lake Erie
Hours: 1–5 p.m., Monday–Friday. 10 a.m.–5 p.m., Saturday and Sunday, during the school year. 10 a.m.–5 p.m., daily, mid-June–Labor Day. Call ahead to schedule group and school tours.
Admission: Free
Ages: All ages
Plan: Under one hour
Parking: Use metropark lot. Vehicle entrance fee.
Lunch: Classroom/lunchroom and picnic tables available. Summer concessions near Lake Erie Metropark wave pool.
Facilities: Bathrooms

With hands-on displays of local plant and animal life, the center focuses on the local area's coastal environment, ecology, and cultural and water fowling history. Special seasonal programs and children's nature workshops are offered throughout the year. Of special note is September's annual Hawk Fest, celebrating the annual migration of hundreds of birds of prey and January's Erie Ice Daze, an old fashioned ice harvest festival. A new 1.5-mile nature trail traverses the coastal marsh, two islands linked by dykes, and the Lake Erie and Detroit River shorelines with 1700 feet of boardwalk and a 350-foot bridge.

Petting Farm

Maybury State Park Petting Farm

20145 Beck Road, Northville
248-349-8390

Location: Entrance off Eight Mile Road, six miles west of I-275
Hours: Park: 8 a.m.–10 p.m., Memorial Day–Labor Day. After Labor Day, park closes at dusk. Farm: 10 a.m.–5 p.m., daily, year-round.
Admission: $25/group farm tour.
Ages: All ages
Plan: Short visit

Parking: $4 vehicle entrance fee. $20 yearly permit fee.

Lunch: Picnic area

Facilities: Outhouses, nearby playscape, bike trails, cross-country ski rentals, and trails. Group hayrides and individual horseback riding at riding stables; call for reservations, 248-347-1088. Hayrides without reservations, weekends only, September and October.

Super-sized bunnies, honking geese, and shy turkeys share the spacious two-story barn with cows, pigs, and goats. Visit during early spring and you'll be rewarded with a new crop of animal babies. You'll also meet Farmer Beemer, the Maybury Park ranger, who's usually on hand to answer questions. Maybury playscape, a wooden all-purpose climber, is nearby—if you can pry your little ones away from the animals.

Animals

Michigan State University Barns

Campus, East Lansing
517-355-8383

Location: Between Harrison and Hagadorn, south of Mt. Hope

Hours: 9 a.m.–4 p.m., daily, year-round. Best times of visit, 2–2:30 p.m. during milking at the dairy barn.

Admission: Free

Ages: All ages

Parking: Free on site of barn

Lunch: Fast food and vending machines are located in the Student Union, corner of Abbott and Grand River. Many other restaurants are located on Grand River Avenue, across from campus. For a real treat, try homemade ice cream and homemade cheese (MSU invented chocolate cheese) at the MSU Dairy Store, located next to the Dairy Plant on Farm Lane. 517-355-8466.

Facilities: Bathrooms are located in each of the barns

If you're in the area, drop in, walk through, and say hello to the cows, pigs, horses, and sheep in the Dairy Barn, Swine Barn, Horse Barn, and Sheep Barn. Small Animal Day, usually held 9 a.m.–4 p.m., the last Saturday in April, is an orgaVarienized program offering children a chance to touch and see baby animals.

Gardens

Michigan State University Horticultural Demonstration Gardens

4-H Children's Garden
MSU Campus, East Lansing
517-355-0348 (general information)
517-353-6692 (children's garden)

Website: www.mi4hfdtn.org
Location: South side of the campus, near the Plant and Soil Sciences Building. Entrance is off Bogue Street, between Wilson Road and Service Drive.
Hours: Dawn to dusk, April 1–October 31. Docent-led tours available; call ahead.
Admission: Free; minimal fee for tours
Ages: All ages
Plan: Short visit
Parking: $1 parking tokens, 8 a.m.–5 p.m. weekdays
Lunch: School groups can eat lunch in the outdoor amphitheater. Fast food and vending machines are located in the Student Union, corner of Abbott and Grand River. Many other restaurants are located on Grand River Avenue, across from campus. For a real treat, try homemade ice cream and homemade cheese (MSU invented chocolate cheese) at the MSU Dairy Store, located next to the Dairy Plant on Farm Lane. 517-355-8466.
Facilities: Bathrooms in building adjacent to Plant Soil Science Building

This $3 million complex of specialty gardens features a 4-H Children's Garden rich in imaginative play. Walk through the door of the "Secret Garden" and you'll find an Alice-in-Wonderland maze, topiary animals (sculpted bushes and trees), model trains, a wooden train climber, treehouse climber, dance chimes, and 65 theme gardens, including the pizza garden of herbs, an enchanted garden of miniature vegetables, and Jack the Giant Killer's garden of towering sunflowers.

Insects

The Minibeast Zooseum and Education Center

6907 West Grand River Avenue,
Watertown Township
517-886-0630

Location: 1/2 mile east of exit 90 off I-96 or exit 81 off M-69

Hours: School year: 1–7 p.m., Tuesday. 1–5 p.m., Wednesday–Friday. 10 a.m.–4 p.m., Saturday. June–August: 10 a.m.–5 p.m., Tuesday–Saturday. 1–5 p.m., Sunday. School tours and traveling school programs are available. Call for reservations.

Admission: $3.50 adults, $2.50 childrens ages 3–12 and seniors.

Ages: All ages

Plan: Under one hour

Parking: Free on site

Lunch: For fast food and family restaurants, hop back on the freeway and exit at Saginaw Road.

Facilities: Gift shop sells mini-beast related, educational items from books to puzzles.

This brand new museum offers insect-lovers a chance to come face to face with and learn about all sorts of creepy crawlies including spiders, worms, snails, millipedes, and a tarantula or two.

Petting Farm

Mott Farm

6140 Bray Road, Flint
810-760-1795

Location: Just north of Flint. Follow I-475 off either I-75 or I-69 to Carpenter Road (exit 11). Same entrance as Crossroads Village/Huckleberry Railroad.

Hours: 10 a.m.–5 p.m., Monday–Friday. 11 a.m.–5 p.m., Saturday, Sunday and holidays, year-round. Large groups should call for reservations.

Admission: $1/person. Hayrides are available to groups.

Ages: Preschool–early elementary

Plan: Short visit

Parking: Free on site

Lunch: Picnic areas

Facilities: Portable toilets

Mott Petting Farm's many barns are full to the brim with animals gentle enough to pet and feed. Children will enjoy a quick visit to the farm before or after a visit to Crossroads Village/Huckleberry Railroad.

Working Farm

Mt. Bruce Station

6440 Bordman Road, Romeo
810-798-2568

Location: In the northwest corner of Macomb County, north of the village of Romeo and just south of Bordman Road.

Hours: The farm hosts a Sheep and Wool Festival, 10 a.m.–5 p.m. Saturday and Sunday, at the end of September. The Farm Wool Shop is open year-round, 10 a.m.–5 p.m., Thursday–Saturday. The shop sells "Michigan Farm Woolies," one-of-a-kind hand-knit woolen goods, and naturally dyed fibers and yarns. "Woolly Country Classroom" is also offered on Saturday afternoons throughout the year.

Admission: Entrance fee for Sheep and Wool Festival and for classes.

Ages: All ages

Plan: Short visit

Parking: During the festival, park at neighboring farms just west of site. For shop customers, park on site.

Lunch: Downtown Romeo offers several family owned restaurants

Facilities: During the festival, sheep-themed hands-on activities, music, children's games, demonstrations, gifts, and foods.

Mt. Bruce Station is a beautifully restored, 50-acre sheep ranch nestled in northwest Macomb County's gently rolling pasturelands. The owners, Yvonne and Peter Uhlianuk, run a flourishing cottage industry, creating naturally dyed yarns, hand-woven and knit woolen goods, and fresh meat from their purebred Corriedale and Romney sheep. Each September, they welcome the public to their farm for the Sheep and Wool Festival, where families can step back in time, watch demonstrations, and take workshops to learn sheep shearing, shirting, carding, spinning, weaving, felting and dyeing, animal care, and shepherding.

Nature Preserve

Nankin Mills Interpretive Center

33175 Ann Arbor Trail, Westland
734-261-1990

Location: On Hines Drive, east of Ann Arbor Trail
Hours: Groups can call year-round to book field trips and scout badge activities
Admission: Price varies with program. Please call.
Ages: All ages
Plan: Under one hour
Parking: Free on site, use lot on Hines Drive side of building
Lunch: Picnic tables and grassy areas throughout Hines Drive–Nankin Mills area. Restaurants along Wayne Road.
Facilities: Bathrooms

Hands-on exhibits, please-touch displays, computer screens, and live animals offer a historic look at the Rouge River, its native animals, and the people who were drawn to its shores, from the Native Americans and settlers to the grist-mill workers and Henry Ford.

Nature Center, Trails

The Nature Center at Friendship Woods

30300 Hales, Madison Heights
248-585-0100

Location: In the midst of 36 forested acres, in the heart of Madison Heights, south off 13 Mile, between John R and Dequindre.
Hours: Noon–5 p.m. Tuesday, Saturday, and Sunday. 10 a.m.–8 p.m., Wednesday. 10 a.m.–5 p.m., Thursday and Friday. Closed Monday. "Super Saturdays," 12:30 p.m., offer children ages 4–8 a free movie, story, and live animal experience. Free guided walks, 3 p.m. first Saturday of each month. Call for birthday parties and scout badge opportunities.
Admission: Free. Some classes charge a fee.
Ages: All ages
Plan: Short visit
Parking: Lot on site
Lunch: Cookies on sale at gift shop. There are plenty of restaurants dotting nearby John R and Dequindre
Facilities: Bathrooms. Gift shop sells creative and inexpensive nature gifts and birthday party favors.

Children will feel completely at home at this cozy log cabin nature center, chock full of kind docents who enjoy sharing their knowledge with youngsters. In addition, there are furs, hides, skins, and other realia to touch and feel, and aquariums filled with fish, turtles, and snakes. Kids can play games at a computer inside a simulated cave and explore nature inside a mini-log cabin. Take a family stroll along the 1 1/3 miles of paved and marked trails surrounding the center.

Nature Center, Trails

Ojibway Park and Nature Center

5200 Matchette Road, Windsor
Ontario, Canada
519-966-5852

Website: www.city.windsor.on.ca/ojibway
Location: Next to Windsor Raceway off Highway 3
Hours: Trails: dawn–dusk. Center: 10 a.m.–5 p.m., daily
Admission: Free
Ages: All ages
Plan: Short visit
Parking: Free in adjacent lots
Lunch: Picnic tables
Facilities: Restrooms. Bird books and birdseed for sale

Ojibway Park offers an 160-acre forest and prairie clearing with shady picnic areas. The nature center is devoted to exhibits and displays on wildlife. Children are encouraged to handle the displays and get to know the center's snakes and turtles.

Zoo

Potter Park Zoo

1301 South Pennsylvania Avenue, Lansing
517-483-4221

Location: 4 blocks south of I-496
Hours: Zoo buildings: 9 a.m.–6 p.m., daily, Memorial Day–end of June. 9 a.m.–7 p.m., July–Labor Day. 9 a.m.–5 p.m. daily, after Labor Day. Park: 8 a.m.–dusk, daily, year-round.
Admission: $5 adult non-residents, $3 adults residents, $1 children, ages 3–15, under 3 free.
Ages: All ages
Plan: Short visit
Parking: $1.50 vehicle, $5 oversized vehicle on weekends
Lunch: Picnic areas and food concessions (summer only)
Facilities: Bathrooms, gift concessions

Children will enjoy visiting this zoo located in hilly Potter Park. They'll find a variety of animals as well as activities. There are over 400 animals, including large cats, primates, kangaroos, Sumatran Tiger, and penguin, farmyard with farm animals, bird and reptile building, small children's contact center, playground, and in the summer, pony and camel rides. The "Michigan Backyards Habitat" exhibit offers a nature trail through urban, suburban, and rural backyards.

Zoo, Petting Farm
Ruby Farms of Michigan

6567 Imlay City Road, Ruby
810-324-2662

Location: Just west of Port Huron
Hours: 11 a.m.–5 p.m., Friday–Sunday, September–Christmas
Admission: Free. Small charge for petting zoo and rides.
Ages: Especially geared for preschool and early elementary
Plan: Short visit
Parking: Free on site
Lunch: Cider mill/restaurant
Facilities: Bathrooms, gift shop

Ruby Farms offers city children a chance to frolic in the country, pet and feed a variety of farm animals, as well as watch several exotic zoo-type animals. The farm offers fresh cider from its cider mill/restaurant, and in November and December, cut-your-own Christmas trees.

Nature Center, Trails
Seven Ponds Nature Center

3854 Crawford Road, Dryden
810-796-3200

Location: North of Pontiac, east off M-24 on Dryden Road
Hours: 9 a.m.–5 p.m., Tuesday–Sunday. 2 p.m. Sunday family programs or nature walks, year-round.
Admission: $2 adults, $1 children
Ages: All ages
Plan: Short visit

Parking: Free on site
Lunch: Picnic area
Facilities: Bathrooms. Gift shop and bookstore with children's books and bird-feeding supplies.

Children are encouraged to touch and explore at the Seven Ponds Nature Center. Inside the Interpretive Building, there are natural history collections of skins, insects, and minerals, a touch table for handling items, and an observation beehive for close inspection of bee activity. Outside, there are trails.

Trout Farm

Spring Valley Trout Farm

12190 Island Lake Road, Dexter
734-426-4772

Website: www.springvallytroutfarm.com
Location: I-94 west to exit 167 (Dexter), then four miles west of Dexter to Island Lake Road
Hours: Spring and fall: 9 a.m.–6 p.m., Saturday and Sunday. Memorial Day–Labor Day: 9 a.m.–6 p.m., Wednesday–Sunday.
Admission: $3 for fishermen, $2 for non-fishermen, under 4 free. You pay per pound for all you catch; fish can't be thrown back into the pond. Fish are packaged in ice free of charge. There is a small fee for cleaning the fish.
Ages: 2 and up for fishing
Plan: Short visit
Parking: Free on site
Lunch: Vending machines, snacks, picnic areas with grills
Facilities: Bathroom

For a first fishing experience, you can't beat Spring Valley Trout Farm. With admission, you are given all the equipment you need—life jacket (for children under 9), pail, poles, hooks, and worms. Helpful staff members show you how to cut off a section of worm, snag it on the hook, and toss your line into the spring-fed pond. The fact that you are guaranteed a catch is the most amazing part for children (and you'll notice adults get very excited, too). For little ones, there is a small children's pond.

Planetarium

Starlab

Lewis E. Wint Nature Center
Independence Oaks County Park
9501 Sashabaw Road, Clarkston
248-625-6473

Website: www.co.oakland.mi.us
Location: 2 1/2 miles north of I-75 on Sashabaw Road. Starlab is set up inside a nature center classroom.
Hours: By appointment only; for school and civic groups. Families are welcome to sign up for workshops or attend evening "Star Parties," held four times a year, at the beginning of each new season.
Admission: $50/first program; $40 additional show on site. Starlab travels to sites; $100/first program, $40 additional show.
Ages: First grade and up
Plan: 45-minute show
Parking: On site. Park entry fee.
Lunch: Covered picnic sites nearby
Facilities: The nature center includes a hands-on exhibit room and 10 miles of outdoor trails.

Starlab planetarium presentations are intimate star shows for all ages.

Nature Center

Sterling Heights Nature Center

42700 Utica Road, Sterling Heights
810-739-6731

Location: Van Dyke and Utica Roads, one block east of Van Dyke
Hours: June–August: 10 a.m.–5 p.m., Tuesday–Saturday. 1–5 p.m., Sunday. School year: 1–5 p.m., Tuesday–Friday. 10 a.m.–5 p.m., Saturday. 1–5 p.m., Sunday.
Admission: Free
Ages: 3 and up
Plan: Short visit
Parking: Free on site
Lunch: Picnicking is permitted. Auditorium may be used as a lunchroom.
Facilities: Bathrooms

The Sterling Heights Nature Center, part of the city's parks and recreation department, sits on seven acres overlooking the Clinton River. The dis-

play room features hands-on natural science experiences. There are live snakes, turtles and fish,
nature puzzles, mystery boxes, and animal skins.
Family nature movies are shown 7 p.m., Tuesday.
Nature classes and programs are also offered for
children and adults.

Nature Preserve, Trails

University of Michigan-Dearborn Environmental Study Area

News and Information, Dearborn
313-593-5338

Location: On the grounds of the Henry Ford Fair
Lane Estate, 4901 Evergeen Road, west of
Fairlane Town Center
Hours: Dawn–Dusk
Admission: Free
Ages: All ages
Plan: Short visit
Parking: Lot adjacent to Ford estate powerhouse
Lunch: Picnicking is not allowed. The Ford
estate's Pool Restaurant is open 11 a.m.– 2 p.m.,
Monday–Friday, year-round. Many restaurants are
available in Fairlane Town Center.
Facilities: Self-guided nature trails, maps avail-
able in parking lot boxes

Nature lovers are encouraged to visit the
sprawling nature area on the Rouge River that was
once part of Henry Ford's estate. Special seasonal
nature hikes are held throughout the year, including a Maple Syrup walk in March. Year-round
classes are also held for mini-naturalists.

Planetarium

University of Michigan Exhibit Museum Planetarium

1109 Geddes, Ann Arbor
734-764-0478 (reservations)
734-763-6085 (taped information)

Location: Fourth floor of the U of M Exhibit
Museum, corner of Geddes and Washtenaw
Avenues on the U of M campus
Hours: Planetarium shows: 10:30 and 11:30 a.m.,
12:30, 1:30, 2:30, and 3:30 p.m., Saturday. 1:30,
2:30, 3:30 p.m. Sunday. 1, 2, and 3 p.m.,

Monday–Friday, during July and August. Museum hours: 9 a.m.–5 p.m., Monday–Saturday. Noon–5 p.m., Sunday.

Admission: Planetarium show, $3.25 adults, $3 seniors and children 12 and under. Museum, free. Tickets go on sale one hour before each show. Special Christmas Shows are offered during December and at extra times during vacation week. Groups may pre-arrange shows at convenient times.

Ages: All ages. Certain shows are recommended for grades 3 and up.

Plan: Shows are approximately 35 minutes, with question-answer session following show.

Parking: Use street meters or Fletcher Street parking lot. On weekends, staff lot behind museum is available.

Lunch: Many restaurants on campus

Facilities: Bathrooms. Gift shop with many inexpensive dinosaur and natural history items. Planetarium is air conditioned; museum is not.

While most families come to the Exhibit Museum to see dinosaurs, the planetarium offers another trip into the exciting realm of natural science and creates a realistic image of the night sky on its 360° dome. Shows are imaginative and most interesting for children 5 and up.

Greenhouse, Trails

University of Michigan Matthaei Botanical Gardens

1800 North Dixboro Road, Ann Arbor
734-998-7061

Location: Take US-23 north, exit at Geddes Road, and turn right. At Dixboro Road, turn left. Gardens are 1 1/2 miles on your right.

Hours: Conservatory: 10 a.m.–4:30 p.m., daily. Grounds: 8 a.m.–sunset. Group tours available. Call three weeks in advance.

Admission: For conservatory, $3 adults, $1 children grades K-12. U of M students and members are free. Grounds are free.

Ages: All ages

Plan: Short visit

Parking: Free on site

Lunch: You'll find restaurants going west on Geddes or driving into U of M's campus

Facilities: Bathrooms. Gift shop with T-shirts, mugs, and botanical items.

It's perpetual summer in the Matthaei Botanical Gardens Conservatory. Lush tropical plants with vivid reds and pinks, exotic banana and lemon trees, and huge exotic cacti capture children's attention. They will also enjoy peering into two ponds full of gliding koi. Four outdoor trails are marked for a self-guided stroll revealing seasonal changes. Free maps are available in the conservatory. Families will also enjoy seasonal events and classes. Of special note is October's Fall Festival.

Trails

West Bloomfield Trail Network

West Bloomfield Parks and Recreation
248-738-2500

Location: The 4.25 mile trail runs from the West Bloomfield Woods Nature Preserve (Arrowhead Road, south of Pontiac Trail) to Sylvan Manor Park (On Woodrow Wilson, south of Orchard Lake Road and west of Middlebelt)
Hours: Dawn–dusk
Admission: Free
Ages: All ages
Plan: As long as you want to hike or bike
Parking: Free in parking lot of Nature Preserve
Lunch: Picnic facilities at Sylvan Manor Park
Facilities: Handicapped accessible restroom at Arrowhead Road entrance

A former railroad line, the quiet hike/bike/cross country ski trail meanders through a variety of natural habitats that many wildlife species call home.

Bird Sanctuary

West Bloomfield Woods Nature Preserve

West Bloomfield Parks and Recreation
248-738-2500

Location: Going north on Orchard Lake Road, turn west onto Pontiac Trail and drive 1 1/2 miles to Arrowhead. Turn left. The nature preserve parking lot is a mile ahead. Or discover the nature preserve while hiking or biking the West Bloomfield Trail Network.
Hours: Dawn–dusk. Call the West Bloomfield Parks and Recreation for the dates of regularly

scheduled naturalist-led tot nature walks. Or book your own group walk.

Admission: Free. Nominal fee for tot walks or group tours.
Ages: All ages
Plan: Short visit
Parking: Free on site
Lunch: Head south on Orchard Lake Road and you'll find a restaurant mecca

The 162-acre preserve was the first Michigan location to receive national recognition as an Urban Wildlife Sanctuary. It hosts more than 100 bird species and a great blue heron rookery. It's also home to red fox, mink, weasel, white-tailed deer, and blue-spotted salamander. At the edge of a lime-green prehistoric-looking swamp you'll see the great blue heron rookery. Dead trees with jagged limbs and hollowed-out trunks sprout magically from the still water. On top, a village of oblong nests—more than 90—crown the limb tops. Herons perch gracefully on each nest, silhouetted by the morning mist. This preserve offers kids a full sensory nature experience.

Working Farm

Wolcott Mill Farm Learning Center

65775 Wolcott Road, Ray Township
810-752-5932
810-749-5997 (group tour)

Website: www.metroparks.com
Location: Off Wolcott Road, about 1 1/2 miles north of 29 Mile Road, southeast of Romeo
Hours: 9 a.m.–5 p.m., daily, open to the public. 9 a.m.–5 p.m., Tuesday–Friday for group tours. Milking demonstrations, 10 a.m. daily. Scout badge opportunities in spring and fall. Special family programming year-round.
Admission: Fall and spring hayrides and winter sleigh rides, as scheduled, $2 adults, $1.50 children and seniors. Small fee for some programs.
Ages: All ages
Plan: Short visit
Parking: Free
Lunch: Bring a picnic
Facilities: Bathrooms, picnic tables, pop machine

Come down to the farm and introduce the kids to cows, sheep, chicks, and geese. During fall weekends, take a lazy, narrated hayride through the corn field, visit a haunted dairy barn, make your way through a Sudan grass maze, and take home a dozen freshly laid eggs. Wolcott Mill Farm Learning Center is a modern working farm where the rangers enjoy sharing farm stories and farming techniques with visitors. Special programs include Easter Egg Hunt and a Halloween Maze.

Nature Center/Trails

Woldumar Nature Center

5539 Lansing Road, Lansing
517-322-0030

Location: Southwest Lansing, one mile north of I-96, off Lansing Road exit.
Hours: Trails: Dawn–dusk. Center: 9 a.m.–5 p.m., Monday–Friday; weekend hours vary.
Admission: Trails: $1/person. Center is free. Fee for special seasonal events. $2/person (minimum $20) for 2-hour naturalist-led program.
Ages: All ages
Plan: Short visit
Parking: Free in lot
Lunch: Space available for groups only
Facilities: Bathrooms and gift shop in nature center
The 188-acre nature preserve offers a variety of habitats, including a beech and maple hardwoods forest, spruce and pine plantation, Grand River frontage and pond, as well as a variety of wildlife—deer, fox, and great blue herons. The nature center offers animal mounts, a bird feeding observation area, and reading area.

8
Seasonal Harvest

TIP

After picking your favorite crop, be sure to schedule time to bake together. Let each child find a special recipe. If you're lucky, you'll have an apple cake or some blueberry muffins to freeze and enjoy on a snowy day.

Here are enough farmers' markets, u-pick farms, and cider mills to keep you out of doors and full of fresh foods all year long. Kids love bustling farmers' markets. Take your little red wagon to pull the kids and the crops, and be sure to peek under produce-laden tables; you just might find bunnies hidden in crates.

Or pick the produce yourself at Michigan's u-pick farms. Many offer a variety of activities during harvest season, from blue-grass music and hay rides to petting farms and candle dipping. How can you resist freshly picked strawberries in June, raspberries in July, peaches in August, or apples, cider, and donuts in September? During October, many farms offer Halloween hayrides and ghost barns, plus pumpkin and gourd picking. Beginning Thanksgiving weekend, Christmas tree farms open for business, offering a hay wagon ride out to the field to choose your own Christmas tree. "Quick Look Lists" list farms according to their u-pick crop. Use these lists for handy reference.

Farmers' Markets

Ann Arbor Farmers' Market

407 North Fifth Avenue, Ann Arbor
734-761-1078
734-662-4221 (Kerrytown)

Location: Next door to Kerrytown, Catherine Street and Fifth Avenue
Hours: January–April: 8 a.m.–3 p.m., Saturday. May 1–Christmas: 7 a.m.–3 p.m., Wednesday and Saturday. Artisan Market, 11 a.m.–4 p.m., Sunday, May–December.

Brighton Farmers' Market

Grand River and Main Street, Brighton
810-227-5086 (Chamber of Commerce)

Location: Cedar Street lot at the Mill Pond
Hours: 8 a.m.–1 p.m. Saturday, May–October

Chelsea Farmers' Market

Chelsea
734-475-1145

Location: In parking area behind Main Street, between Park and Middle Streets in downtown Chelsea
Hours: 8 a.m.–1 p.m. Saturday, May–October.

Eastern Market

2934 Russell, Detroit
313-833-1560

Location: 2 blocks east of I-75, take Mack Avenue exit
Hours: Stores and restaurants, 8 a.m.–4 p.m., Monday–Friday, year-round. Market, 6 a.m.–5 p.m., Saturday, year-round. Closed Sunday, except for the Annual Flower Day, 5 a.m.–4 p.m., the Sunday following Mother's Day.

The area's largest, most boisterous and aromatic farmers' market. In addition to fresh fruits and vegetable stalls, the market's specialty stores offer fresh baked goods, spices, nuts, cheeses, coffees, wines, meat, and shellfish. Bring a wagon or stroller to carry your kids and purchases and get ready for a crush of colorful people. Arrive early Saturday morning to be sure of a parking space. Parking can be found along Russell or Riopelle, or in lots north of farmers' sheds or in the parking structure in the middle of the market. May's Annual Flower Day is a carnival of flowers, plants, shrubs, strolling clowns, artists, singers, dancers, musicians, and more.

Farmington Farmers' Market

The Village Commons, Farmington
248-473-7276

Location: In the parking lot of the Village Commons, two blocks east of Farmington Road, on Grand River.
Hours: 9 a.m.–2 p.m., Saturday, mid-May–October

Flint City Market

420 East Boulevard Drive, Flint
810-766-7449

Location: Robert T. Longway exit off I-475
Hours: 6:30 a.m.–5:30 p.m., Tuesday, Thursday, and Saturday, year-round

Lapeer Farmers' Market

576 Liberty, Lapeer
810-667-0341

Location: Liberty at Nepessing, in front of the historic courthouse
Hours: 10 a.m.–2 p.m. Wednesday and 9 a.m.–2 p.m. Saturday, May–October

Livonia Farmers' Market

29350 West Chicago, Livonia
734-446-2538

Location: At the historic Wilson Barn on the corner of Middle Belt and West Chicago
Hours: 8 a.m.–3 p.m. Saturday, July–September

Meridian Township Farmers' Market

Central Park, Marsh Road, Okemos
517-349-1200

Location: Ingham County
Hours: 8 a.m.–6 p.m., Wednesday. 8 a.m.–2 p.m., Saturday, July–October.

Mount Clemens Farmers' Market

37685 South Gratiot, Mount Clemens
810-469-2525

Location: Downtown Mount Clemens.
Hours: Summer: 9 a.m.–9 p.m., Monday–Saturday. 9 a.m.–6 p.m., Sunday. Rest of year: 9 a.m.–8 p.m., Monday–Saturday. 9 a.m.–5 p.m., Sunday.

Northville Farmers' Market

Seven Mile Road, Northville
248-349-7640 (Chamber of Commerce)

Location: Seven Mile Road and Sheldon Road, at the Northville Downs parking lot
Hours: 7 a.m.–5 p.m., Thursday, May–October

Plymouth Farmers' Market

Plymouth
734-453-1540 (Chamber of Commerce)

Location: At "The Gathering," across from Kellogg Park, on Penniman and Main Streets
Hours: 7:30 a.m.–12:30 p.m., Saturday, first week in May to mid-October

Pontiac Farmers' Market

2350 Pontiac Lake Road
248-858-5495

Location: Just west of Telegraph Road
Hours: 6:30 a.m.–2 p.m., Tuesday, Thursday, Saturday, May 1–Christmas. After Christmas, 6:30 a.m.–2 p.m., Saturday only.

Port Huron Main Street Farmers' Market

Huron Avenue, Port Huron
810-985-8843

Location: 300 block of Huron Avenue, downtown Port Huron
Hours: 9 a.m.–4 p.m. Saturday, May–October

Royal Oak Farmers' Market

316 East Eleven Mile Road, Royal Oak
248-548-8822

Location: Two miles east of Woodward, two blocks east of Main Street
Hours: Farm market: 7 a.m.–2 p.m. Saturday, year-round. Plus, 7 a.m.–1 p.m., Friday, May–Christmas. Antique market: 7 a.m.–4 p.m., Sunday, year-round.

Ypsilanti Farmers' Market

Depot Town, Ypsilanti
734-483-1100 (City Hall)

Location: In Depot Town, Cross Street just east of Huron River Drive
Hours: 7 a.m.–3 p.m., Wednesday and Saturday.

U-Pick Farms and Cider Mills

Here is a sampling of the most popular farms and cider mills in the greater Detroit area. To help you find the site closest to your home, check the county in which each farm or cider mill is located. Also, be sure to call ahead for directions and hours. Hours vary depending on the season, the crop, and the weather.

Almar Orchards

1431 Duffield, Flushing
810-659-6568

Location: Genesee County
Hours: 9 a.m.–6 p.m., Monday–Saturday; noon–6 p.m., Sunday, year-round
Activities: Cider mill, farm market, hayrides, petting zoo with llamas, reindeer, goats, and horses

Apple Charlie's and South Huron Orchard and Cider Mill

38035 South Huron Road, New Boston
734-753-9380

Location: Wayne County
Hours: 8 a.m.–dark, daily, August–December.
Activities: U-pick apples, cider mill, farm market, bakery, gift shop, farm animals, hayrides, group tours

Ashton Orchards and Cider Mill

3925 Seymour Lake Road, Ortonville
248-627-6671

Location: Oakland County
Hours: 10 a.m.–5 p.m., Monday–Saturday. Noon–6 p.m., Sunday, year-round
Activities: Cider mill and farm market

Beck's Cider Mill

1660 Maple Rapids Road, St. Johns
517-224-4309

Location: Clinton County
Hours: Fall season
Activities: Cider, donuts, farm market, children's

play area, weekend hayrides. Group hayrides and bonfires by appointment.

Blake's Almont Farm

Van Dyke and Hough Road, Almont
810-798-3251

Location: Lapeer County
Hours: June–October
Activities: U-pick strawberries, cherries, apples, country store, weekend harvest activities

Blake's Big Apple Orchard

71485 North Avenue, Armada
810-784-9710

Location: Macomb County
Hours: 8 a.m.–6 p.m., daily, April–December
Activities: U-pick strawberries, cherries, apples, pears, pumpkins, raspberries, peaches, and Christmas trees. Group tours, produce store, fudge shop, bakery, haunted house, animal petting farm, wagon rides, and train rides through the orchard on weekends.

Blake's Orchard and Cider Mill

17985 Armada Center Road, Armada
810-784-5343

Location: Macomb County
Hours: 8 a.m.–6 p.m., daily, mid-June–December
Activities: U-pick strawberries, cherries, vegetables, raspberries, pumpkins, apples and pears, wagon and pony rides, miniature train rides, haunted barn, cider mill, Christmas trees, farm market, weekend activities, group tours

Brookwood Fruit Farm

7845 Bordman Road, Almont
810-798-8312

Location: Lapeer County
Hours: 9 a.m.–5 p.m. daily, July–April.
Activities: U-pick cherries, peaches, pears, apples, red raspberries, plums

Coon Creek Orchard

78777 Coon Creek Road, Armada
810-784-5062

Location: Macomb County
Hours: 8 a.m.–6 p.m., daily, late June–October.
Activities: U-pick strawberries, cherries, raspberries, plums, pears, apples, pumpkins, cider mill, farm market, gift shop, petting farm, "Indian Village" group tours

Crossroads Village Cider Mill

G-6140 Bray Road, Flint
810-736-7100

Location: Genesee County
Hours: 10 a.m.–5 p.m., Monday–Friday. 11 a.m.–6 p.m., Saturday and Sunday, Memorial Day–Labor Day. 11 a.m.–6 p.m., weekends only, through September.
Activities: Cider press demonstration. The mill is part of the Huckleberry Railroad/Crossroads Village complex.

Davies Orchard

40026 Willow Road, New Boston
734-654-8893

Location: Wayne County
Hours: 9:30 a.m.–6 p.m., daily, mid-September–end-October
Activities: U-pick apples

DeGroot's Strawberries

4232 Bull Run Road, Gregory
517-223-9311
Location: Livingston County
Hours: 8 a.m.–8 p.m., June–July
Activities: U-pick strawberries

Deneweth's Pick Your Own Strawberry Farms

16125 22 Mile Road, Macomb Township
810-247-5533

Location: Macomb County
Hours: 8 a.m.–9 p.m., June–July
Activities: U-pick strawberries, wagon rides to and from field

Dexter Cider Mill

3685 Central Street, Dexter
734-426-8531

Location: Washtenaw County
Hours: 9 a.m.–5 p.m., late August–mid-November
Activities: Cider press demonstrations, donuts

Diehl's Orchard and Cider Mill

1479 Ranch, Holly
810-634-8981

Location: Oakland County
Hours: 9 a.m.–6 p.m. daily, mid-August–October 30. 9 a.m.–5 p.m. daily, October 31–late December.
Activities: U-pick pumpkins, country shop with cider, donuts, apples, jams, jellies, popcorn. Wagon rides and entertainment on weekends during fall; Ciderfest last weekend in September.

Driver's Berry Farm

Doane Road, South Lyon
248-437-1606
248-437-8461

Location: Livingston County
Hours: 8 a.m.–8 p.m., daily, July, August–October
Activities: U-pick early and late raspberries, blueberries, pumpkins

Erie Orchards

1235 Erie Road, Erie
734-848-4518

Location: Monroe County
Hours: 9 a.m.–7 p.m., Monday–Saturday. 11 a.m.–6 p.m., Sunday, mid-July–Christmas
Activities: U-pick blueberries, peaches, apples, pumpkins, and Christmas trees. Cider press and donut-making demonstrations. Weekend entertainment, pony rides, animal petting farm and hayrides. Group and school tours available.

Erwin Orchards

61475 Silver Lake, South Lyon
248-437-0150

Location: Oakland County
Hours: 9 a.m.–6 p.m., daily
Activities: U-pick apples, pumpkins. Group tours, wagon rides, haunted barn, country store. Erwin Orchards grows dwarf apple trees, just the right height for young pickers.

Franklin Cider Mill

7450 Franklin Road, Franklin
248-626-2968

Location: Oakland County
Hours: Saturday before Labor Day–Sunday after Thanksgiving: 7 a.m.–6 p.m., Monday–Friday. 8 a.m.–6 p.m., Saturday and Sunday.
Activities: Cider-press demonstrations, food stand selling apples, seasonal foods, donuts

Hy's Cider Mill

6350 Thirty-Seven Mile Road, Romeo
810-798-3611

Location: Macomb County
Hours: 11 a.m.–6 p.m., Saturday and Sunday. September–Halloween
Activities: U-pick apples, cider, donuts, and wagon rides for apple pickers

Jeffery's Blueberries

3805 Cribbins Road, Avoca
810-324-2874

Location: St. Clair County
Hours: 10 a.m.–7 p.m., Monday–Saturday; noon–5 p.m. Sunday, summer months
Activities: U-pick blueberries

Koan's Orchards

12183 Beecher, Flushing
810-659-8720

Location: Genesee County
Hours: 8 a.m.–6 p.m., Monday–Saturday; 9 a.m.–6 p.m. Sunday, mid-September–May 31
Activities: Cider mill, donuts, farm market

Long Family Orchard and Farm

Commerce Lake Road, Commerce Township
248-360-3774

Location: Oakland County
Hours: May–Thanksgiving: 3–6 p.m., Monday–Friday. 10 a.m.–5 p.m., Saturday and Sunday.
Activities: U-pick asparagus, strawberries, cherries, apples, and pumpkins, farm market

McCarron's Orchard

7456 West Carpenter, Flushing
810-659-3813

Location: Genesee County
Hours: Hours vary with the season, open year-round
Activities: Cider mill, fruit market, bakery specializing in homemade fruit pies

Makielski Berry Farm

7130 Platt Road, Ypsilanti
734-572-0060

Location: Washtenaw County
Hours: 8 a.m.–8 p.m., daily during September–November
Activities: U-pick fall red raspberries

Mary's Farm Market

474453 Ford Road, Canton Township
734-981-2866

Location: Wayne County
Hours: U-pick, 10 a.m.–dusk, Saturday and Sunday during October. Farm market, 9 a.m.–7 p.m., daily.
Activities: U-pick pumpkins, corn maze, group hayrides, and bonfires

Meyer's Farm

48120 West Eight Mile Road, Northville
248-349-0289

Location: Oakland County
Hours: 9 a.m.–dusk, daily, October
Activities: U-pick pumpkins

Middleton Berry Farm

2120 Stoney Creek Road, Oakland
248-693-6018

Location: Oakland County
Hours: Hours vary depending on crop, June–October
Activities: U-pick strawberries, spring and fall raspberries, vegetables and pumpkins, petting farm, wagon rides, Halloween activities. Group tours available.

Middleton Cider Mill

46462 Dequindre, Utica
810-731-6699

Location: Macomb County
Hours: 8 a.m.–6 p.m., daily September–Halloween
Activities: Pony rides on the weekends, wild geese and ducks, donuts, cider, candy, goodies

Miller's Big Red

4900 West Thirty-Two Mile Road, Washington
810-752-7888

Location: Macomb County
Hours: 9 a.m.–6 p.m., daily, May–early December. 9 a.m.–6 p.m., daily, September and October for apples, pumpkins, and fall group tours
Activities: U-pick strawberries, apples, raspberries, and pumpkins, hayrides, cider mill, fresh produce, bakery, flowers, October haunted house, and hayrides

Montrose Orchards

12473 Seymour, Montrose
810-639-6971

Location: Genesee County
Hours: January–April 15: Noon–5:30 p.m., daily. April 16–December 31: 8 a.m.–6 p.m., Monday–Saturday. 10 a.m.–6 p.m., Sunday.
Activities: U-pick strawberries, blueberries, and pumpkins, winery, bakery, gift shop, craft shop, cider mill, hay wagon rides, animals, and tours

Navarre Farms

1485 Bates Lane, Monroe
734-241-0723

Location: Monroe County
Hours: May–early July: 8 a.m.–8 p.m., Monday–Friday. 8 a.m.–6 p.m., Saturday and Sunday.
Activities: U-pick asparagus

Oak Haven Farm

7515 Grange Hall Road, Ortonville
248-634-5437

Location: Oakland County
Hours: October: 10 a.m.–6:30 p.m., Sunday–Thursday. 10 a.m.–8 p.m., Saturday and Sunday. Petting farm, maze and hayrides, 11 a.m.–6 p.m., Saturday and Sunday.
Activities: U-pick pumpkins, cider, donuts, petting farm, hay maze, craft cabin. School tours, by reservation.

Obstbaum Orchards and Cider Mill

9252 Currie Road, Salem Township
248-349-5569

Location: Washtenaw County
Hours: 10 a.m.–6 p.m., Saturday and Sunday, mid-September–Thanksgiving
Activities: U-pick apples, cider and donuts, farm market with candies, butters, syrups, preserves, dried flowers, and wreaths

Paint Creek Cider Mill and Restaurant

4480 Orion Road, Rochester
248-651-8361

Location: Oakland County
Hours: Cider Mill and Country Store: 9 a.m.–6

p.m., daily, during fall. 10 a.m.–5 p.m., Saturday and Sunday, rest of year. Restaurant: Call for hours, open year-round. Dinner, Monday–Friday. Lunch and dinner, Saturday. Brunch and dinner, Sunday.

Activities: Cider, donuts, baked goods, candy, honey. Restaurant, pub, large mill water wheel, and trails.

Pankiewicz Farms Cider Mill

10387 Lindsey Road, Casco
810-727-9051

Location: St. Clair County
Hours: Weekends only, October–December
Activities: Cider, donuts and goodies

Parmenter's Northville Cider Mill

714 Baseline Road, Northville
248-349-3181

Location: Wayne County
Hours: 10 a.m.–8 p.m., daily, Saturday before Labor Day–Sunday before Thanksgiving
Activities: Cider-press demonstrations, country store with cider, donuts, caramel apples, honey, jam, candy, play area

Parshallville Cider Mill

8507 Parshallville Road, Fenton
810-629-9079

Location: Livingston County
Hours: 10 a.m.–6 p.m., daily, Labor Day–mid-November
Activities: Cider press demonstrations, donuts, wagon rides

Plymouth Orchards and Cider Mill

10685 Warren Road, Plymouth
734-455-2290

Location: Washtenaw County
Hours: 9 a.m.–7 p.m., daily, September and October. 10 a.m.–6 p.m., daily, November–second weekend in December.

Activities: U-pick pumpkins. Cider-press demonstrations, petting farm, wagon rides, country market. Group tours available.

Potter Farm

8684 McKean Road, Willis
734-461-6348

Location: Washtenaw County
Hours: 8 a.m.–7 p.m., daily, June
Activities: U-pick strawberries

Porters Orchard and Cider Mill

12160 Hegel, Goodrich
810-636-7156

Location: Genesee County
Hours: 9 a.m.–6 p.m., Monday–Saturday. Noon–6 p.m., Sunday, July–April. Noon–6 p.m., Monday–Saturday. Closed Sunday, May and June.
Activities: Cider mill, bakery, farm market

Pumpkin Factory

48651 Harris, Belleville
734-461-1835

Location: Wayne County
Hours: 9:30 a.m.–9 p.m., daily, October
Activities: Halloween costumes, u-pick pumpkins, bakery, cider, goodies, gift shop, hayride, haunted cornfield

Pumpkin Patch

32285 Sibley Road, New Boston
734-753-4586
Location: Wayne County
Hours: 10 a.m.–dark, October
Activities: U-pick pumpkins, hayrides, pony rides, petting farm

Quality Dairy Cider Mill

500 East Saginaw Street, Lansing
517-487-4635

Location: Ingham County
Hours: Daily, September–October 31
Activities: Cider mill

Rapp Orchard

63545 Van Dyke, Romeo
810-752-2117

Location: Macomb County
Hours: 8:30 a.m.–6 p.m. daily, early July (cherries) and October (pumpkins). Store hours: 8:30 a.m.–7 p.m., daily, July–October. Closes at 6 p.m., daily, November–June.
Activities: U-pick cherries and pumpkins, farm store

Rochester Cider Mill

1525 Rochester Road, Rochester
248-651-4224

Location: Oakland County
Hours: 9 a.m.–6 p.m., daily, September–November. 9 a.m.–5 p.m., weekends, after Thanksgiving–New Year's Eve.
Activities: Group tours available. Cider press and donut-making demonstrations, petting farm, antique tools and farm equipment on display, farm store with caramel apples, candy, apples, and other fall goodies.

Rowe's Produce Farm

10570 Martz Road, Ypsilanti
734-482-8538
Location: Washtenaw County
Hours: June: 7 a.m.–8 p.m., daily. July–September: 8 a.m.–7 p.m., Monday–Saturday. 8 a.m.–6 p.m., Sunday.
Activities: U-pick strawberries, raspberries, beans, and tomatoes, farm market

Spicer Orchards Farm Market and Cider Mill

10411 Clyde Road, Fenton
810-632-7692

Location: Livingston County
Hours: U-pick and farm store: 8 a.m.–6 p.m., daily, June–November. 9 a.m.–6 p.m., daily, rest of year.
Activities: U-pick strawberries, cherries, blueberries, raspberries, asparagus, apples, and pumpkins, farm market, country craft store, cider mill,

wagon rides, cider and donut-making demonstrations, kids' crafts, petting farm

Stony Creek Orchard and Cider Mill

2961 West Thirty-Two Mile Road, Romeo
810-752-2453

Location: Macomb County
Hours: 9 a.m.–6 p.m., daily, early September–Christmas. 9:30 a.m.–5:30 p.m., Wednesday–Sunday, January–March.
Activities: U-pick apples, pumpkins, wagon rides, farm market with cider, donuts, jams

Sweet Seasons Orchards

15787 Allman Road, Concord
517-524-8535

Location: Jackson County
Hours: 10 a.m.–6 p.m. daily, September 1–Christmas Eve
Activities: Cider mill, donuts, goodies

Trabbic Farms Pumpkin Patch

1560 East Sterns Road, Erie
734-848-4049
Location: Monroe County
Hours: 10 a.m.–7 p.m., daily during October.
Activities: U-pick pumpkins

Uncle John's Cider Mill

8614 North US-27 Street, St. Johns
517-224-3686
Location: Clinton County (30 minutes north of Lansing)
Hours: 9 a.m.–8 p.m., daily, September and October. 9 a.m.–6 p.m., daily, rest of year
Activities: During the fall harvest season, u-pick pumpkins, cider-press demonstration, gift shop, baked goods, apples, wagon rides, Halloween family fun house, weekend bands and craft and car shows, petting farm, and train rides. Holiday gift items, November–December.

Upland Hills Farms
481 Lake George Road, Oxford
248-628-1611

Location: Oakland County
Hours: Pumpkin Festival: 10 a.m.–5 p.m.,
Saturday and Sunday, October
Activities: Pumpkin Festival: Hayride, u-pick
pumpkins, playground, haunted house, petting
farm, pony rides, country store, fall goodies

Verellen Orchards and Cider Mill
63260 Van Dyke, Romeo
810-752-2989

Location: Macomb County
Hours: 8 a.m.–7 p.m. Monday–Saturday; 8 a.m.–6
p.m., Sunday, year-round
Activities: U-pick strawberries, cherries, already
picked apples, farm market, cider and donuts

Wasem Fruit Farm
6580 Judd Road, Augusta Township
734-482-2342

Location: Washtenaw County
Hours: 9 a.m.–6 p.m., daily, September–Halloween
Activities: U-pick apples and pumpkins, cider mill,
farm market, group tours

Weier's Cider Mill
603 West Thirteenth Street, Monroe
734-242-7396

Location: Monroe County
Hours: 8 a.m.–5 p.m., Monday–Friday, September–mid-November
Activities: Cider mill

Westview Orchards and Cider Mill of Romeo
65075 Van Dyke, Romeo
810-752-3123

Location: Macomb County
Hours: 8 a.m.–7 p.m., daily, depending on season

Activities: U-pick cherries, apples, raspberries, and pumpkins, cider mill, farm market, group tours

Wiard's Orchards

5565 Merritt Road, Ypsilanti
734-482-7744

Location: Washtenaw County
Hours: 9 a.m.–6 p.m., daily, May–November. Country Fair: Saturday and Sunday, September–October. Christmas trees, Saturday and Sunday, December.
Activities: U-pick strawberries, cherries, peaches, pears, apples, pumpkins, Christmas trees, country store with seasonal goodies, and fall cider press demonstrations. Country Fair weekends in September and October feature haunted houses, petting farm, craft booths, entertainment, train, pony and wagon rides.

William Lutz

11030 Macon Road, Saline
734-429-5145

Location: Washtenaw County
Hours: Dawn–dusk, 9 days during October, for those who pay one fee to "rent-a-tree" and then are welcome to all the apples that the tree produces. The last Sunday in October is open to the public for a final "clean sweep" of the orchards. Apples then are priced by the bushel.
Activities: Rent-a-tree program

Windy Ridge Orchard and Cider Mill

9375 Saline-Milan Road, Saline
734-429-7111

Location: Washtenaw County
Hours: 10 a.m.–6 p.m., Thursday–Sunday, weekend after Labor Day–weekend after Halloween. Reopen during Christmas season for trees.
Activities: U-pick pumpkins, Christmas trees, hayrides, cider and donuts, retail apples, antiques, bakery, petting animals

Wolcott Orchards

3284 West Coldwater Road, Mt. Morris
810-789-9561

Location: Genesee County
Hours: 9 a.m.–5 p.m., daily, year-round. Closed July.
Activities: During the fall season, apples, cider-press demonstration, bakery, gift shop, weekend hayrides. Group tours available. Apple Festival last full weekend in September.

Yates Cider Mill

1990 East Avon Road, Rochester
248-651-8300

Location: Oakland County
Hours: 9 a.m.–7 p.m., daily, late August–October. 9 a.m.–5 p.m., daily, November.
Activities: Group tours available weekdays for a minimum charge. Cider-press demonstration, donuts, apples, pies and seasonal foods, fudge shop, picnic area, water wheel, trails.

Zabinsky Blueberry Farm

11024 Beach Road, Dexter
734-426-2900

Location: Washtenaw County
Hours: 8 a.m.–8 p.m., late-July–Labor Day
Activities: U-pick blueberries

Quick-Look Lists

During the spring, summer, and fall, Michigan's farms are bursting with vegetables, berries, apples, pumpkins, and cider. Here is a listing of u-pick farms and cider mills arranged to help you see at a glance which farms offer which crops. Often, farms close or change their u-pick policy depending on that season's weather conditions. PLEASE CALL AHEAD TO VERIFY HOURS AND LOCATION.

U-PICK SUMMER FRUITS

Strawberries

Season: Mid-June–early July

Blake's Almont Farm, Almont. 810-798-3251.

Blake's Big Apple Orchard, Armada. 810-784-9710.

Blake's Orchard and Cider Mill, Armada.
810-784-5343.

Coon Creek Orchard, Armada. 810-784-5062.

DeGroot's Strawberries, Gregory. 517-223-9311.

Deneweth's Pick Your Own Strawberry Farms,
Shelby Township. 810-247-5533.

Long Family Farm and Orchard, Commerce
Township. 248-360-3774.

Middleton Berry Farm, Oakland. 248-693-6018.

Miller's Big Red, Washington. 810-752-7888.

Potter Farm, Willis. 734-461-6348.

Rowe's Produce Farm, Ypsilanti. 734-482-8538.

Spicer Orchards Farm Market and Cider Mill,
Fenton. 810-632-7692.

Verellen Orchards, Romeo. 810-752-2989.

Wiard's Orchards, Ypsilanti. 734-482-7744.

Blackberries and raspberries

Season: Early July–early August

Blake's Big Apple Orchard, Armada. 810-784-9710.

Blake's Orchard and Cider Mill, Armada.
810-784-5343.

Coon Creek Orchard, Armada. 810-784-5062.

Driver's Berry Farm, South Lyon. 248-437-1606.

Middleton Berry Farm, Oakland. 248-693-6018.

Cherries

*Season: Early July–early August for sweet and
sour cherries*

Blake's Almont Farm, Almont. 810-798-3251.

Blake's Big Apple Orchard, Armada. 810-784-9710.

Blake's Orchard and Cider Mill, Armada.
810-784-5343.

Brookwood Fruit Farm, Almont. 810-798-8312.

Coon Creek Orchard, Armada. 810-784-5062.

Long Family Orchard and Farm, Croswell. 810-360-3774.

Rapp Orchard, Romeo. 810-752-2117.

Spicer Orchards Farm Market and Cider Mill, Fenton. 810-632-7692.

Verellen Orchards, Romeo. 810-752-2989.

Westview Orchards and Cider Mill of Romeo, Romeo. 810-752-3123.

Wiard's Orchards, Ypsilanti. 734-482-7744.

Blueberries

Season: Mid-July–mid-August

Driver's Berry Farm, South Lyon. 248-437-1606.

Erie Orchards, Erie. 734-848-4518.

Jeffery's Blueberries, Avoca. 810-324-2874.

Montrose Orchards, Montrose. 810-639-6971.

Spicer Orchard Farm Market and Cider Mill, Fenton. 810-632-7692.

Zabinsky Blueberry Farm, Dexter. 734-426-2900.

Peaches

Season: August–September

Blake's Big Apple Orchard, Armada. 810-784-9710.

Blake's Orchard and Cider Mill, Armada. 810-784-5343.

Brookwood Fruit Farm, Almont. 810-798-8312.

Coon Creek Orchard, Armada. 810-784-5062.

Erie Orchards, Erie. 734-848-4518.

Wiard's Orchards, Ypsilanti. 734-482-7744.

Pears

Season: August–September

Blake's Big Apple Orchard, Armada. 810-784-9710.

Blake's Orchard and Cider Mill, Armada. 810-784-5343.

Coon Creek Orchard, Armada. 810-784-5062.

Wiard's Orchards, Ypsilanti. 734-482-7744.

Fall Raspberries

Season: Late August–October

Blake's Almont Farm, Almont. 810-798-3251.

Blake's Big Apple Orchard, Armada. 810-784-9710.

Blake's Orchard and Cider Mill, Armada.
810-784-5343.

Brookwood Fruit Farm, Almont. 810-798-8312.

Coon Creek Orchard, Armada. 810-784-5062.

Driver's Berry Farm, South Lyon. 248-437-1606.

Makielski Berry Farm, Ypsilanti. 734-572-0060.

Middleton Berry Farm, Oakland. 248-693-6018.

Miller's Big Red, Washington. 810-752-7888.

Rowe's Produce Farm, Ypsilanti. 734-482-8538.

Spicer Orchards Farm Market and Cider Mill,
Fenton. 810-632-7692.

Westview Orchards and Cider Mill of Romeo,
Romeo. 810-752-3123.

U-Pick Apples

Season: Late August–November

Apple Charlie's and South Huron Orchard and
Cider Mill, New Boston. 734-753-9380.

Blake's Almont Farm, Almont. 810-798-3251.

Blake's Big Apple Orchard, Armada. 810-784-9710.

Blake's Orchard and Cider Mill, Armada.
810-784-5343.

Brookwood Fruit Farm, Almont. 810-798-8312.

Coon Creek Orchard, Armada. 810-784-5062.

Davies Orchard and Cider Mill, New Boston.
734-654-8893.

Erie Orchards, Erie. 734-848-4518.

Erwin Orchards, South Lyon. 248-437-4701.

Hy's Cider Mill, Romeo. 810-798-3611.

Miller's Big Red, Washington. 810-752-7888.

Obstbaum Orchards and Cider Mill,
Salem Township. 248-349-5569.

Spicer Orchards Farm Market and Cider Mill,
Fenton. 810-632-7692.

Stony Creek Orchard and Cider Mill, Romeo.
810-752-2453.

Wasem Fruit Farm, Augusta Township.
734-482-2342.

Westview Orchards and Cider Mill of Romeo,
Romeo. 810-752-3123.

Wiard's Orchards, Ypsilanti. 734-482-7744.

William Lutz, Saline. 734-429-5145.

U-Pick Pumpkins

Season: October

Blake's Big Apple Orchard, Armada. 810-784-9710.

Blake's Orchard and Cider Mill, Armada.
810-784-5343.

Coon Creek Orchard, Armada. 810-784-5062.

Davies Orchard and Cider Mill, New Boston.
734-654-8893.

Diehl's Orchard, Holly. 248-634-8981.

Driver's Berry Farm, South Lyon. 248-437-1606.

Erie Orchards, Erie. 734-848-4518.

Erwin Orchards, South Lyon. 248-437-4701.

Kensington Metropark Farm Center, Milford.
248-685-1561.

Long Family Orchard and Farm, Commerce
Township. 248-360-3774.

Mary's Farm Market, Canton Township.
734-981-2866.

Meyer's Farm, Northville. 248-349-0289.

Middleton Berry Farm, Oakland. 248-693-6018.

Miller's Big Red, Washington. 810-752-7888.

Montrose Orchards, Montrose. 810-639-6971.

Oak Haven Farm, Ortonville. 248-634-5437.

Plymouth Orchards and Cider Mill, Plymouth.
734-455-2290.

Pumpkin Factory, Belleville. 734-461-1835.

Pumpkin Patch, New Boston, 734-753-4586.

Rapp Orchards, Romeo. 810-752-2117.

Spicer Orchards Farm Market and Cider Mill,
Fenton. 810-632-7692.

Stony Creek Orchard and Cider Mill, Romeo.
810-752-2453.

Trabbic Farms Pumpkin Patch, Erie. 734-848-4049.

Uncle John's Cider Mill, St. Johns. 517-224-3686.

Upland Hills Farms, Oxford. 248-628-1611.

Wasem Fruit Farm, Augusta Township.
734-482-2342.

Westview Orchards and Cider Mill of Romeo,
   Romeo. 810-752-3123.

Wiard's Orchards, Ypsilanti. 734-482-7744.

Windy Ridge Orchard and Cider Mill, Saline.
   734-429-7111.

Cider Mills

Season: Late August–December

Almar Orchards, Flushing. 810-659-6568.

Apple Charlie's and South Huron Orchard and
   Cider Mill, New Boston. 734-753-9380.

Ashton Orchards and Cider Mill, Ortonville.
   248-627-6671.

Beck's Cider Mill, St. Johns. 517-224-4309.

Blake's Orchard and Cider Mill, Armada.
   810-784-5343.

Coon Creek Orchard, Armada. 810-784-5062.

Crossroads Village Cider Mill, Flint. 810-736-7100.

Dexter Cider Mill, Dexter. 734-426-8531.

Diehl's Orchard and Cider Mill, Holly.
   248-634-8981.

Erie Orchards, Erie. 734-848-4518.

Franklin Cider Mill, Franklin. 248-626-2968.

Hy's Cider Mill, Romeo. 810-798-3611.

Koan's Orchards, Flushing. 810-659-8720.

McCarron's Orchard, Flushing. 810-659-3813.

Middleton Cider Mill, Utica. 810-731-6699.

Miller's Big Red, Romeo. 810-752-7888.

Montrose Orchards, Montrose. 810-639-6971.

Obstbaum Orchards and Cider Mill,
   Salem Township. 248-349-5569.

Paint Creek Cider Mill, Rochester. 248-651-8361.

Pankiewicz Farms Cider Mill, Casco. 810-727-9051.

Parmenter's Northville Cider Mill, Northville.
   248-349-3181.

Parshallville Cider Mill, Fenton. 810-629-9079.

Plymouth Orchards and Cider Mill, Plymouth.
   734-455-2290.

Porters Orchard and Cider Mill, Goodrich.
   810-636-7156.

Quality Dairy Cider Mill, Lansing. 517-487-4635.

Rochester Cider Mill, Rochester. 248-651-4224.

Spicer Orchards Farm Market and Cider Mill,
   Fenton. 810-632-7692.

Stony Creek Orchard and Cider Mill, Romeo.
 810-752-2453.

Sweet Seasons Orchard, Concord. 517-524-8535.

Uncle John's Cider Mill, St. Johns. 517-224-3686.

Verellen Orchards and Cider Mill, Romeo.
 810-752-2989.

Wasem Fruit Farm, Ypsilanti. 734-482-2342.

Weier's Cider Mill, Monroe. 734-242-7396.

Westview Orchards and Cider Mill of Romeo,
 Romeo. 810-752-3123.

Wiard's Orchards, Ypsilanti. 734-482-7744.

Windy Ridge Orchard and Cider Mill, Saline.
 734-429-7111.

Wolcott Orchards, Mt. Morris. 810-789-9561.

Yates Cider Mill, Rochester. 248-651-8301.

U-Pick Vegetables

Season: All summer

Blake's Orchard and Cider Mill, Armada.
 810-784-5343.

Long Family Orchard, Commerce Township.
 248-360-3774.

Middleton Berry Farm, Oakland. 248-693-6018.

Navarre Strawberry Farm, Monroe. 734-241-0723.

Rowe's Produce Farm, Ypsilanti. 734-482-8538.

Spicer Orchards Farm Market and Cider Mill,
 Fenton. 810-632-7692.

U-Pick Christmas Trees

The abundance of Christmas tree farms in Southern Lower Michigan makes it easy for families to pick and cut their own tree. Many farms also offer a variety of holiday attractions, including horse-drawn wagon rides, visits with Santa, craft shops, and refreshments. So start a new family tradition. Dress warmly; bring a saw in case the farm doesn't supply one; bring twine to secure the tree to your car; and don't forget to bring along your camera. Most Christmas tree farms open Thanksgiving weekend and stay open through Christmas Eve, but call ahead to be sure trees are still available.

Arend Tree Farms, 3512 Notten Road, Grass
 Lake. 734-475-7584.

Arend Tree Farms 2 & 3, 12870 South M-50, Brooklyn. 517-592-2006.

Asplin Farms, 12190 Miller Road, Lennon. 810-621-4780.

Blake's Big Apple Orchard, 71485 North Avenue, Armada. 810-784-9710.

Blake's Orchard and Cider Mill, 17985 Armada Center Road, Armada. 810-784-5343.

Boughan's Tree Farm #1, 15851 Martinsville Road, Belleville. 734-697-9600.

Boughan's Tree Farm #2, 44020 Hull Road, Belleville. 734-699-6483.

Broadview Christmas Tree Farm, 4380 Hickory Ridge Road, Highland. 248-887-8733.

Candy Cane Christmas Tree Farm #1, 4780 Seymour Lake Road, Oxford. 248-628-8899.

Candy Cane Christmas Tree Farm #2, 2401 Farnsworth Road, Lapeer. 248-628-8899.

Chaprnka Tree Farm, 10421 West Coldwater Road, Flushing. 810-659-9329.

Coldsprings Farm, 4250 Park Lake Drive, Dexter. 734-475-7584.

Croswell Berry Farm, Croswell. 810-679-3273.

Erie Orchards, 1235 Erie Road, Erie. 734-848-4518.

Fodor's Christmas Tree Farm, 3738 Burtch Road, Grass Lake. 517-522-4982.

Green Tee, 2233 Oakville Waltz Road, New Boston. 734-654-6427.

Hillside Farm, 4714 U.S. 12, Tipton. 313-274-0681.

Howell Nature Center, 1005 Triangle Lake Road, Howell. 517-546-0249.

Huff Tree Farm, 1500 West Wardlow, Highland. 248-887-4230.

Huron Christmas Farm, 32100 King Road, New Boston. 734-753-9288.

Kelley's Frosty Pines, 7600 Hitchcock Road, White Lake. 248-698-1674.

Marlin Bliss Tree Farm, 13437 Todd Road, Ida. 734-269-2346.

Matthes Evergreen Farm, 13416 Lulu Road, Ida. 734-269-6244.

Mosher Tree Farm, 7155 North Territorial Road, Dexter. 734-426-5271.

Opper-Land Pines, 59500 Frost, New Haven. 810-749-9888.

Pleasant Knoll Tree Farm, 3080 Oak Grove Road, Howell. 517-546-2954.

Ruby Tree Farm, 6567 Imlay City Road, Ruby. 810-324-2662.

Runyan's Country Tree Farm, 10235 Webster Road, Clio. 810-687-2476.

Skyhorse Station Evergreen Plantation, 11000 Roberts Road, Stockbridge. 517-851-7017.

Smiths Farm, 7242 East Mt. Morris Road, Otisville. 810-653-6187.

Summer Gardens, 77033 Van Dyke, Romeo. 810-752-7379.

Sun Tree Farms, 3640 Judd Road, Saline. 734-429-3666.

Thornhollow Tree Farm, 44387 Hull Road, Belleville. 734-699-3709.

Tollander Tree Farm #1, Bryce Road between Rabidue and Cribbins Roads, Port Huron. 810-985-8951.

Tollander Tree Farm #2, 7747 Imlay City Road, Port Huron. 810-985-8951.

Tollander Tree Farm #3, 5680 Griswold Road, Port Huron. 810-985-8951.

Trim Pines Farm, 4357 East Baldwin, Grand Blanc. 810-694-9958.

Waldock Tree Farm, 3090 Dutcher, Howell. 517-546-3890.

Warren's Tree Farm, 8366 Spicer Road, Brighton. 810-231-4335.

Wiard's Orchards, Ypsilanti. 734-482-7744.

Windy Ridge Orchard and Cider Mill, 9375 Saline-Milan Road, Saline. 734-429-7111.

9
Parks

TIP

Keep a "picnic bag" with blanket, plastic tablecloth, napkins, cups, plates, and cutlery in your car just in case you and the kids are in the mood for an impromptu picnic.

Beaches, picnic tables, creative playgrounds, and wild water slides—the map of southeastern lower Michigan is dotted with city, county, state, and national parks. The Detroit Parks and Recreation Department operates over 200 neighborhood parks and play lots, including Belle Isle and the riverfront parks. The Huron-Clinton Metropolitan Authority operates 13 popular metroparks offering a wide range of seasonal activities from nature centers and beaches to boat ramps and toboggan runs.

Macomb County's Freedom Hill is an outdoor concert and festival site; Oakland County's eight developed parks offer wave-action pools, beaches, a refrigerated toboggan run, and cross-country skiing. Wayne County's six parks criss-cross the county, offering boating, hiking, a nature interpretive center, picnicking, a water park, and special events. The Michigan State Department of National Resources oversees parks offering family beaches, horseback riding, and a petting farm. There are also Windsor City Parks, Canadian National Parks, and Ann Arbor-area and Lansing-area parks within a short drive.

This chapter also includes a sampling of unusual parks and water parks. Be sure to check your city's parks and recreation department for a catalog of seasonal activities, classes, family events, vacation camps, sports leagues, and neighborhood parks. Many area programs also offer activities for children with disabilities.

Detroit Parks

For general information and location of city playgrounds and play lots, call 313-224-1100. Here is a sampling of Detroit's best family parks.

Belle Isle

313-852-4075

Location: East Jefferson at Grand Boulevard, 2½ miles east of the RenCen
Hours: Grounds are open 24 hours, daily. All buildings are open year-round. Food concessions and the zoo are open April–October. Check individual listings for specific hours of buildings.
Admission: All facilities charge a nominal fee.

Facilities: Playscape—a creative playground, waterslides and beach, Aquarium, Dossin Great Lakes Museum, Nature Center, Anna Scripps Whitcomb Conservatory, Zoo, covered picnic area, and golf course.

You'll see the giant slide as you drive across the bridge onto the island. It's part of Playscape, an imaginative playground made up of timbers of all sizes and shapes, a fireman's pole, tree house, suspended bridge, tire swings, and other play equipment. Visit Belle Isle just for this playground—open all year—or be sure to leave time at the end of your visit to the other sites. During the summer, have a cool thrill riding down the water slides. Your kids won't want to leave unless you promise they'll be back soon.

Chene Park

2600 East Atwater, Detroit
313-393-0292

Location: Along the Detroit River between Chene and DuBois Streets, just east of the RenCen
Hours: Outdoor amphitheater offers a summer season of concerts and programs
Admission: Price varies with event
Facilities: Outdoor amphitheater hill in the summer.

Hart Plaza

313-877-8077

Location: Jefferson Avenue, along the Detroit River, just west of the RenCen
Hours: Always open
Admission: Free
Facilities: Outdoor plaza, Noguchi fountain, benches, walkway along the river, summertime food concessions, wintertime ice-skating

Hart Plaza epitomizes summertime in the city. It's home to the ethnic festivals each summer weekend from May to Labor Day, Freedom Festival activities during the July Fourth weekend, and the Montreux Jazz Festival in early September. Even on a day without a festival, the plaza is busy and lively. Kids will enjoy running around the Noguchi fountain's "shower" and walking along the river, watching for barges. During the winter, families can ice-skate on a large outdoor rink.

St. Aubin Park

1930 East Atwater, Detroit
313-259-4677

Location: Atwater and St. Aubin, along the Detroit River, just east of the RenCen
Hours: Always open
Admission: Free
Facilities: Creative play area, marina, picnic areas, river overlooks, bicycle paths, and walkways

This riverfront family park offers an imaginative, marine-inspired children's playground and the dock for the Diamond Jack, a narrated boat cruise.

Huron-Clinton Metroparks

Thirteen metroparks, with over 23,480 acres of parkland, offer a wide variety of recreation for residents of Livingston, Oakland, Macomb, and Wayne counties. The parks are open year-round, but call ahead; hours may vary from park to park and for different activities and seasons. Young children enjoy the "tot lots," fantasy playground villages located at the following metroparks: Hudson Mills, Indian Springs, Lake Erie, Lower Huron, Metro Beach, and Willow. Families also enjoy visiting the well-staffed, hands-on nature centers located at Indian Springs, Kensington (which also has a farm center), Lake Erie, Metro Beach, Oakwoods, and Stony Creek. Wolcott Mill Metropark now boasts two sites, one a historic grist mill, the other a Farm Learning Center.

Vehicle permits are required ($2 weekdays, Wednesdays are free; $3 weekends and holidays; $15 annual, $8 senior citizen annual). Huron-Clinton Metropolitan Authority is located at 13000 High Ridge Drive, Brighton. For toll-free information, call 1-800-47-PARKS. Cross-country ski/golf information, 1-800-234-6534. Website, www.metroparks.com

Delhi Metropark

East Delhi Road, Ann Arbor
Call Hudson Mills Metropark for information
734-426-8211
1-800-477-3191

Fifty-acre park along the Huron River, five miles northwest of Ann Arbor. Picnic sites with shelters and stoves, playfields, creative playscape, fishing sites, swings, and slides. Canoe rentals available May–September. Call Skip's Canoe Livery, 734-769-8686.

Dexter-Huron Metropark

Huron River Drive, Dexter
Call Hudson Mills Metropark for information,
734-426-8211
1-800-477-3191

A riverside park with 122 acres, 7 1/2 miles northwest of Ann Arbor. Shady picnic sites with tables and stoves, swings, slides, playfields, and fishing sites.

Hudson Mills Metropark

8801 North Territorial Road, Dexter
734-426-8211
1-800-477-3191

A multi-purpose park of 1,504 acres, located 12 miles northwest of Ann Arbor, on North Territorial Road at the crossing of the Huron River. Picnic sites, swings, slides, tot lot, playing fields, hike-bike trail, nature trail, fishing. 18-hole disc golf course and 18-hole golf course. The Activity Center has food service, tennis, basketball and shuffleboard courts, softball diamond, and, during the summer, bicycle rental. During the winter, the Activity Center offers ski rental, indoor food service, and cross-country ski trails.

Huron Meadows Metropark

8765 Hammel Road, Brighton
810-231-4084
1-800-477-3193

A 1,540-acre park, located six miles south of Brighton. Picnic sites and Golf Center building with food service, driving range, and 18-hole golf course. During the winter, there is cross-country skiing and ski rental.

Indian Springs Metropark

5200 Indian Trail, White Lake
248-625-7280
1-800-477-3192

A 2,232-acre park located near Clarkston, nine miles northwest of Pontiac. A six-mile bike-hike trail, picnic sites, 18-hole golf course, tot lot, nature trails and center, and cross-country skiing.

Kensington Metropark

2240 West Buno Road, Milford
248-685-1561
1-800-477-3178

This 4,337-acre multi-purpose park, located near Milford and Brighton, offers summertime boat rental, 18-hole golf course, bike-hike trail, picnic sites, fishing sites, the Island Queen—a 66-passenger sternwheeler, boat launches, two beaches with bathhouses, heated showers, playgrounds, and food service. The Farm Center (including hay/sleigh rides and food service) and Nature Center are open year-round. During the winter, the park offers cross-country ski trails and rentals, ice-skating, tobogganing, and sledding.

Lake Erie Metropark

32481 West Jefferson, Rockwood
734-379-5020
1-800-477-3189

A 1,600-acre park located in Brownstown Township between Gibraltar and Rockwood, along Lake Erie. During the summer, the park offers picnic sites, wooden playscape, tot lot, volleyball and basketball courts, 18-hole golf course, marina and boat launch, and entertainment. The "Great Wave," a large wave-action pool with bathhouse, food service building, and wet shop, is open 9:30 a.m.–8 p.m., daily, Memorial Day–Labor Day. Cross-country skiing, rental, and ice-skating during the winter. The Marshlands Museum and Nature Center is open year-round.

Lower Huron Metropark

17845 Savage Road, Belleville
734-697-9181
1-800-477-3182

A 1,237-acre park located along the Huron River near Belleville, with shore fishing, picnic-playfield sites, 18-hole golf course, tot lot, bike-hike trail, nature trails, tennis, basketball, and volleyball courts, and horseshoe equipment. The swimming pool with water slide, bathhouse, and food service is open 9:30 a.m.–7 p.m., weekdays; 10:30 a.m.–8 p.m., weekends and holidays, Memorial Day–Labor Day. Winter facilities include cross-country ski trails and three ice rinks.

Metro Beach Metropark

31300 Metropolitan Parkway, Mount Clemens
810-463-4581
1-800-477-3172

A 770-acre park located along Lake St. Clair, five miles southeast of Mount Clemens. Summer facilities include Olympic-size outdoor swimming pool with one-flume water slide, miniature Adventure Golf, 18-hole golf course, shuffleboard, horseshoe and tennis courts, beach, boat ramp, beach shop, food service, voyageur canoe tours, trackless train, and picnic sites. Pool hours: 10 a.m.–6 p.m., weekdays. 10 a.m.–dusk, weekends and holidays, Memorial Day–Labor Day. A nature center, bike-hike trails, and tot lot village are open all year. Cross-country ski trails, ice-skating, and ice-fishing are available during winter.

Oakwoods Metropark

Willow Road, Flat Rock
734-782-3956
1-800-477-3182

A 1,719-acre park located five miles northeast of Flat Rock and adjacent to Willow Metropark offers a nature center, interpretive trails, bike and roller blade trails, voyageur canoe tours, picnic sites, and cross-country skiing.

Stony Creek Metropark

4300 Main Park Road, Washington
810-781-4242
1-800-477-7756

A 4,461-acre park located six miles north of Utica and northeast of Rochester. Two beaches with bathhouses, heated showers, food service, picnic sites, swings and slides, bike-hike trails, bike rentals, 18-hole golf course, boat launching, voyageur canoe tours, sailboard rental and lessons, nature trails, and nature center. During winter, cross-country skiing and rental, ice-fishing, ice-skating, and toboggan hills.

Willow Metropark

South Huron, Huron Township
734-697-9181 (Lower Huron Metropark)
1-800-477-3182

A 1,531-acre park located between Flat Rock and New Boston offers shuffleboard, tennis and basketball courts, food service, playfields, bike-hike trail, 18-hole golf course, bike and boat rental, and picnic sites with tables and stoves. The large tot lot is open April–October. The Olympic-size swimming pool is open 9:30 a.m.–7 p.m., weekdays; 10:30 a.m.–8 p.m., weekends and holidays, Memorial Day–Labor Day. Winter facilities include cross-country ski trails and rental, snack bar, ice-skating, and sledding hill.

Wolcott Mill Metropark

63841 Wolcott Road, Ray Township
810-749-5997
1-800-477-3175

A 2,380-acre park located along the banks of the north branch of the Clinton River, between Twenty-Six and Thirty-One Mile Roads in Macomb County. The park includes a 150-year-old gristmill open to the public 10 a.m.–5 p.m., Monday–Friday. 10 a.m.–7 p.m., Saturday and Sunday, May–October. 10 a.m.–5 p.m., daily, April and November. Call for group tours.

Wolcott Mill Farm Learning Center

65775 Wolcott Road, Ray Township
810-752-5932
810-749-5997 (group tours)

A working farm located off Wolcott Road, about
1.5 miles north of 29 Mile Road, southeast of
Romeo. Offers fall hayrides and Sudan grass maze,
year-round tours and classes, and holiday and seasonal family events. 9 a.m.–5 p.m., daily, open to
the public. 9 a.m.–5 p.m. Tuesday–Friday for group
tours. Milking demonstrations, 10 a.m., daily.

Lansing-Area Parks

Fitzgerald Park

133 Fitzgerald Park Drive, Grand Ledge
517-627-7351

The 76-acre park is most famous for its 300-mil-
lion-year-old rock formations that jut majestically
from the shore of the Grand River. 60-foot sandstone ledges provide brave rock climbers a chance
to try the sport. The park also offers picnicking, fishing, canoeing and canoe rentals, cross-country skiing, recreation game area, and naturalist services.

Frances Park

2600 Moores River Drive, Lansing
517-483-4277

The park features a formal rose garden with
150 varieties of roses, woodland trail, and two
overlooks onto the Grand River.

Lake Lansing

Marsh Road and Lake Drive, Haslett
517-676-2233

Seven miles from downtown Lansing. Lake
Lansing Park-South offers a beach with supervised
swimming, snack bar-bathhouse, picnic grounds
and shelters, volleyball and shuffleboard courts,
horseshoes, pedal boat livery, and creative play-

ground with "tyke track" for toddlers. Lake Lansing Park-North offers picnic areas and shelters, playgrounds, volleyball and basketball courts, horseshoes, ball field, and hiking and cross-country ski trails. Lake Lansing Boat Launch provides private boat owners access to lake.

Louis F. Adado Riverfront Park and River Trail

300 North Grand Avenue, Lansing
517-483-4277

Riverside Park is home to many of Lansing's festivals, including Labor Day's Riverfest. River Trail offers six miles of paved scenic walkway along the Grand and Red Cedar Rivers. Things to see along the walk include the Turner-Dodge House, Potter Park Zoo, and the Brenke River Sculpture and Fish Ladder, where spawning salmon and steelhead fight their way upstream during September.

Washington Park

2516 South Washington Avenue, Lansing
517-483-4277

This city-center park offers lighted tennis courts and, during winter, an outdoor ice-skating rink.

Macomb County Parks and Recreation

Freedom Hill County Park

15000 Metroparkway, Sterling Heights
810-979-7010

This 100-acre park, located on Metroparkway (Sixteen Mile) between Utica and Schoenherr Roads, offers an open-air amphitheater, bandstand, covered pavilions, picnic areas, basketball and volleyball courts, tot lot, hike and bike trails, BMX track, radio-controlled race car and truck track, and conference/banquet facilities. During the summer, Freedom Hill is busy with weekend festivals and weekday evening outdoor movies.

Michigan State Parks

Michigan state parks dot the map offering sandy beaches, forest trails, and recreation facilities. Parks are open 8 a.m.–10 p.m., daily, year-round. Vehicle permits are required ($4 daily, $20 annual, $5 annual for seniors). Administrative offices are located in Lansing. Michigan State Parks: 517-373-9900. For camping reservations, call 1-800-44-PARKS. Here is a sampling of popular parks in southeastern lower Michigan. Website: www.dnr.state.mi.us

Bald Mountain Recreation Area

1330 East Greenshield Road, Lake Orion
248-693-6767
248-814-9193 (gun range)

This 4,637-acre park offers picnic sites, playground, beach, beach house and concession, boat rental, gun range, hiking and cross-country skiing trails.

Dodge No. 4 State Park

4250 Parkway, Waterford
248-666-1020

A 139-acre park located off Cass Elizabeth Lake Road offering picnic sites, playground, beach, beach house and concession, boat rental, riding stable, gun range, cross-country ski and snow mobile trails, and ice-skating.

Highland Recreation Area

5200 East Highland Road, White Lake
248-889-3750

This 5,524-acre park offers picnic sites, playground, beach, beach house, camping sites, bridle paths, cross-country ski trails, riding stable, and walking trails.

Holly Recreation Area

8100 Grange Hall Road, Holly (offices)
248-634-9751

This 8,000-acre park, located east of exit 101 off I-75 North, offers campgrounds, including two mini-cabins sleeping four, and a log cabin for six. In addition, there are beaches and hiking and cross-country ski trails.

Island Lake Recreation Area

12950 East Grand River, Brighton
810-229-7067

This 3,466-acre park offers picnic sites, canoe rental, playground, beach, beach house, concession, and bike trails.

Lakeport State Park

7605 Lakeshore Road, Lakeport
810-327-6224

A 565-acre park along Lake Huron offering picnic sites, playground, beach, beach house, and concession.

Maybury State Park

20145 Beck Road, Northville
248-349-8390

This 944-acre park offers picnic sites, bike/hike trails, paved mountain bike trail, petting farm, cross-country ski rental and trails, playscape, fishing pond, horse trails, and riding stables.

Ortonville Recreation Area

5779 Hadley Road, Ortonville
248-627-3828

Beaches, hiking, boating, picnic areas, cabins, camping, gun range.

Pontiac Lake Recreation Area

7800 Gale Road, Pontiac
248-666-1020

A 3,700-acre park with camping, and picnic sites, playground, beach, beach house and concession, archery range, horse trails and riding stables.

Proud Lake Recreation Area

3500 Wixom Road, Milford
248-685-2433

A 3,614-acre park offering hiking trails, camping and picnic sites, playground, beach, beach house, and concession.

Seven Lakes State Park

8100 Grange Hall Road, Holly (offices)
248-634-7271

Located west of exit 101 off I-75 North, Seven Lakes offers 76 modern campground sites, public beach, boat rental, hike/bike and snow mobile trails.

Sterling State Park

2800 State Park Road, Monroe
313-289-2715

This 1,000-acre park offers picnic sites, playground, beach, beach house, concession, campsites with facilities, and bike trails.

Oakland County Parks

Eight developed parks in Oakland County offer family beaches, picnic sites, boat rental, wave-action pools and water slides, nature trails, and much more. Parks are open year-round. Summer hours are 8 a.m. to one hour after sunset, daily. Winter hours are 8 a.m.–sunset, 9 a.m.–4 p.m. for golf courses, weather permitting. But call ahead; hours may vary from park to park and for different activities and facilities.

Daily vehicle pass is $5 for Oakland County residents, $8 for non-residents. Annual vehicle pass is $25 for residents, $45 for non-residents. For general information, 248-858-0906, or 1-888-OCPARKS.

Addison Oaks

1480 West Romeo Road, Leonard
248-693-2432

A 793-acre park located 9 miles north of Rochester that offers camping, swimming, picnicking, boat rental, mountain bike rental, fishing, hiking and nature trails, plus winter cross-country ski trails, ice-fishing, and ice-skating.

Glen Oaks

30500 Thirteen Mile Road, Farmington Hills
248-851-8356

This 18-hole golf course, located between Orchard Lake and Middlebelt Roads, offers banquet facilities and, during the winter, cross-country skiing.

Groveland Oaks

5990 Grange Hall Road, Holly
248-634-9811

The 360-acre park located at Dixie Highway and Grange Hall Road offers a sandy beach, swimming lake, a large, imaginative playscape, and a flume water slide that splashes into Stewart Lake. There are also camping, picnicking, and boat and coaster bike rentals.

Independence Oaks

9501 Sashabaw Road, Clarkston
248-625-0877

This 1,062-acre park located on Sashabaw Road, 2 1/2 miles north of I-75, offers ten miles of marked nature and cross-country ski trails, a nature interpretive center, 200-seat amphitheater, boat rental, picnicking, fishing, swimming, soft ball field, volleyball court, horseshoe pit, ice-skating, cross-country ski rental and many facilities for the handicapped.

Orion Oaks

Orion Township
248-858-0906

Undeveloped park with limited access for hiking, fishing, and non-motorized boating.

Red Oaks Water Park

1455 East Thirteen Mile Road, Madison Heights
248-585-6990

Keep cool bucking the waves and whooshing around the curves in Red Oak's large wave-action pool and three water slides. Food service and inner tube and raft rental are available.

Red Oaks Golf Course

29600 John R, Madison Heights
248-541-5030

Nine-hole golf course; cross-country skiing in winter.

Springfield Oaks

12451 Andersonville Road, Davisburg
248-625-8133

The Youth Activities Center and outdoor arenas host August's annual 4-H Fair; the 18-hole golf course offers cross-country skiing in the winter, plus banquet facilities.

Waterford Oaks

1780 Scott Lake Road, Waterford
248-858-0913 (activity center)
248-858-0918 (water park)
248-858-5433 (tennis complex)
248-858-0915 (BMX track)
248-975-4440 ("The Fridge")

This 145-acre park located between Watkins and Scott Lake Roads offers a wave-action pool, giant two-flume "Slidewinder" water slides, water chute raft ride, and, for small children, a creative wet playground. Also, bicycle motorcross track; games complex with platform tennis, tennis, volleyball, shuffleboard, and horseshoe courts; activities center; picnicking; hiking trail, and from November–March, "The Fridge" a refrigerated toboggan run.

White Lake Oaks

991 South Williams Lake Road, White Lake
248-698-2700

An 18-hole golf course with cross-country skiing
and rental during the winter, plus banquet facilities.

Wayne County Parks

For exact location, activities, and hours of each
park, call the main information number, 734-261-
1990, 9 a.m.–5 p.m., weekdays. Administrative
offices are at 33175 Ann Arbor Trail, Westland,
open 8 a.m.–4:30 p.m., Monday–Friday. 8 a.m.-8
p.m., Thursday. 8 a.m.–1 p.m., Saturday. Park
grounds are open dawn to dusk daily.

Bell Creek Park and Lola Valley Park

Redford

Neighboring parks along the Bell branch of the
Rouge River, Bell Creek offers softball and baseball diamonds, soccer field, tennis courts, picnic
shelter, and play structure; Lola Valley offers natural beauty and picnic tables.

Elizabeth Park

Trenton
734-675-8051 (pony ranch)

The state's oldest county park offers softball
and baseball diamonds, tennis courts, tourist
lodge, 52-slip marina, riverwalk, handicapped fishing dock, speed-skating rink, pony and sleigh
rides, concessions, and picnic shelter.

Lower Rouge Parkway

Dearborn to Canton Township

This 12-mile parkway along three Rouge River
forks offers baseball and softball diamonds, football and soccer field, tennis courts, picnic tables,
and nature trails.

Middle Rouge Parkway

(commonly known as Edward Hines Park)
Dearborn to Northville

This 17 1/2-mile parkway along the scenic banks of the Middle Rouge River offers softball and baseball diamonds, a 17 1/2-mile bike and hike trail, bridle paths, picnicking sites and shelters, playground equipment, tennis courts, football and soccer fields, fishing, canoe, and paddleboat livery, a wooded arboretum and nature interpretive center, plus, during the winter, sledding and toboggan hills, ice-skating, and cross-country skiing. During the winter holidays, it's the home of the Wayne County Light Fest.

Warren Valley Golf Course

26116 West Warren, Dearborn Heights
313-561-1040

A 36-hole course with cross-country skiing, rental, and lessons in winter. Plus club house with banquet hall.

William P. Holliday Forest and Wildlife Preserve

Westland

Picnicking and 12 miles of marked nature trails.

Windsor City Parks and Canadian National Parks

Take a family walk through downtown Windsor's city parks and explore Canada's national parks located in Southern Ontario.

Website: www.city.windsor.on.ca/parkrec

Coventry Gardens and Peace Fountain

Two miles east of downtown Windsor on
Riverside Drive East at Pillette Road
519-253-2300

During the summer, the Peace Fountain is illuminated with ever-changing patterns of colored lights and water.

Fort Malden National Historic Park

100 Laird Avenue
Amherstburg, Ontario, Canada
519-736-5416

Location: From the tunnel, take Riverside Drive (Highway 18) to Amherstburg. Turn right at Alma Street, left at Laird Street. Approximately 25 minutes from tunnel.

Hours: May–October: 10 a.m.–5 p.m., daily. Rest of year: 1–5 p.m., Sunday–Friday, closed Saturday.

Admission: $2.50 adults, $2 seniors, $1.50 children 12 and under. 5 and under free.

Ages: All ages

Plan: Short visit

Parking: Free lot in front of fort

Lunch: Picnic areas along fort's grassy avenues

Facilities: Visitor Center, bathrooms, benches along Detroit River

Built in 1796 by the British, Fort Malden saw action during the War of 1812. Today, her four remaining buildings sit among rolling hills and grassy avenues. Kids will enjoy almost everything about this fort. The video is only six minutes long, and costumed guides demonstrate musket firing and other nineteenth-century military routines, plus children are allowed to try on military costumes. Best of all, the hills and avenues are perfect for running and rolling. After your visit, drive down a block to Austin "Toddy" Jones Park, located at the corner of Laird Avenue South and North Street. Here you'll find creative slides and swings, plus a wooden fort climber.

Navy Yard Park

Dalhousie Street, Amherstburg

Behind the historic Park House Museum on Dalhousie Street in Amherstburg, overlooking the Detroit River. There are park benches for picnicking and old anchors for creative photos of the kids.

Point Pelee National Park

South of Leamington, Ontario
519-322-2371 (recorded information)
519-322-2365 (visitor center)

Location: From Detroit, take the Ambassador Bridge to Windsor. From Windsor, follow Route 3 to Leamington. Prominent signs give directions to the park. About an hour's drive from the bridge.
Hours: Visitor Center: 10 a.m.–5 p.m., March–April. 8 a.m.–6 p.m., May. 10 a.m.–6 p.m., June–August. 10 a.m.–5 p.m., September–October. 10–4 p.m., weekdays; 10 a.m.–5 p.m., weekends, November–March. Grounds: 6 a.m.–9:30 p.m., daily, year-round.
Admission: $3.25 adults, $2.40 seniors, $1.60 children, $8.55 family, children under 3 are free (Canadian dollars)
Ages: All ages
Plan: Full day
Parking: On site
Lunch: Picnic sites
Facilities: Visitor Center with exhibits and theater, boardwalk, two observation towers, nature and bicycle trails. Canoe and bicycle rental April–Labor Day. Ice-skating and cross-country skiing during winter, weather permitting.

This well-kept park becomes a bird-watcher's paradise in early May and August through October as migratory birds stop along their routes. Monarch butterflies are also plentiful during the summer through mid-September. A wide variety of activities are available throughout the year that appeal to children of all ages.

Queen Elizabeth II Gardens, Jackson Park

Tecumseh Road and Ouellette Street, Windsor
519-253-2300

This formal flowering garden located five minutes from the tunnel includes a six-acre rose garden with 450 different varieties. Kids will enjoy the maze-like shrubbery and the grounded Lancaster Memorial Bomber, a large World War II Royal Air Force Bomber.

Neighborhood Playscapes

Say goodbye to playgrounds with ho-hum metal slides and standard swings. Playscapes—those custom-designed, volunteer-built, multi-level wooden play environments with giant tubular slides, suspension bridges, colorful climbers, and imaginative towers—are popping up all over the metro area. Here are some of the area's best kept secrets. Please remember that school playscapes are not open to the public while school or summer programs are in session. Try school playscapes in the evening or on weekends. Most playscapes have signs posting public hours.

Allen Park

Cabrini Catholic Church
At Wick and Lawrence

Ann Arbor

Mixer Park
1519 Fuller Road
At Fuller Road and Maiden Lane

Birmingham

Springdale Park
On Strathmore, the first street north of Big Beaver, off Woodward

Bloomfield Hills

Detroit Country Day Lower School
3003 West Maple
On Maple Road, between Lahser and Cranbrook

Brighton

Downtown Brighton, on Mill Pond at Main and
St. Paul Streets

Detroit

Belle Isle Playscape
Belle Isle, Detroit

Farmington Hills

Gill Elementary School
21195 Gill Road
Between 8 and 9 Mile, on Gill Road

Grosse Ile

Adventure Island
Outside Township Hall
8841 Macomb

Huntington Woods

Burton Elementary School
26315 Scotia
At Scotia and Nadine, just south of Eleven Mile
and west of Woodward

Northville

Maybury State Park
20145 Beck Road

Novi

Community Sports Park
At the corner of Eight Mile and Napier Roads

Oak Park

Jewish Community Center
15110 West Ten Mile Road
Off Ten Mile Road, just east of Greenfield

Plymouth

On Ann Arbor Trail, between Sheldon and
Beck Roads

Royal Oak

The Detroit Zoological Park

Sterling Heights

DeKrieser Elementary
17 Mile Road and Dodge Park

Troy

Boulan Park
On Crooks Road, north of Big Beaver, on the
west side of the road

West Bloomfield

Doherty Elementary School
3575 Walnut Lake Road, just east of Orchard
Lake Road

Ealy Elementary School
5475 Maple Road, between Orchard Lake and
Middlebelt Roads

Green Elementary School
4500 Walnut Lake Road, Orchard Lake and
Farmington Roads

Unusual Parks

Take a trip back to the wild west and to prehistoric times or play in a barrier-free environment.

Illuminated Cascades

Sparks Foundation County Park
Brown Street, Jackson
517-788-4320 day
517-788-4227 night

Location: Exit 138 at junction of I-94 and US-127
Hours: Illuminated Cascades: 7:30–11 p.m., daily,
Memorial Day–Labor Day. All other park facilities:
Sunrise–10 p.m., Memorial Day–Labor Day.
Admission: For falls, $2 adults and children 6 and
up weekdays. $3 weekends, holidays, and special
events. Children 5 and under free. Group rates
available.

Ages: All ages
Plan: Half day visit; spend an evening
Parking: Free on site
Facilities: Picnic and playground areas, paddle-boats and miniature golf, Cascades museum and gift shop.

Summer evenings, the Cascades, a 500-foot hill of six spraying fountains, comes to life in vivid color. Live bands, fireworks, and entertainment add to the thrill. Families can also enjoy paddle-boats, miniature golf, and other park facilities.

Mixer Playground

Fuller Park
1519 Fuller Road, Ann Arbor
734-994-4263

Location: Fuller Road and Maiden Lane
Hours: Dawn to dusk, daily
Admission: Free for park. $3 adults, $2.50 children for pool.
Ages: All ages; purposely designed to offer wheel chair accessibility
Plan: Short visit
Parking: Free in lot adjacent to playground
Lunch: Small snack bar
Facilities: The Fuller Park pool is open Memorial Day–mid-September.

Mixer Playground is a barrier-free, two-story, creative wooden playscape with slides and crawl spaces. Built entirely by community volunteers, the play area is designed to offer accessibility to all children.

Penny Whistle Place

G-5500 Bray Road, Flint
810-736-7100
1-800-648-7275

Location: I-475 and Carpenter Road (exit 11), adjacent to Crossroads Village
Hours: 10 a.m.–6 p.m., Monday–Saturday. Noon–6 p.m., Sunday. Memorial Day–August 22; weekends until Labor Day, weather permitting.
Admission: $3.50 children ages 3–12. $1 ages 12 and up. 2 and under are free. Group rates available.
Ages: 3–10 year olds
Plan: Half day visit
Parking: Free on site

Lunch: Concessions, picnic tables
Facilities: Bathrooms, drinking fountains, benches for parents

At Penny Whistle, a creative playground, children can explore, climb, and become daring adventurers in a safe environment. Toddlers play in a sandbox with creative dump trucks large enough to sit on, zoom down the Tube Slides, and march around the Punch Bag Forest. Older children will love diving into layers of orange balls in the Ball Crawl, soaring over an abyss in the Cable Glide, and pumping water and sound at the Music Pump. Parents can sit up close to watch, give their children a hand, or become adventurers themselves. Attendants are also on hand to help children.

Prehistoric Forest

US-12, Onsted (Irish Hills)
517-467-2514

Location: On US-12 in Irish Hills
Hours: 10:30 a.m.–7 p.m., weekdays, 10:30 a.m.–8 p.m. weekends, Memorial Day–Labor Day
Admission: $6 adults, $4 children 4 to 16, 3 and under free.
Ages: Preschoolers
Plan: Short visit
Parking: Free on site
Lunch: Picnic sites. Stagecoach Stop U.S.A. is down the road.
Facilities: Bathrooms, gift shop

Prehistoric Forest, a kitschy representation of Mesozoic life, is for dinophiles with a taste for the tacky. The safari train takes you "deep" into the forest where more than 40 prehistoric beasts dwell in vivid cartoon color. A guide walks you through part of the tour, cracking dino jokes. Parents have ample opportunity to snap photos of their little Flintstones grinning on the back of a neon-colored Brontosaurus.

Stagecoach Stop, U.S.A.

7203 US-12, Onsted (Irish Hills)
517-467-2300

Location: On US-12 in Irish Hills, seven miles west of M-50 and M-52 intersection
Hours: 10:30 a.m.–5:30 p.m., Tuesday–Friday; 10:30 a.m.–6:30 p.m., Saturday and Sunday,

Memorial Day–Labor Day. Closed Mondays.
Admission: $10 adults, $6 children 12 and under and seniors, 3 and under free. Includes admission to Eisenhower Presidential Car. Group rates available.
Ages: All ages
Plan: Half day visit
Parking: Free on site
Lunch: Restaurant, ice cream parlor, concessions, fudge shop, picnic tables
Facilities: Bathrooms, gift shop, outdoor amphitheater, Western chapel

Walk along an 1880's Wild West town. Visit the general store, carriage house, saw mill, and blacksmith shop. Take a wild game train ride. Visit the petting farm and kiddie rides. Don't be surprised if the townsfolk get rowdy and a street fight begins. Just sit on the bleachers and see who's going to win. Special events are held throughout the summer in the outdoor amphitheater, and old-Western style weddings are held in the chapel.

Water Parks

Buck the wild waves, whoosh around the curves of a monster slide, and take a bumper boat ride. Michigan's water parks keep you cool.

Belle Isle Water Slides

Belle Isle Park, Detroit
313-852-4059

Location: Beside the beach on the north side of the island
Hours: Noon–8 p.m. daily, Memorial Day–Labor Day
Admission: $3 all day pass
Ages: Children must be at least 43 inches tall and wear swim gear
Plan: Half-day or full-day visit
Parking: Free
Lunch: Concessions located at golf course, picnic tables and shelters nearby
Facilities: Bathhouse

Both children and teens will enjoy twisting and turning along three water slides—six-feet, 19-feet and 31-feet tall—all dropping into a splash pool. Patrons can stay all day but are asked to clear the pool every 45 minutes and go to the end of the line, ensuring that everyone has a chance to experience the cool thrill.

Chandler Park Family Aquatic Center

12600 Chandler Park Drive, Detroit
313-822-7665

Location: East of I-94, at Connor and Chandler Park Drive
Hours: 11 a.m.–8 p.m., daily, Memorial Day–Labor Day.
Admission: Wayne County residents: $6 adults weekdays, $7 adults weekends, $4 children weekdays, $5 children weekends, free for under age 2. The admission price doubles for non-residents. Group rates for birthday parties.
Ages: All ages. Must be 48 inches or taller for waterslide. Please supervise small children carefully.
Plan: All day
Parking: Free on site
Lunch: Concessions and shaded tables
Facilities: Wet shop sells sunglasses, bathing suits, and beanie babies. Bathhouse with changed area, showers, and rental lockers. Swim lessons available.

Stay cool at the new 80-acre aquatic center. Just for tots, there's "Tadpole Place," a 4,800-square-foot water play area full of climbing structures and waterfalls. "Splash Down," a tube water slide, offers families a wild ride in an inner tube, down a twisting, 203-foot-long slide. The "Way Cool Wave Pool" alternates calm water with three-foot waves, and on the "Body Slide," children over 48 inches can whoosh down 161 feet, through tunnels and dips. The park also offers a Friday evening concert series and a Monday afternoon kiddie entertainment series.

Four Bears Water Park

3000 Auburn Road, Utica
810-739-5863

Website: www.fourbearswaterpark.com
Location: Auburn Road, between Ryan and Dequindre, seven miles east of I-75, just off M-59
Hours: 10 a.m.–3 p.m. weekdays. 11 a.m.–7 p.m., weekends, Memorial Day–June 15. 11 a.m.–7 p.m., daily, through Labor Day.
Admission: $12.95 over 48 inches, $6.95 under 48 inches, under 3 years and over 65 years free. $5 beach and picnic access. Group rates and season pass available.

Ages: All ages
Plan: Full day visit
Parking: Free. Next to entrance and across the street.
Lunch: Restaurant, vending machines, concessions, picnic tables
Facilities: Bathrooms, beach house with showers and lockers. Gift shop selling beach paraphernalia and Four Bears souvenirs.

Wear your bathing suit, pack a change of clothes and a picnic lunch, and plan on a full day of water activities at Four Bears. Young children will enjoy the kiddie rides, playground, bumper boats, splash pool, and miniature water slide. Older children will want to play miniature golf, practice their swings at the batting cages, take a turn on the 50-foot triple water slide, or ride the go-carts. The whole family will enjoy the paddle boats and riding the speed slide into the man-made lake.

Groveland Oaks Water Slide

5990 Grange Hall Road, Holly
248-634-9811

Location: Groveland Oaks County Park, Dixie Highway at Grange Hall Road
Hours: 10:30 a.m.–5:30 p.m., daily, Memorial Day–Labor Day
Admission: Water slide 50 cents/ride or $5/day.
Ages: Recommended 5 and up
Plan: Half day-full day visit
Parking: $5 Oakland County residents vehicle entry fee, $8 non-residents vehicle fee
Lunch: Concession stands
Facilities: Bathrooms, beach, paddleboats, canoe, rowboat, and waterbug (one-person paddleboat) rental

Groveland Oaks offers an added attraction to family beach visits. Now you can ride a water slide and splash right into the lake.

Lake Erie Metropark Wave Pool

32481 West Jefferson, Rockwood
734-379-5020

Location: Brownstown Township between Gibraltar and Rockwood, along Lake Erie
Hours: 9:30 a.m.–8 p.m., Saturday and Sunday.

11 a.m.–7 p.m., Monday–Friday. Memorial Day–Labor Day.

Admission: $4 adults, $3 children ages 15 and under. $1.50 twilight (5 p.m.–closing weekdays, 6 p.m.–closing weekends and holidays). Raft rental $1.50 per raft.

Ages: All ages. Small children need to be closely supervised.

Plan: Half day-full day visit

Parking: $2 daily weekday vehicle permit, $3 weekend permit, $15 annual vehicle permit

Lunch: Snack bar and picnic tables adjacent to pool area

Facilities: Bathrooms, coin lockers, wet shop with beach paraphernalia and rafts

Throughout the day, the pool alternates periods of three-foot waves with intervals of calm. Be sure to arrive early enough to rent a raft. It's more fun to ride the wild waves on a raft.

Red Oaks Waterpark

1455 East Thirteen Mile Road, Madison Heights
248-585-6990

Location: Between John R and Dequindre

Hours: 11 a.m.–7 p.m., Memorial Day–Labor Day

Admission: $7.75 Oakland County residents, $10.00 non-residents, $3.75 seniors. Children 30–43 inches, $3 Oakland County residents, $4 non-residents, children under 30 inches free. Twilight discounts after 4 p.m. Fees for raft and lounge chair rental.

Ages: All ages. Supervise small children closely.

Plan: Half day–full day visit

Parking: Free on site

Lunch: Concessions, picnic areas, and grills

Facilities: Bathrooms, beach house, playscape, carpeted pool deck, raft and lounge chair rental at admission window. Swim lessons are available.

Red Oaks offers the largest wave-action pool in Michigan. Be sure to arrive early to rent a raft. It's more fun to ride the waves on a raft. Whoosh down the three-flume water slide and splash down into a separate pool. What a wild way to beat the summer's heat.

Rolling Hills Family Water Park

7660 Stony Creek, Ypsilanti
734-482-FUNN

Location: Rolling Hills County Park, Textile and Stony Creek Roads

Hours: 11 a.m.–8 p.m. daily, Memorial Day–Labor Day

Admission: $3.50 weekdays, $4.50 weekends and holidays. Children under 36 inches are free. $2.50 after 5 p.m. weekdays.

Ages: Must be 36 inches or taller to use water slide. Small children should be carefully supervised in wave pool.

Plan: Half day–full day visit

Parking: $3 vehicle entry fee for Washtenaw County residents; $6 non-residents.

Lunch: Concessions, picnic tables and picnic pavilion in county park

Facilities: Water park offers a wave pool, three water slides—a body slide, tube slide, and kiddie slide—and an activity pool for small children. Rolling Hills County Park offers hiking trails, sand volleyball, play area, and disc golf course.

During the dog days of summer, small children can play in their own activity pool and whoosh down their own miniature water slide, while older children enjoy the two water slides and a wave-action pool.

Veterans Park Water Slide

2150 Jackson Road, Ann Arbor
734-761-7240

Location: At the juncture of Jackson and Maple Roads

Hours: 1–8 p.m., Monday–Friday. Noon–8 p.m., Saturday and Sunday, Memorial Day–Labor Day.

Admission: $3 adults, $2.50 children. 3 and younger are free.

Ages: For water slide, children must be at least 42 inches tall.

Plan: Half day–full day visit

Parking: Free on site

Lunch: Concessions

Facilities: Bathrooms, showers, lockers, skateboard ramp, tennis courts, baseball diamond

Veterans Park offers a full range of water and summer fun. Bring your swim suits, skateboards, and tennis rackets.

Waterford Oaks Water Park

1700 Scott Lake Road, Waterford
248-858-0918

Location: Waterford Oaks County Park, Scott Lake Road between Pontiac Lake Road and Dixie Highway

Hours: 11 a.m.–7 p.m., daily, Memorial Day–Labor Day

Admission: $10 Oakland County residents, $13 non-residents. Children 30–43 inches, $7 Oakland County residents, $9.50 non-residents, children under 30 inches free. Twilight discounts after 4 p.m. Fees for tube, raft, or lounge chair rental. Swim lessons are available.

Ages: All ages. Supervise small children carefully.

Plan: Full day visit

Parking: Free on site

Lunch: Snack bar, grills, and picnic areas

Facilities: Bathrooms, inflatable rafts available for purchase, beach house. Also in park—tennis, shuffleboard, and volleyball courts.

Take the plunge from Waterford Oaks' dual flume, 340-foot long "Slidewinder" water slide. Body surf in the three-foot waves that alternate with calm periods in the large wave-action pool. Ride a raft and whoosh down a 55-foot-tall twisting chute into a pool or stay cool with the little ones in a creative wet playground, offering over 30 interactive activities including waterjets, waterfalls, and waterslides.

10
Best Rides in Town

TIP

Just when your children are starting to nod off or lose interest in the zoo, park, or village, hop on an old-fashioned train, boat, or hay wagon. After the slow-moving ride, you'll be ready to continue your visit recharged.

Motion and excitement. That's what this chapter is all about. Here are all the best rides in town—on land, sea, and air. There are urban trolleys, miniature trains, old-fashioned stern-wheelers, country hay wagons, sleighs, hot-air balloon rides, and Detroit's own People Mover.

Hot-Air Balloon

Adventures Aloft

Kerr Hardware, 222 South Cedar, Mason
517-676-3740

Location: South of Lansing, off US 127
Hours: Several hours before sunset, Monday–Friday; sunrise and sunset Saturday and Sunday, weather permitting, year-round.
Admission: $150/person, $275/two people, $350/three people
Parking: Free at Kerr Hardware

The three-hour adventure begins at Kerr Hardware. Participants ride out to the fairgrounds or park, enjoy an hour balloon ride, and celebrate afterwards with grape juice or champagne. Flight certificates are awarded to all fliers.

Train

Bluewater Michigan Chapter of the National Railway Historical Society

Royal Oak
248-541-1000

The Bluewater Chapter offers a variety of historic tours and fall color excursions May–October in Southern Lower Michigan and Southwestern Ontario. Call for brochure and dates.

Trolley

Blue Water Trolley

Blue Water Area Transit, Port Huron
810-987-7373

Location: Ride begins on Quay Street, but you can catch the trolley at any intersection along the route.

Hours: 10:45 a.m.–5:30 p.m., Tuesday–Thursday. 11:15 a.m.–9 p.m., Friday. 10:45 a.m.–4:15 p.m., Saturday. No Sunday or Monday runs. Early June–Labor Day. Chartered group tours available after normal operating hours and on Sunday and Monday.
Admission: 10 cents
Parking: Use downtown parking lots or street parking

Take a 40-minute tour through downtown Port Huron and along the river front. You'll pass historic homes and have a panoramic view of the Blue Water Bridge and the Thomas Edison Statue.

Hot-Air Balloon
Capt. Phogg

2470 Grange Hall Road, Fenton
248-634-3094

Website: www.balloonride.com
Location: 1 1/4 miles west of I–75 north, off exit 101
Hours: Flying times: Sunrise and two hours prior to sunset, daily, year-round, weather permitting.
Admission: $189/person. Not suggested for small children; older children must be at least four feet tall.
Parking: Free in lot

The three-hour program includes pre-flight briefing in the balloon showroom, watching the inflation process, a 45-minute to one-hour flight, and afterwards, a champagne ceremony in which each participant is awarded a flight certificate and balloon pin.

Historic Steam Engine
Coe Rail

840 North Pontiac Trail, Walled Lake
248-960-9440

Location: On Pontiac Trail, just north of Maple Road
Hours: 1 and 2:30 p.m., Sunday, mid-April–October.
Admission: $8 adults, $7 children 2 to 10 and seniors. Group rates and group charters available.
Parking: Free on site
Facilities: Beverages and snacks for sale on board train.

All aboard for a one-hour ride on a restored 1917 Erie Lakawanna passenger train, with narration and magic show. School groups and birthday parties welcome. Adult dinner train rides are offered aboard the Michigan Star Clipper, 7 p.m., Tuesday–Thursday and Saturday, 7:30 p.m., Friday, and 5 p.m., Sunday, year-round.

Coach Ride

Crown Coach, Inc.

Birmingham
248-360-1373

Location: Coach rides begin on Woodward near the Midtown Café, in downtown Birmingham.
Hours: 7 p.m.–1 a.m., Friday and Saturday, May 1–January 1.
Admission: $30 for half-hour ride; $60 for one-hour ride, with four people. $5/each additional person (coach seats a maximum of six people).
Parking: Adjacent lots and metered street parking
   Ride in an old-fashioned carriage through downtown and residential Birmingham. Pack a picnic or sparkling cider and celebrate a family milestone.

Downtown Transit System

Detroit People Mover

313-962-7245

Location: There are 13 stations along the 2.9 mile route around downtown Detroit
Hours: 7 a.m.–11 p.m., Monday–Thursday. 7 a.m.–midnight, Friday. 9 a.m.–midnight, Saturday. Noon–8 p.m., Sunday. Round-trip rides are approximately 15 minutes long.
Admission: 50 cents, children 5 and under free. Exact change is needed, and token machines selling 50-cent coupons for dollar bills are located in all stations.
Parking: Many people find it convenient to park in Greektown and use the station on the third floor of Trapper's Alley, or park in RenCen lots off Jefferson and use the station on the second level of the Millender Center
   There's nothing that will make you feel more like a tourist than sailing above the street level and catching a brilliant view of the Detroit River. The People Mover is one of Detroit's best thrills. For a

mere 50 cents, you can ride as much as you want, peek into office buildings, view each station's wonderful public art, and feel on top of the world.

Detroit Trolley

1301 East Warren, Detroit
313-933-1300

Location: The trolley runs from Washington and Grand Circus Park to Mariner's Church on Jefferson
Hours: Every 15 minutes, 7 a.m.–8 p.m., daily during the winter. 7 a.m.–midnight, daily during the summer. Doesn't run Thanksgiving Day, Christmas Day, and New Year's Day.
Admission: 50 cents, exact change
Parking: Best bet—park in RenCen lots and catch the trolley in front of the Visitor's Center at Jefferson, east of Beaubien

Ride the red trolleys and experience downtown Detroit by land after cruising by air on the People Mover. Kids will especially enjoy the old-fashioned pace and the bells.

Detroit Zoo Train

8450 West Ten Mile Road, Royal Oak
248-398-0903

Ride the miniature train for 50 cents each way. There are two stations, one at the entrance, the other at the back of the zoo, near the Log Cabin Learning Center.

Boat Ride

Diamond Jack's River Tours

Detroit River, Detroit
313-843-7676 (recorded information)
313-843-9376 (group tours)

Website: www.diamondjack.com
Location: St. Aubin Park and Hart Plaza docks along the Detroit River
Hours: 2, 4, and 6 p.m. from Hart Plaza; 2:15, 4:15, and 6:15 p.m. from St. Aubin, Tuesday–Sunday, end of May–August. Same times, Friday–Sunday, September.
Admission: $12 adults, $11 seniors, $9 children 6–16. Under 6 are free. Group rates and charters are available for a minimum of 25 passengers.
Parking: For St. Aubin Park, use lot adjacent to park. For Hart Plaza, use Ford Auditorium parking structure or Miller Parking lot across the street.

Enjoy summer aboard a former Mackinac Island ferry boat. The Diamond Jack offers a two-hour, narrated river boat cruise along the Detroit River, filled with Detroit River history and gossip.

Paddle Wheel

Genesee Belle

Crossroads Village
6140 Bray Road, Flint
810-736-7100
1-800-648-PARK

Location: Crossroads Village dock is adjacent to the carousel. Evening cruises depart from Stepping Stone Falls, across Mott Lake from the village.
Hours: Daily afternoon cruises during the summer. Wednesday lunch and dinner cruises by reservation. Evening cruises from Stepping Stone Falls, 7 p.m. Sunday, mid-May to end of August.
Admission: Daytime: $3.75 adults, $2 children 12 and under, under 1 free. Crossroads Village admission ticket required. Evening: $4.50 adults, $3.50

children 12 and under, under 1 free.
Parking: Free on site

Step back in time and enjoy a 45-minute cruise along Lake Mott in an old-fashioned paddle wheel. Entertainment is included on weekend cruises.

Antique Vehicle Rides, Hay & Sleigh Rides
Greenfield Village

20900 Oakwood Boulevard, Dearborn
313-271-1620
313-982-6150 (24-hour information)

Website: www.hsmgv.org

During the season (Memorial Day–Labor Day), visitors can choose a variety of old-fashioned rides, each at an additional fee above admission. There are narrated carriage tours, 30-minute steam engine train rides (the train is open through October), a 1913 carousel, antique car rides, and a 15-minute ride on a old-fashioned sternwheeler, the *Suwanee.* I would recommend the train ride. For $3, you can ride back and forth through the village all day. Evening hay rides are offered during the fall, and sleigh rides through the closed village during the winter, weather permitting.

Old-fashioned Train
Huckleberry Railroad

Crossroads Village
6140 Bray Road, Flint
810-736-7100

Lean out the windows and catch a breeze. The Huckleberry Railroad is a delightful 45-minute ride on an old-fashioned steam engine. Take a scary ride on the ghost train during October, a Christmas ride during December, and a Bunny Train ride prior to Easter.

Steamboat
Island Queen

Kensington Metropark
2240 West Buno Road, Milford
248-685-1561
1-800-47-PARKS

Website: www.metroparks.com
Location: Kensington Boat Rental
Hours: Noon–6 p.m., daily, Memorial Day–Labor Day. Weekends only, Labor Day–mid-September. Group charters available at other times.
Admission: $2 adults, $1.50 children and seniors, 12 and under. Five and under free.
Parking: $3 vehicle entry fee on weekends, $2 fee on weekdays, free on Wednesdays

Step back into history on the 66-passenger, diesel-powered paddlewheel. The 45-minute ride on Kent Lake is a refreshing and relaxing change of pace during summer's dog days.

Hay & Sleigh Rides

Kensington Farm Center's Hay and Sleigh Rides

2240 West Buno Road, Milford
248-685-1561
1-800-47-PARKS

Website: www.metroparks.com
Location: Farm Center
Hours: Every 30 minutes, noon–4 p.m., week-ends. Group charters available at other times.
Admission: $2 adults, $1.50 children and seniors.
Parking: Free on site

Ride through Kensington's fields, ripe with shimmering corn during the fall, the bare skeletal corn shucks silhouetted against the white sky in winter. Kids love the sturdy horses, the old-fashioned hay wagon, and red sleigh. Each ride is approximately 20-minutes long. Warm up and have a snack at the Country Store.

Hot-Air Balloon

Michigan Balloon Corporation

P.O. Box 96, Holly
1-800-968-8368

Location: Flights leave from Seven Lakes State Park, Holly
Hours: Sunrise and two hours before sunset, year-round, weather permitting.
Admission: $175/person, group rates available.
Parking: State Park daily vehicle permit, $4.

Three-hour adventure includes briefing, inflation, one-hour balloon ride and a champagne or sparkling juice toast. All participants are awarded Michigan Balloon souvenirs.

Train

Michigan Transit Museum

North Gratiot Avenue, Mount Clemens
810-463-1863

Website: www.alexxi.com/mtm
Location: North Gratiot Avenue and Joy Boulevard
Hours: 1, 2, 3, and 4 p.m., every Sunday, last Sunday in May–last Sunday in September
Admission: Train ride only: $5.50 adults, $2.75 children 4 to 12, under 3 free. $2 adults, additional for Selfridge Military Air Museum.
Parking: Free on site

Take a 45-minute ride back into time on the 1924 diesel locomotive. Banjo and harmonica music crackle over the loudspeaker; inside the train car are faded ads: "Lux soap flakes—only 10 cents a box." The train goes through the Selfridge Military Base and stops at the Selfridge Military Air Museum for those who want to get off. Passengers are picked up one hour later. Plan on an hour stay at the museum. The 4 p.m. ride does not drop off passengers.

Boat

Pelee Island Transportation

Pelee Island, Ontario, Canada
519-724-2115

Website: http://bmts.com/~northland
Location: Docks are located in Kingsville and Leamington
Hours: Boats leave several times a day, spring–fall. Call for specific times and location.
Admission: $5.25 adults, $2.75 child, under 6 free. $11.50 vehicle
Parking: Free on site

Take a three-hour round trip cruise across Lake Erie from Kingsville or Leamington to Pelee Island and back. Or take a ride along with your car and spend some time exploring Pelee Island by car. Vehicle reservations must be made in advance.

Old-fashioned Trolley
Royal Oak Trolley

Royal Oak
248-547-4000

Location: 16 stops throughout downtown Royal Oak
Hours: Noon to midnight, Sunday–Wednesday. Noon–1 a.m., Thursday–Saturday, year-round.
Admission: 50 cents/person.

Hitch a ride through downtown Royal Oak on an antique trolley.

Hayrides
Rushlow's Arabians

29242 Bredow, Huron Township
734-782-1171

Location: At the corner of Middlebelt and Bredlow, six miles south of Metro Airport
Hours: One-hour rides daily, weather permitting, by appointment only
Admission: Rates vary with group size. Evening rides include bonfires.
Parking: Free on site

Bring the gang out for an old-fashioned hayride. For groups, the Rushlow family provides a barn if you'd like to hold a barn dance; you bring the refreshments. In addition, birthday parties and horseback riding lessons are offered on site.

Hot-Air Balloon

Sky Adventures

4191 Locust Valley Lane, Oxford (office)
248-628-1000

Location: Flights begin at Mr. B's, just north of downtown Oxford
Hours: Several hours before sunset, daily. Several hours after sunrise on Saturday and Sunday. All flights weather permitting, year-round. Peak season is April–November.
Admission: $145/person for groups of 5 or more. $150/person for groups of 2–4. $185 for 3–4 people in a private party. $225/two people. $165/one person. Children must be at least five years old.
Parking: Free on site

Meet at the saloon, drive out with the chase vehicles to the flight site, take an hour-long balloon ride, and then celebrate the flight with a champagne (real or non-alcoholic) ceremony, which includes cheese, crackers, souvenir balloon pin, and champagne glass. Sunrise weekend flights celebrate with donuts and champagne.

Train

Southern Michigan Railroad

320 South Division Street, Clinton
517-423-7230 (Tecumseh information)

Location: Three blocks south of US-12
Hours: Trains leave Clinton at 11 a.m., 1, and 3 p.m. and leave Tecumseh at noon, 2, and 4 p.m.,

Sunday, June–September. Group rides may be scheduled at other times. Color tours offered in October.

Admission: Varies with ride. Yearly membership available

Parking: Free on site

The Southern Michigan Railroad takes you on a one-hour-and-20-minute ride between Clinton and Tecumseh, two charming small towns. It is a wonderful way to introduce your children to train travel, enjoy fall scenery, and browse through Tecumseh's restored shopping district.

Miniature Train

Starr-Jaycee Park Train

Thirteen Mile Road, east of Crooks, Royal Oak
248-544-6680 (Royal Oak Recreation)

Free train rides are offered noon–4 p.m. on the first full weekend of every month, May–November, weather permitting.

Hay and Sleigh Rides

Wolcott Mill Farm Learning Center

65775 Wolcott Road, Ray Township
810-752-5932
810-749-5997 (group tour)

Location: Off Wolcott Road, about 1 1/2 miles north of 29 Mile Road, southeast of Romeo

Hours: Call to schedule, Saturdays and Sundays

Admission: Fall and spring hayrides and winter sleigh rides, $2 adults, $1.50 children and seniors.

Parking: Free on site

Take a lazy hay or sleigh ride through the rows of corn and around the 100-acre field of crops.

11
That's Entertainment

TIP

Introduce your children to live music and theater early, but try to match your child's age and temperament to the show and venue. Children ages six and younger do best at Youtheatre's Wiggle Club shows and the Detroit Symphony Orchestra's Tiny Tots performances.

Children love live performances. Whether it's a folk concert, puppet show, holiday classic, or outdoor concert, the Detroit area has it all. The biggest children's show in town is Youtheatre at the Millennium Centre, offering Saturday and Sunday, October–May performances of the best in mime, drama, dance, music, and puppetry from around the country. The Youtheatre's Wiggle Club is a series designed for three to five year olds. Older children find plenty of interest in the remaining "Movin' Up" lineup.

For an introduction to classical music, bring your elementary and middle school-aged children to Orchestra Hall for the Detroit Symphony Orchestra's Young People's Concert Series, selected Saturdays throughout the school year. In addition, the DSO's Tiny Tots series, held at Farmington Hills' Mercy Auditorium, is specially designed for preschoolers. Older children will enjoy concerts, dances, and shows at Detroit's grand theaters—the Fisher, Fox, Detroit Opera Theater, Music Hall, or Orchestra Hall. For first-time theater-goers, check the local library or parks and recreation department for children's theater series which are especially geared for preschoolers and usually last less than an hour. Metro Detroit also offers families a variety of arts and craft venues where kids can create masterpieces.

Theater, Music

Aaron DeRoy Theatre

Jewish Community Center
6600 West Maple, West Bloomfield
248-661-1000

Location: Maple Road, just west of Drake Road
Showtime: Evening and Sunday matinee performances
Tickets: Prices vary depending on performance
Ages: Preschool and up
Parking: Free on site

Family shows, musicals, and concerts are offered throughout the year. During November's Jewish Book Fair week, there are children's programs held on Sunday afternoon. In addition, JET, the Jewish repertory theater, offers a series of adult plays (248-788-2900).

Family Shows
Act I Series

Wharton Center for the Performing Arts
MSU Campus, East Lansing
517-432-2000
1-800-WHARTON

Website: www.msu.edu/wharton
Location: Corner of Bogue, Shaw Lane, and Wilson Road
Showtime: 1:30 and 4 p.m. Sundays, September–April
Tickets: $6.50/person
Ages: Preschool–elementary
Parking: Parking structure attached, $4

Act I, a family theater series, runs throughout the school year with a lineup of plays, puppets, and music. Wharton Center also brings in the best of dance, music, and theater, and presents Michigan State University Theater Department shows.

Tea Time
Afternoon Tea at the Ritz-Carlton

Dearborn
313-441-2100

Location: On the southwest corner of Southfield Road and Hubbard Drive
Showtime: 2–4 p.m., Tuesday, Wednesday, Thursday, and Saturday. Call for advance reservations. Special Spring Teddy Bear children's teas, year-round specialty teas and Christmas teas.
Tickets: $22 six-course tea, $17 four-course tea. Holiday and theme teas have higher prices.
Ages: Older elementary school and up
Parking: Free in adjacent lot

Dress up and enjoy an elegant afternoon at The Ritz. This outing is a perfect opportunity to share with Grandma and Grandpa.

Tea Time
Afternoon Tea at Fiona's Tea House

945 Beech Street, Detroit
313-967-9314

Location: Between the Lodge and Third, three blocks north of Michigan Ave.
Showtime: 9 a.m.–4 p.m. Tuesday–Thursday for lunch. 2–4 p.m. Tuesday–Thursday for tea. 9:30 a.m.–2 p.m. and 5–10 p.m. Friday for lunch and dinner. 10 a.m.–3 p.m. Sunday brunch. Call ahead to book birthday parties and children's teas.
Tickets: Afternoon tea: $15 adults, $12 children. For children's tea, minimum number of people is 15; maximum 25
Ages: Recommended for ages 3 and up
Parking: Free parking on street

Enter the 100-year-old red brick cottage and travel back to a gracious time of lace curtains, starched white linen table cloths, pink roses, and floral china tea cups. Owner Fiona Palmer offers little sprites more treats than they can possible eat, and enjoys throwing old-fashioned birthday tea parties for well-behaved children.

Tea Time

Afternoon Tea at the Townsend Hotel

Birmingham
248-642-7900, ext. 7159

Location: Downtown Birmingham
Showtime: 3–5 p.m., Tuesday–Sunday. 3–5 p.m., daily during December. Call for advance reservations. Theme teas are offered throughout the year and include a January Japanese Tea, April Mad Hatter's Tea, and Dicken's Old-Fashioned Christmas Tea.
Tickets: $22.95. Special theme teas have a higher price. Birthday party packages are available.
Ages: Older elementary school and up
Parking: Metered lot just west of the hotel

It's time to introduce your children to the rewards of good manners. Surround yourself with plush furniture, fine china, silver, and gentle music. Enjoy scones, tea sandwiches, and sinfully rich confections. Raise your pinkies and drink soothing tea. Believe it or not, your children will rise to the occasion.

Music

Ann Arbor Symphony Orchestra

Michigan Theatre
603 East Liberty, Ann Arbor
734-994-4801

Location: Liberty and State Streets
Showtime: Six evening subscription concerts each year, September–May. No concerts during November and February. Special December holiday sing-along is a family matinee.
Tickets: $16–$29 adult, $4 off ticket price for children. $2 off for seniors and students.
Ages: 5 and up
Parking: Street parking, nearby lots

Children will especially enjoy the early December "Sing-Along with Sam", which includes songs lead by Conductor Sam Wong, plus refreshments and a visit with Santa, held at the Bethlehem Church of Christ on Fourth Avenue.

Toy Lending Library/Disabilities

The Arc Lekotek

26049 Five Mile Road, Redford
313-532-8524

Location: 1 1/2 blocks west of Beech Daly
Showtime: Call for appointment; available weekdays, evenings, and Saturday
Tickets: $75/year per child. Fee assistance available upon request.
Ages: Birth–21 years
Parking: Free on site

Arc Lekotek is a non-profit toy lending library offering positive play experiences for families whose children are mentally or physically disabled. All family members are encouraged to come to the play appointment and, with the help of a trained play leader, learn how best to use the toys with their mentally or physically impaired youngster. Up to six toys can be borrowed each visit.

Music

The Ark

316 South Main, Ann Arbor
734-761-1451
734-763-8587 (U of M Union ticket office)

Location: Between William and Liberty on west side of Main Street
Showtime: Matinee performances, Sunday afternoons for children's concerts. Adult folk, pop, and jazz performances are offered selected weekdays and weekend evenings.
Tickets: $5 adults, $3 children (children's concerts)
Ages: Preschool and up
Parking: Free on site

Peter "Madcat" Ruth, the Chenille Sisters, Gemini, and other Ann Arbor and national folk notables make annual appearances at this small, intimate folk club, which offers children's concerts almost once a month. Be sure to try the non-alcoholic ginger beer.

Fun & Games

The Art Castle

1093 East Long Lake Road, Troy
248-680-1127

Location: Long Lake Road, just east of Rochester Road
Showtime: 12:30–6 p.m., Monday–Thursday. 12:30–7:30 p.m., Friday. 10 a.m.–6 p.m., Saturday. Noon–5 p.m., Sunday. Year-round. Extended hours during the summer.
Tickets: Plaster molds are $4.25 and up; magnets and pins are also available
Ages: Preschool–adult
Parking: Free on site

Children of all ages will enjoy painting a plaster figure or plaque. The Art Castle holds birthday parties and offers group discounts.

Multi-Cultural Art

ArtVentures

Ann Arbor Art Center
117 West Liberty Street, Ann Arbor
734-994-8004

Location: Studio is on second floor, above the Art Center gallery
Showtime: Open to the public 1–4 p.m. the first Sunday of every month. Birthday parties and groups can call to arrange special times.
Tickets: Free on first Sunday of every month. Group rates also available.
Ages: Preschool–adult
Parking: Pay lot behind the Art Association; enter off Ashley or Williams Streets.

Groups of 10 or more can have some crafty fun and learn about the art and architecture of diverse cultures. Adult staff help children create simple projects like puppets, windsocks, collages, or jewelry. Feat of Clay, located on the Art Center's third floor, offers another creative outing for older children.

Family Theater

Baldwin Public Library

300 West Merrill, Birmingham
248-647-1700

Location: Downtown Birmingham
Showtime: Saturday or Sunday, during the school year
Tickets: Free
Ages: 6 and up
Parking: Use metered adjacent lots or street parking
Advance registration is necessary for a free hour's worth of fun from local performers.

Music

Birmingham-Bloomfield Symphony Orchestra

248-645-2276

Location: Temple Beth El, 7400 Telegraph Road, Birmingham.
Showtime: Six concerts held weekend evenings, October–June. "Between the Holidays" during December.

Tickets: $20 and $15
Ages: 5 and up
Parking: Free
Older children will enjoy the well-respected BBSO's classical music and pops concerts during the school year.

Family Shows
Birmingham Community House

380 South Bates, Birmingham
248-644-5832

Website: www.communityhouse.com
Location: On Bates between Merrill and Townsend
Showtime: Several Saturday performances throughout the year
Tickets: Depends on event
Ages: Preschool and up. Children under 5 must have adult chaperones.
Parking: Use street parking or nearby lots
The Community House offers families a variety of mime, music, magic, dance, storytelling, and drama performed by traveling troupes and local entertainers.

Theater
BoarsHead Theatre

425 South Grand Avenue, Lansing
517-484-7800 (office)
517-484-7805 (box office)

Location: Downtown Lansing, off I-496
Showtime: Evening and matinee performances, September–May
Tickets: $15–$25, Main Stage productions; $5–$6, Family Shows. Ask about discount tickets and dinner discount programs.
Ages: Ages vary depending on shows.
Parking: Free
Professional theater offering a wide variety of productions. During the Christmas season and early spring, the theater offers plays for families with small children.

Theater

Bonstelle Theatre

3424 Woodward Avenue, Detroit
313-577-2960

Location: Woodward and Elliott, one block south of Mack
Showtime: 8 p.m., Friday and Saturday. 2 p.m., Sunday
Tickets: Regular series, $7.50–$10. Holiday shows, $6 children 12 and under. Children's shows, $3. Group rates available.
Ages: Generally shows for adult audience with a family show each holiday season. Every few years *A Christmas Carol* is performed.
Parking: Free in lot adjacent to theater on Elliott

Talented Wayne State University undergraduate theater students perform classic plays running the gamut from Shakespeare to Tennessee Williams.

 Music

Brunch with Bach

Detroit Institute of Arts
5200 Woodward, Detroit
313-833-2323

Location: Kresge Court Cafe
Showtime: 11:30 a.m., second Sunday of each month; breakfast starts at 11 a.m.
Tickets: $22 adults, $11 children. Reserve tickets at least a month in advance. $5 stairway seats for concert only, first-come, first-served basis.
Ages: Primarily an adult activity available to mature children, recommended 10 years and older
Parking: Use Detroit Science lot on John R, $3

Sophisticated children with a penchant for classical music and adult foods (like quiche and endive salad) will enjoy sitting in the hushed Kresge Court, quietly eating brunch while listening to a piano or string concert. Come prepared with pencil and paper for sketching, a perfect antidote for the young and sometimes restless.

Family Shows
Chrysler Theatre

Cleary International Centre
201 Riverside Drive West, Windsor, Ontario
519-252-8311 (administration office)
1-800-387-9181(box office)
519-252-6579 (box office)

Location: Riverside Drive West and Ferry Street, one block west of Ouellette Avenue
Showtime: Evenings and matinees, weekdays and weekend, depending on show.
Tickets: $10–$40 (Canadian funds)
Ages: For children's shows, preschool and elementary school
Parking: Metered street parking, lots across the street near the river, also in back of the auditorium

Several children's shows are offered, each appealing to families with young children. The Windsor Symphony Orchestra also offers a family concert series at Chrysler Theatre.

Family Shows
Clawson Parks and Recreation Children's Series

509 Fisher Court, Clawson
248-589-0334

Location: Hunter Community Center
Showtime: 2 p.m., Saturday or Sunday, January–March
Tickets: $2
Ages: Preschool–early elementary
Parking: Free on site

A children's concert series offering families a variety of classic tales and performances by local magicians, musicians, and comedians.

Special Events
Cobo Arena

301 Civic Center Drive, Detroit
313-983-6616

Website: www.olympiaentertainment.com
Special events and concerts are held at the arena.

Special Events

Cobo Conference and Exhibition Center

1 Washington Boulevard, Detroit
313-877-8111

Cobo Center hosts the annual Auto Show in January, Home Furniture and Flower Show in March, and the Christmas Carnival in December.

Family Shows, Summer Series

Cohn Amphitheatre at
Independence Oaks County Park

9501 Sashabaw Road, Clarkston
248-625-6473

Website: www.co.oakland.mi.us
Location: 2 1/2 miles north of I-75, on Sashabaw Road
Showtime: Matinees and evening performances throughout the year
Tickets: Prices vary according to program
Ages: All ages
Parking: Vehicle entry fee: $5 Oakland County resident, $8 non-resident
The Independence Oaks Amphitheatre offers a variety of entertaining and educational family shows that focus on Michigan history and Michigan's natural resources.

Family Shows

Cranbrook Summer Children's Theatre

248-645-3678

Location: Cranbrook Education Community, 1221 North Woodward, Bloomfield Hills
Showtime: Public performances at St. Dunstan's Theatre or the outdoor Greek Theatre are held at the end of summer classes in late July. One set of performances involve students in third through fifth grades, the other grades 9–college.
Tickets: Moderate prices
Ages: All ages
Parking: Free on site
Your children will enjoy watching their peers perform folk and fairy tales or modern musicals.

Opera, Theater, Dance, Family Shows

Detroit Opera House

1526 Broadway, Detroit
313-874-SING (tickets)
313-237-3200 (administrative office)

Location: Broadway at Grand Circus Park
Showtime: Michigan Opera Theatre's season runs fall and spring. In addition, the Detroit Opera House hosts a dance series, musicals, variety shows, and special events like the Detroit Symphony Orchestra's "Nutcracker Suite."
Tickets: Prices vary with show. Family discount rates and subscriptions are available.
Ages: General season, upper elementary–adult
Parking: $6–$8. Detroit Opera House parking garage on Broadway and John R, surface lot at the Broadway-Randolph People Mover Station, surface lot north of the Detroit Athletic Club on Madison, or Grand Circus underground.

The elegantly restored home of the Michigan Opera Theatre has a seating capacity of 2,900 and is one of the world's best settings for grand operas with a 75,000-square-foot stage house and an orchestra pit capacity for nearly 100 musicians.

Puppet Theater

Detroit Puppet Theater

25 East Grand River, Detroit
313-961-7777

Location: On Grand River, between Farmer and Woodward
Showtime: Noon and 2 p.m., Saturdays. Groups may be scheduled during weekdays. PuppetArt also offers traveling performances.
Tickets: $6.50 adults, $5 children, $4 groups of 20 or more
Ages: All ages
Parking: Free in lot at Grand River and Library, just east of the theater

Detroit's first puppet theater in 40-odd years offers a repertoire of dramatic, classic puppet shows for all ages. Owned and operated by PuppetArt, a troupe of Russian-American theater arts professionals, the theater performs folktales with large, hand-made, and lavishly costumed marionette and rod puppets, beautiful, colorful sets, and classical and folk music. Puppets are on display inside the cozy puppet theater and in large picture windows facing the street. Workshops on how to make puppets are offered after the 2 p.m. performance.

Theater

Detroit Repertory Theatre

13103 Woodrow Wilson, Detroit
313-868-1347

Location: Exit the Northbound Lodge Freeway at Glendale. Exit at Elmhurst off Southbound Lodge Freeway
Showtime: November–June: 8:30 p.m., Thursday and Friday. 3 and 8:30 p.m., Saturday. 2 and 7:30 p.m., Sunday.
Tickets: $15
Ages: 12 and up
Parking: Free parking lots
　　Professional equity actors theater performs modern dramas in a 200-seat theater.

IMAX Theater

Detroit Science Center
IMAX Dome Theatre

5020 John R, Detroit
313-577-8400

Website: www.sciencedetroit.org
　　The IMAX Theatre's 360° domed ceiling draws you into the movie, creating a sense that you are moving with the motion on the screen. Children will enjoy this excitement.

Music

Detroit Symphony Orchestra
Tiny Tots Series

Mercy High School Auditorium
29300 11 Mile Road, Farmington Hills
313-576-5111

Website: www.detroitsymphony.com

Location: Off Middlebelt Road, just north of 11 Mile Road
Showtime: 10:15 a.m. and 11:45 p.m., selected Saturdays, February–May
Tickets: $10
Ages: 3–6
Parking: Free on site

Targeted to the smallest concert-goers and their parents, Tiny Tots offers three 45-minute Detroit Symphony Orchestra concerts that introduce kids to the symphony and the sounds of its instruments. Each concert includes a narrator, plenty of visual excitement, audience participation, and, of course, favorite classical pieces.

Music

Detroit Symphony Orchestra Young People's Concerts

Orchestra Hall
3711 Woodward Avenue, Detroit
313-576-5111

Website: www.detroitsymphony.com
Location: Between Warren and Mack, one mile south of the DIA
Showtime: 11 a.m., Saturday. Usually six concerts each season. October–June.
Tickets: $8–$31
Ages: All ages, but 6–10 would derive the greatest enjoyment
Parking: $5, lots on Parsons and on Woodward.

These light classical concerts are designed to familiarize children with serious music in a fun way. The Detroit Symphony plays along with dance, mime, puppets, and guest conductors.

Special Event

Disney on Ice

The newest Disney animated movie is brought to three-dimensional life in a week of matinee and evening performances during March and November at Joe Louis Arena.

Family Theater
Family Entertainment Series

Sponsored by Livonia Parks and Recreation
Civic Center Library Auditorium
32777 Five Mile Road, Livonia
734-466-2410

Location: Five Mile and Farmington Roads
Showtime: 2 p.m., selected Sundays during the year
Tickets: $4/person
Ages: Preschool–10
Parking: Alongside the library
Local magicians, youth theaters, musicians, and storytellers offer families relaxing entertainment on Sunday afternoons.

Children's Series
Family Fun

Fairlane Town Center
18900 Michigan Avenue, Dearborn
313-593-1370

Location: Performances are in the Fountain Court, in the middle of the mall.
Showtime: 4 and 6 p.m., Saturdays, spring and fall
Tickets: Free
Ages: Preschool–elementary
Parking: Mall lot
Kids will enjoy taking a break from shopping to enjoy a performance lineup that includes national and local puppeteers, musicians, dancers.

Fun & Games

Feat of Clay

Ann Arbor Art Center
117 West Liberty, Ann Arbor
734-327-9552

Location: Between Ashley and Main, just west of the U of M campus. On the third floor.
Showtime: 1–6 p.m., Tuesday–Thursday. 1–9 p.m., Friday. 10 a.m.–6 p.m., Saturday. Noon–5 p.m., Sunday.
Tickets: Bisqueware, $2–$30. Studio time: $7/hour for adults, $4.50/hour for children ages 12 and under, with minimum of one hour, which includes glazes, tools, instructional support, and firing. Group rates and birthday parties available.
Ages: Elementary–adult
Parking: Street meters or pay lot behind building

Feat of Clay is an upscale and more artsy version of the typical plaster playhouses. Pick out white bisqueware, create your own combination of glaze colors and designs, and the results: a piece of functional pottery to use or display. Bisqueware pieces include tea cups, mugs, pasta bowls, pitchers, tiles, plates, and doggie bowls. Since the prices are higher and the techniques a little more sophisticated, it's best for older elementary school children and adults. Also visit the Art Center's Gallery, Kid's Activity Center, and Gallery Shop. The Center's ArtVentures offers another creative outing.

Theater

Fisher Theatre

West Grand Boulevard at Second, Detroit
313-872-1000 (information)
313-871-1132 (group sales)
248-645-6666 (Ticketmaster)

Website: www.fisherdetroit.com
Location: West Grand Boulevard and Second Avenue
Showtime: 8 p.m., Tuesday–Saturday. 2 p.m., Saturday and Sunday. 7:30 p.m., Sunday.
Tickets: $20–$65
Ages: Most plays are geared for an adult audi-

ence; occasionally there are plays and musicals appropriate for a young audience.

Parking: Use lots adjacent to the theatre, $6.

The Fisher Theatre is housed in a landmark building and is one of Detroit's major "Broadway" playhouses.

Family Shows

Flint Youth Theatre at Bower Theater

1220 East Kearsley, Flint
810-760-1018

Location: Flint's Cultural Center

Showtime: Weekday and weekend performances, throughout the year

Tickets: $5–$7. Group rates available.

Ages: Preschool and up

Parking: Free on site

Flint Youth Theatre offers talented local children a chance to take workshops and classes and perform several shows throughout the year.

Theater

Flint Youth Theatre at Whiting Auditorium

1241 East Kearsley, Flint
810-760-1138

Location: Downtown Flint

Showtime: Public performances vary during the school year. Field Trips for schools, 10 a.m. and noon weekdays.

Tickets: $10 adults, $ 8 children

Ages: Preschool and up

Parking: Free on site

A series of four touring shows includes puppets, plays, and musical tales.

Theater

Fox Theatre

2211 Woodward, Detroit
313-983-6611 (information)
248-433-1515 (tickets by phone)
248-645-6666 (Ticketmaster)

Website: www.fisherdetroit.com

Location: On Woodward, two blocks south of I-75

Showtime: Evening and matinee performances
Tickets: Prices vary with performances
Ages: While most shows are geared for an adult audience, the Rockettes Christmas show is scheduled for December, *Sesame Street Live!* for January, and *Rugrats Live!* for March.
Parking: Lot across the street between John R and Woodward, Fox parking tower on north side of theater, underground lot at Grand Circus Park.

The Fox is an opulently beautiful, landmark Detroit theater you won't want to miss.

Music, Festivals

Freedom Hill

15000 Metroparkway, Sterling Heights
810-979-7010

Location: On Metroparkway (Sixteen Mile) between Utica and Schoenherr Roads
Showtime: Concerts and festivals are scheduled May–September
Tickets: Prices vary with concert; many festivals are free
Ages: All ages
Parking: $3–$5 on site

Freedom Hill offers families a chance to enjoy an outdoor concert. Ethnic festivals and outdoor movies are also held here during the summer.

Fun & Games

Fun with Plaster

6718 Orchard Lake Road, West Bloomfield
248-932-5210

Location: Just south of Maple Road
Showtime: 11 a.m.–6 p.m., Tuesday–Saturday. Noon–5 p.m. Sunday.
Tickets: Average plaster mold is $4.95, plus $1 for paint. Group and birthday party rates available.
Ages: Preschool–adult
Parking: Free

Try your hand at painting plaster molds; leave the mess behind you and take home a finished masterpiece.
Second location: 33405 Grand River, Farmington. 248-442-2690

Theater

Gem and Century Theatres

333 Madison Avenue, Detroit
313-963-9800 (box office)
248-645-6666 (Ticketmaster)

Location: Around the block from the Detroit Opera House
Showtime: Evening and matinee performances
Tickets: Prices vary with performances
Ages: While most shows are geared for an adult audience, older children will enjoy the cabaret atmosphere.
Parking: Lots adjacent to theaters

Take a trip back to an ornate 1920's movie house in these authentically restored, intimate theaters, now offering a variety of musical plays and revues.

Lunch Theater

Genitti's Hole-in-the-Wall

108 East Main Street, Northville
248-349-0522

Location: Downtown Northville
Showtime: 11:30 a.m., Saturday lunch, followed by show. Performances are held throughout the year.
Tickets: $11.55 adults, $9.55 children includes lunch and show
Ages: Preschool–elementary
Parking: On Main Street or in lot east of the restaurant

Sit family style in the restaurant and enjoy a hearty Italian lunch of salad, soup, pasta, chicken, and dessert. A lighthearted and lively performance full of audience participation follows in the small, intimate adjacent theater. Come dressed in costume for Halloween performances.

Summer Series

Giggles Gang

Oakland Mall
14 Mile Road at I-75, Troy
248-585-6000

Location: In center court
Showtime: 1 and 6 p.m., several Wednesdays during July and August
Tickets: Free
Ages: Preschool–elementary
Parking: Free in mall lots

Local magicians, theater groups, storytellers, and musicians entertain families during the summer.

Family Shows

Grosse Pointe Children's Theatre

Grosse Pointe War Memorial
32 Lakeshore Drive, Grosse Pointe Farms
313-881-7511

Location: William Fries Auditorium, Grosse Pointe War Memorial, Lakeshore Drive near Fisher Road
Showtime: Matinees and evenings, selected Saturdays and Sundays
Tickets: Prices vary with show
Ages: All ages
Parking: Free on site

The Grosse Pointe Children's Theatre, made up of school-aged children, performs several energetic shows throughout the year, including one for the December holidays. Birthday parties and groups receive special recognition before the performance.

IMAX Theater

Henry Ford Museum IMAX Theatre

20900 Oakwood Boulevard, Dearborn
313-271-1570
1-800-747-IMAX

Website: www.hfmgv.org
Location: Southfield Freeway and Oakwood Boulevard
Hours: Every hour on the hour. 10 a.m.–5:30 p.m., Sunday–Thursday. 9 a.m.–8:30 p.m., Friday. 9 a.m.–9:30 p.m., Saturday.
Admission: $7.50 adults, $6.50 children ages 5–12 and seniors, $6 children 4 and under. Ticket prices are separate from museum or village admission. Combination tickets are available. Henry Ford Museum or Greenfield Village and IMAX: $17.50 adults, $16 seniors, $12.50 children ages

5–12, $6 children 4 and under. Henry Ford Museum and Greenfield Village and IMAX: $28 adults, $27 seniors, $19 children ages 5–12, $6 children 4 and under.
Ages: Kindergarten and up
Plan: Each movie is 35–45 minutes, but plan on a whole-day visit and enjoy the other museums and historic village on site
Parking: Free lot
Lunch: Café, snack bar, concession stand
Facilities: Bathrooms, drinking fountain, coat check, stroller availability

Henry Ford Museum's new 420-seat theater shows both two- and three-dimensional IMAX movies on its huge, 62x80-foot flat screen, with six-track digital surround sound. The movies tie into the programming at the village and include educational and unique subjects. Be sure to call ahead to reserve your tickets.

Hilberry Theatre

4743 Cass, Detroit
313-577-2972

Website: www.comm.wayne.edu/theatre
Location: Corner of Cass and Hancock.
Showtime: The Hilberry offers first-rate adult shows in evening and matinee performances, October–May. A children's show is performed 10:30 a.m., Monday–Saturday for approximately two weeks, end of June–early July.
Tickets: $10–$17 for regular series; $4 for July's children's show. Group rates available.
Ages: Middle school and high school for adult series, ages 3–11 for the children's show.
Parking: Two lots across Cass from the theater, $3 fee

The Hilberry is a repertory company of talented Wayne State University graduate students who perform seven classic and modern plays each season. Children will enjoy summer's special children's play, often a fractured fairy tale or original story. After summer performances, cast members are on hand to give autographs.

Silent Films and Organ Concerts
Historic Baldwin Theatre

415 South Lafayette, Royal Oak
248-541-6430

Location: Between Ten and Eleven Mile Roads
Showtime: 8 p.m., Saturday, 2 p.m., Sunday. Each silent movie is accompanied by live organ music.
Tickets: $8
Ages: All ages
Parking: Municipal parking

Travel back to the days before "Talkies" became the rage, and enjoy a classic silent movie with organ music accompaniment. Baldwin Theatre is also the home of Stagecrafters, a community theater and youth theater.

Movie Theater, Organ Concerts
Historic Redford Theatre

17360 Lahser Road, Detroit
313-537-1133
313-537-2560 (information line)

Location: On Lahser Road, just north of Grand River
Showtime: 8 p.m., Friday and Saturday, 2 p.m., Saturday. Each movie is preceded by a half-hour organ concert.
Tickets: $2.50, except for specials or concerts
Ages: All ages
Parking: Free on site

Thanks to the Motor City Theatre Organ Society's loving restoration of the historic Redford Theatre and its Barton three-manual, 10-rank pipe organ, your kids can travel back to the time when Saturday at the movies meant big screens and live organ music. Local musicians give an organ concert before each classic movie. Schools are invited to schedule a silent movie with organ accompaniment during school hours.

Special Events

Jack Breslin Student Events Center

1 Birch Road, MSU Campus, East Lansing
517-432-5000

Location: Harrison and Shaw, on the west end of campus
Showtime: Evening and matinee performances
Tickets: Prices vary depending on show
Ages: Ages vary depending on show
Parking: Many lots near center

The center hosts rock concerts, country concerts, musicals, and annual visits by the rodeo, Disney on Ice, and Ringling Bros. and Barnum & Bailey Circus.

Family Shows

Jewish Community Center

15110 West Ten Mile Road, Oak Park
248-967-4030

Location: Ten Mile Road, just east of Greenfield Road
Showtime: Selected Sunday matinees, held throughout the year
Tickets: Prices vary depending on show
Ages: 3–7
Parking: Free on site

The center offers afternoon performances of local and national storytellers, children's theater, musicians, and puppetry.

Jewish Theater

JET (Jewish Ensemble Theatre)

Aaron DeRoy Theater
Jewish Community Center
6600 West Maple Road, West Bloomfield
248-788-3583 (information)
248-788-2900 (box office)

Website: www.comnet.org/JET
Location: On the lower level of the Jewish Community Center
Showtime: 7:30 p.m., Wednesday, Thursday and Sunday. 2 p.m., Sunday matinee, and occasionally

Wednesday matinee. 8 p.m. Saturday.
Tickets: $13–$23
Ages: Generally middle school–adult
Parking: Jewish Community Center lot

JET is a professional theater which offers a yearly series of four plays plus a festival of on-stage play readings from new plays. Most of the plays have themes of interest to the Jewish community or have Jewish authors. JET also offers educational outreach projects, including plays for school groups.

Special Events

Joe Louis Arena

600 Civic Center Drive, Detroit
313-983-6606

Website: www.detroitredwings.com

The arena hosts Ringling Bros. and Barnum & Bailey Circus, Disney on Ice, and a host of rock concerts. Parents who want to take their children to a rock concert, but let the children enjoy the concert without them, can wait in the "Parents' Room."

Family Shows

Junior Theatre

co-sponsored by Ann Arbor Civic Theatre and Ann Arbor Community Education and Recreation
2275 Platt Road, Ann Arbor
734-971-2228 (tickets)
734-971-0605 (information)

Website: www.a2ct.org
Location: Ann Arbor Civic Theatre Playhouse, Platt south of Washtenaw
Showtime: Two shows during the school year, plus "The Strolling Players" tour during the summer.
Tickets: $6 adults, $5 children
Ages: Elementary–middle school
Parking: Free on site

Children's theater performed by talented Ann Arbor area middle and high school students.

Fun & Games

Kaput Kapot

151 South Bates, Birmingham
248-594-8423

Location: off of Maple Road in downtown Birmingham
Showtime: 1–8 p.m., Tuesday–Thursday. Noon–5 p.m., Wednesday, Friday, and Saturday. By appointments only on Sunday and Monday. Call to schedule private parties.
Tickets: Bisqueware, $3–$60. Studio time: $6/hour with minimum of one hour, which includes glazes, tools, instructional support, and firing. Birthday and adult parties available.
Ages: 7 and up
Parking: Metered parking and parking structure on block away

Kaput Kapot is another upscale glaze-your-own-pottery studio. Pick out white bisqueware, create your own combination of glaze colors and designs, and end up with a piece of functional pottery to use or display. Bisqueware pieces include tea cups, mugs, pasta bowls, pitchers, tiles, plates and doggie bowls. Since the prices are higher and the techniques a little more sophisticated, it is best for older elementary school children and adults.

Family Shows

Kids Koncerts

Southfield Centre for the Arts
24350 Southfield Road, Southfield
248-424-9022

Location: On the east side of Southfield Road, just north of 9½ Mile Road
Showtime: 1:30–2:15, once-a-month on Saturday
Tickets: $3.25. Group of 10 or more, $2.50.
Ages: 4–10
Parking: Free on site

Once-a-month, throughout the year, Southfield Parks and Recreation brings to the stage a series of clowns, mimes, musicians, and magicians to entertain area families.

Historical Reenactments
Living History Encampments

Travel back in time and experience the sights, sounds, and smells of the Revolutionary War, War of 1812, and the Civil War. Reenactment festivals are popping up all over Southeastern Michigan and offer families a wonderful day-long immersion in the past. Here is a sampling of popular annual festivals.

Civil War Remembrance, Memorial Day Weekend, Greenfield Village, Dearborn. 313-271-1620.

Heritage Festival, Memorial Day Weekend, Rochester Municipal Park, Rochester. 248-656-0999.

Rendezvous on the Rouge, second weekend in June, Ford Field, Dearborn. 313-565-3000.

Civil War Muster, second weekend in June, Kensington Metropark, Milford. 248-685-1561.

Civil War Reenactment, mid-June, The Burgh, Civic Center Drive and Berg Road, Southfield. 248-827-0701.

Civil War Weekend, end of June, Crossroads Village, Flint. 810-736-7100.

Civil War Re-Creation, early July, Nike County Park, Newport. 734-654-8265.

Waterford Summer Festival, end of July, Waterford. 248-623-9389.

Ypsilanti Heritage Festival, mid-August, Riverside Park and Depot Town, Ypsilanti. 734-483-4444.

Tin Cups and Hard Tacks, mid-August, Michigan Historical Museum, Lansing. 517-373-3559.

War of 1812 Battle Reenactments, mid-August, Lake Erie Metropark, Rockwood. 734-379-5020.

Cascades Civil War Muster, end of August, Cascades Park, Jackson. 517-788-4320.

Old French Town Days, end of August. Hellenberg Park, Monroe. 734-243-7137.

Rendezvous on the Huron, first weekend in September. Kensington Metropark Farm Center, Milford. 248-685-1561.

Revolutionary War Encampment, first weekend in September. Fort Malden National Historic Site, Amherstburg. 519-736-5416.

Railroad Days, end of September. Greenfield Village, Dearborn. 313-271-1620.

Somewhere in Time, September. Elizabeth Park, Trenton. 734-261-1990.

Dearborn Civil War Days, first weekend in October. Commandant's Quarters, Dearborn. 313-565-3000.

Fall Festival: A Blast to the Past, first Saturday in October. University of Michigan Matthaei Botanical Gardens, Ann Arbor. 734-998-7061.

Wolcott Mill Civil War Muster, first weekend in October, Wolcott Mill Metropark, Ray Township. 810-749-5997.

Family Shows, Family Movies
McMorran Place Theatre

701 McMorran Boulevard, Port Huron
810-985-6166 (information)
810-985-1922 (hot line)

Website: www.mcmorran.com
Location: Downtown Port Huron, McMorran Boulevard and Huron Avenue
Showtime: Evening and matinee performances of children's plays are offered throughout the year. Family movies (rated G and PG) are offered 7 p.m., daily.
Ages: Depends on specific show.
Tickets: Prices vary with performances
Parking: On site

McMorran Place Theatre offers a variety of family entertainment year-round, including movies, concerts, dance, and theater.

Theater

Macomb Center for the Performing Arts

44575 Garfield Road, Clinton Township
810-286-2222 (box office)
810-286-2268 (group rates)

Location: Garfield and Hall (M-59) Roads, near Lakeside Mall
Showtime: Sunshine Series: 10 a.m., 1, and 3:30 p.m., Saturdays, September–May. Family Series and Special Events offer matinee and evening performances
Tickets: $7 and up
Ages: Preschool–adult
Parking: Free on site

The Sunshine Series brings national and local professional children's theater troupes to the Macomb Center stage, performing classic stories, fairy tales, puppetry, and magic. In addition, the Family Series and Special Events include holiday specials, musicals and dance.

Fun, Magic

Magic Club McDonald's

10945 Allen Road, Allen Park
313-386-9401

Location: Two miles east of Telegraph at the corner of Allen Road and Goddard Road
Showtime: 6 p.m., Monday
Tickets: Free show with your meal
Ages: Preschool–adult
Parking: Free at restaurant

Business as usual on Monday evenings includes burgers, fries, happy meals, and disappearing bunnies. Local magicians perform informal, light-hearted, audience-participatory shows for families. Arrive early to stake out a table and play in the cheery playscape where a talking Ronald McDonald resides. Magicians also entertain once a week at a White Lake McDonald's, 9615 Highland Road. 248-698-2424.

Lunch Theater

Maplewood Family Theatre

31735 Maplewood, Garden City
734-525-8846

Location: Maplewood Community Center
Showtime: 12:30 p.m., Saturday, once a month,
October–April.
Tickets: $6 includes food and show
Ages: All ages
Parking: Free on site
   Enjoy a light meal and a performance by a local
children's theater troupe.

Theater

Marquis Theatre

135 East Main, Northville
248-349-8110

Location: Downtown Northville
Showtime: Selected matinee performances for the
public and school groups throughout the year
Tickets: $7
Ages: Preschool and up
Parking: Metered parking on street or in municipal
lots
   Come to the Marquis Theatre, a national historic landmark in Northville, sink into plush red vel-
vet seats, and munch on buttery popcorn as you
watch a lively rendition of a children's classic or a
popular musical. All shows are suitable for families;
three are geared specifically to children and performed during spring, summer, and winter.

 Video Arcade

Marvin's Marvelous Mechanical Museum and Emporium

Hunter's Square Shopping Plaza
31005 Orchard Lake Road, Farmington Hills
248-626-5020

Website: www.marvin3m.com
Location: On Orchard Lake Road, just south of
Fourteen Mile Road
Showtime: 10 a.m.–9 p.m., Monday–Thursday. 10

a.m.–11 p.m., Friday and Saturday. 11 a.m.–9 p.m. Sunday.
Tickets: 25 cents–$1 for most machines and rides. A dollar bill changer is located near the rides.
Ages: Preschool and up
Parking: Free lot on site

Line your pockets with quarters and get ready for a cacophony of blips and beeps. Over 300 mechanical games, kiddie rides, and authentic old-fashioned pinball machines make this indoor ride emporium a child's dream come true. Toddlers will love the variety of rides and the circus atmosphere. Older children will want to try to outwit the "metal grabbers" and snag a special prize, or shoot ducks and enemies on beautifully restored machines, many built in the early part of the century. There's plenty of room for birthday parties.

Theater

Masonic Temple

500 Temple, Detroit
313-832-5900 (information)
313-871-1132 (group sales)

Website: www.masonicdetroit.com
Location: Temple and Second
Showtime: Matinee and evening performances depending on show
Tickets: $20–$65
Ages: Generally geared to an adult audience, although many shows are of interest to children of all ages
Parking: Use area lots, $5–$8

The Masonic Temple Theatre, a designated historic building with a seating capacity of over 4,000 seats, is one of the area's most beautiful and largest theatrical houses. It hosts dance concerts and touring shows, including musicals with spectacular sets.

Music, Summer Series

Meadow Brook Music Festival

Oakland University, Rochester
248-377-0100 (information)
248-645-6666 (Ticketmaster)

Location: Walton Boulevard, between Adams and Squirrel Roads
Showtime: Matinees for children's series; evenings for concert series, June–September.
Tickets: Prices vary with show; pavilion and lawn tickets available
Ages: Children's shows are geared for preschool to upper elementary. Many DSO Friday evening concerts are suitable for the whole family and include fireworks or a laser show.
Parking: $6 parking on site
 The Music Festival hosts the Detroit Symphony Orchestra and other musicians, and offers classical, jazz, and pops programs. Bring blankets and lawn chairs and picnic on the lawn before and after the concert.

Theater

Meadow Brook Theatre

Oakland University, Rochester
248-377-3300 (box office)
248-370-3316 (group sales)

Location: Walton Boulevard between Adams and Squirrel Roads, on the campus of Oakland University
Showtime: Matinee and evening performances depending on play. Student discount tickets always available day of performance.
Tickets: $19.50–$35
Ages: Generally an adult audience, but many plays are appropriate for 11 and up
Parking: Free on site
 Seven plays are offered each season; several offer special school matinees. The annual December favorite, *A Christmas Carol,* is fun for the entire family.

Puppet Shows

Meadowbrook Village Mall Puppet Theatre

82 North Adams Road, Rochester
248-375-9451

Location: The puppet theater is located in a storefront space inside the mall.

Showtime: During the school year: 7 p.m., Monday–Friday. 11 a.m., 1, and 3 p.m., Saturday. 1, and 3 p.m., Sunday. During the summer: 11 a.m., 1, 3, and 7 p.m., Monday–Friday. 11 a.m., 1, and 3 p.m., Saturday. 1 and 3 p.m., Sunday.
Tickets: Free
Ages: Preschool–early elementary
Parking: Free in adjacent lot

Each month, a new classic fairy tale adaptation is presented, offering parents and their small children a 25-minute respite from shopping. Children sit on miniature bleachers and are mesmerized by the small puppet stage. Narration, dialogue, and music are taped, but the puppet manipulation is live.

Opera, Music, Dance, Theater

Michigan Opera Theatre

1526 Broadway, Detroit
313-237-SING (information)
313-237-7894 (group sales)

Website: www.motopera.org
Location: The Detroit Opera House, Broadway at Grand Circus Park
Showtime: 8 p.m., Friday and Saturday, 2 p.m., Sunday matinees, 7:30 p.m., Sunday. Five operas offered during fall and spring season. The Opera House also hosts a dance series, musicals, and special events.
Tickets: Prices vary with show. Group rates available.
Ages: 7 and up for most operas
Parking: $6–$8. Detroit Opera House parking garage on Broadway and John R, surface lot at the Broadway-Randolph People Mover Station, surface lot north of the Detroit Athletic Club on Madison, or Grand Circus underground

The Michigan Opera Theatre often offers a special student matinee for one of its shows with great appeal for children. A question-and-answer session follows the performance. The MOT also provides traveling "Community Programs" for performances in the schools and special American Sign Language performances for the hearing-impaired.

Special Event

Michigan Renaissance Festival

Holly
248-634-5552 (office)
1-800-601-4848

Location: One mile north of Mt. Holly, Inc., on Dixie Highway (US 10) between Pontiac and Flint
Showtime: 10 a.m.–7 p.m., weekends and Labor Day Monday, mid-August–September, rain or shine
Tickets: $14.95 adults, $ 11.75 seniors, $5.95 children 5–12, under 5 free. Group prices available.
Ages: All ages
Parking: Free on site

Enter a sixteenth-century village dell and take part in the ribald merrymaking. Children will enjoy old-fashioned rides, strolling costumed players, and entertainment—puppet shows, dance, juggling, and jousting. Gnaw on a turkey leg or roasted corn, shop for handmade art wares, and watch craft demonstrations in the village marketplace.

Dance

Music Hall

350 Madison Avenue, Detroit
313-963-7680
313-963-2366 (tickets)

Location: Corner of Madison Avenue and Brush Street. Take Madison Avenue exit off I-75
Showtime: Times vary.
Tickets: Prices vary.
Ages: Mature children for dance series and special events.
Parking: $5 in lighted lots, located on all four sides of theater

Music Hall offers a first-rate dance concert series, including the Dance Theatre of Harlem, plus a variety of gospel shows, musicals, and well-known entertainers.

Family Shows

Oakland University Department of Music, Theater and Dance

Varner Hall, Oakland University campus,
Rochester
248-370-2030 (information)
248-370-3013 (box office)

Location: I-75 and University Drive, Oakland University campus
Showtime: A variety of performances, September–April
Tickets: $4–$12
Ages: 6–12 years
Parking: Free on site

The Department of Music, Theater and Dance includes children's shows and activities and a family holiday show in December.

Youth Concerts, Music

Orchestra Hall

3711 Woodward Avenue, Detroit
313-576-5111

Website: www.detroitsymphony.com
Location: Between Warren and Mack, one mile south of the DIA
Showtime: Young People's Concerts, 11 a.m., Saturdays. Adult series of classical, pops, and jazz, 8 p.m., Thursday and Friday, 10:45 a.m., Friday, 8:30 p.m., Saturday, 3 p.m., Sunday. Season runs September–June. Special December holiday events, like the annual "Nutcracker," offer more matinee and evening performances.
Tickets: $8–$31 for youth concerts, $18 and up for adult concerts.
Ages: 6–10 for the youth concerts and holiday specials, middle school and up for the adult concerts
Parking: $5, lots on Parsons and on Woodward

Historic Orchestra Hall is the proud home of the Detroit Symphony Orchestra.

Fun & Games

The Painted Pot

421 Walnut Boulevard, Rochester
248-652-8255

Location: University and Fourth Street
Showtime: Noon–9 p.m., Tuesday–Thursday. 10 a.m.-6 p.m., Friday and Saturday. Noon–5 p.m., Sunday. Closed Monday.
Tickets: Bisqueware, $1–$60. Studio time: $7/hour with minimum of one hour, which includes glazes, tools, instructional support, and firing. Group rates and birthday parties available.
Ages: Elementary–adult
Parking: Metered parking in front and lot in back

An upscale and artsy paint-your-own-pottery studio with a party room seating up to 75. Choose from a variety of tea cups, banks, mugs, pasta bowls, pitchers, tiles, plates, and doggie bowls. Create your own combination of glaze colors and designs, and the results: a piece of functional pottery to use or display.

Music, Special Events

The Palace

Two Championship Drive, Auburn Hills
248-377-0100 (information)
248-645-6666 (Ticketmaster)

Website: www.palacenet.com
Nationally known rock groups and entertainers, dazzling special events, as well as the Detroit Pistons, Vipers, and Shock take center stage at the Palace. Arrive early and enjoy the two-story family entertainment atrium, where fans can browse through rock star memorabilia in the Celebrities Hall of Fame and relive Piston history playing computer games, watching the giant video wall, and browsing through the Pistons Hall of Fame. During selected rock concerts, parents without tickets may stay and relax in the "Quiet Room," which is actually the Palace Club. For easiest access to the Club, parents should enter Gate One off Lapeer Road and enter the Palace through the Administration Entrance next to the West Entrance. After the concert, meet the kids on the first floor of the Atrium.

Theater, Children's Theater

The Performance Network
"Goodtime Saturdays"

Huron Street, Ann Arbor
734-663-0681 (box office)

Location: On Huron, between Main and Fourth
Showtime: Varies with show
Tickets: Moderate prices
Ages: Preschool–elementary
Parking: Use structure on Fourth and Washington
The Performance Network is a 143-seat "black box" theater offering innovative theater and new plays for children, families, and adults.

Music

Pine Knob Music Theatre

Clarkston
248-377-0100 (information)
248-645-6666 (Ticketmaster)
Website: www.palacenet.com
Location: Sashabaw Road, off I-75
Showtime: Concert series, evenings, late May–early September
Tickets: Both pavilion and lawn tickets are available
Ages: All ages
Parking: $6 on site
Pine Knob offers the area's largest outdoor music and entertainment lineup throughout the summer. Relax on the lawn with a picnic or sit in the pavilion. Parents can drop off children at concerts and wait in the "Parents' Park."

Fun & Games

Plaster Playhouse

43063 Hayes, Sterling Heights
810-566-0666

Location: Lakeshore Plaza at Hayes and Nineteen Mile Road
Showtime: School year: 3–7 p.m., Tuesday–Friday. 10 a.m.–6 p.m., Saturday. Noon–5 p.m. Sunday. Summer: Noon–6 p.m., Monday–Friday. Noon–5 p.m., Saturday. Closed Sunday.

Tickets: Average plaster mold is $5. $1.25 additional for paint.
Ages: Preschool–adult
Parking: Free

Plaster Playhouse offers children a chance to become artists and take home their painted creations.

Fun & Games

Plasterworks

3050 Union Lake Road, Union Lake
248-360-9920

Location: Corner of Union Lake and Commerce Lake Roads, in Commerce Town Center
Showtime: Summer: 10 a.m.–6 p.m., Monday–Friday. 10 a.m.–8 p.m., Saturday. Noon–6 p.m., Sunday. School year: Noon–6 p.m., Monday–Friday. 10 a.m.–8 p.m., Saturday. Noon–6 p.m., Sunday.
Tickets: $1.25 for the paint. $4.75 and up for the plaster mold. Group rates and birthday party packages available.
Ages: Preschool–adult
Parking: Free on site

At the Plasterworks, kids of all ages can choose a modern plaster mold and in less than an hour, turn it into a colorful work of art. The atmosphere is informal, and the adult supervision encouraging.
Second location: 42114 Ford Road, Canton. 734-981-3930

African American Theater

Plowshares Theatre Company

Anderson Theater
Henry Ford Museum
20900 Oakwood Boulevard, Dearborn
313-872-0279 (box office)

Location: Performances are held in the museum's Anderson Theater
Showtime: 7:30 p.m., Thursday–Friday. 3 and 8 p.m. Saturday. 6 p.m., Sunday.
Tickets: $18 evening, $15 matinee
Ages: Middle school and up
Parking: Free parking lot

Michigan's only African American professional theater company offers comedies, new works, and Michigan premiers of African American plays.

Music, Special Events

Pontiac Silverdome

1200 Featherstone, Pontiac
248-456-1600

Website: www.stadianet.com/silverdome
The silverdome hosts a variety of special events and trade shows and the Detroit Lions, expected through the 2001 season.

Theater, Dance

Power Center

121 Fletcher, Ann Arbor
734-763-3333

Ann Arbor's modern facility hosts concerts, dance, theater, and music series. The kids will love the reflecting glass windows.

Summer Series

Puppets in the Park

Bloomer Park
7581 Richardson Road, West Bloomfield
248-738-2500

Location: Richardson Road, 1/2 mile east of Haggerty Road
Showtime: 1–2 p.m., one weekday in July and August
Tickets: Free
Ages: Preschool and early elementary
Parking: Free on site
On a balmy summer day, watch a puppet show while enjoying a picnic lunch.

Theater

Purple Rose Theatre

137 Park Street, Chelsea
734-475-5817

Location: On Chelsea's main street
Showtime: 8 p.m., Wednesday–Saturday. 3 p.m., Saturday matinee. 2 p.m., Sunday matinee.
Tickets: $25 Friday–Saturday. $20 Wednesday, Thursday, and Sunday.
Ages: Ages vary with each show
Parking: Lot behind theater
The intimate, 119-seat theater, owned by actor Jeff Daniels, features live contemporary plays for both families and adults. Dine nearby at the Common Grille (734-475-0470) before the performance.

Theater

Quirk Theatre

13 Quirk, Ypsilanti
734-487-1221

Location: On the Eastern Michigan University campus
Showtime: Evenings and matinees
Tickets: Prices vary with show
Ages: While most shows are geared for an adult audience, there are several children's shows offered throughout the year.

Parking: On site

The EMU Players perform a holiday play in December and several adaptations of children's classics throughout the year.

Special Event

Ringling Bros. and Barnum & Bailey Circus

The beginning of October is the time the "Greatest Show On Earth" comes to the Joe Louis Arena.

Theater

Riverwalk Theatre

228 Museum Drive, Lansing
517-482-5700 (information)
517-372-0945 (box office)

Location: Adjacent to Impression 5 Museum
Showtime: Children's shows are 7:30 p.m., Friday; 2 and 4:30 p.m., Saturday and Sunday.
Tickets: Prices vary depending on show
Ages: 3–10 for children's shows.
Parking: Free in Impression 5 lot

Whether it's a children's show with thematic elements tying into a special Impression 5 exhibit, or a musical comedy, Riverwalk's 250-seat theater-in-the-round offers an intimate experience.

Special Event

Royal Hanneford Circus

This circus comes to the Palace in March with lots of animal acts plus death-defying stunts, clowns, and glitter.

Comedy Club

The Second City

2301 Woodward Avenue, Detroit
313-965-2222 (tickets)

Website: www.secondcity.com
Location: Second City Theater building just north of the Fox

Showtime: 8 p.m., Wednesday, Thursday, and Sunday. 8 and 10:30 p.m. Friday and Saturday. Free improv after Friday and Saturday late show.
Tickets: $12–$19.50
Ages: Use your discretion; the material uses adult humor
Parking: Parking deck on Montcalm, or across the street, usually $5

Chicago's and Toronto's famed comedy club goes Motown. Don't miss seeing metro Detroit's talented performers spoof the local scene. For before or after meals, try America's Pizza Cafe, serving lunch and dinner daily, 313-964-3122, or Hockeytown Cafe, 313-965-9500. Second City also offers a comedy camp for kids, July and August.

Special Event

Sesame Street Live!

The Sesame Street gang takes the stage at the Fox Theatre for a wild and noisy show, held for almost two weeks during the end of January.

Summer Series

Shain Park Concerts

Shain Park
Martin and Henrietta, Birmingham
248-644-1807 (Parks and Recreation)
Location: Two blocks west of Woodward, one block south of Maple
Showtime: 7 p.m., every Thursday, June–August
Tickets: Free
Ages: All ages
Parking: Use metered lots and street parking

Pull up a patch of earth and settle in for a lively outdoor concert in the middle of downtown Birmingham. Kids can play on the climbers and swings in the park while you listen to the music.

Special Event

Shrine Circus

The State Fairgrounds Coliseum hosts the colorful and noisy annual Shrine Circus in March.

Family Series, Movies
Stage IV Events

State Wayne Theatre
35310 Michigan Avenue, Wayne
734-326-4600

Location: One block west of Wayne Road
Showtime: Varies with show
Tickets: $5 adults, $3.50 children
Ages: Preschool and elementary
Parking: In lot

City of Wayne Parks and Recreation offers a family series of seasonal fare and youth theater, including a Halloween show and Storytime with Santa. Plus, the State Theatre offers second-run movies at discount prices.

Family Shows
Stagecrafters Youth Theatre

Baldwin Theatre
415 South Lafayette, Royal Oak
248-541-6430

Location: Between Ten and Eleven Mile Roads
Showtime: Matinee and evening
Tickets: $5
Ages: Preschool and up
Parking: Free on site

Young children will enjoy watching their favorite fairy tales and children's musicals performed by drama students ages 8–17, during the Youth Theatre's winter and summer productions. The Stagecrafters also offer an adult season of drama and musicals, September–June. Older children would enjoy many of these productions.

Family Shows, Special Events
State Fairgrounds

1120 West State Fair Avenue, Detroit
313-369-8250

The State Fairgrounds hosts children's theater performances and dog and horse shows throughout the year, the Shrine Circus in March, and the annual Michigan State Fair at the end of August.

Summer Concerts

Bring your lawn chairs, blankets and picnic suppers. If it's summer, it's time for free music under the stars. Here's a list of concert series offered by local parks and recreation departments.

Ann Arbor:
Gallup Park on Saturdays, 734-662-9319; West Park on Wednesdays, 313-994-2300, ext. 228.

Birmingham:
Shain Park on Thursdays, 248-644-1807.

Bloomfield Hills:
Christ Church Cranbrook carillon concerts on Sunday, 248-644-5210.

Farmington:
Downtown Gazebo on Fridays, 248-473-7276.

Grosse Pointe Farms:
Grosse Pointe War Memorial on Wednesdays, 313-881-7511

Livonia:
In selected parks on Sundays, 734-466-2412

Novi:
North lawn of Civic Center on Thursdays, 248-347-0400.

Oak Park:
Shepard Park on Tuesdays, 810-691-7555.

Plymouth:
Kellogg Park on selected evenings, 734-416-4278.

Royal Oak:
Detroit Zoo, just inside the front gate on Wednesdays, 248-398-0903

Southfield:
Civic Center and Berg Road Gazebo on Wednesdays; Sun Bowl behind 3000 Prudential Town Center on Sundays, 248-424-9022.

Sterling Heights:
Dodge Park on Thursdays, 810-977-6123, ext. 200.

Troy:
Civic Center lawn, Big Beaver Road, on Wednesdays, 248-524-3484.

Waterford:
Hess-Hathaway Park on selected evenings, 248-623-2449.

Wayne County:
In selected parks on Wednesdays, 734-261-1990

Westland:
William P. Faust Public Library Performance
Pavilion on Sundays, 734-722-7620
Wyandotte:
Bishop Park on Wednesdays, 734-246-4505.

Summer Series

Summer Fun Series

Downtown Farmington
248-473-7276

Location: Under the tent on Grand River east of
Farmington Road
Showtime: Generally 10:30 a.m., noon, and 1 p.m.,
Wednesday, mid-June–mid-August
Tickets: Free or minimal workshop fee
Ages: Preschool–elementary
Parking: Use downtown store lots

Series highlights Michigan entertainers and
offers a lineup of storytelling, puppetry, songs,
comedy, magic, and playlets.

Summer Family Series

Summer in the City

151 Martin Street, Birmingham
248-433-3550

Location: On Martin Street, in front of City Hall, in
downtown Birmingham
Showtime: 6:30 p.m., Friday, July and August
Tickets: Free
Ages: Preschool and up
Parking: Use street meters or downtown parking
structures

Bring blankets, lawn chairs and a picnic supper
and settle in for an enthusiastic family performance
by local musicians, dancers, puppeteers, and
singers.

Outdoor Movies

Summer Movies

Here's a trend that's getting bigger every year.
It's the 90's version of the 50's drive-in movies.
Several Metro Detroit parks are showing big
screen, outdoor movies on summer evenings.

Many even charge families by the carload. Bring lawn chairs or blankets and lots of snacks. Call ahead for a schedule.

Ford Lake Park, Ypsilanti. 734-483-0774.

Freedom Hill County Park, Sterling Heights. 810-979-7010.

Wayne County Park, various locations. 734-261-1990.

West Bloomfield Parks and Recreation, 734-738-2500.

Multi-Cultural Art
Sunday Funday

Sponsored by the Arts League of Michigan
313-964-1104

Location: Museum of African American History, 315 East Warren, Detroit.
Showtime: 3–4:30 p.m. Sunday, once a month
Tickets: Free with museum admission. Sunday Funpack, $4/person includes museum admission, light lunch, free gifts, and coupons
Ages: Preschool–adult
Parking: Free on site

Nationally and locally known artists, dancers, writers, and musicians demonstrate their craft and then lead families in hands-on workshops. Past experiences have included creating Egyptian jewelry and learning how to sing "Scat."

Family Shows
Temple Beth El Fisher Concert Series

7400 Telegraph Road, Bloomfield Hills
248-851-1100

Website: www.tbeonline.com
Location: Telegraph, just south of Maple Road
Showtime: 12:45 p.m., Sunday. Three 45-minute concerts each year.
Tickets: Free
Ages: Preschool–fourth grade
Parking: Free on site

The Loren B. Fisher Cultural Art Series offers three free performances for families during the year, offering local singers, magicians, clowns, children's opera, and theater.

Special Events

UniverSoul Circus

The nation's only all-black circus unfurls its big top at Detroit's Chene Park at the end of September and offers international aerialists, unicyclists, equestrians, clowns, elephants, and tigers, plus a look at African American history.

Family Entertainment

Upstage Magic Theatre

The Wunderground
110 South Main Street, Royal Oak
248-546-1123

Location: At Main Street and Eleven Mile, on the second floor above Ace Hardware
Showtime: Weekend shows, May–August. Store hours are noon–6 p.m., Monday–Saturday. Extended hours and Sunday hours during the summer.
Tickets: $6 adults, $5 children
Ages: All ages
Parking: Metered lot behind store

The 100-seat Upstage Magic Theatre's performances of puppeteers, magicians, jugglers, poets, and storytellers is a perfect way to pass the time while waiting for a table at a popular Royal Oak restaurant or for a respite in the middle of a shopping Saturday. The Wunderground also offers kids of all ages a variety of puzzles and magic tricks, taro cards, yo-yo's, crystal balls, and juggling supplies. In addition, magic classes are offered throughout the year.

Children's Theater

Wild Swan Theater

416 West Huron, Ann Arbor (office)
734-995-0530

Website: www.comnet.org/wildswan
Location: Six public performances are held at Towsley Auditorium, Clark and Golfside Roads, on the

campus of the Washtenaw Community College, Ann Arbor Township. The group also performs for schools, libraries, museums and festivals.

Showtime: Friday evening, Saturday and Sunday afternoons. School performances, 10 a.m. and 1 p.m., Friday.
Tickets: $8 adults, $6 children
Ages: Preschool–adult
Parking: Free on site

Wild Swan Theater recreates folktales with dazzling wit and creativity, using masks, theater, music, and dance. In addition, American Sign language is part and parcel of the performance, so the production is accessible to the hearing impaired. Those with visual impairments can call ahead to request audio description tapes. Call for a schedule of children's and family workshops. "Dramatically Able," a video and handbook, offers teachers and workshop leaders a blueprint for adding dramatic play into the classroom.

Music

Windsor Symphony Orchestra

Chrysler Theatre
201 Riverside Drive
Windsor, Ontario, Canada
1-800-387-9181(box office)
519-252-6579 (box office)

Location: Chrysler Theatre, Clearly International Centre, Riverside Drive West and Ferry Street, one block west of Ouellette Avenue
Showtime: Family shows, 2 p.m., Sunday. Pops, 2:30 p.m., Sunday. Classical series, 8 p.m., Saturday.
Tickets: $20–$30 (Canadian funds)
Ages: 2 and up
Parking: Metered street parking, lots across the street near the river and in back of the auditorium

At family concerts, the emphasis is on fun as classical music is brought to life with art, mime, and humorous conducting.

Family Shows

Young People's Theater

734-996-3888 (ticket information tape)

Location: Performances held in different Ann Arbor auditoriums.

Showtime: Four or five family shows a year, evening and weekend matinee performances. YPT also offers year-round acting classes.

Tickets: Minimal fees

Ages: Shows are geared to an audience of all ages. Children 5 and up perform and act as stagehands.

Parking: Depends on location

Young People's Theater offers talented children a chance to perform in a variety of shows, from folk and fairy tales to modern musicals. Performances are energetic and creative and perfect for the entire family.

Fun & Games

You're Fired

6925 Orchard Lake Road, West Bloomfield
248-851-5594

Location: On The Boardwalk

Showtime: Noon–9 p.m., Tuesday–Thursday. 10 a.m.–5 p.m., Friday and Saturday. Noon–5 p.m., Sunday

Tickets: Bisqueware, $3.50 and up. Studio time: $8/hour with minimum of one hour, which includes glazes, tools, instructional support, and firing. Group rates and birthday parties available.

Ages: Older elementary–adult

Parking: Lot in front of store

You're Fired is an upscale and more artsy version of the typical plaster playhouses. Pick out white bisqueware, create your own combination of glaze colors and designs, and the results: a piece of functional pottery to use or display. Bisqueware pieces include candlesticks, serving pieces, picture frames, little boxes, vases and tea services.

Family Shows

Youtheatre

Millennium Centre
15600 J.L. Hudson Drive, Southfield
248-557-PLAY (7529) (box office)
248-557-4338 (administrative office)

Website: www.youtheatre.org
Location: Public performances at Millennium Centre. Three school field trip locations: Millennium Centre; Macomb Center for the Performing Arts, 44575 Garfield Road, Clinton Township; Michigan Theater, 603 East Liberty, Ann Arbor.
Showtime: 11 a.m. and 2 p.m., Saturday, 2 p.m., Sunday, October–May. School field trip matinees 10 a.m. and 12:30 p.m., weekdays. "Playshops," hands-on, creative theater arts workshops, are held 9:30–10:30 a.m., before each Saturday morning performance. Reservations are required for Playshops.
Tickets: $9. Subscription, group and advance purchase discounts available. Playshops, $8
Ages: Wiggle Club shows are geared for age 3–6. Movin' Up shows are geared for ages 7 and up.
Parking: Parking is free at the Millennium Centre and Macomb Center for the Performing Arts. Meter parking is available near Michigan Theater.

For almost four decades, Youtheatre has offered the finest and largest children's theater season in metro Detroit, presenting the best in mime, dance, puppetry, performance arts, and theater from around the country. Youtheatre offers a great birthday party and scout outing package. Teachers should call to receive a brochure of field trip performances. Beginning October 2000, Youtheatre moves to the new Millennium Centre. Shows scheduled March–May 2000 are in the old location, Music Hall, 350 Madison Avenue, Detroit.

Family Shows

Youtheatre at Michigan Theater
"Not Just For Kids"

603 East Liberty, Ann Arbor
734-668-8397

Location: West of State Street, just off the U of M campus
Showtime: Weekend afternoons, October–May
Tickets: $8.50 for Michigan Theater members, $10 general admission
Ages: Preschool and up
Parking: Use parking lot on Maynard and East Liberty

Youtheatre brings the best in children's theater, music, and puppetry to Ann Arbor.

Youth Theater
Youth Theater Opportunities

If your son or daughter is an aspiring actor, there are a number of Metro Detroit theater groups that offer young thespians a chance to perform. In addition, many offer year-round classes and summer workshops.

All of Us Express, Lansing: 517-699-3690

Ann Arbor Junior Theatre: 734-971-0605

Ann Arbor Young Actors Guild: 734-930-1614

Avon Players Rochester: 248-608-9077

Bloomfield Youth Theatre: 248-433-0885

Cotton Candy Players, Northville: 248-349-8110

Detroit Dance Collective, Royal Oak:
    248-546-4949

Flint Youth Theatre, Flint: 810-760-1018

Henry Ford Community College Children's
    Theatre, Dearborn: 313-845-9817

J.A.R. (Junior Actors of Ridgedale) Players,Troy:
    248-689-6240

Macomb Junior Players, Clinton Township:
    810-228-9525

Mosaic Youth Theatre of Detroit: 313-554-1422

Novi Youth Theatre: 248-347-0400

Peddy Players Theatre Company Youth Theatre,
    Detroit: 313-871-1051

Popcorn Players, Birmingham: 248-644-5832

Shameless Rainbow Youth Theater, Ann Arbor:
    734-663-0681

Southgate Community Players Young People's
    Theatre: 313-292-4159

Stagecrafters, Royal Oak: 248-541-6430

Ted E. Bear Productions, West Bloomfield:
    248-661-1000

Tinderbox Productions, Redford: 313-535-8962

Tree House Players, Grosse Pointe:
    313-881-7511

Wayne's World Youtheatre: 734-721-7400

Young People's Theater, Ann Arbor:
    734-996-3888

12
Cheering for the Home Team

TIP

Minor league teams, like the Vipers who play at the Palace, the Toledo Mud Hens, and Lansing Lugnuts, offer families a less expensive alternative to big league games. You'll also find friendly mascots, lots of promotional giveaways, and autograph-signing players.

Detroit is not just Hockey Town. We're Sports City. Love baseball? Check out the Tigers in Comerica Park, their brand new, state-of-the-art stadium. A hockey fan? We've got the back-to-back Stanley Cup champion Red Wings and on the college level, great hockey (with rowdy cheering fans) at U of M, MSU, and at the new WSU hockey stadium at the State Fair Coliseum. A football fan? Cheer for the Lions at the Silverdome and then at their new Detroit stadium in 2002. Or spend a fall afternoon cheering for the Wolverines at the newly enlarged Big House, and the Spartans at Spartan Stadium. Into basketball? Catch the Pistons and the Shock, Detroit's two professional basketball teams, at the Palace.

To avoid disappointing your children, send away for tickets early. And when you go, be ready to part with a lot of cash. Most children go to sporting events as much for the food as for the game. Don't forget to check the team schedules for special promotions. Many professional sports offer free gifts to the first several thousand patrons at a certain game. Your children will be thrilled to leave with a free calendar, mug, T-shirt, visor, cap, ball, or Beanie Baby.

Pro Football

Detroit Lions

Pontiac Silverdome
1200 Featherstone Road, Pontiac
248-335-4151
248-645-6666
(Ticketmaster to charge tickets by phone)

Website: www.Detroitlions.com
Location: M-59 and Opdyke Road. The team hopes to move into their new Detroit stadium by the 2002 season.
Season: August–December
Tickets: $35, $20
Lunch: The Main Event, a full service restaurant, plus lots of concessions
Parking: Lot on site. $10 fee, shuttle available.
Highlights: Occasional promotions offer free calendars, posters, or growl towels

Pro Basketball

Detroit Pistons

The Palace
Two Championship Drive, Auburn Hills
248-377-0100 (information)
248-371-2055 (group rates)
248-645-6666
(Ticketmaster to charge tickets by phone)

Website: www.palacenet.com
Location: I-75 and M-24
Season: November–April
Tickets: $10–$28
Lunch: Lots of choices including the Palace Grille, Domino's Pizza, kosher hot dogs, deli stand, and Mexican stand
Parking: Lot on site. $6 fee.
Highlights: There are special promotions throughout the season when fans 16 and younger receive Pistons T-shirts, basketballs, mugs, wristbands, baseball caps, mouse pads, gym bags, or pennants. We took three boys to one game and came home with three new basketballs. In the two-story family entertainment atrium, fans can relive Piston history playing computer games, watching the giant video wall, and browsing through the Pistons Hall of Fame. Challenge your favorite player to a slam dunk contest in the interactive video game Virtual Hoops, shop at the team superstore, and browse through rock star memorabilia in the Celebrities Hall of Fame.

Pro Hockey

Detroit Red Wings

Joe Louis Arena
600 Civic Center Drive, Detroit
313-983-6606 (recorded information)
313-471-3099 (group rates)
248-645-6666
(Ticketmaster to charge tickets by phone)

Website: www.detroitredwings.com
Location: Civic Center at the Riverfront, downtown Detroit
Season: October–April
Tickets: $20–$72

Lunch: Lots of concessions, including Little Caesar's Pizza
Parking: Use Joe Louis parking lot, adjacent to arena on Atwater Street. $7 fee.
Highlights: There are several special games when fans are given calendars or pucks

Pro Indoor Soccer

Detroit Rockers

The Palace
Two Championship Drive, Auburn Hills
248-366-6254 (information)
248-645-6666
(Ticketmaster to charge tickets by phone)

Location: I-75 and M-24
Season: October–March
Tickets: $11 general seats, $16 reserved seats
Lunch: Lots of choices, including the Palace Grille, Domino's Pizza, deli stand, and Mexican stand
Parking: Lot on site, $6 fee.

Pro Women's Basketball

Detroit Shock

The Palace
Two Championship Drive, Auburn Hills
248-377-0100 (information)
248-371-2055 (group rates)
248-645-6666 (Ticketmaster)

Website: www.detroitshock.com
Location: I-75 and M-24
Season: Early June-August
Tickets: $5–20
Lunch: Lots of choices including the Palace Grille, Domino's, deli stand, and Mexican stand
Parking: Lot on site, $6 fee.
Highlights: Cheer the team on with Zap the team mascot. Free give-away and family halftime entertainment. Before, during, and after the game, enjoy the new two-story family entertainment atrium where you can play computer games, watch the giant video wall, browse through the Pistons Hall of Fame, challenge your favorite player to a slam dunk contest in the interactive video game Virtual Hoops, shop at the team superstore, and browse through rock star memorabilia in the Celebrities Hall of Fame

Pro Baseball

Detroit Tigers

Comerica Park
2100 Woodward, Detroit
313-471-BALL (information and group sales)
248-25-TIGER (charge by phone)

Location: Off Woodward in Foxtown
Season: April–October
Tickets:
Lunch: Lots of food choices, including the gotta-have ballpark frank. Families can eat before the game in the 16,000-square-foot open-air patio.
Parking: Use Comerica Park structure or downtown lots
Highlights: The new, 40,000-seat stadium boasts the biggest scoreboard in sports—10 stories high and nearly a city block long. Comerica Park also features a walking hall of fame museum with base-

ball artifacts and interactive displays in the main concourse. The Tigers offer a schedule of special games when gifts of T-shirts, mugs, tote bags, notebooks, baseball cards, and even Beanie Babies are given out. After the games on Mondays, children can run the bases, and on Fridays there are fireworks/laser shows. In addition, kids love Paws, the larger-than-life, plush-stuffed Tiger mascot, and can join the Detroit Tigers Kids' Club and receive special membership freebies. Entry blanks are available at the stadium.

Pro Baseball Farm Team

Detroit Tiger Triple-A Farm Team

Toledo Mud Hens
Ned Skeldon Stadium
2901 Key Street, Maumee, Ohio
419-893-9483

Website: www.mudhens.com
Location: On Key Street, between Heatherdowns and Anthony Wayne Trail
Season: April–September.
Tickets: $6.50 box, $5 reserved, $4 general
Lunch: Concessions
Parking: Free
Highlights: You'll love the informality and small-town feeling at the Ned Skeldon Stadium. Every seat is close to the field and you'll get to shake hands with the mascot—Muddy the Mud Hen. The players are happy to give autographs, so bring along your minor league cards.

Minor League Hockey

Detroit Vipers

The Palace
Two Championship Drive, Auburn Hills
248-377-0100 (information)
248-371-2055 (group rates)
248-645-6666 (Ticketmaster)

Website: www.palacenet.com
Location: I-75 and M-24
Season: October–early April
Tickets: $5–$20
Lunch: Lots of choices, including the Palace

Grille, Domino's Pizza, kosher hot dogs, deli stand, and Mexican stand

Parking: Lot on site, $6 fee.

Highlights: Free give-aways and halftime entertainment. Before, during, and after the game, enjoy the two-story family entertainment atrium where you can play computer games, watch the giant video wall, browse through the Pistons Hall of Fame, challenge your favorite player to a slam dunk contest in the interactive video game Virtual Hoops, shop at the team superstore, and browse through rock star memorabilia in the Celebrities Hall of Fame.

Auto Racing

Flat Rock Speedway

14041 South Telegraph Road, Flat Rock
734-782-2480

Location: One mile south of Flat Rock on Telegraph Road

Season: 5:30 p.m. qualifying, 7 p.m. race, Saturday. Special events on Sunday. Mid-Apri–mid-September.

Tickets: $8–$15 adults, $3 children 6–12, under 6 free

Lunch: Concessions

Parking: Free on site

Basketball

Harlem Globetrotters

The Palace hosts the hilarious hoopsters in their annual January Motown visit.

Harness Racing

Hazel Park Raceway

1650 East Ten Mile Road, Hazel Park
248-398-1000

Location: Ten Mile, between Dequindre Road and Couzens

Season: 7:30 p.m., Monday, Tuesday, Thursday–Saturday, early April–mid-October. No races on Wednesday or Sunday.

Tickets: $2 clubhouse and grandstand.
Lunch: Two clubhouse restaurants, grandstand concessions
Parking: Use lots surrounding raceway, free.

Harness Racing
Jackson Harness Raceway

200 West Ganson, Jackson
517-788-4500

Location: Jackson and Ganson Roads
Season: 7:30 p.m., Wednesday, Friday, and Saturday. 3 p.m., Sunday. April–June and August–mid-October.
Tickets: Free on Wednesday, $2 Friday, Saturday, and Sunday
Lunch: Concessions, clubhouse restaurant
Parking: $1

Minor League Baseball
Lansing Lugnuts

Oldsmobile Park
505 East Michigan Avenue, Lansing
1-800-945-NUTS
517-485-4500

Location: Between Cedar and Larch Streets, just north of Michigan Avenue, 3 blocks east of the Capitol
Season: April–September
Tickets: $6, $5.50, $4.50
Lunch: Stadium fare including hotdogs, popcorn, peanuts
Parking: Metered street parking, ramps on North and South Grand Avenue lead to parking structures.
  Lansing's going nuts over their Kansas City affiliate baseball team. Join Big Lug, the team mascot, in the 10,000-seat stadium, and after the game, shop for souvenirs at Nuts and Bolts, the official store for red and black Lugnuts merchandise on Washington Square.

Rodeo

Longhorn World Championship Rodeo

Saddle up the gang and bring them to the Palace for the annual rodeo every February.

Auto Racing

Michigan International Speedway

12626 US-12, Brooklyn
517-592-6671, 517-592-6672
1-800-354-1010 (ticket office)

Website: www.penske.com
Location: M-50 and US-12
Season: Special event races are held on weekends, June–August
Tickets: $30–$75 depending on event. $5 discounts for children 12 and under.
Lunch: Elias Brothers Big Boy concession.
Parking: Free on site

College Sports

Michigan State University Spartans— Go Spartans!

220 Jenison Field House, East Lansing
517-355-1610

Website: www.msu.edu
Location: MSU Campus: Football—Spartan Stadium. Basketball—Jack Breslin Student Events Center. Hockey—Munn Arena.
Season: Football—September–November. Basketball—November–March. Hockey—October–March.
Tickets: Football $32–$38, basketball $11–$20, hockey $7–$14
Lunch: Concessions
Parking: Most lots around the Football Stadium and Jennison Field House charge $4–$5

Harness Racing
Northville Downs

301 South Center, Northville
248-349-1000

Location: Seven Mile and Sheldon Roads
Season: Live racing hours vary with season; call ahead for specific times. Generally, nightly 7:30 p.m. post times.
Tickets: $2. Children must be 12 years or older
Lunch: Clubhouse restaurant, grandstand concessions
Parking: Use lots surrounding site

Pro Hockey
Port Huron Border Cats

215 Huron Avenue, Port Huron
810-982-2287

Website: www.bordercats.com
Location: One block north of Military Street Bridge
Season: October-March
Tickets: $8.25, $10.25, $12.25
Lunch: The Hack, one block away
Parking: Lot on site. $2 fee.
Highlights: Bridges the Cat Mascot and cheerleaders. Ice promotion activities include "Chuck the Puck" where you can win a team jersey, the "$10,000 Shoot Out," and "Shoot for a Car."

Harness Racing
Sports Creek Raceway

4290 Morrish Road, Swartz Creek
810-635-3333

Location: 7 miles west of Flint, off I-69 at Morrish Road, Exit #128
Season: Mid-October–first weekend of April
Tickets: $2.50 grandstand, $4.50 clubhouse. All ages are welcome, but only 18 and older can place bets.
Lunch: Club house restaurant and grandstand concessions
Parking: Free

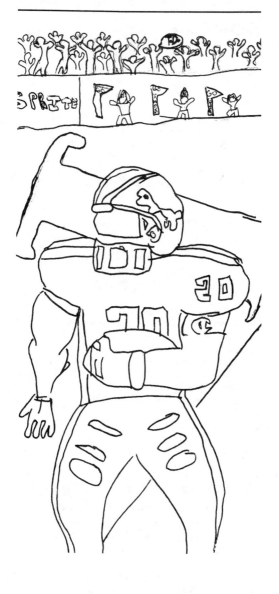

College Sports
University of Detroit Titans

4001 West McNichols Road, Detroit
313-993-1700

Website: http://www.udmercy.edu
Location: Calihan Hall, on Fairfield between Puritan and McNichols (Six Mile Road)
Season: November–March (Basketball)
Tickets: $7–$10
Lunch: Concessions
Parking: Use adjacent lot.

College Sports
University of Michigan Wolverines — Go Blue!

1000 South State Street, Ann Arbor
734-764-0247

Website: www.mgoblue.com
Location: U of M Campus: Football—U of M Stadium. Basketball—Crisler Arena. Hockey—Yost Field House.
Season: Football—September–November, Basketball—November–March. Hockey—October–March.
Tickets: Football $35, basketball $15, $12, hockey $9–$17
Lunch: Concessions
Parking: Use lots surrounding sites or park on campus and walk to the stadium or arenas

Amateur Auto Racing
Waterford Hills Road Racing

Waterford Road, Waterford
Independence Township
248-623-0070

Location: Six miles north of Pontiac and/mile east of Dixie Highway (U.S. 24)
Season: Begins 8 a.m. Saturday; 10 a.m. Sunday, May–September.

Tickets: $5, under 12 free. $5 additional for Pit Pass.
Lunch: Concessions
Parking: Free in lot

College Sports
Wayne State University Warriors

The Matthaei Complex
5101 John C. Lodge, Detroit
313-577-4280

Location: Lodge Expressway (M-10) and Warren: Football—WSU Stadium. Basketball—Matthaei Building. Hockey—State Fair Coliseum, 8 Mile Road at Woodward Avenue.
Season: Football—September–November. Basketball—November–March. Hockey—October–February.
Tickets: Tickets are available at box office on day of game. Football: $5 adults, $3 students, $1 with I.D., children 12 and under. Basketball: $3 adults, $2 students, $1 children 12 and under. Hockey: $10 adults reserved, $8 general, $4 children.
Lunch: Concessions
Parking: Use street along Lodge Service Drive or adjacent to sports facilities. State Fair Coliseum, located at 8 Mile Road and Woodward, has a parking lot.

Harness Racing
Windsor Raceway

Windsor, Ontario, Canada
313-961-9545 or 519-969-8311

Website: www.windsorraceway.com
Location: Highway 18 and Sprucewood, about three miles from the Ambassador Bridge
Season: 7:30 p.m., Tuesday, Wednesday, Friday–Sunday, October–April.
Tickets: $3.50 clubhouse, $2.50 grandstand, children under 12 free
Lunch: Concessions and restaurant
Parking: Lot on site, free.

Wrestling

World Championship Wrestling

The Palace, Two Championship Drive,
Auburn Hills
248-377-0100 (information)
248-645-6666 (Ticketmaster)

Location: I-75 and M-24
Season: Hulk Hogan and his gang of comic wrestlers invade the Palace
Tickets: $15–$30
Lunch: Lots of choices, including Domino's Pizza and kosher hot dogs
Parking: Lot on site. $6 fee.

13
Burning Off Energy

A SAMPLING OF PARTICIPANT SPORTS

TIP

Offer your kids safe, noncompetitive experiences by trying out some of the sports listed in this chapter. Follow up with lessons or leagues if they have fun or want to learn more.

Kids are always full of energy and raring to play. Here's a sampling of sites where they can burn off one or two hours of energy. You can find places for Little Leaguers' batting and fielding practice, friendly fishing holes where kids are assured of a catch, area municipal pools, and ice-skating rinks. You have your pick of places that rent canoes and cross-country skis, and offer bumper bowling, sledding, snow-shoeing, kite flying, horseback riding, go-karts, and miniature golf.

Kids can experience a variety of unusual sports, like archery, disc golf, laser tag, five-pin bowling, whirlyball, and paintball. In addition, indoor basketball courts, indoor soccer fields, and indoor playgrounds, wall climbing, rodeo experiences, and kids' ski clubs are also listed.

To help your selection, sports are listed alphabetically. I have intentionally omitted specific hours and prices because they fluctuate so rapidly. Please call for directions, hours, and fees.

Archery

It's okay for Jason to play William Tell, just don't fall for the apple-on-the-head trick. You can rent equipment or bring your own, and play for one hour during open shooting.

Detroit Archers

5795 Drake Road, West Bloomfield
248-661-9610

Double Action Indoor Shooting Center

32411 Dequindre, Madison Heights
248-588-4488

Pontiac Lake Recreation Area

7800 Gale Road, Pontiac
248-666-1020

River Bends Park

River Bends Road, off Ryan Road, just north or
Auburn Road, Shelby Township
810-731-0300

Starlight Archery Co.

21570 Groesbeck, Warren
810-771-1580

Target Sports

30482 North Woodward, Royal Oak
248-549-2122

Basketball

Bring the kids, pay one price, and spend the day shooting hoops in the area's basketball centers. Most have volleyball playing time, video games, food concessions, birthday party packages, leagues, lessons, and for little players, smaller, portable backboards.

Basketball America

257 West Clarkston, Lake Orion
248-693-5858

Features: Nine small courts, one regulation court, volleyball, rollerblade hockey

Basketball City

16400 Eastland, Roseville
810-778-1120

Features: Six full courts, 4-on-4 courts

Basketball City

15100 Northline Road, Southgate
313-285-1120

Features: Six full courts

Basketron

25855 Ford Road, Dearborn Heights
313-563-8766

Features: Whiffle basketball played from electronic bumper cars, arcade

Joe Dumars Fieldhouse

45300 Mound Road, Shelby Township
810-731-3080

Features: Indoor and outdoor basketball and volleyball courts, roller hockey rink, restaurant, fitness center, arcade

Metro Hoops

43655 Utica Road, Sterling Heights
810-731-HOOP

Features: Three small courts, volleyball

The Sports Academy

42930 West Ten Mile Road, Novi
248-380-0800

Features: Two courts, batting cages

Batting Cages

Here's your chance to be MVP (Most Valuable Parent) and indulge your child in a Tiger fantasy. Most area batting cages are open April to October and offer slow-pitch and fast-pitch in both softball and hardball. The sites provide bats and batting helmets; bring mitts if there are fielding cages.

Apple SportsPlex Family Entertainment Center

3700 Lansing Road, Lansing
517-485-7070

Features: Batting cages, in-line roller skating, roller-hockey, floor hockey, miniature golf, driving range, video arcade, concessions, and pro shop

Canton Softball Center Complex

4655 West Michigan Avenue, Canton
734-483-5624

Features: Batting cages (April-October), restaurant, concessions, softball diamonds

C.J. Barrymore's Sports and Entertainment

21750 Hall Road, Clinton Township
810-469-2800

Features: Batting cages, softball diamonds, go-carts, kiddie karts, miniature golf, video arcade, lasertron, driving range, family restaurant, indoor/outdoor concessions

Four Bears Water Park

3000 Auburn Road, Utica
810-739-5863

Features: Batting cages, miniature golf, water slides, bumper boats, go-carts, restaurant

FunTyme Adventure Park

800 North Hogsback Road, Mason
517-676-1942

Features: Batting cages, miniature golf, indoor and outdoor driving range, go-carts, waterpark, and concessions

FunTyme Adventure Park

6295 East Saginaw Highway, Grand Ledge
517-627-6607

Features: Batting cages, miniature golf, indoor and outdoor driving range, go-carts, waterslide, and concessions

FunTyme Adventure Park

3384 James Phillips Drive, Okemos
517-332-7944

Features: Batting cages, miniature golf, indoor driving range, video arcade, go-carts, and concessions

Grand Slam Baseball Training Center

3530 Coolidge Highway, Royal Oak
248-549-7100

Features: Batting cages, fielding cages, pro shop, snack bar

Home Plate Sports Center

32909 Harper, St. Clair Shores
810-296-5655

Features: Batting cages

Midway Golf Range

22381 Van Born, Taylor
313-277-9156

Features: Batting cages, bumper cars, trampolines, go-carts, miniature golf, driving range

Oasis Golf/Tru Pitch Batting Cages

39500 Five Mile Road, Plymouth
734-420-4653

Features: Batting cages, miniature golf

Red Oaks Golf Dome and Sports Village

29601 John R, Madison Heights
248-548-1857

Features: Batting cages, go-carts, miniature golf, indoor and outdoor driving range, playscape, snack bar

The Sports Academy

42930 West Ten Mile Road, Novi
248-380-0800

Features: Batting cages, hitting and pitching tunnels, two basketball courts, concession, birthday party rooms

Sport-Way

38520 Ford Road, Westland
734-728-7222

Features: Batting cages, go-carts, miniature golf

Bicycling

Rent bicycles-built-for-two or single seaters and take a spin with the kids, April–October.

Agnes' Bike Rental

Honest John's Bar
416 Field, Detroit
313-824-1243

Features: Rental, summer only

Freedom Hill County Park

15000 Metroparkway, Sterling Heights
810-979-7010

Features: Bicycle Motorcross (BMX) track

Gallup Park Livery

3000 Fuller Road, Ann Arbor
734-662-9319

Hudson Mills Metropark

8801 North Territorial Road, Dexter
734-426-8211

Kensington Metropark

2240 West Buno Road, Milford
248-685-1561

Richfield Park BMX Track

Richfield Park, Richfield Township
810-736-7100 (Genesee County Parks)
810-653-3414 (Track director)

Features: BMX track, open daily mid-April–end of September. Races May–September, but no bike rentals

Riverfront Cycle

507 East Shiawasee Street, Lansing
517-482-8585
1-888-536-1600

Stony Creek Metropark

4300 Main Park Road, Washington
810-781-4242

Waterford Oaks

2800 Watkins Lake Road, Pontiac
248-858-0915

Features: Bicycle motocross (BMX) track, weekly practices and races, and BMX rentals, May–August

Willow Metropark

South Huron, Huron Township
734-697-9181

Boating

Take your children out to sea every summer on a wild boat ride. Paddle under bridges, talk to the fish, spin some yarns, and have a picnic. Surrounded by lakes and rivers, Metro Detroit offers a variety of boat rentals.

Addison Oaks

1480 West Romeo Road, Leonard
248-693-2432

Features: Rowboat and paddleboat rental on Buhl Lake and Adams Lake

Argo Park Livery

1055 Longshore Drive, Ann Arbor
734-668-7411

Features: Canoe, kayak and rowboat rental, snacks, and fishing supplies

The Boat Rental Club

24400 East Jefferson
Jefferson Beach Marina, Boat Slip B1
St. Clair Shores
810-779-2888

Features: Powerboats and sailboats up to 35 feet long

Charlie's Boat and Bait Market

13468 La Plaisance Road, Monroe Township
734-241-1545

Features: Fishing boats

Crosswinds Marsh

Haggerty and Oakville-Waltz Road, Sumpter
Township
734-261-1990

Features: Canoe rental

Delhi Metropark–Skip's Canoe Rentals

3780 Delhi Court, Ann Arbor
734-769-8686

Features: Canoe and kayak rental on Huron River.

Fitzgerald Park

133 Fitzgerald Park Drive, Grand Ledge
517-627-7351

Features: Canoe rental on Grand River

Gallup Canoe Livery

3000 Fuller Road, Ann Arbor
734-662-9319

Features: Canoe, paddleboat, rowboat and bicycle rental, snacks, and live bait

Great Water Yachts

24400 East Jefferson, St. Clair Shores
810-778-7030

Features: Yacht rental on Lake St. Clair

Groveland Oaks

5990 Grange Hall Road, Holly
248-634-9811

Features: Paddleboat, canoe, rowboat, and one-person "waterbug" rental on Stewart Lake

Heavner's Canoe and Cross Country Ski Rentals

2775 Garden Road, Milford
248-685-2379

Features: Canoe, paddleboat, and kayak rental on the Huron River

Independence Oaks

9501 Sashabaw Road, Clarkston
248-625-0877

Features: Rowboat, paddleboat, canoe rental on Crooked Lake

Kensington Metropark

2240 West Buno Road, Milford
248-685-1561

Features: Paddleboat and rowboat rental on Kent Lake

Middle Rouge Parkway

Joy Road and Hines Drive, Livonia
734-261-1990

Features: Canoe and paddleboat rental on Middle Rouge River

Pine Lake Marina

3599 Orchard Lake Road, Orchard Lake
248-682-2180

Features: Water ski boats and ski school on Pine Lake

Roy's Boat Harbor

32715 South River Road, Harrison Township
810-463-1479

Features: 14- or 16-foot boats with outboard motors

Seven Lakes State Park

8100 Grange Hall Road, Holly
248-634-7271

Features: Row boats, paddleboats, and canoes

Stony Creek Metropark

4300 Main Road, Washington
810-781-4242

Features: Paddleboat, rowboat, and canoe rental on Stony Creek Lake

William M. Burchfield Park

881 Grovenberg Road, Holt
517-676-2233

Features: Pedal boat, kayaks, and canoe rentals on Grand River

Wolynski Canoe Rental

2300 Wixom Trail, Milford
248-685-1851

Features: Kayaks

Bumper Bowling

For preschoolers, bumper bowling is the greatest invention since Barney. Children are protected against bowling gutter balls by plastic tubing that sits in the gutters. Throw the ball any which way, and it's bound to bounce off the bumper, careen down the lane and knock off a few pins. Here is a sampling of area lanes offering bumper bowling on a regular basis. Call ahead to find out when lanes are open and to request the bumpers. Bumper bowling is always a great party idea. For more information, call the Bowling Proprietors Association of Greater Detroit, 248-559-5207.

Astro Lanes

32388 John R, Madison Heights
248-585-3132

Bel-Aire Lanes

24001 Orchard Lake Road, Farmington
248-476-1550

Belmar II

3351 West Road, Trenton
734-675-8319

Bowl One

1639 East Fourteen Mile, Troy
248-588-4850

Cherry Hill Lanes

300 North Inkster Road, Dearborn Heights
313-278-0400

Cherry Hill Lanes North

6697 Dixie Highway, Clarkston
248-625-5011

Colonial Lanes

1950 South Industrial Highway, Ann Arbor
734-665-4474

Drakeshire Lanes

35000 Grand River, Farmington Hills
248-478-2230

Five Star Lanes

2666 Metropolitan Parkway, Sterling Heights
810-939-2550

Friendly Ark Sterling Lanes

33200 Schoenherr, Sterling Heights
810-979-5200

Friendly Bronco Lanes

22323 Ryan Road, Warren
810-756-8200

Friendly Merri-Bowl Lanes

30950 Five Mile Road, Livonia
734-427-2900

Galaxy Lanes

2226 East Hill, Grand Blanc
810-695-2700

Garden Bowl

4120 Woodward Avenue, Detroit
313-833-9850

Harbor Lanes

25419 Jefferson, St. Clair Shores
810-772-1200

Hartfield Lanes

3490 West Twelve Mile Road, Berkley
248-543-9338

Holiday Lanes

3101 East Grand River Avenue, Lansing
517-337-2695

Liberty Bowl

17580 Frazho, Fraser
810-725-2228

Luxury Lanes and Lounge

600 East Nine Mile Road, Ferndale
248-544-0530

Mayflower Lanes

26600 Plymouth Road, Redford
313-937-8420

Metro Bowl

5141 Luther King Jr. Boulevard, Lansing
517-882-0226

Novi Bowl

21700 Novi Road, Novi
248-348-9120

Oakwood Blue Jackets Bowl

850 South Oakwood Boulevard, Detroit
313-841-1351

Pampa Lanes

31925 Van Dyke, Warren
810-264-8877

Plum Hollow Lanes

21900 West Nine Mile Road, Southfield
248-353-6540

Pro Bowl-East

2757 East Grand River Avenue, East Lansing
517-337-1709, 517-337-1700

Pro Bowl-West

2122 Martin Luther King Jr. Boulevard, Lansing
517-321-7522

Recreation Bowl

40 Crocker Boulevard, Mount Clemens
810-468-7746

Redford Bowl

25815 Grand River, Detroit
313-531-2271

Regal Lanes

27663 Mound Road, Warren
810-751-4770

Rose Bowl Lanes

28001 Groesbeck, Roseville
810-771-4140

Royal Scot Golf and Bowl

4722 West Grand River Avenue, Lansing
517-321-3071

Sylvan Lanes

2355 Orchard Lake Road, Sylvan Lake
248-682-0700

Thunderbird Lanes

400 West Maple, Troy
248-362-1660

Troy Lanes

1950 East Square Lake Road, Troy
248-879-8700

Universal Lanes

2101 East Twelve Mile, Warren
810-751-2828

Woodland Lanes

33775 Plymouth Road, Livonia
734-522-4515

Ypsi-Arbor Lanes

2985 Washtenaw, Ypsilanti
734-434-1110

Cross-Country Skiing

It's possible to cross-country ski almost everywhere in Metro Detroit, from city, county, state, and national parks, to golf courses, ski resorts, and nature preserves. Many area ski shops and resorts rent equipment on a daily basis. Here is a sampling of sites that rent equipment and offer scenic trails.

Addison Oaks

1480 West Romeo Road, Leonard
248-693-2432

Glen Oaks
30500 Thirteen Mile Road, Farmington Hills
248-851-8356

Heavner's Canoe and Cross Country Ski Rental
2775 Garden Road, Milford
248-685-2379

Howell Nature and Conference Center
1005 Triangle Lake Road, Howell
517-546-0249

Hudson Mills Metropark
8801 North Territorial Road, Dexter
734-426-8211

Huron Hills Ski Center
3465 East Huron River Drive, Ann Arbor
734-971-6840

Huron Meadows Metropark
8765 Hammel Road, Brighton
810-231-4084

Independence Oaks
9501 Sashabaw Road, Clarkston
248-625-0877

Indian Springs Metropark
5200 Indian Trail, Clarkston
248-625-7870

Kensington Metropark
2240 West Buno Road, Milford
248-685-1561

Lake Erie Metropark
32481 West Jefferson, Rockwood
734-379-5020

Lake Lansing Park-North
Lake Drive, Haslett
517-676-2233

Maybury State Park

20145 Beck Road, Northville
248-349-8390

Metro Beach Metropark

Metropolitan Parkway, Mount Clemens
810-463-4581

Rolling Hills County Park

7660 Stony Creek Road, Ypsilanti Township
734-484-7669

Stony Creek Metropark

4300 Main Park Road, Washington
810-781-4242

White Lake Oaks

991 South Williams Lake Road, White Lake Twp.
248-698-2700

Willow Metropark

South Huron, Huron Township
313-697-9181

Woldumar Nature Center

5539 Lansing Road, Lansing
517-322-0030

Disc Golf

If you like throwing Frisbees and want a new challenge, try disc golf. On a 9- or 18-hole course, participants throw Frisbee-like discs into a raised basket, trying to play or beat the par on each hole. Like golf, disc golf courses offer hazards and other challenging obstacles. Children five and up who are able to throw a Frisbee will enjoy the game. Here are a sampling of courses located at public parks. Some offer equipment and free score cards for use. Others ask you to bring your own trusty Frisbee.

Addison Oaks County Park

1480 West Romeo Road, Leonard
248-693-2432

Brown Park

South of Packard Road between
Stone School Road and Platt Road, Ann Arbor
734-994-2780

Firefighters' Park

On the north side of Square Lake Road,
between Crooks and Coolidge, Troy
248-524-3484 (Parks and Recreation)

Hudson Hills Metropark

8801 North Territorial Road, Dexter
734-426-8211

Rolling Hills County Park

7660 Stony Creek Road, Ypsilanti Township
734-484-3871

Starr-Jaycee Park

On the south side of Thirteen Mile Road,
east of Crooks Road, Royal Oak
248-544-6680 (Parks and Recreation)

Stony Creek Metropark

Lakeview Picnic Area
Enter on Twenty-Six Mile Road,
west of M-53 (Van Dyke), Washington
810-781-4242

Wagner Park

On Detroit Avenue, between Rochester and Main
(Livernois), Royal Oak
248-544-6680 (Parks and Recreation)

Downhill Skiing

Five area ski resorts offer southeastern
Michiganians an easy escape to the slopes.
Generally open from November to March, they
offer rental, instruction, ski shop, and restaurant.
Some offer snowboarding rentals and instruction.

Alpine Valley

6775 East Highland, Milford
248-887-4183

Mt. Brighton Ski Area

4141 Bauer Road, Brighton
810-229-9581

Mt. Holly, Inc.

13536 South Dixie Highway, Holly
248-634-8269

Pine Knob Ski Resort

Sashabaw Road and I-75, Clarkston
248-625-0800

Riverview Highlands Ski Area

15015 Sibley Road, Riverview
734-281-4255

Fishing

Sure you can rent a rowboat and take along all your fishing gear. But if you want a hassle-free fishing trip, head over to a trout farm, where fishing is fun, quick, and everyone is guaranteed a catch.

G.B.'s Fishin' Hole

71201 Coon Creek, Armada
248-784-8354

Spring Valley Trout Farm

12190 Island Lake Road, Dexter
734-426-4772

Five-Pin Bowling

Everything about five-pin bowling is weird and fun. Bowling balls are small and lightweight. You hold them with your entire hand and not with your fingers; there are no finger holes. The score is calculated by the point value of each pin you knock down and you can actually have three tries each turn unless you get a strike or spare.

Parkview Lanes

1055 Ottawa Street, Windsor, Ontario, Canada
519-254-7360

Playdium Recreation

4985 Wyandotte Street East, Windsor,
Ontario, Canada
519-945-3111

Go-Carting

Treat your little daredevils to a fast ride around the go-cart track. Children under approximately 52–58 inches can ride around only on an adult's lap.

C.J. Barrymore's Sports and Entertainment

21750 Hall Road, Clinton Township
810-469-2800

Features: Go-carts, kiddie karts, batting cages, softball diamonds, miniature golf, video arcade, lasertron, driving range, pro shop, family restaurant, indoor/outdoor concessions

Four Bears Water Park

3000 Auburn Road, Utica
810-739-5863

Features: Go-carts, batting cages, miniature golf, water slides, bumper boats, restaurant

FunTyme Adventure Park

800 North Hogsback Road, Mason
517-676-1942

Features: Go-carts, batting cages, miniature golf, indoor and outdoor driving range, waterslide

FunTyme Adventure Park

6295 East Saginaw Highway, Grand Ledge
517-627-6607

Features: Go-carts, batting cages, miniature golf, indoor and outdoor driving range, waterslide

FunTyme Adventure Park

3384 James Phillips Drive, Okemos
517-332-7944

Features: Go-carts, batting cages, miniature golf, indoor driving range, waterslide

Midway Golf Range

22381 Van Born, Taylor
313-277-9156

Features: Go-carts, batting cages, bumper cars, miniature golf, driving range, trampolines

Red Oaks Golf Dome and Sports Village

29601 John R, Madison Heights
248-548-1857

Features: Go-carts, batting cages, miniature golf, indoor and outdoor driving range, playscape, and snack bar

Sport-Way

38520 Ford Road, Westland
734-728-7222

Features: Go-carts, batting cages, miniature golf

Van Dyke Sport Center

32501 Van Dyke, Warren
810-979-2626

Features: Go-carts, miniature golf, indoor/outdoor driving range, video arcade, pool tables, restaurant, concessions, pro shop

Hiking

The area's many arboretums, parks, and nature centers offer a variety of self-guided hiking trails.

Horseback Riding

Get along little doggies, time for some horsing around. Here is a sampling of area ranches that offer riding by the hour, year-round, weather permitting. Many also offer riding lessons for all ages.

Dodge Park #4

4250 Parkway, Pontiac
248-666-1020

Great Western Riding Stable Company

5444 Bates, Mount Clemens
810-749-3780

Hell Creek Ranch

10866 Cedar Lake Road, Pinckney
734-878-3632

Highland Recreation Area Riding Stables

5300 Highland, White Lake
248-887-4349

Oakwood Riding Stables

2991 Oakwood, Ortonville
248-627-2826

Maybury State Park

20145 Beck Road, Northville
248-349-8390

Oakland County 4-H Horseback Riding for Handicappers

248-858-0889

Pontiac Lake Riding Stable

Pontiac Lake Recreation Area
3480 Teggerdine Road, White Lake Township
248-625-3410

Sundance Riding Stables

9250 Nixon Road, Grand Ledge
517-627-5500

Sundown Riding Stables

71700 Romeo Plank Road, Armada Township
810-752-PONY

Wildwood Equestrian Center

Exceptional Equestrian Program
(Horseback riding for the handicapped)
3935 Seven Mile Road, South Lyon
248-486-7433

HORSEBACK RIDING LESSONS

While the following stables do not offer open riding by the hour, they do offer group or private riding lessons for children of all ages. Most start with age 7; some even run classes for under-5 on the same horse with Mom or Dad. Many also offer summer camp programs.

Bridlewood Farms Equestrian Center

930 South Williams Lake Road,
White Lake Township
248-360-4740

Evergreen Stable

16333 Lowery Road, Chelsea
734-475-7449

Hadley Hill Farm

1344 South Hadley Road, Ortonville
248-627-2356

Haverhill Farms

2986 McKeachie, White Lake Township
248-887-2027

Just A Folly Farm

1555 North Baldwin Road, Oxford
248-628-5879

Maybury State Park

20145 Beck Road, Northville
248-347-1088

Rochester Hills Stables

P.O. Box 173, Romeo
810-752-9520, 810-752-6020

Rushlow's Arabians

29242 Bredow, Huron Township
734-782-1171

Showcase Stables

7447 Pontiac Trail, Northville
248-437-0889

Spring Brook Stables

42500 Ryan, Sterling Heights
810-739-8622

Stoney Creek Farm

1460 Mead Road, Rochester
248-651-3398

Stoney Ridge Farms

9970 Liberty Road, Chelsea
734-663-3509

Windemere Equestrian Center

20615 Dunham, Clinton Township
810-465-2170

Ice-Skating

Celebrate winter by taking a twirl on the area's many indoor rinks during family open skating. Or enjoy the real thing—bundle up and skate out in the open, with snowflakes falling all around you. Here is a sampling of the area's indoor and outdoor rinks. Skate rental is noted.

Addison Oaks

1480 West Romeo Road, Leonard
248-693-2432

Features: Outdoor rink

Adray Sports Arena

14900 Ford Road, Dearborn
313-943-4098

Features: Indoor rink

Allen Park Civic Arena

15800 White Street, Allen Park
313-928-8303

Features: Indoor rink

Berkley Ice Arena

2300 Robina, Berkley
248-546-2460

Features: Indoor rink, skate rental

Birmingham Ice Sports Arena

2300 East Lincoln, Birmingham
248-645-0730
248-645-0731

Features: Indoor rink, skate rental

Buhr Park Ice Rink

2751 Packard Road, Ann Arbor
734-971-3228

Features: Outdoor rink, skate rental

Canfield Ice Arena

2100 Kinloch, Dearborn Heights
313-561-1960

Features: Indoor rink

Charles L. Bowers Farm

1219 West Square Lake Road, Bloomfield Hills
248-645-4830

Features: Outdoor rink

Clark Park

1400 Scotten, Detroit
313-297-9328

Features: Outdoor rink, skate rental

Compuware-Oak Park Arena

13950 Oak Park Boulevard, Oak Park
248-538-0009

Features: Indoor rink

Compuware Sports Arena

14900 Beck Road, Plymouth
248-737-7373

Features: Indoor rink, skate rental

Devon-Aire Ice Arena

9510 Sunset, Livonia
734-425-9790

Features: Indoor rink

Drake Sports Park

Drake Road, south of Maple Road,
West Bloomfield
248-738-2500

Features: Outdoor rink

Eddie Edgar Ice Arena

33841 Lyndon, Livonia
734-427-1280

Features: Indoor rink

Farmington Hills Ice Arena

35500 Eight Mile Road, Farmington Hills
248-478-8800

Features: Indoor rink, skate rental

Garden City Ice Arena

200 Long Cabin Drive, Garden City
734-261-3490 (Parks and Recreation)

Features: Indoor rink, skate rental

Great Lakes Sport City

34400 Utica Road, Fraser
810-294-2400

Features: Indoor rink, skate rental

Hart Plaza

Jefferson at Woodward, Detroit
313-877-8077

Features: Outdoor rink, skate rental

Highland Recreation Area

M-59 east of US-23, White Lake
248-889-3750

Features: Outdoor rink

Holly Recreation Area

8100 Grange Hall Road, Holly
248-634-9751

Features: Outdoor rink

Independence Oaks

9501 Sashabaw Road, Clarkston
248-625-0877

Features: Outdoor rink

Inkster Civic Arena

27077 South River Park, Inkster
313-277-1001

Features: Indoor rink

Jack Adams Ice Arena

10500 Lyndon, Detroit
313-935-4510

Features: Indoor rink, skate rental

John Lindell Ice Arena

1403 Lexington Boulevard, Royal Oak
248-280-3990

Features: Indoor rink, skate rental

Kennedy Ice Arena

3131 West Road, Trenton
734-676-7172

Features: Indoor rink

Kensington Metropark

2240 West Buno Road, Milford
248-685-1561

Features: Outdoor rink

Lake Erie Metropark

32481 West Jefferson, Rockwood
734-379-5020

Features: Outdoor rinks

Lakeland Ice Arena

7330 Highland (M-59), Waterford
248-666-2090

Features: Indoor rink, club skating only

Lansing Ice Arena

1475 Lake Lansing Road, Lansing
517-482-1596

Features: Indoor rink, skate rentals

Lincoln Park Community Center

3525 Dix, Lincoln Park
313-386-4075

Features: Indoor rink, skate rental

Lower Huron Metropark

17845 Savage Road, Belleville
734-697-9181
1-800-477-3182

Features: Outdoor rinks

McMorran Place Complex

701 McMorran Boulevard, Port Huron
810-985-6166

Features: Two indoor rinks

Melvindale Ice Arena

4300 South Dearborn, Melvindale
313-928-1200

Features: Indoor rinks, skate rental

Metro Beach Metropark

Metro Parkway at Jefferson
Mount Clemens
810-463-4581

Features: Two outdoor rinks

Mount Clemens Ice Arena and Fitness Center

200 North Grosbeck, Mount Clemens
810-307-8202

Features: Indoor rinks, skate rental

Novi Ice Arena

42400 Arena Drive, Novi
248-347-1010

Features: Indoor rink, skate rental

Plymouth Cultural Center

525 Farmer, Plymouth
734-455-6623

Features: Indoor rink, skate rental

Redford Ice Arena

12400 Beech Daly, Redford
313-387-2757

Features: Indoor rink, skate rental

River Rouge Arena

141 East Great Lakes, River Rouge
313-842-0670

Features: Indoor rink

Rolling Hills County Park

7660 Stony Creek Road, Ypsilanti Township
734-484-7669

Features: Outdoor rink

St. Clair Shores Civic Arena

20000 Stephens, St. Clair Shores
810-445-5350 (Parks and Recreation)

Features: Indoor rinks

Southfield Sports Arena

26000 Evergreen Road, Southfield
248-354-9357

Features: Indoor rink, skate rental

Southgate Ice Arena

14700 Reaume Parkway, Southgate
734-246-1342

Features: Indoor rink

Stony Creek Metropark

4300 Main Park Road, Washington
810-781-4242

Features: Outdoor rink

University of Michigan-Dearborn Ice Arena

4901 Evergreen Road, Dearborn
313-593-5673

Features: Indoor rink, staff and students only

Veterans Ice Arena

2150 Jackson Road, Ann Arbor
734-761-7240

Features: Indoor rink, skate rental

Wallace Ice Arena

550 Lone Pine Road, Bloomfield Hills
248-645-3186

Features: Indoor rink

Washington Park

2516 South Washington Avenue, Lansing
517-483-4232

Features: Outdoor and indoor rinks, skate rentals

Waterford Oaks County Park

1780 Scott Lake Road, Waterford
248-975-4440 ("The Fridge")

Features: Outdoor rinks

Wayne Community Center

4635 Howe Road, Wayne
734-721-7400

Features: Indoor rink, skate rental

Wayne County Parks

734-261-1990

Features: Outdoor rinks at almost every park

Westland Sports Arena

6210 North Wildwood, Westland
734-729-4560

Features: Indoor rink, skate rental

Willow Metropark

South Huron, Huron Township
734-697-9181

Features: Three outdoor rinks

Yack Arena

3131 Third Street, Wyandotte
734-324-7265

Features: Indoor rink

Yost Ice Arena

1000 South State Street, Ann Arbor
734-764-4600

Features: Indoor rink, skate rental

Indoor Playgrounds

Let it rain, sleet, hail, or snow. We're covered. The indoor playground craze has blanketed Detroit with brightly colored Willy Wonka lands of chutes and ladders, plexiglass tunnels, and ballswims. Geared for ages 2–10, the playgrounds require parents to stay and actually encourage them to join their children on the playscape. You'll check your shoes, so be sure to wear socks. Parents will also want to rent knee pads. Malls and stores have also gotten into the act with creative playgrounds and castle-scapes.

Art Van Kids Castle

27775 Novi Road, Novi
248-348-8922

Art Van Kids Castle

14055 Hall Road, Shelby Township
810-566-1490

Art Van Kids Castle

22035 Eureka Road, Taylor
734-287-4000

Art Van Kids Castle

6500 14 Mile Road, Warren
810-939-2100

Art Van Kids Castle

8300 Wayne Road, Westland
734-425-9600

Breakfast Playground

Lakeside Mall
14000 Lakeside Circle, Sterling Heights
810-247-1744

Discovery Zone

5038 Miller Road, Flint
810-230-6800

Discovery Zone

105 East Thirteen Mile Road, Madison Heights
248-585-7940

Discovery Zone

13745 Lakeside Circle, Sterling Heights
810-566-6801

Discovery Zone

7390 South Haggerty Road, West Bloomfield
248-788-9393

Fairlane Frog Hop

Fairlane Town Center
Michigan Avenue, Dearborn
313-593-1370

Jeepers!

Great Lakes Crossing
4000 Baldwin, Auburn Hills
248-972-3200

Jeepers!

Macomb Mall, 32233 Gratiot, Roseville
810-296-6569

Jeepers!

Northland Mall, Southfield
248-557-5500

Jeepers!

Wonderland Mall, Livonia
734-762-5118

Kid Kingdom

42599 Ford Road, Canton
734-981-0711

Kid Kingdom

2107 West Stadium Boulevard, Ann Arbor
734-769-1700

Sparky's

Livonia Mall
Seven Mile and Middlebelt Road, Livonia
248-477-3333

Indoor Soccer

Play soccer year-round at these indoor arenas which offer leagues, clinics, camps, and birthday parties.

Soccer Zone

6833 Center Drive, Sterling Heights
810-939-6400

Features: Indoor soccer, in-line hockey rinks, pro-shop, and concession

Soccer Zone

41550 Grand River, Novi
248-374-0500

Features: Indoor soccer, in-line hockey rinks, pro-shop, and concession

Total Soccer

34300 Utica Road, Fraser
810-294-8848

Features: Indoor soccer, concession

Total Soccer

1319 Lexington, Royal Oak
248-288-2110

Features: Indoor soccer, concession

Total Soccer

22200 Beech Road, Southfield
248-352-5690

Features: Indoor soccer, concession

Total Soccer

30990 Wixom Road, Wixom
248-669-9817

Features: Indoor soccer, concession

Wide World Sports Center

2140 Oak Valley Drive, Ann Arbor
734-913-4625

Features: Indoor soccer, roller hockey and lacrosse field

Kite Flying

Learn how to make and fly kites at family workshops held during spring at area parks and nature centers, including Maybury State Park, Kensington Metropark Nature Center, and Independence Oaks County Park.

Kite lovers can also fly kites every Wednesday, from 5:30 p.m. until dusk, May–September, as weather permits, on the soccer fields of Schoolcraft College, 18600 Haggerty Road,

Livonia. Experienced kite fliers will be happy to help beginners. For information, Kites & Things, 734-454-3760. Website: www.skyburner.com

Laser Tag

Jump into a video game–inspired experience where you can "take out" the enemy with a trusty laser gun. First, suit up with a Star Trek–like metal headpiece, battery pack, and laser gun. Then, enter the dark and foggy game room, where "danger" lurks behind neon-outlined city buildings or fantasy space.

Laser Quest

33800 Gratiot Avenue, Clinton Township
810-790-5555

Laser Quest

31401 John R, Madison Heights
810-616-9292

Laser Quest

7277 Nankin, Westland
734-266-0888

Laser Storm

4790 South Hagadorn Road, Suite 152,
East Lansing
517-333-8276

Lasertron

C.J. Barrymore's Sports and Entertainment
21750 Hall Road, Clinton Township
810-469-2800

Mulligan's Golf Center

3951 Joslyn Road, Auburn Hills
248-332-4653

Phazer Land

31166 Grand River, Farmington
248-442-7880

Sparky's

Livonia Mall
Seven Mile and Middlebelt Road, Livonia
248-477-3333

U.S. Blades and Laser World

5700 Drake Road, West Bloomfield
248-661-4200

Miniature Golf

Test your putting skills against green hills, blue lagoons, colorful windmills, or wishing wells. Time to show the kids the difference between a bogey and an eagle. Here is a sampling of area miniature golf sites. Most are open seasonally during the summer and early fall. At Brighton's Golf-O-Rama you won't have to worry about the weather; the miniature golf course is indoors.

Apple SportsPlex Family Entertainment Center

3700 Lansing Road, Lansing
517-485-7070

C.J. Barrymore's Sports and Entertainment

21750 Hall Road, Clinton Township
810-469-2800

Ford Road Miniature Golf

29060 Ford Road, Garden City
734-425-9816

Four Bears Water Park

3000 Auburn Road, Utica
810-739-5863

FunTyme Adventure Park

800 North Hogsback Road, Mason
517-676-1942

FunTyme Adventure Park

6295 East Saginaw Highway, Grand Ledge
517-627-6607

FunTyme Adventure Park

3384 James Phillips Drive, Okemos
517-332-7944

Golden Bear Golf Center

3500 Edgar Street, Royal Oak
248-549-4653

Golf-O-Rama

2944 South Old US-23, Brighton
810-227-9322

Mulligan's Golf Center

54300 Ten Mile Road, South Lyon
248-437-2850

Jawor's Golf Center

32900 Gratiot, Roseville
810-293-9836

King Park Golf

G-5140 Flushing Road, Flushing
810-732-2470

Marino Sports Center, Inc.

38951 Jefferson, Mount Clemens
810-465-6177

Mauro's Miniature Golf

600 East Nine Mile Road, Hazel Park
248-547-2331

Metro Beach "Shipwreck Lagoon"

Metro Parkway at Jefferson, Mount Clemens
810-463-4581

Midway Golf Range

22381 Van Born, Taylor
313-277-9156

Mulligan's Golf Center

3951 Joslyn Road, Auburn Hills
248-332-4653

Oak Park Mini-Golf

14300 Oak Park Boulevard, Oak Park
248-691-7555

Oasis Golf/Tru-Pitch Batting Cages

39500 Five Mile Road, Plymouth
734-420-4653

Sport and Fun

30749 Grand River, Farmington Hills
248-471-4700

Red Oaks Golf Dome and Sports Village

29601 John R, Madison Heights
248-548-1857

Sport-Way

38520 Ford Road, Westland
734-728-7222

Ted's Southgate Golf Center

14600 Reaune Parkway, Southgate
734-246-1358

Van Dyke Sport Center

32501 Van Dyke, Warren
810-979-2626

Willow Creek "Walk in the Woods" and "Sport Mountain" Miniature Golf

3120 South Lapeer Road, Lake Orion
248-391-1230

Ypsilanti Putt-Putt

2675 Washtenaw, Ypsilanti
734-434-2838

Paintball

This game, popular in North and South America, Europe, and Australia, is catching on in Metro Detroit. Teams play against each other on an indoor or outdoor playing field, using paint pellets and guns. Not recommended for children younger than twelve.

Battlegrounds Paintball

13199 US-12, Saline
734-397-2255

Hell Survivors, Inc.

125 Pearl, Pinckney
734-878-5656

Paintball Arena

34 Rapid Street, Pontiac
248-333-2557

Splat Ball City Playing Field

1580 East Grand Boulevard, Detroit
313-925-2489 (on site)
313-875-7549 (office)

Rock 'N' Bowl

This new bowling alley trend combines bowling with dancing. Music is provided by a live band or deejay. Often there are contests and prizes. Friendly Ark in Sterling Heights gears their events to 9–14 year olds, and Detroit's Garden Bowl features live bands or dee jays on Friday and Saturday nights and attracts an older crowd. Here is a sampling of other Rock 'N' Bowls. Call ahead to check out the ages of the crowd.

Bel-Aire Lanes

24001 Orchard Lake Road, Farmington
248-476-1550

Five Star Lanes

2666 Metropolitan Parkway, Sterling Heights
810-939-2550

Galaxy Lanes

2226 East Hill, Grand Blanc
810-695-2700

Luxury Lanes and Lounge

600 East Nine Mile Road, Ferndale
248-544-0530

Sylvan Lanes

2355 Orchard Lake Road, Sylvan Lake
248-682-0700

Thunderbird Lanes

400 West Maple, Troy
248-362-1660

Troy Lanes

1950 East Square Lake Road, Troy
248-879-8700

Rodeo

Your little cowboys and cowgirls sure won't get the blues learning how to rope 'em and ride 'em. This club teaches children rodeo skills.

Youth Rodeo Club

Lapeer County MSU Extension, 810-667-0343
Stan Williams, 810-798-8277

Rollerblading

Pull on your spandex, helmet, knee and elbow pads and get ready for indoor in-line skating. Most Metro Detroit roller-skate arenas now rent rollerblades or allow skaters to bring their own rollerblades, but reserve the right to inspect them at the door. Call ahead. Be sure to check out the list of roller rinks, too.

Roll at the Dome

Pontiac Silverdome
1200 Featherstone, Pontiac
810-456-1646 (hotline)

U S Blades

5700 Drake Road, West Bloomfield
248-661-4200

The following parks offer roller-skate, rollerblade, and safety gear rental and instruction spring through fall. Call for hours and location within the park.

Indian Springs Metropark

5200 Indian Trail, White Lake
248-969-0547

"Roll in the Park"

Hines Drive, Wayne County Parks
734-261-1990

Stony Creek Metropark

4300 Main Park Road, Washington
248-969-0547

Roller-Skating

The music's on, the lights are blinking. Put the kids into continuous motion at the roller rink. Here is a sampling.

Ambassador Skating Rink

96 West Fourteen Mile, Clawson
248-435-6525

Bonaventure Roller Skating Center

24505 Halstead Road, Farmington Hills
248-476-2200

The Great Skate

29100 Hayes, Roseville
810-777-4300

Northland Roller Rink

22311 West Eight Mile Road, Detroit
313-535-1443

The Rink, Inc.

50625 Van Dyke, Utica
810-731-5006

Riverside Roller Arena

36635 Plymouth, Livonia
734-421-3542

Rolladium

4475 Highland, Waterford Township
248-674-0808

Roller-Cade

2130 Schaefer, Detroit
313-386-5710

Shores Skateland

35020 Klix, Clinton Township
810-792-0901

Skateland Fun Zone

23911 Allen Road, Woodhaven
734-671-0220

Skateland West

37550 Cherry Hill, Westland
734-326-2800

Skateworld of Troy

2825 East Maple Road, Troy
248-689-4100

Skatin' Station

8611 Ronda Drive, Canton
734-459-6400

Shooting Ranges

The following ranges offer safe, single load shooting. Children of all ages with adult supervision are welcome. Bring your own guns or use those supplied by the course.

Bald Mountain

1330 Greenshield, Lake Orion
248-693-6767

Dodge Park No. 4

4250 Parkway, Pontiac
248-666-102

Ortonville Recreation Area

Ortonville
248-627-3828

River Bends Park

River Bends Road, off Ryan Road, just north or
Auburn Road, Shelby Township
810-731-2645

Ski Clubs for Kids

Here's a chance to get your little snow bunnies
out on the slopes. From November to March,
weather permitting, area ski clubs offer weekly
chaperoned ski trips, equipment rental, lessons,
and a chance to earn patches and pins.

Blizzard Ski School

248-559-9754

Bloomfield Hills Ski Club

Sponsored by Bloomfield Hills Recreation
248-433-0885

Grosse Pointe Ski Hi Club

Sponsored by Grosse Pointe War Memorial
313-881-7511

Jim Dandy Ski Club

313-345-8997

Oak Park Student Ski Club

Sponsored by Oak Park Recreation
248-691-7555

Troy Downhill Ski Program

Sponsored by Troy Parks and Recreation
248-524-3484

Winter Walden Ski Club

248-855-1075

West Bloomfield Ski Club

248-738-2500

Sledding

Many city and country parks, nature preserves, arboretum, and golf courses offer toboggan runs and sledding sites. Thrill-seekers will want to take the 1,000-foot plunge down "The Fridge," the refrigerated toboggan slide at Waterford Oaks County Park. Here is a sampling.

Beverly Hills Village Park

Beverly (131/2 Mile Road), west of Southfield Road, Beverly Hills
248-646-6404 (City office)

Bloomer State Park

John R at Bloomer Road, Rochester
248-652-1321

David Shepherd Park

Oak Park Boulevard, west of Coolidge, Oak Park
248-691-7555 (Recreation Department)

Highland Recreation Area

M-59 east of US-23, White Lake
810-889-3750

Holly Recreation Area

8100 Grange Hall Road, Holly
248-634-9751

Kensington Metropark

2240 West Buno Road, Milford
248-685-1561

Madison Heights Civic Center

Thirteen Mile Road, Madison Heights
248-588-1200 (City Hall)

Middle Rouge Parkway (Edward Hines Parkway)

Cass-Benton area between Six and Seven Mile Roads, Northville
734-261-1990

Pontiac Lake Recreation Area

7800 Gale Road, Pontiac
248-666-1020

River Bends Park

Off Ryan Road, just north of Auburn Road,
Shelby Township
810-731-2645

Rolling Hills County Park

7660 Stony Creek, Ypsilanti
734-484-7669

Southfield Civic Center–Evergreen Hills

26000 Evergreen Road, Southfield
248-354-9603

Stony Creek Metropark

4300 Main Park Road, Washington
810-781-4242

Waterford Oaks County Park

1650 Scott Lake Road, Waterford
248-975-4440

Features: "The Fridge," a refrigerated toboggan slide

Willow Metropark

I-275 at South Huron Road, Huron Township
734-697-9181

Snowshoeing

Strap on those big mesh paddles and hit the
trails. The following site offers snowshoe rental,
instruction, and trails.

Lewis E. Wint Nature Center

Independence Oaks County Park
9501 Sashabaw Road, Clarkston
248-625-6473

Swimming

Municipal pools, recreation centers, and area
YMCAs—for a small fee you can beat the heat in
both indoor and outdoor pools. Even with life-
guards on duty, be sure to supervise your kids.
Here is a sampling of area pools.

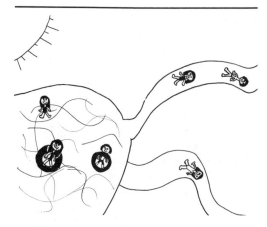

Beech Woods Recreation Center

22200 Beech Road, Southfield
248-354-9510

Features: Outdoor pool

Buhr Park Pool

2751 Packard Road, Ann Arbor
734-971-3228

Features: Outdoor pool

Detroit Recreation Department Pools

313-224-1180
There are 17 locations.

Brennan Recreation Center, 21415 Plymouth,
Detroit, 313-935-4428. Features: Outdoor pool

Brewer Recreation Center, 4535 Fairview, Detroit,
313-267-7152. Features: Indoor pool

Brewster-Wheeler Recreation Center,
637 Brewster, Detroit, 313-833-9777.
Features: Indoor pool

Butzel-Adams Recreation Center, 10500 Lyndon,
Detroit, 313-935-3119. Features: Indoor pool

Butzel Family Center, 7737 Kercheval, Detroit,
313-267-7125. Features: Indoor pool

Considine Center, 8904 Woodward, Detroit,
313-876-0131. Features: Indoor pool

Gatliff Memorial Pool, 970 Merrill Plaisance,
Detroit, 313-935-3276. Features: Outdoor pool

Heilmann Recreation Center, 19601 Crusade, Detroit, 313-267-7153. Features: Indoor pool

Johnson Recreation Center, 8640 Chippewa, Detroit, 313-578-7590. Features: Indoor pool

Kemeny Recreation Center, 2260 South Fort, Detroit, 313-297-9332. Features: Indoor pool

Maheras Recreation Center, 12550 Avondale, Detroit, 313-852-4045. Features: Outdoor pool

Palmer Park, 313-935-3276. Features: Outdoor pool

Patton Recreation Center, 2301 Woodmere, Detroit, 313-297-9337. Features: Indoor pool

Rouge Park, 22000 Joy Road, Detroit, 313-852-4523. Features: Outdoor pool

Stone Pool, 4595 Fourth Street, Detroit, 313-833-3990. Features: Outdoor pool

Williams Recreation Center, 8431 Rosa Parks Boulevard, Detroit, 313-898-6584. Features: Indoor pool

Young Recreation Center, 2751 Robert Bradby Drive, Detroit, 313-877-8008. Features: Indoor pool

Fuller Pool

1519 Fuller Road, Ann Arbor
734-994-4263

Features: Outdoor pool

Jewish Community Center Pool

1511 West Ten Mile Road, Oak Park
248-967-4030

Features: Indoor pool. Non-member must be accompanied by member and pay a fee.

Jewish Community Center Pool

6600 West Maple Road, West Bloomfield
248-661-1000

Features: Indoor/Outdoor pool. Non-member must be accompanied by member and pay a fee.

Metro Beach Metropark Pool

Metro Parkway at Jefferson, Mount Clemens
810-463-4581

Features: Outdoor pool

Oak Park Municipal Pool

14300 Oak Park Boulevard, Oak Park
248-691-7555

Veterans Pool

2150 Jackson Road, Ann Arbor
734-761-7240

Features: Outdoor pool and water slide

Wayne Aquatic Center

4635 Howe, Wayne
734-721-7400

Features: Indoor pool for residents and nonresidents. Small fee for non-members.

William Costicks Activity Center Pool

28600 Eleven Mile Road, Farmington Hills
248-473-1834

Features: Indoor pool

Willow Metropark

South Huron, Huron Township
734-697-9181

Features: Outdoor pool

YMCA Pools

Ten area YMCAs have indoor pools. Non-members pay a fee. Included in this list are also YMCAs without pools; swim lessons are often given in nearby schools.

Birmingham, 400 East Lincoln, Birmingham, 248-644-9036

Downriver, 3211 Fort Street, Wyandotte, 734-281-2600

Eastside, 10100 Harper, Detroit, 313-921-0770

Farmington, 28100 Farmington Road, Farmington Hills, 248-553-4020

Huron Valley, 305 Caroline Street, Milford, 248-685-3020. No pool

Lakeshore Family, 23401 East Jefferson, St. Clair Shores, 810-778-5811. No pool

Livonia Family, 14255 Stark Road, Livonia, 734-261-2161

Macomb, 10 North River Road, Mount Clemens, 810-468-1411

North Oakland County, 116 Terry, Rochester, 248-651-9622. No pool

Northwestern, 21755 West Seven Mile Road, Detroit, 313-533-3700

Plymouth Community Family, 248 Union Street, Plymouth, 734-453-2904. No pool

South Oakland, 1016 West Eleven Mile Road, Royal Oak, 248-547-0030

Warren Area Family, 8777 Common Road, Warren, 810-751-1050. No pool

Wayne/Westland, 827 South Wayne Road, Westland, 734-721-7044

Western, 1601 Clark Street, Detroit, 313-554-2136

Trampoline

Children four years and older can flip and leap to their heart's content.

M.V. Trampoline Center

22381 Van Born, Taylor
313-277-9156

U S Blades and Laser World

5700 Drake Road, West Bloomfield
248-661-4200

Features: Bungee jump trampoline, laser tag, video games, rollerblading, playscape

Voyageur Canoe Rides

Learn how fur traders and early explorers traversed the Great Lakes by booking passage in a 34-foot, 18-passenger voyageur canoe ride. From spring through fall, naturalist-led canoe rides offer both history and nature lessons and often feature a light breakfast or lunch. Everyone is expected to paddle, so children must be at least six years old.

Metro Beach Metropark Nature Center

Metropolitan Parkway, Mt. Clemens
810-463-4581

Oakwoods Metropark Nature Center

Willow Road, Flat Rock
734-782-3956

Stony Creek Nature Center

4300 Main Park Road, Washington
810-781-4242

Wall Climbing

Looking for the ultimate sporting experience? How about scaling a fake rock-encrusted wall? Your Sylvester Stallone-wanna be's will wanna try wall climbing.

Ann Arbor Climbing Gym

324 West Ann, Ann Arbor
734-761-4669

Features: 12 ropes on a series of steel walls, plus cave; shoe and harness rental and instruction

Gibraltar Climbing Company

3901 Huron Church Road, Windsor
519-966-7625

Features: 14 ropes plus bouldering cave; shoe and harness rental and instruction

Planet Rock

34 Rapid Street, Pontiac
248-334-3904

Features: Wall climbing for ages 5 and older; shoe and harness rental and instruction

REI

17559 Haggerty, Northville
248-347-2100

Features: Climb a pinnacle; free shoe and harness rental

Vertical Ventures Rock Climbing and Wilderness Program

667 Snyder Road, East Lansing
517-336-0520

Features: Back packing, hiking and mountain climbing. Adventure summer camps in Oak Park and Grand Ledge.

Whirly Ball

This sport is a combination of bumper car, basketball, and jai-alai. Kids ages 10 and up can participate. Prices run about $145/hour (ten people share the court and the cost).

Whirly Ball Fun Center

G-4007 Corona, Flint
810-230-9154

Whirly Ball of Michigan

19781 Fifteen Mile Road, Clinton Township
810-792-4190

Whirly Ball West

5700 Drake Road, West Bloomfield
248-788-8900

Whirly Ball Ann Arbor

640 Phoenix, Ann Arbor
734-975-6909

14
Michigan at Work—Tours

Don't be afraid to move up close to the guide during the tour. And encourage your children to become mini-reporters and ask a lot of questions.

Everyone enjoys peeking behind the scenes. Children especially benefit from seeing people at work and watching made-in-Michigan products being born. This chapter lists Michigan companies and cottage industries that still welcome families and groups with a regularly scheduled tour. While most of the tours are within a two-hour drive from Detroit, I have also included tours farther away to help you plan your overnight adventures.

There are also many community sites that will take small groups on a tour, provided you call first and arrange a mutually convenient time. Try police and fire stations, courthouses, hospitals, theaters, fast-food restaurants, grocery stores, butcher shops, radio and TV stations, even your own job site. You are limited only by your imagination. Many of the museums, historic villages and homes, and science and nature sites listed in this book offer tours to school and civic groups; several theaters offer school field trips.

Farming

Amon Orchard

8066 North US-31, Traverse City
616-938-9160, 1-800-937-1644

Location: 1 1/2 miles north of Acme on US-31
Hours: Call for tour reservation, May–October
Admission: $1 includes trolley ride
Ages: All ages
Parking: Free on site

Tour the cherry orchard on a trolley and learn why Traverse City is the Cherry Capital of the World. After the tour, visit the barnyard petting farm and then browse through the wide selection of specialty cherry foods and freshly picked fruits in the farm market.

Industry

Amway Corporation

7575 East Fulton Street East, Ada
616-787-6701

Location: M-21 (Fulton Road), 12 miles east of downtown Grand Rapids and 11 miles west of the I-96 Lowell exit
Hours: One-hour tour. 8:30 a.m.–noon, 1–5 p.m.,

Monday–Friday. Closed holidays. Two-week advance reservations are required for groups of ten or more. Tours for the handicapped are available upon advance request. Groups smaller than ten do not need reservations, but should arrive 15 minutes early.

Admission: Free

Ages: Children under 16 should be accompanied by a parent

Parking: Free on site

Freebies: Tour souvenir

Tour the extensive Amway World Headquarters and learn all about the growth, products, and markets of one of the world's largest direct-selling companies. The self-guided tour includes films, a computer-generated show of the factory production area, and hands-on displays.

Arts and Crafts

Arts & Scraps

17820 East Warren, Detroit
313-640-4411

Location: Between Cadieux and Mack

Hours: 11 a.m.–6 p.m., Tuesday and Thursday. 11 a.m.–4 p.m., Saturday. Also by appointment. Adult workshops, teacher training, group field trips, day camps, and birthday parties are available.

Admission: Free. Children can stuff a bag full of artistic scraps for a very modest price.

Ages: Preschool and up

Parking: Free in front or in back of building

Arts & Scraps offers parents and early elementary teachers a rainy day treasure trove of scraps and odds and ends—everything that children need for creative expression. Kids will enjoy peeking into barrels and looking through boxes, "shopping" for items they can paint, color, glue, and cut into special projects.

Food

Bakers Delight

33896 Dequindre, Sterling Heights
810-268-8000

Location: 141/2 Mile Road and Dequindre, in the Melody Plaza

Hours: Retail hours: 9 a.m.–7 p.m,. Monday–Friday, 9:30 a.m.–5:30 p.m., Saturday. Workshops are scheduled after school: call at least three months in advance. Minimum 10; maximum 24 children.
Admission: $5/person
Ages: First grade and up.
Parking: Adjacent to store

Workshops are offered around holiday time. Owner Celia Shears helps children create panoramic sugar eggs for Easter, panoramic sugar balls for Mother's Day, and graham cracker houses for Christmas. Scout groups are also welcome.

Natural Wonder

Bear Cave Resort

4085 Bear Cave Road, Buchanan
616-695-3050

Location: Six miles south on Red Bud Trail from Highway 31
Hours: 9 a.m.–4:30 p.m., daily, May 15–October 31. Advance reservations are needed for groups. Tours run approximately 25 minutes.
Admission: $3 adults, $1.50 children ages 5–12, under 5 are free
Ages: All ages
Parking: Free at Bear Cave Resort
Freebies: Cave booklet

Michigan's only natural cave is approximately 150 feet long and 15 feet high at its tallest. Walk down 40 feet under the ground and take a self-guided tour along a paved and lighted walkway. An audio tape narration tells stories of a cave monster and points out stalagtites, stalagmites, wall fossils, and nature's etchings. Folk legend also claims that a nearby water-filled cavern was once a hiding place for runaway slaves on the Underground Railroad. After the tour, take a walk along the St. Joseph River.

Industry

Besser Company

801 Johnson Street, Alpena
517-354-4111

Website: www.besser.com

Location: North of Alpena, Johnson Street and US 23 north
Hours: Call two weeks ahead to schedule visit.
Admission: Free
Ages: Only middle school age and up can go through the factory. Younger children are welcome to visit the offices.
Parking: Free on site
Freebies: Pencils with logo and industry literature

One-hour tour of offices and factory offers a historical display about the Besser Company, a walk through the computer design offices, and the steel assembly line where concrete block-making machinery mixers are made.

Industry

Bissel, Inc.

2345 Walker NW, Grand Rapids
616-453-4451

Website: www.bissel.com
Location: Take I-96 west past Grand Rapids to exit 28. Turn left on Walker.
Hours: One-hour tour offered morning and afternoon, weekdays, September-April. Schedule three weeks ahead
Admission: Free
Ages: Recommended middle school and up
Parking: Free on site
Freebies: After the tour, visitors can go to the adjacent factory outlet store and receive a discount on their purchases

Tour the factory that manufactures home care products. Watch shampoo bottles blown and sweeper motors assembled.

Farming

Calder Brothers Dairy Farm

9334 Finzel Road, Carleton
734-654-2622

Location: South Stoney Creek and Finzel Roads. Carleton is about 45 minutes south of downtown Detroit, off I-75 south.
Hours: 10 a.m.–8:30 p.m., Monday–Thursday and Sunday. 10 a.m.–9 p.m., Friday and Saturday, June–mid-September. 10 a.m.–7:30 p.m., daily,

rest of year. Call ahead to schedule tours. 4 p.m. milking demonstration daily.

Admission: $5.75 tour
Ages: All ages
Parking: Free on site
Freebies: Ice cream cone

Milk a cow by hand, bottle feed a calf, watch a cow being machine milked, and see how milk is stored for transport to the Calder Brothers processing plant. Kids will also enjoy petting the other animals—peacocks, dogs, burros, deer, llamas, pot belly pigs, chickens, and geese. The tour also includes a hayride.

Arts & Crafts

The Candle Factory

301 Grand View Parkway
Traverse City
616-946-2280, 616-946-2850

Location: South side of Grandview Parkway, one block west of downtown
Hours: Generally 9:30 a.m.–6 p.m., Monday–Saturday; 10 a.m.–5:30 p.m., Sunday, year-round. Extended hours seasonally. To view candle making, call ahead; production hours fluctuate.
Admission: Free
Ages: All ages
Parking: Free on site

Surround yourself with candles and their heavenly fragrance. Kids will enjoy peeking into the candlemaking area to see how candles are hand-carved and hand-dipped. The Candle Factory sells a wide variety of hand-made candles.

Ecology

Candy Cane Christmas Tree Farm

4780 Seymour Lake Road, Oxford
248-628-8899

Location: Seymour Lake Road, 1/2 mile east of Sashabaw Road
Hours: Noon–5 p.m., weekdays. 9 a.m.–5 p.m., weekends, mid-April–mid-May. Call for appointments.
Admission: $3
Ages: Preschool–early elementary
Parking: Free. Park along driveway

Freebies: One small tree with planting instructions

Enjoy an ecology talk explaining why trees are important to the earth, then walk through the tree farm and listen to the spring birds, busy in the farm's bird houses. Each child receives a 18–24-inch tree to take home to replant. During November–Christmas, the farm sells Christmas trees.

Farming

Carousel Acres

12749 Nine Mile Road, South Lyon
248-437-PONY

Location: 1 1/2 miles west of Pontiac Trail
Hours: 1 1/2–2-hour experiences offered daily, spring, summer, and fall, by reservation only. Other options include a Mobile Petting Farm that brings the farm animals to your special event.
Admission: Depends on size of group
Ages: All ages
Parking: Free

Carousel Farms offers children a private hands-on farm experience. Tour the barn, take a pony ride, and pet bunnies, chickens, pygmy goats, dairy calves, lambs, and a llama. Baby animals abound in spring. Special events include an Easter Egg Hunt and Halloween Family Fun Days. Ten one-week day camp sessions are available for ages 4–12 during the summer.

Farming

Childs Place Buffalo Ranch

12770 Roundtree Road, Hanover
517-563-8249

Location: 18 miles southwest of Jackson
Hours: 9 a.m.–4 p.m., Tuesday–Sunday, year-round
Admission: $35 minimum for eight-person hayride, $5/person for hayride, $1 to walk around
Ages: All ages
Parking: Free on site

No need to travel out west to see Buffalo. Just hop aboard a covered wagon hayride at this buffalo breeding ranch, ride into the pasture, and you'll be surrounded by approximately 100 buffalo. Offer them ears of corn; they'll eat from your hand and might even let you pet them. Buffalo meat and buffalo products—jewelry, coats, moccasins, and rugs—are on sale at the ranch outpost. Horseback riding by the hour and half-hour is also offered.

Food

Chocolate Vault, Ice Cream Parlour and Candy Shoppe

110 West Chicago, Tecumseh
517-423-7602

Location: Downtown Tecumseh
Hours: 9 a.m.–10 p.m., Monday–Saturday. Noon–10 p.m., Sunday
Admission: Free
Ages: All ages
Parking: Street parking

Kids will enjoy looking through a window and watching employees hand dip a variety of centers and other goodies into an 80-pound chocolate melter. Come prepared to indulge in an ice cream sundae and your favorite candies.

Utilities

Cook Energy Information Center

Red Arrow Highway, Bridgman
616-465-6101

Location: Between exits 16 and 23, off I-94. South of St. Joseph.
Hours: 10 a.m.–5 p.m. Tuesday–Sunday. Closed December 15–January 15 and major holidays. Groups 10 or more must call ahead for a reservation; under 10 people can just drop by.
Admission: Free
Ages: All ages
Parking: Free on site

The 45-minute tour includes three entertaining and educational theater presentations. The first explains energy today and in the future. The second shows a working model of a nuclear power plant and the third, a wide-screen visual tour of the plant. In addition, visitors can walk along a scenic trail through the dunes and picnic on a terraced patio overlooking Lake Michigan. A private dining room accommodates large groups, by reservation only.

Food

Cook's Farm Dairy

2950 Seymour Lake Road, Ortonville
248-627-3329

Location: Take I-75 north to M-15 north. Go one mile east on Seymour Lake Road
Hours: Half-hour–45-minute tours. Summer: 9 a.m.–10 p.m., Monday–Saturday. Noon–10 p.m., Sunday. Winter: 9 a.m.–8 p.m., Monday–Saturday. Noon–8 p.m., Sunday. Call to schedule tours for groups of ten or more.
Admission: $3
Ages: All ages
Parking: Free on site
Freebies: Ice cream cone and glass of Cook's chocolate milk

Tours start in the cow barn. After meeting new-born calves, you are taken into the production plant for a dry run of the process that turns cows' milk into ice cream and chocolate milk. The tour ends in the ice cream parlor/farm store.

Food

Dakota Bread Company

6879 Orchard Lake Road, West Bloomfield
248-626-9110

Location: On the east side of Orchard Lake Road, 1/4 mile south of Maple Road
Hours: One-hour tours are offered Wednesday mornings by reservation only; call several months in advance.
Admission: $4/child
Ages: 4 and up
Parking: Free in lot
Freebies: Cookies, a small sample bread to take home and/or the bread each child created

Children don white baker's aprons and, surrounding a large butcher block, roll a small piece of dough into a shape. The mini-bakers watch the hopper turning grain into flour, the giant bread hook mixing up dough, and the cutting and weighing of big globs of freshly made dough. Cookies and songs follow. Children are invited to come back later to pick up their small bread.

Arts & Crafts

Davisburg Candle Factory

634 Davisburg Road, Davisburg
810-634-4214

Location: I-75 north to exit 93 (Dixie Highway), downtown Davisburg

Hours: 10 a.m.–5 p.m., Monday–Saturday, year-round. In addition, noon–4 p.m., Sunday, August–December 25. For groups of ten or more, schedule in advance. Also call in advance to be sure the taper line is running.

Admission: $20 refundable deposit

Ages: All ages

Parking: Free on street

Watch tapers being dipped into hot wax colors and suspended to dry. This is done courtesy of a wonderful homemade taper line contraption. Kids will enjoy watching it run. You'll love the sweet musky, cinnamon smell of the candles. A candle shop with a variety of candles and accessories is located upstairs.

Mining

Delaware Copper Mine

On The Keweenaw Peninsula, Kearsage
906-289-4688

Location: 12 miles south of Copper Harbor, in Kearsage.

Hours: 10 a.m.–5 p.m. daily, mid-May–June and September–October, self-guided tours only. 10 a.m.–6 p.m., daily, July and August, guided tours.

Admission: $8 ages 13 and up, $4 ages 6–12, 5 and under free. Self-guided tour: $7 adults, $4 children.

Ages: All ages

Parking: Free on site

Go deep into the bowels of the earth and take a guided 35–45 minute underground tour of a former copper mine. Above ground, see a mining museum, prehistoric mining pits, and the ruins of nineteenth century mining buildings. Afterwards, pet deer in the petting farm and shop in the gift shop. Dress warmly.

History

Detroit Historical Museum

5401 Woodward Avenue, Detroit
313-833-1805

Website: www.detroithistorical.org
Location: In Cultural Center, across from the Detroit Institute of Arts
Hours: Wednesday–Sunday. Tours are only scheduled through a written application; call to have an application sent to your group. Minimum group 10; maximum 60 children.
Admission: $2/child
Ages: Preschool–high school
Parking: Lot on west side of building. $3 on weekends

A docent-guided tour of the exhibits and a hands-on activity help children understand Detroit's history.

Utilities

Detroit Water and Sewage Department—Northeast Water Treatment Plant

11000 East Eight Mile Road, Detroit
313-964-9570

Location: Eight Mile and Van Dyke
Hours: One-hour tour, 9 a.m.–2 p.m., Monday–Friday. Call two weeks in advance to schedule tour.
Admission: Free
Ages: Minimum suggested age 12 years. Group maximum is 20 people; minimum is five people.
Parking: Free on site

Watch the pumps and cisterns working as they bring in raw water, purify, and filter it and pump it out to Metro Detroit households.

 Industry

Dow Visitor's Center

47 Building, Midland
517-636-8658

Location: State and Ellsworth Streets
Hours: 2 1/2-hour tour, 9:30 a.m.–noon, Monday.

1–3:30 p.m., Friday. Call at least two weeks in advance to schedule tour.
Admission: Free
Ages: Minimum age fourth grade
Parking: Free on site
Freebies: A pen

Tour one of the world's largest and most diversified specialty chemical production facilities. Watch a slide presentation about Dow's earliest beginnings and learn about the many chemical, plastic, and agricultural products manufactured at this site. Then walk through the Saran Wrap plant and see production and shipping first hand.

Farming

Erie Orchards and Cider Mill

1235 Erie Road, Erie
734-848-4518
734-847-8695

Location: Just west of Telegraph Road on Erie Road, south of Monroe
Hours: Call to arrange one-hour tour, Monday–Friday, during the fall.
Admission: $4.50/person includes tour, apple picking, hayride, one pumpkin, glass of cider, and donut, teacher gift
Ages: Preschool and up
Parking: Free on site
Freebies: Children receive coloring sheets.

Look behind the scenes at an apple orchard, starting with a hayride through the orchard full of 3,500 dwarf trees. Pick apples, then walk into the grading room and cold storage room. Watch how cider and donuts are made, pick apples and pumpkins, and then relax with a complimentary glass of cider and a fresh donut.

Food

Fenn Valley Winery

6130 122nd Avenue, Fennville
616-561-2396

Website: www.fenvalley.com
Location: Exit 34 off I-96
Hours: Self-guided tours during business hours. During winter 1–5 p.m., daily. During summer, extended hours.

Admission: Free
Ages: All ages
Parking: Free on site
Freebies: Free tastings of house wines and non-alcoholic beverages

Watch a 17-minute wine-processing video, peer into the warehouse from the second-story observation windows, and taste several house wines. For kids, there are non-alcoholic tastings and a chance to poke their heads through the faceless cardboard cutouts on the winery lawn and become a German boy and girl. Browse through the store and buy Fenn Valley wines to enjoy at home.

Utilities

Fermi 2 Power Plant

6400 North Dixie Highway, Newport
734-586-5228

Location: I-75 exit 21 Newport Road to North Dixie
Hours: Two-hour tour offered at mutually convenient times, day or evening, by reservation only. Groups should call three to five weeks in advance. Families are often added on to large groups; please call for appointment.
Admission: Free
Ages: Interest level fourth grade and older.
Parking: Free on site
Freebies: Free literature on Fermi 2 and nuclear power

Watch a videotape about the future of nuclear power, take a bus tour of the cooling towers, walk through the control room simulator, play energy-related video games, and use a power-generating bicycle.

Fire Safety

Fire Headquarters

24477 Lahser Road, Southfield
248-827-0720

Location: Just south of Ten Mile Road
Hours: A thirty-minute tour. Mornings, Monday–Wednesday or special arrangements for evening tours. Call ahead. For groups of Southfield residents or businesses only.
Admission: Free

Ages: Kindergarten–eighth grade
Parking: Limited parking on the side of the station
Freebies: Fliers and helmets when available

Tour the stationhouse and see how firefighters live and work and watch a demonstration of fire equipment. A Public Education Officer talks about fire safety.

Industry

Ford Motor Company
Wixom Assembly Plant

28801 Wixom Road, Wixom
248-344-5358

Location: Wixom Road and I-96, approximately three miles west of Twelve Oaks Mall
Hours: Two-hour walking tour, Friday only. Written reservation requests only, at least six months in advance: Plant Tours, Ford Motor Company, Wixom Assembly Plant, 28801 Wixom Road, Wixom, MI 48393-0001. Include the number of people, your requested Friday date, and your daytime phone.
Admission: Free
Ages: Age 12 or older
Parking: Free in visitor lot

Walk through the plant and watch Ford's luxury cars being born. The Lincoln Town Car, and Lincoln Continental are produced here.

Transportation

Four Winns Boat Company

925 Frisbie, Cadillac
616-775-1351

Website: www.fourwinns.com
Location: North end of Cadillac in the Cadillac Industrial Park
Hours: 1 and 2 p.m. Monday–Friday. Call ahead at least 24 hours in advance to reserve tour time. One-hour tour.
Admission: Free
Ages: 10 and up, accompanied by an adult.
Parking: Free on site
Freebies: Boat catalog

Walk through the boat factory and watch performance boats and sports boats being made from start to finish.

Industry

Frank Industries, Inc.

3950 Burnsline Road, Brown City
810-346-2771

Location: 65 miles north of Detroit, near I-69.
Hours: 9 a.m.–4:30 p.m., Monday–Friday. Call ahead to reserve tour time.
Admission: Free
Ages: All ages. Children must be accompanied by an adult
Parking: Free on site
Freebies: Brochures

Walk through the factory and watch conveyor belts and assembly lines as robots and people create recreational vehicles, including vans, campers, and motor homes.

Food

Frankenmuth Brewery, Inc.

425 South Main, Frankenmuth
517-652-6183

Location: Tuscola and South Main
Hours: 11 a.m.–6 p.m., Monday–Friday. 10 a.m.–7 p.m., Saturday. Noon–6 p.m., Sunday. Tours offered every hour on the hour. Last tour starts one hour prior to closing.
Admission: $2.50 adults, $1.25 ages 13–20, children under 12 are free.
Ages: All ages
Parking: Free on site
Freebies: Free samples of beer for those age 21 and over

After a six-minute video on the brewing process, walk right into the brewery and see up close how beer is made. You'll marvel at the large copper kettles and fermenting tanks and enjoy watching the fill-er-up process of the bottling line. Beer, pretzels, souvenir glasswear and wearables can be purchased at the gift shop.

Industry

GM Lansing Car Assembly Plants

Body Plant and Chassis Plant
517-885-9676 (tour reservations)

Website: www.oldmobile.com
Website: www.alero.com
Location: Two plants, the Body Plant and Chassis Plant.
Hours: Call to schedule a tour Monday–Friday. Both tours can be scheduled on the same day
Admission: Free
Ages: Must be at least 12 year old
Parking: Parking lots nearby
Freebies: Brochures and pamphlets about tour

Follow cars from the drawing board to the end of the assembly line with two tours. Start at the Body Plant and watch as state-of-the-art robots transform raw metal into car bodies. Then at the Chassis Plant, motors, seats, interior trim, and other features are added. Watch the final step as computers check out the finished cars in mock road tests.

Industry

GM Truck Group

G-3100 Van Slyke Road, Flint
810-236-4978

Location: Exit 116 off I-75 north and go east to Van Slyke. Turn north and go about 1/2 mile. Turn in at Gate 6.
Hours: By appointment, Monday–Friday. Call far in advance.
Admission: Free
Ages: Suggested minimum 6 years
Parking: Free in visitors lot. Use Gate 6
Freebies: Gifts vary

Put on your safety glasses and get ready for a sight and sound show. This one-hour tour gives you an up-close look at the creation of a four-door pickup truck from start to finish.

Farming

Green Meadow Farm

6400 Hollister Road, Elsie
517-862-4291

Website: ww.greenmeadowfarm.com
Location: Northeast of Lansing
Hours: 9 a.m.–4 p.m. Monday–Friday. Saturday tours are also available if necessary. Call ahead to arrange a tour time.
Admission: Free
Ages: All ages
Parking: Free on site
Freebies: For groups, goodie bags with Dairy Industry promotion pencils, erasers, stickers, and more

Children learn the ins and outs of dairy farming, tour the feed barns, maternity barns, calf barns, and cow barns. Milking is a 24-hour operation at Green Meadow Farm, so children are always guaranteed a first-hand look at the milking process.

Arts and Crafts

The Groove Gallery "Bead Parties"

106 South Main Street, Royal Oak
248-398-8162

Location: At Main Street and Eleven Mile, on the second floor above Ace Hardware
Hours: Hours vary with the season. Call ahead to book a 1–1 1/2-hour party.
Admission: Minimum charge, $80/group. "Bead Party" includes a finished beaded project, $10/child. "Tie Dye Party" includes dyeing a cotton T-shirt, $10/child. Groups can be as small as three, as large as 15 people.
Ages: 7 and up
Parking: Metered lot behind store

The Groove Gallery is a boutique that sells beads, jewelry, incense, candles, and unique gifts. Bead Parties and Tie Dye Parties offer scout groups and birthday parties a chance to create, with assistance, a beaded necklace, anklet or bracelet, or tie dye shirt. $4 bead packets are also on sale for parents who would like to have their bead party at home.

Mining

Gypsum Mine Tour

Michigan Natural Storage
1200 Judd SW, Grand Rapids
616-241-1619

Location: Chicago Drive and Burlingame Street
Hours: 1¼-hour tour, 8 a.m.–5 p.m., Monday–Friday, by appointment only
Admission: $2 adults, $1.50 junior high students, $1.25 elementary students and seniors. $30 minimum charge.
Ages: All ages
Parking: Free on site
Freebies: You can keep the rocks you find

Go down into the mine, hear about the history and geology of gypsum mining, and spend some time exploring for rocks. The mine is currently used by local businesses for natural cold storage.

Food

Hiram Walker and Sons, Unlimited

2072 Riverside Drive, Windsor
519-561-5499

Location: Walker Road and Riverside Drive
Hours: May–August: 9 and 10 a.m., noon, 1 and 2 p.m. Monday–Friday. September–April: 2 p.m., Monday–Friday. The tour begins in the company store.
Admission: Free
Ages: All ages. Small children must be accompanied by an adult
Parking: Free in lot on Montreal, off of Riverside Drive, one light east of Walker Road
Freebies: Postcards

Tour the distillery and bottling plant, then browse through the company store, where you can purchase Hiram Walker products and also mugs, shirts and hats with the company name and logo.

Animals

Hoegh Pet Casket Company

317 Delta Avenue, Gladstone
906-428-2151

Location: Off Highway 41 on Delta Avenue
Hours: 8 a.m.–4 p.m., Monday–Friday, year-round. Groups of 10 or more should call to arrange tour time. Drop-in tours are approximately 25 minutes; group tours are 45 minutes.
Admission: Free
Ages: All ages. Small children must be accompanied by an adult.
Parking: Free on site
Freebies: Souvenirs with company logo

For 30 years, Hoegh Industries has been one of America's only pet casket manufacturers. Tour the plant and watch the complete manufacturing of pet caskets. A model pet cemetery is also located in the back of the plant. Movies of real pet cemeteries and a question and answer session are added to group tours. Here's a tour worthy of Stephen King.

Food

Homestead Sugar House Candies

11393 Homestead Road, Beulah
616-882-7712

Location: 31 miles south of Traverse City
Hours: 9:30 a.m.–5 p.m., daily, Memorial Day–Labor Day. 9:30 a.m.–4 p.m. daily after Labor Day.
Admission: Free
Ages: All ages
Parking: Free
Freebies: Candies

Watch hand-dipped maple cream candies and rum brandy cherries being created by the candy makers at the Homestead Sugar House. Then browse, buy, and try a few new sugar or sugarless treats.

Industry

ICT Shelby "Man-Made Gemstones"

1330 Industrial Drive, Shelby
616-861-2165

Location: Shelby exit off I-31, north of Muskegon.
Hours: 9 a.m.–5:30 p.m. Monday–Friday, noon–4 p.m. Saturday. Call to schedule tours for groups of 10 or more.
Admission: Free
Ages: All ages

Parking: Free on site

Begin the half-hour tour with a short slide film presentation in the 50-seat theater, then browse through the gems on display and have a hands-on experience trying to shape a "gem" on the faceting machine. The retail store sells gemstones, and for children, crystallized stone souvenirs.

Mining

Iron Mountain Iron Mine

US-2, Vulcan
906-774-7914

Location: Nine miles east of Iron Mountain, on US-2
Hours: 9 a.m.–6 p.m., daily, Memorial Day–Labor Day. 9 a.m.–5 p.m., daily, Labor Day–October.
Admission: $5.50 adults, $4.50 children ages 6–12, under 6 free. Bring sweatshirts—the mine is chilly.
Ages: All ages
Parking: Free on site

Don raincoats and hard hats and ride an underground train one quarter-mile through underground drifts and tunnels. Your tour guide will point out geological formations and mining equipment. You'll come away with a first-hand understanding of the dangers of the mining industry. Browse in a gift shop after the tour.

Clothing

Iverson Snowshoe Company

Box 85, Maple Street, Shingleton
906-452-6370

Website: www.seekwilderness.com
Location: Off M-28, two blocks past intersection of M-94 and M-28
Hours: 8 a.m.–3:30 p.m., Monday–Friday, year-round. Call ahead to set up a tour.
Admission: Free
Ages: All ages
Parking: Free

Ten-minute tours demonstrate how wood is bent and rawhide shoes are laced, as workers create snowshoes. The retail showroom sells trout fishing net, miniature snowshoes for decorations, hats, scarves, mittens, T-shirts, snowshoes, and lodge furniture.

Cultural

Japanese Cultural Center and Tea House

1315 South Washington Avenue, Saginaw
517-759-1648

Location: Ezra Rust Drive and South Washington Street, across from the Saginaw Zoo
Hours: March–November tours: Noon–4 p.m., Tuesday–Saturday. December–February: closed. Gardens: April–May and October–November, 9 a.m.–4 p.m., Tuesday–Saturday. June–September, 9 a.m.–8 p.m., Tuesday–Saturday. Gardens closed in December. Formal tea offered second Saturday of every month at 2 p.m., year-round. Call ahead to schedule groups of 15 or more.
Admission: Formal tea, $6/person. Tour of garden and tea house plus informal tea service (green leaf tea and sweets), $3 adults, $2 children 12 and under and students. School groups should ask about origami craft and video.
Ages: All ages
Parking: Use tea house parking lot or zoo parking lot across the street

Experience the serenity and simple beauty of the Japanese garden and tea house. Children will especially enjoy creating an origami figure and, if they are adventurous, tasting a sweet gelatin candy and green tea.

Food

Jiffy Baking Mixes Chelsea Milling

201 North Street, Chelsea
734-475-1361

Website: www.jiffymix.com
Location: Downtown Chelsea
Hours: 8:30 a.m.–1:30 p.m., Monday–Friday, by reservation only
Admission: Free
Ages: All ages, but for children 5 and under, there must be one adult for each child.
Parking: Free on site
Freebies: Begin your tour with a piece of Jiffy cake and a beverage and then take home a sample Jiffy mix

Start with a slide presentation of the production of Jiffy mixes, then take a 1 1/2-hour guided tour of the noisy, busy plant and warehouse. You'll love seeing the little Jiffy mix boxes looking like toy soldiers as they come around on the assembly line.

Farming

Kellogg Farm

10461 North 40th Street, Hickory Corners
616-671-2507

Location: Halfway between Battle Creek and Kalamazoo
Hours: 8 a.m.–sunset daily, year-round. 1 1/2-hour guided tours available by reservation only. Free self-guided trail.
Admission: Depends on size of group
Ages: 3 and up
Parking: Free on site

Take a 1/4-mile walk around the grounds and through the barns of the modern dairy farm. Children will learn about breeding, crop systems research, and animal nutrition. Milking is done three times a day, at 7 a.m., 12:30, and 7 p.m. W.K. Kellogg Forest and Kellogg Bird Sanctuary are nearby. Weary travelers will want to stop for a homemade meal at the historic Hickory Inn at the four-way crossroads in downtown Hickory Corners, 616-671-4362.

Food

Kilwins Quality Confections

355 Division Road, Petoskey
616-347-4831

Website: www.kilwins.com
Location: Northeast of the downtown shopping district
Hours: 15-minute tour, offered 10:30 and 11 a.m., 2 and 2:30 p.m., Monday–Thursday, Memorial Day–Labor Day. Large groups can call to arrange tours throughout the year. Call ahead for times.
Admission: Free
Ages: All ages
Parking: Free on site
Freebies: A sample chocolate

This is a heavenly tour for chocoholics. Walk through the candy-making rooms and drool over 500-pound chocolate melters, watch the candy conveyor belts merrily chugging along, and then (yum!) taste a special sample. After your tour, you can buy candy in the gift shop.

Animals

Leader Dog for the Blind

1039 South Rochester Road, Rochester
810-651-9011

Website: www.leaderdog.org
Location: Avon and Rochester Roads
Hours: 11/2–2-hour family tour, held one Sunday afternoon each month except June, July, August, and December. Call for exact dates. Tour registration is requested.
Admission: Free
Ages: All ages. Please note: Tours are available for families only, not for scout or school groups.
Parking: Free on site
   The walking lecture tour takes visitors through the kennels and offers information about the facility. A 20-minute movie explores the special bond between leader dogs and their blind owners.

Transportation/Toys

Lionel Trains Visitor Center

26750 Twenty-Three Mile Road,
Chesterfield Township
810-949-4100, ext. 1211

Location: Gratiot and 23 Mile Road
Hours: 45-minute–one-hour tours. 10 a.m., 3, and 4 p.m. Wednesday and Thursday. 10 a.m., 1:30, and 2:30 p.m., Friday. 9, 10, 11 a.m., and noon, Saturday. Closed Sunday–Tuesday and holiday weekends. Call ahead to reserve your tour time.
Admission: Free
Ages: All ages
Parking: Free on site
Freebies: Catalogs, pins, and hats
   A ten-minute video offers Lionel Trains history and production process. Visitors are introduced to Lionel's founder, Joshua Lionel Cowen, who invented the first electric car and moveable track in 1900. Footage of today's train factory shows trains being molded, painted, and decorated. The highlight of the tour is the Visitor Center, where ten

miniature trains roar through tunnels, over and around bridges and up and down hills on the detailed 560-square-foot village display. Kids will enjoy pushing buttons that operate the train accessories.

Arts & Crafts
Little Dipper Candle Shoppe

415 North Fifth Avenue, Ann Arbor
734-994-3912

Location: Kerrytown
Hours: 10 a.m.–6 p.m., Monday–Friday. 9 a.m.–6 p.m., Saturday. Noon–5 p.m., Sunday. Large groups should call ahead to reserve times.
Admission: $1.50 for one pair of dipped candles
Ages: All ages
Parking: Use metered lot adjacent to Kerrytown
   Kids will enjoy choosing their own small tapers and then dipping them in the color of their choice. The store's fragrance is a pleasure for the noses in your family.

Arts & Crafts
Mary Maxim, Inc.

2001 Holland Avenue, Port Huron
810-987-2000

Location: Holland and Pine Grove Avenue
Hours: 9:30 a.m.–6 p.m., Monday–Saturday. 9:30 a.m.–9 p.m., Friday. Noon–5 p.m., Sunday. July–January. Call at least one week in advance to arrange a tour.
Admission: Free
Ages: School-age children through adult
Parking: Free on site
Freebies: Coffee and cookies, a special tour bag with a complimentary gift, and Mary Maxim catalog
   Enjoy a snack and watch a demonstration of needlework at this leading manufacturer of needlecraft kits. Then browse through the retail store.

Animals

Michigan Humane Society— Central Shelter

7401 Chrysler Drive, Detroit
313-872-3400

Michigan Humane Society— Genesee County

G-3325 South Dort Highway, Burton
810-744-0511

Michigan Humane Society—North

3600 Auburn Road, Rochester Hills
248-852-7420

Michigan Humane Society—West

37255 Marquette, Westland
734-721-7300

Each office will take children through the kennels, infirmary, and office, 10 a.m.–5 p.m., Monday–Friday. Call to arrange a convenient tour time for your group.

Government

Michigan State Capitol

Capitol Avenue, Lansing
517-373-2353 (Monday–Friday)
517-373-2348 (weekends)

Website: www.mileg.org
Location: Between Allegan and Ottawa Streets
Hours: 9 a.m.–4 p.m., Monday–Friday. 10 a.m.–3 p.m., Saturday. Closed Sunday. Groups of ten or more should call to schedule a tour several weeks in advance of visit.
Admission: Free
Ages: All ages
Parking: Meters on street, reserved areas for buses behind Capitol on Walnut Street or at Historical Museum

Tour the elegant state capitol, restored to its 1879 splendor. Visit the old Supreme Court, and current Senate and House viewing galleries and committee rooms. Don't forget to notice the portraits of former Michigan governors, located on the second floor rotunda, near the Governor's executive office and reception rooms.

Farming

Michigan State University Botany Greenhouse and Butterfly House

MSU Campus, East Lansing
517-355-0229

Location: Just north of Farm Lane and East Circle Drive
Hours: 8 a.m.–5 p.m., Monday–Friday. 10 a.m.–2 p.m., Saturday and Sunday. Groups of ten or more must call ahead to schedule tours. Families can drop in during open hours.
Admission: For tours: $1.50 adults, $1 seniors, 75 cents children, with a minimum of $20/group. Donations are requested of drop-in visitors.
Ages: All ages
Parking: Use the large orange and blue parking structure on Grand River, behind the Student Book Store

Kids will love wandering through the 25,000-square-foot greenhouses where 3,000 species from rainforest, subtropical, and desert climes dwell. There are special collections of orchids, ferns, and—don't get too close—carnivorous plants. The Butterfly House has several species of free flying butterflies. Don't go home without treating the kids to MSU's answer to Ben and Jerry. At the MSU Dairy Store, homemade ice cream is a bargain and you can try chocolate cheese, a Spartan invention. Located next to the Dairy Plant on Farm Lane.

Farming

Michigan State University Dairy Store

1140 South Anthony Hall, MSU Campus,
East Lansing
517-355-8466

Location: On Farm Lane, between Shaw Lane and Wilson
Hours: May–Halloween: 9 a.m.–8 p.m., Monday–Friday. 10 a.m.–7 p.m., Saturday. 11 a.m.–6 p.m., Sunday. November 1–April: 9 a.m.–7 p.m., Monday–Friday. Noon–5 p.m., Saturday and

Sunday. Schedule tours at least two weeks in advance. 20 people minimum for tour.
Admission: Free
Ages: All ages
Parking: Pay lot north of building on Shaw Lane
    See how ice cream, yogurt, and cheese are processed and taste the homemade results as MSU gives Ben and Jerry a run for their money. At the MSU Dairy Store, a double scoop of homemade ice cream is under $3.

Farming

Michigan State University Farm Tours

MSU Campus, East Lansing
517-355-4458 (Alumni Center)

Location: All barns are located south of campus. Swine barn on Forest Road; sheep barn on Hagadorn Road; cow barn on College Road. Barn tours can begin at Student Union or at one of the barns; check with your tour guide.
Hours: Barns are open for self-guided tours or pre-arranged group tours, 8 a.m.–4 p.m., Monday–Saturday. Figure approximately 30 minutes for each barn.
Admission: Free
Ages: All ages
Parking: Use lots close to barns
    Meet the animals and learn how they live and what they eat, and watch cows being milked in the dairy barn.

Animals

Michigan State
Veterinary School Vet-A-Visit

College of Veterinary Medicine
Michigan State University, East Lansing
517-355-5165

Location: Bogue and Wilson, near Wharton Center
Hours: 9 a.m.–4 p.m., Saturday, usually held mid–April
Admission: Free
Ages: All ages
Parking: Use Wharton Center lot
    Exhibits, demonstrations, live animals, and a Teddy Bear Clinic invite youngsters to peek behind

the scenes at MSU's Veterinary School. This is a perfect tour for veterinary wannabe's and animal lovers.

Food

Morley Candy Makers, Inc.

23770 Hall Road, Clinton Township
810-468-4300

Location: On Hall Road, between Gratiot and Groesbeck
Hours: 1½-hour tours, 10 a.m., 1 p.m., Tuesday–Thursday, September–Mother's Day. Call many months ahead, especially for popular spring reservations.
Admission: Free
Ages: First grade and up. Minimum 25; maximum 50. Adult supervision required for every five children.
Parking: Free in front of office
Freebies: Free candy samples

Watch a slide presentation on the history of chocolate and the history of Morley Candy Makers, a Michigan company since 1919. Then, walking along an observation walkway, peek into the production and packing plant and witness chocolate candies being created, tended, and packaged. End up in the retail store for a few free samples and a chance to buy some candy and chocolate topping to take home.

Cultural

Nokomis Learning Center

5153 Marsh Road, Okemos
517-349-5777

Website: www.nokomis.org
Location: ¼ mile north of Meridian Mall, along Marsh Road
Hours: 10 a.m.–5 p.m., Tuesday–Friday. Noon–5 p.m., Saturday. Closed Sunday and Monday. 1½-hour tours are offered for 15 or more; call ahead.
Admission: $2/person
Ages: Kindergarten and up
Parking: Free on site

Children learn about the heritage of the Woodland Indians of the Great Lakes—the

Ojibway, Ottawa, and Potawatomi tribes known as "The People of the Three Fires." Tours include a short lecture, demonstration, game, and craft.

Animals

Oakland County Animal Control

1700 Brown Road, Auburn Hills
248-858-0863

Location: West of M-24 on Brown Road
Hours: 45-minute–one-hour tour, 10 a.m.–4:45 p.m., Tuesday–Thursday. 10 a.m.–5:45 p.m., Monday and Friday. Call to schedule a tour.
Admission: Free
Ages: All ages
Parking: Free on site

Watch an educational video, tour the kennels, and meet the dogs who are waiting for adoption.

Media

Observer and Eccentric Newspapers

36251 Schoolcraft, Livonia
734-591-0500

Location: Corner of Schoolcraft and Levan
Hours: Tours offered during office hours on Wednesday mornings. Call ahead to reserve tour. Maximum group size is 25, minimum size is 10.
Admission: Free
Ages: 10 and up
Parking: Free on site

See up close how a modern newspaper is created. The tour takes you through the advertising, composing, and editing offices, through the photo lab and plate room, and from a viewing deck, you can watch the paper actually being printed.

Arts & Crafts

O'Neill Pottery

1841 Crooks Road, Rochester
248-375-0180

Location: Between Avon and M-59
Hours: Call two weeks in advance to schedule a tour or hands-on workshop

Admission: 1 1/2-hour hands-on workshop: $7 per person to create a ceramic work and have it glazed and fired (work is ready two weeks from date of workshop). Minimum 10 people.
Ages: All ages
Parking: Free on site

Children will enjoy visiting this centennial home, now the studio of working potter Helen O'Neill. Learn about clay work, watch her work on the potter's wheel, and then walk around the three-acre grounds and feed the farm animals living in the barn. Older children or adults may choose the hands-on workshop and create their own ceramic work.

The Palace

Two Championship Drive, Auburn Hills
248-377-8278

Location: Take exit 81, Lapeer Road, off I-75. Turn onto South Drive and go to West entrance.
Hours: Tours offered Monday–Friday. Call ahead to arrange a tour. Groups of all sizes can be accommodated. Families can be added on to larger groups.
Admission: Tour: $5 adults, $3 children. Special tour packages with lunch available upon request.
Ages: Preschool and up
Parking: Free on lot

Peek behind the scenes into the multimillion dollar Palace broadcast center, owners' suites, Hall of Fame, press box, locker rooms, and take a peek at Piston championship trophies. Learn Pistons, Vipers, and Shock lore. If you're lucky, you might even catch a glimpse of a player or coach. Your preteens and teens will nominate you best parent of the year.

Pelee Island Winery

455 Sea Cliff Drive, Country Road 20,
East Kingsville, Ontario, Canada
519-733-6551
1-800-59-PELEE

Website: www.peleeisland.com
Location: Downtown Kingsville. Take Ambassador

Bridge over and follow the Huron Line to Highway 3, all the way to Kingsville (about one hour from the bridge).

Hours: One-hour tours. Noon, 2, and 4 p.m., daily, year-round.

Admission: $3 adults, $2 seniors, 18 and under free

Ages: All ages

Parking: Free on site

See a video of the history of Pelee Island and its winery, walk through the processing plant, see rooms used for bottling, fermentation, and laboratory. After the tour, sample the wines and browse in the gift shop.

Arts & Crafts

Pewabic Pottery

10125 East Jefferson, Detroit
313-822-0954

Website: www.pewabic.com

Location: On East Jefferson between Cadillac and Hurlbut Streets, across from Waterworks Park, 31/2 miles east of downtown Detroit

Hours: Gallery: 10 a.m.–6 p.m., Monday–Saturday. Guided tours by appointment only. Hands-on workshops are scheduled at times convenient for group and instructor. Call two weeks in advance to schedule a guided tour or hands-on workshop. Individuals are welcome to drop in for a self-guided tour, as well as browse in galleries and gift shop.

Admission: Guided tour, with minimum 15 people: $3/person. 11/2-hour hands-on workshop: $12/child to have work glazed and fired (work is ready four weeks from date of workshop).

Ages: Minimum 5 years for tour or workshop.

Parking: Free on site

Pewabic Pottery is a historic, turn-of-the-century pottery, famous for its contemporary ceramics. Children are allowed to tour the workshops and galleries, but they will benefit more from participating in hands-on workshops that explore clay works. Classes for adults and children are also available.

Phoenix Memorial Laboratory

2301 Bonisteel Boulevard, Ann Arbor
734-764-6220

Website: www.umich.edu/~mmpp
Location: Bonisteel Boulevard and Murfin
Hours: 8:30 a.m.–3 p.m., Monday–Friday. Call to arrange a tour.
Admission: Free
Ages: First grade and up
Parking: Meter parking

Tour the nuclear reactor plant and laboratory. Kids will enjoy peering into the azure pool surrounding the nuclear reactor and watching demonstrations that show the radioactivity of various materials.

Quincy Mine Hoist No. 2

US-41, Hancock
906-482-3101

Website: www.quincymine.com
Location: Near Hancock, on US-41
Hours: 9:30 a.m.–6 p.m., daily, May–mid-October. Restricted hours Memorial Day–mid-June and Labor Day–mid-October. Last tour leaves 5:30–6 p.m.
Admission: $12.50 adults, $7 children ages 6–13. Surface tour only—$7.50 adults, $3 children.
Ages: All ages
Parking: Free on site

Don hardhats and raincoats and travel on a tram 700 feet underground into an abandoned copper mine. The 1½-hour tour demonstrates copper mining operations and equipment.

Farming

Real Life Farm

48700 Geddes Road, Canton
734-495-0822, 313-451-7856

Location: Between Beck and Denton Road. Just ten minutes west of Metro Airport.
Hours: 3–4 hour springtime tours, 10 a.m.–2 p.m.,

Monday–Friday. Four-hour fall tours, 10 a.m.–midnight, Monday–Saturday. All tours require 25-person minimum. Call ahead to schedule.

Admission: Spring tour: $5/person. Fall tour: $8.50/person. Summer day camp.

Ages: Spring tours are geared to preschool and elementary children. Fall tours are for all ages.

Parking: Free on site

Meet Farmer Don and experience spring on the farm with a 30-minute hayride, horseback ride in the corral, and hands-on activities, including bottle feeding and hand feeding animals and milking nanny goats or cow. Fall tours include hayride, horseback ride, bonfire-cookout, petting farm, and use of the barn for square dancing. No alcohol is permitted on the farm premises.

Saginaw Water Works

522 Ezra Rust, Saginaw
517-759-1640

Location: Across from the Saginaw Zoo

Hours: One-hour tour, offered 8 a.m.–4:30 p.m. Monday–Friday. Large groups should call two weeks in advance for reservations; groups with less than 10 people can drop in during hours.

Admission: Free

Ages: Minimum age fourth grade

Parking: Free on site

Watch a movie that explains how water is treated and purified, then walk through the treatment plant. Kids will enjoy the sights and sounds of pumps and gushing water.

Food

St. Julian Winery

716 South Kalamazoo, Paw Paw
616-657-5568

Website: www.st.julian.com

Location: 1/4 mile north of I-94 on M-40. Paw Paw is about 15 miles west of Kalamazoo.

Hours: 20–30-minute tour held every half-hour, 9 a.m.–4 p.m., Monday–Saturday. Noon–4 p.m., Sunday. Call to schedule a large tour.

Admission: Free

Ages: All ages
Parking: Free on site
Freebies: Wine tasting for adults, non-alcoholic juice for kids

Begin with a ten-minute informational video, then walk through the cellars, crushing room, bottling room, and warehouse in this guided tour that shows you how wine is made using both state-of-the-art equipment and old-world methods.

Scrap Box

581 State Circle, Ann Arbor
734-994-4420

Location: Off State Street, one block south of I-94
Hours: 10 a.m.–6 p.m., Tuesday. 2–6 p.m., Wednesday, Thursday, Friday. 10 a.m.–2 p.m., Saturday. Arrange for group workshops during hours the store is closed to regular business.
Admission: Free
Ages: 4 and up
Parking: Free on site

At the Scrap Box, junk comes in all sizes and shapes. Children can look through bins and boxes of foam, wood, plastic, paper, cardboard, and cork discards and fill a grocery bag for a small fee. Creativity and playfulness will turn the scraps into treasures. This is the perfect place to stock up on materials for rainy day projects. Birthday parties and classroom field trips can be scheduled.

Food

Stahl's Bakery

51021 Washington, New Baltimore
810-725-6990

Location: Washington and Main Streets, downtown New Baltimore
Hours: Call several weeks ahead to arrange a Monday–Thursday morning tour
Admission: Free
Ages: All ages
Parking: Free on site
Freebies: A "belly button cookie" (chocolate chip butter cookie)

Step into the sweet, humid cloud of Stahl's Bakery and watch bread made the old-fashioned way, by a fraternity of flour-dusted young men wearing white aprons. Kids will enjoy watching large batches of dough kneaded by hand and made into loaves, and watching the bakers take out finished loaves with long bread oars called "peels."

Food

Tabor Hill Winery

185 Mt. Tabor Road, Buchanan
616-422-1161
1-800-283-3363

Website: www.taborhill.com
Location: Two miles south of Baroda
Hours: May 1–November 30: Winery: 8 a.m.–5 p.m., Monday and Tuesday. 8 a.m.–9 p.m., Wednesday–Saturday. Noon–9 p.m., Sunday. Tours: noon–4:30 p.m., daily, every half-hour. Restaurant: 11:30 a.m.–3 p.m. and 5:30–9 p.m., Wednesday–Saturday. Noon–9 p.m., Sunday. December 1–April 30: Winery: 8 a.m.–5 p.m., Monday–Thursday. 8 a.m.–9 p.m., Friday. 11 a.m.–9 p.m., Saturday. Noon–9 p.m., Sunday. Tours by appointment only. Restaurant: 5:30–9 p.m., Friday. 11:30 a.m.–3 p.m., and 5:30–9 p.m., Saturday. 11:30 a.m.–3 p.m., Sunday.
Admission: Free
Ages: All ages
Parking: Free on site
Freebies: Free wine tastings and non-alcoholic tastings for children

The guided winery tour takes you through the winery, out to the vineyard, and into the cellar, where you see the bottling line. Taste the many house wines, browse in the retail shop, and stay for lunch or dinner in the casual restaurant. During the winter, bring your own skis and cross-country ski through the vineyards.

Sports

United States Olympic Education Center

Meyland Hall
Northern Michigan University, Marquette
906-227-2888

Location: On the corner of Wright and Tracy Streets, on the edge of campus
Hours: 8 a.m.–5 p.m., Monday–Friday, year-round. Expanded summer hours. Call ahead to schedule a tour.
Admission: Free
Ages: All ages
Parking: Guest parking on campus

Twenty-minute tour of training facility includes a short video, a peek into the weight room, sports medicine room, athletes' housing, and boxing facility.

Government

United States Post Office— George W. Young Facility

1401 West Fort, Detroit
313-226-8667

Location: Between Trumbull and Eighth Streets
Hours: Monday–Friday. Schedule tours at least two weeks in advance.
Admission: Free
Ages: All ages
Parking: Free lot just east of the building on Eighth Street.

Take a behind-the-scenes look at what happens to a letter after it as been flipped into the neighborhood collection box and trucked downtown. Watch envelopes fed into and spit out of state-of-the-art sorting machines.

Food

Walker's Candies

1033 Wyandotte Street East, Windsor
519-253-2019

Location: About two minutes from the tunnel
Hours: 9 a.m.–5 p.m., Monday–Friday. Group

tours only; call ahead to schedule. Tours are approximately 45 minutes.
Admission: $1/person
Ages: All ages
Parking: Free on site
Freebies: Taste three different chocolate candies

Chocoholics will enjoy learning where chocolate comes from, touring the small candy-making facilities, and watching employees hand-dip candy. The tour ends in the retail store for your buying pleasure.

Food

Warner Vineyards

706 South Kalamazoo, Paw Paw
616-657-3165
616-657-3654 (restaurant)

Location: 1/4 mile north of I-94 on M-40. Paw Paw is approximately 15 miles west of Kalamazoo.
Hours: 10 a.m.–5 p.m., daily, year-round. Self-guided champagne tours.
Admission: Free
Ages: All ages
Parking: Free on site
Freebies: Champagne and wine tasting for adults

Watch how champagne is made. Travel through the tierage vaults and riddling rooms to the finishing room where champagne is corked and labeled. End the tour with a champagne-tasting session.

Farming

Wiard's Orchards

5565 Merritt, Ypsilanti
734-482-7744

Website: www.wiards.com
Location: Four miles south of Ypsilanti
Hours: 10 a.m.–2 p.m., Tuesday, Wednesday and Thursday, September–October. Arrive 15 minutes early. Call to reserve tour time. Minimum 20 people.
Admission: Half-hour school group tours are $4.95/person; teachers are free. One-hour pumpkin picking tours are $6/person. "Boo Barn," $1/person. 45-minute adult orchard tours are $3.75/person. The farm also offers 40-minute Spooky Hayrides on October evenings for groups

of 25 or more. $11 includes the hayride, bonfire, and marshmallows.

Ages: All ages
Parking: Free
Freebies: The school tour includes cider and a donut and each child takes home "an apple for each hand." The pumpkin tour includes the school tour plus one small pumpkin for each child. Adult tours include donuts, cider, and coffee.

Visit a bustling working farm. Take a tractor-drawn hay wagon ride through the orchards, pick apples or pumpkins, and watch how cider is made. End your visit at the animal petting farm and hay barn and enjoy cider and donuts at the picnic area.

Farming

Wicks' Apple House

52281 Indian Lake Road, Dowagiac
616-782-7306

Location: East of Benton Harbor, off M-140
Hours: 8 a.m.–6 p.m., Tuesday–Sunday, Memorial Day–November. Cider mill is open Saturday and Sunday, mid-September–October. Tours on Wednesday only. Call ahead to schedule a tour.
Admission: A visit to the farm is free. Tours: $1.50 includes beverage and donut.
Ages: All ages
Parking: Free on site
Freebies: Bag with apples, candies, and apple brochure

Experience autumn at this full-service centennial farm. Wednesday group tours show visitors the cider operation—the cider press and the jug and processing room. The farm also has a farm market with fresh produce and apples, cider mill, bakery, restaurant, and gift shop. Cider Fest, the second weekend in October, features entertainment and wagon rides.

Media

WKBD UPN 50

26905 West Eleven Mile Road, Southfield
248-350-5050

Location: Between Inkster and Telegraph
Hours: 1¼-hour tour. 9 a.m.–6 p.m., Monday,

Tuesday, Thursday, Friday. Call at least two weeks in advance to arrange an appointment

Admission: Free

Ages: 7 and up. Group, 6 minimum; 30 maximum

Parking: Free on site

Walk through the TV station, peeking into sales and business offices, engineering and news rooms. See the news set, weather board, and master controls up close, and sit in on a taping if your tour corresponds to show time.

Farming

W. K. Kellogg Experimental Forest

7060 North 42nd Street, Augusta
616-731-4597

Location: Halfway between Battle Creek and Kalamazoo, approximately two miles north of Augusta

Hours: 8 a.m.–sunset, daily. Closed major holidays. 1 1/2-hour tours are offered to groups year-round, by reservation only.

Admission: Free recreation use, fee for group tours

Ages: All ages

Parking: Free on site

Take a wildflower, tree identification, animal homes, or maple syrup tour through the quiet 700-acre, one-million-tree forest, or enjoy hiking, biking, walking, or cross-country skiing. March's Maple Syrup Open House is open to the public. Kellogg Farm and Kellogg Bird Sanctuary are nearby. Weary travelers will want to stop for a homemade meal at the historic Hickory Inn at the four-way crossroads in downtown Hickory Corners, 616-671-4362.

Clothing

Wolverine World Wide, Inc.

465 Wolverine Street, Rockford
616-866-5500

Location: 15 minutes north of Grand Rapids

Hours: Tours set up at convenience of group; call at least one week in advance

Admission: Free

Ages: Third grade and up

Parking: Free on site

Watch famous Hush Puppy shoes being made in this half-hour tour that includes the heat, steam, and pressure areas, assembly line, and an up-close look at materials used for soles.

Arts & Crafts
Wooden Shoe Factory
447 US-31 at 16th Street, Holland
616-396-6513

Location: Two miles west of I-96 from Grand Rapids
Hours: 8 a.m.–4:30 p.m., Monday–Saturday
Admission: Free
Ages: All ages
Parking: Free on site

Kids will enjoy watching serious shoemakers turn blocks of wood into wooden shoes or "klompens" using 100-year-old machinery and old-fashioned hand carving. After the tour, browse around the gift shop, full of Dutch imports, wooden toys, and homemade fudge.

Medical Research
Wright & Filippis, Inc.
2845 Crooks Road, Rochester
248-829-8213

Location: M-59 and Crooks
Hours: 1–1 1/2-hour tour. 8 a.m.–4 p.m., Monday–Friday. Call to schedule tours.
Admission: Free
Ages: Minimum age 6 years
Parking: Free on site

Children acquire a better understanding of the physically challenged when they visit Wright & Filippis, a firm that researches and develops high-tech products for the disabled and adaptive sports and recreation products. Tour groups learn the difference between an orthosis and prosthesis, tour the workshops, and try out the wheelchairs.

15
Programs for the Schools

A SAMPLING OF TRAVELING PROGRAMS

TIP

Encourage your school's PTO or PTA to set aside funds for bringing in several traveling programs each year. Many schools run bake sales, candy sales, or auctions to raise funds specifically for cultural enrichment.

The Detroit area is full of talented actors, dancers, artists, and musicians who will bring their art into the schools. There are also traveling science and history programs, sponsored by area museums and individuals, which offer school children new ideas in an entertaining format. Here is a sampling of traveling programs available for school, church, synagogue, library, or civic organizations. Fees are not listed because they fluctuate with each booking, depending on the size of the group and traveling distance.

Theater

The Actors' Company

Michael Gravame, Warren
248-988-7032

Highly spirited, Broadway-style productions of classic children's tales and major musicals for elementary to middle school age children.

Storytelling

Ami D.

Ami Jackson, Detroit
313-934-8635

Multi-cultural storytelling, accompanied by piano and/or harp and vocals, with audience participation. Ami D. spins folktales and urban stories. Upper elementary–high school and adult.

Science

Ann Arbor Hands-On Museum Outreach

219 East Huron Street, Ann Arbor
734-995-5439

The Ann Arbor Hands-On Museum offers comprehensive science-based workshops for elementary and middle schools designed to enhance curricula through creative and interactive activities, including Human Biology, Magnetism and Sound, Mathematics, Astronomy, and Light. In addition, the museum will produce Family Math, Physics,

Chemistry, or Astronomy Nights at local elementary and middle schools.

Music

Ann Arbor Symphony Orchestra

527 East Liberty, Ann Arbor
734-994-4801

A morning and afternoon weekday concert is offered to area school children in March. Teachers can call for tickets, preparatory materials, and to book a classroom visit by an ensemble or a symphony docent. Geared for upper elementary and middle school.

Drug Education

BABES World

33 East Forest, Detroit
1-800-54-BABES

Engaging puppets teach children about healthy living skills and encourage them to feel good about themselves when they "say no" to drugs and alcohol. For grades preschool–12.

Storytelling

Barbara Schutz-Gruber

Ann Arbor
734-761-5118

Award-winning storyteller whose favorites include folktales from around the world, tales from Michigan and the Great Lakes, medieval legends, ghost stories, and string stories—stories illustrated with figures and shapes created by a simple piece of string. Preschool–high school.

Animals

Binder Park Zoo—Zoomobile Outreach

7400 Division Drive, Battle Creek
616-979-1351

A variety of thematic presentations incorporating role-playing, hands-on activities, and live animals, for preschool–high school age children.

Drug & Crime Prevention

Blue Pigs

Detroit Police Crime Prevention Section
313-596-2521

Through a variety of songs and musical styles, three talented Detroit Police officers offer children information about child protection, drug abuse and awareness, and crime prevention. The approximately 45-minute show is tailored for audiences, elementary–college.

Theater

Boarshead: Michigan Public Theater

425 South Grand Avenue, Lansing
517-484-7800

Theatrical performances for grades K–12, include material derived from oral and written Michigan histories. Also, custom-designed acting and playwriting workshops and school residencies.

Theater

Bonstelle and Hilberry Theatres

Department of Theater,
Wayne State University, Detroit
313-577-3010

Wayne State University's Black Theatre Program offers one touring production, January–May. For high school.

Puppets

Brad Lowe's Fantasy E-FEX Puppets

Lake Orion
248-405-1021

Brad Lowe offers original adaptations of traditional stories, using music and large, colorful hand puppets, as well as costume-character appearances and puppetry demonstrations and workshops. Preschool–adult.

Music, Values
Carol Johnson

Grand Rapids
616-243-6194

Using original material, Carol Johnson accompanies herself on guitar, banjo, or piano and sings of self- worth, the environment, and living and loving joyfully. Appropriate for elementary schools and family events.

Animals
Carousel Acres Mobile Petting Farm

12749 Nine Mile Road, South Lyon
248-437-7669

Children enjoy up-close-and-personal visits with a gaggle of friendly animals as the petting farm travels to your special event. For preschool and elementary age children.

Music, Storytelling, Drug Education
Casey & Mac —
"Songs and Stories for Little People"

Casey Makela, Mikado
517-736-6583

Audience-participatory stories, songs, and music for preschool, elementary, and family audiences. Many programs offer drug resistance messages, self-esteem, and fun. A teacher's guide is available for each program.

Music
Chautauqua Express

Guy Louis, South Lyons
1-800-377-7113

Like the traveling entertainment shows of yesteryear, Guy Louis both entertains and educates children in a variety of themed shows, including American Music, World Music, African American Music, Music Appreciation, and Environmental Concerns. He also uses a variety of unusual and string instruments. For preschool–middle school and family audiences.

Science

"Chemipalooza"

Dow Chemical Company
2020 Dow Center, Midland
1-800-441-4369

"Chemipalooza" makes chemistry exciting to learn. For middle–high school.

Theater

Children's Theatre of Michigan

m'Arch and Janet Marie McCarty, Troy
248-588-2914

Janet Marie and m'Archibald McCarty offer original musical story-theater performances, including tall tales and silly stories, to reinforce and energize reading, English and social studies curriculum, for children of all ages.

History

Clinton Historical Commission

Pat Dewandeler
810-286-1413

Pat and a lineup of colorful speakers offer Clinton Township history presentations and walking tours for school children–adults. Pat will also implement Clinton Township historical research projects in local schools.

History

Cowboy Arizona

Harold Rice
810-463-5972

Hey there, buckaroos, learn all about life on the ranch and the whys and wherefores of cowboy/cowgirl clothes and paraphernalia in a one-hour program with Cowboy Arizona.

Art

Cranbrook Academy of Art Museum

1221 North Woodward, Bloomfield Hills
248-645-3323

Cooperative program bringing children and their ideas into the art museum as well as teaching children curatorial skills.

Science

Cranbrook Institute of Science

1221 North Woodward, Bloomfield Hills
248-645-3229

45-minute outreach program topics for grades K–adult include portable Starlab, anthropology, physics, geology, electricity and magnetism, dinosaurs, environment, Native Americans, and math.

Clowning

Crazy Richard the Madd Juggler

Richard Bassett, East Jordan
616-536-7987

Crazy Richard offers a unique and lively show combining juggling, clowning, mime, and audience involvement. He also offers juggling workshops.

Puppets

Daren Dundee, Entertainer

21175 Carson, Mount Clemens
810-463-1798

Puppeteer/magician Daren Dundee offers a variety of programs for young children and the whole family, incorporating story-telling, comedy, puppetry, and magic.

Ventriloquist

David Stewart

Grand Rapids
616-363-9322

Silly songs and comical situations, with help from an assortment of idiosyncratic dummies including Sidney the orangutan, Harold the little boy, Wendel the Southern bear, Orenthal the pig, and Ima Hag the old lady. For preschool–adults.

Storytelling

Detroit Association of Black Storytellers

Nkenge Abi
313-868-2639

The Association offers a roster of local African American storytellers.

Science

Detroit Audubon Society

1320 North Campbell, Royal Oak
248-545-2929

Speakers with a slide presentation on changing topics are available to clubs and schools.

Dance

Detroit Dance Collective

23 East Adams, Detroit
313-965-3544

Detroit Dance Collective, a professional, modern dance touring company made up of performers who are also dance educators, offers a variety of school performances, classes, and workshops for students, as well as conducting professional seminars for educators. They will design programs to meet the special needs of any group.

History

Detroit Historical Museum "Detroit Storyliving"

5401 Woodward Avenue, Detroit
313-833-1198

Using music and interactive historical adventures for children, a team of eight teaches school children and families Detroit history, including the Great Fire of 1805, Automobile Culture, Auto Migration of 1914, and Detroit's role in the Underground Railroad. Their program, "Detroit Storyliving," travels to schools.

Detroit Institute of Arts— Art to the Schools

5200 Woodward Avenue, Detroit
313-833-7883

Call 9 a.m.–5 p.m., Monday–Friday, for an "Art to the Schools" request form. Scheduling is not handled over the phone. Free 45- to 60-minute art appreciation talks are available for grades 4–6, Tuesdays and Thursdays, October–May. The talks are based on the DIA's collection and are illustrated with slides. The topics include "Native Cultures of America," "Modern Times," "Exploring Art," "African Traditions," "American Life," and "Ancient World."

Storytelling

Detroit Story League

Barbara Shutz-Gruber
734-761-5118

The League offers a roster of local storytellers.

Science

Dr. Zap

Kevin St. Onge, Leslie
517-589-5560

Using magic and theater, Dr. Zap offers a dynamic audience participation performance explaining principles of physics, chemistry, and optics. For grades K–8.

Values

Dolls for Democracy

Jewish Women International
25160 Lahser, Suite 130, Southfield
248-788-4899

"Doll ladies" bring into the classroom 12-inch replica dolls of famous courageous people who have worked for the betterment of humanity. The presentation teaches brotherhood/sisterhood and the importance of perseverance over adversity. The approximately 45-minute biographical presentation is geared to grades 2–6. It's free, but donations are accepted.

Science

Ecology Center

117 North Division, Ann Arbor
734-761-3186

Offers hands-on environmental education and ecology presentations to school children of all ages. Can also call to schedule visit to Recycling and Education Station, 2420 South Industrial Highway, Ann Arbor. In addition, Recycle Ann Arbor, 2950 East Ellsworth, Ann Arbor, 734-662-6288, offers tours.

Dance

Eisenhower Dance

Ann Bak, Rochester
248-362-9329
Performance, demonstration, audience-participation programs, and residency for K–12.

Storytelling

The Fabricators

Milli P. and Ami D., Detroit
313-934-8635

Original folktales and creation stories. Ami and Milli also bring historical characters to life. For upper elementary–high school audiences and adults.

Storytelling, Animals

The Farm Lady

Margaret Schmidt
Maple Woods Homestead
25377 Wixom Road, Novi
248-349-4226

Using live animals, demonstrations, and stories, Margaret Schmidt introduces children to pioneer farm life. She brings Betsy the Pig with "Charlotte's Web," lambs for "Spring on the Farm," and a turkey with her harvest program. For preschool–sixth grade children.

Fitness

Fit-N-Fun Tumblebus

Fraser
810-329-3391

Children play games, sing songs, and learn gymnastics on tumbling equipment and gymnastic bars in the colorful school buses with padded walls and floors.

Theater

For A Good Time Theatre Company

Pat Parker, Saginaw
517-753-7891

History and literature is brought to life with humorous performances by adult professional actors. For grades K–8.

Nature/Recycling

For-Mar Nature Preserve

2142 North Genesee, Burton
810-789-8567

One-hour program geared for K–8 offers lessons on the environment, recycling, nature, and animals.

Music

Gemini

2000 Penncraft Ct., Ann Arbor
734-665-0165
1-800-317-9929

Twin brothers Sandor and Laszlo Slomovits, professionally known as Gemini, offer participatory concerts in elementary schools and for family audiences. The award-winning children's entertainers offer boisterous fun, incorporating a wide range of musical traditions and instruments into their songs.

Theater

Goodtime Network

Becky Fox
734-663-1430

Goodtime Players offer original musical comedies. Shows are approximately 30 to 45 minutes and geared for elementary children and families.

Magic

Gordon Russ

Ferndale
248-879-1943

Magician Gordon Russ involves kids of all ages in delightful mystery adventures and family magic shows.

Music

Harpbeat

Donna Novack and Maria Flurry
734-482-0220
1-800-KID-TUNES (recordings
248-879-1943 (bookings)

Using different languages (including American Sign Language), a variety of musical styles, and harp and percussion instruments, Harpbeat encourages children to sing along. For ages 4–12.

Transportation

Have Trains Will Travel

Gary Rollins
Farmington Hills
248-478-6691

Hands-on, interactive G-scale model train display and rail crossing safety presentation for grades K–12.

Dance

Hole in the Bog Mummers and Morris Dancers

Walt Schlichting
Point Sanilac
810-648-0227

Accompanied by live traditional music and song, the dancers perform age-old Celtic and British dances and raucous mummer's plays featuring the Fool, the Wild Man, Robin Hood, Maid Marion, St. George, and the Hobbyhorse.

Science/Animals

Howell Nature Center

1005 Triangle Lake Road, Howell
517-546-0249

Naturalists bring permanently injured mammals and wildlife into the classroom and teach children about wildlife preservation. The center also offers a high ropes adventure course and overnight facility.

Science

Huron-Clinton Metroparks

1-800-47-PARKS

Free slide and movie programs on southeast Michigan nature for grades K–12. Brochures are mailed in September. Act quickly; the programs are booked on a first-come, first-served basis.

Science

Impression 5 Science Center

200 Museum Drive, Lansing
517-485-8116

Entertaining science shows for grades K–12 introduce children to the world of science.

Storytelling

Jenifer Strauss Ivinskas

Hastings
616-945-4943

High participation, multi-cultural folktales, fairy tales, and legends. Storytelling concerts, residencies, and workshops for grades K–12 and adults.

Storytelling

Jerry Jacoby

Clark Lake
517-529-9110

Jacoby's G-rated stories encourage honesty, respect, responsibility, and better self-esteem. His middle school performances deal with peer pressure and decision making. For grades K–9.

Living History

Jim Neely's Traveling Museum of Living History

Brooklyn
517-592-6451
Neely recreates life in the 1700's through the early 1900's in dramatic first person narrations.

Storytelling, Puppets, Music

Joanne Manshum

Lansing
517-393-4384

Manshum weaves traditional tales and accompanies them on autoharp, hammered dulcimer, and Celtic harp. Manshum also performs stories dressed as a clown, accompanied by large puppets. In addition, she presents close-up puppet shows with hand puppets and offers workshops. For preschool–grade 5.

Music

Josh and Ron's Family Adventure

Ron Coden, Huntington Woods
248-541-3736

Longtime national celebrity musicians Josh White Jr. and Ron Coden blend their voices in an acoustic concert for all ages.

Storytelling

Judy Sima

Southfield
248-644-3951

Judy Sima offers her audience a variety of traditional tales, including ghost stories, children's literature, and humor. Children are encouraged to participate. Storytelling workshops are available for middle school age children to adults, as well as families.

Archeology and Ecology

Kelsey Museum of Archeology

434 South State Street, Ann Arbor
734-764-9304

Hands-on kits include educational materials and artifact reproductions, available to elementary and middle school classrooms.

Storytelling

LaRon Williams

Ann Arbor
734-665-0857

Using characterization, creative sound, and vocalization, Williams weaves stories from around the world, with an emphasis on African and African American tales. For preschool–adult.

Science

Louis E. Wint Nature Center—Starlab

Independence Oaks
9501 Sashabaw Road, Clarkston
248-625-6473

Starlab, a portable, inflatable planetarium, travels to schools for 45-minute, naturalist-led astronomy shows, suitable for first grade and older.

Storytelling

Linda Day

Livonia
248-478-6339

Linda Day weaves folktales, scary stories, humor, and participation tales for preschool–adult audiences. Middle and high school workshops are also available.

Wildlife Education

Little Creatures Co.

Dan Briere, Royal Oak
248-544-2239

Children get an up-close look at creepy crawly bugs, small exotic mammals, reptiles, and amphibians, and learn about animal habitats, food sources, and habits. For ages 4–12.

Science

Living Science Foundation

Plymouth
734-207-8291

Five entertaining, hands-on science shows for grades K–12, including "Tidepool Touch," "Rainforest," "Australian Outback," "Predators of the Deep," and "Natural Science." The Living Science Foundation instructors are widely known for their razzle-dazzle demonstrations and fine teaching skills. Classroom visits over school-wide assemblies preferred.

Animals

Lizard Lady's Reptile Review

Teress Killeen, Clinton
517-424-5099

Meet Fluffy, an iguana; Diva, a 12-foot-long albino Burmese python; and Bob, a 54-year-old red foot tortoise who snores. The Lizard Lady and her husband, the Reptile Wrangler, bring their reptile road show to schools, libraries, and birthday parties. A portion of their proceeds benefits the Rainforest Action Network.

History, Dance

Madame Cadillac Dance Theatre

15 East Kirby, Suite 903, Detroit
313-875-6354

Madame Cadillac Dance Theatre brings the French Colonial period and the history of Detroit's first settlers to life with authentic dance, music, and costumes. Their repertoire includes French court and country dances, "First Lady and the Voyager," and "Two Women of New France." Each show is 50 minutes and appeals to families and children of all ages.

Storytelling, Magic

Marc "Kodiak" LeJarett, Folk Magician

Three Rivers
616-279-6050

Journey with LaJarett as "Kodiak," the mountain man to mythical "Sasquatch County" as he recreates the rich heritage of American folklore.

Music

Marc Thomas

22549 Power, Farmington
248-879-1943, 248-478-0738

Thomas and his puppet, Max the Moose, offer sing-along fun, self-esteem, and reading inspiration concerts for preschool, elementary, and family audiences.

Music, Puppets

Maureen Schiffman

Novi
248-348-5083

Using movement, music, and puppets, Schiffman and her monkey puppet, Coco, engage preschool–elementary children in delightful sing-alongs and participatory concerts.

Aviation History

Michigan Balloon Corporation

Holly
1-800-968-8368

Michigan Balloon Corporation brings a hot air balloon to the schools, teaches children about the history of hot air ballooning from 1783 to the present, and ends with a hands-on demonstration of

how a balloon is inflated. For grades K–12 and adults.

Music, Theater
Michigan Opera Theatre

Community Programs Department
Detroit Opera House, 1526 Broadway, Detroit
313-237-7850

MOT offers top-notch creative traveling performances geared to children of all ages, plus traveling special educational programs such as master classes and workshops that supplement school curriculum. Performances are approximately 45 minutes. Classes and workshops are also offered at the Detroit Opera House during the summer.

Transportation
Miniature Motorways

Kevin Mark, Livonia
734-261-6169

Two six-lane slot car tracks, figure-eight and oval tracks offer children a chance to race two-inch model cars. The track and over 500 model cars are brought to your site. For ages 6 through adult.

Science
Mr. Wizard's Science Assembly Programs

Stan Randall, Walled Lake
1-800-537-0008

An assembly program of entertaining hands-on experiments, created by Don Herbert, better known as "Mr. Wizard," and performed by specially trained assistants. For grades K–8.

Science, Literature, Values
Mobile Ed Productions

26018 West Seven Mile, Redford
313-533-4455, 1-800-433-7459

Mobile Ed Productions offers a variety of educationally exciting programs for K to 12, including "Music Programs," "Self Esteem Programs," "Starlab Planetarium," "Mark Twain," "Chemistry, It Really Matters," "Animals Sensing Their World," "Lights, Camera, Action,"and "All About Us."

Theater

Mosaic Youth Theatre of Detroit

Brian McIntosh, Detroit
313-554-1422

Detroit's talented young adult actors offer a repertory of original educational and entertaining productions for grades K–12 and adults.

Music, Storytelling

Mustard's Retreat

David Tamulevich and Michael Hough
Ann Arbor
734-995-9066

Using a variety of instruments, including dulcimers, penny whistles, guitars, and harmonicas, Tamulevich and Hough perform family concerts full of audience participation, storytelling, lively folk songs, and Irish-type ballads and blues.

Storytelling, Music

Naim Abdur Rauf

Detroit
313-238-1498

Using traditional African drums and wearing traditional African dress, Abdur Rauf offers stories and songs that introduce children to African culture and history.

Puppets

Nancy Henk: Puppets To Go

Clinton Township
810-463-0480

Puppeteer Nancy Henk offers school puppet demonstrations, hands-on workshops, and adaptations of familiar stories using rod, hand, and shadow puppets, for ages 3–12. Henk also offers adult puppetry workshops.

Storytelling, Music
Norina David
Detroit
313-259-9023

David puts on an Underground Railroad performance and African heritage storytelling and song for schools and churches. She also offers theme skits, including a drug awareness program.

Recreation
Oakland County Mobile Recreation Units
248-858-0916

Mobile recreation units offer sports equipment, games, puppet shows, moonwalk, orbitron, skate-mobile, dunk tank, and traveling music show.

Drug & Safety Education
Officer Ollie and Friends
Wayne County Sheriff
1231 St. Antoine, Detroit
313-224-2234

For grades K–1, Officer Ollie offers "Don't Go with Strangers." For preschool–fifth grade, "Eddie Eagle Gun Safety." For grades 2–3, "Be a Winner, Say No to Drugs." For fourth grade, "Vandalism and Shoplifting." For grades 5–8, "Drug and Substance Abuse."

Mime
O.J. Anderson
Ann Arbor
734-668-0163

Using physical comedy and laughter, Anderson bridges the gap of important issues for school age children and adults.

Music

Omni Arts in Education

Claudia Rodgers, Detroit
313-864-3422

This non-profit organization brings professional dancers, visual artists, theater performers, and musicians into Metro Detroit schools to perform and teach children about their specialty.

Music

Peter Madcat Ruth

Ann Arbor
734-761-8518

An internationally acclaimed harmonica virtuoso, Madcat Ruth offers his original blend of folk music, blues, jazz, country, and rock and roll to children and adults of all ages.

Music, Puppets, Storytelling
Professor Ed U. Gator

The Royal American Folklore Theatre
132 South Arlington, Kalamazoo
1-800-435-0398

Using original puppets and theatrical story-telling, the professor engages children in classic Cajun, Creole, French, Irish, and Russian folktales.

Puppets
PuppetART

Detroit Puppet Theater, 25 East Grand River
313-961-7777

Classically trained Russian puppeteers bring their lavish puppet productions to schools and community sites. Each performance uses hand-made marionettes or rod puppets, artistic sets, and classical or folk music. For audiences of all ages.

Theater
Purple Rose Theatre

137 Park Street, Chelsea
734-475-5817

A touring theater company visits schools, pre-senting student theater arts workshops.

Theater, Music
A Reasonable Facsimile

Anne and Rob Burns, Rochester
248-651-2276

Specializing in music and theater from the Renaissance, Anne and Rob Burns offer children of all ages a humorous view of knights, dragons, rogues, and ladies. Dressed in Renaissance costume, they play multiple characters and a variety of musical instruments from the era, including gittern, dulcimer, recorders, fifes, shawms, and percussion. Reasonable Facsimile is available for Renaissance, dance, music, and theater workshops, festivals, assemblies, and concerts.

Puppets, Creative Writing

Red Rug Puppet Theatre

Beth Katz, East Lansing
517-332-8442

Puppeteer Beth Katz performs fairy tales and customized shows for school reading celebrations. Her performances are geared to elementary schools. She also offers puppetry workshops for teachers and preschool-elementary schools.

History

Richard Glaz

The Cooperage, 8832 Dixie, Fair Haven
810-725-2484

A devoted Civil War reenactor and owner of The Cooperage, a Civil War memorabilia museum, Glaz offers living history programs for scout and school groups.

Ventriloquist

Richard Paul

Macomb Township
1-800-579-8051

Ventriloquist Richard Paul offers a variety of comedy-ventriloquism shows with a message.

Dance

Sabsabu Dance Theatre

Marcelle Sashu Amen-Ra, Detroit
313-869-2007

With traditional percussion instruments and costume, Sabsabu Dancers perform traditional and contemporary West African dance-stories, offering a look at the cultural richness of West African folklore and folklife. Amen-Ra is available for dance workshops, classes, and curriculum enrichment.

Magic, Education

Scheer Magic Productions

Doug Scheer, Commerce Township
248-960-4422

Doug Scheer and his many alter egos perform magic shows for children of all ages. Scheer also offers educational shows—"Adventures in Reading," "Pollution Solution," "Uncle Sam's History Show," "Mystery of Science," "Spooktacular Halloween Show," "Arithme-tricks: a Math Magic Show," "The Adventures of Les Trouble," and "Memory Madness"—for elementary schools and youth groups.

Music

Sheila Ritter

Ann Arbor
734-973-0684

Ritter energizes the 2–10 set with a concert of sing-alongs, movement songs, songs from many cultures, and traditional children's favorites.

Music

SongSister Julie Austin

Ann Arbor
734-677-3575

Julie Austin performs solo and with SongBrother David Mosher on a variety of instruments, including guitar, violin, banjo, autoharp, mandolin, jawharp, recorders, and even nose flute. The concerts, geared to preschool–upper elementary school children and their families, mix stories, humor, songs, movement, and educational concepts. Austin also offers music workshops for educators.

Divorce, Values, Drugs

SPACE Presents

26400 Lahser Road, Suite 100, Southfield
248-355-9936

A repertory of original 30-minute plays about issues, including divorce, peer pressure, and drugs, that young people face today, followed by a facilitated discussion. For grades 5–12.

Animals

Species Survival Center
4990 Ann Arbor-Saline Road, Ann Arbor
734-998-0790

Live exotic animals, including leopards, owls, alligators, giant toads, and two-toed sloths, are brought into the classroom for a variety of hands-on presentations. "Rain Forest Animals," "Reptiles and Amphibians," "Animmal Adaptations," "Endangered Species," and "Animal Classification" are geared to grades 1–12 and approximately 50 minutes long. The "Mini Program" for preschool and kindergarten is 25–30 minutes long.

Music, Comedy

The Spoon Man
Jim Cruise, Grand Rapids
1-800-968-7469

Interactive comedian Cruise offers wacky audience participation spoon-playing programs for all ages.

Magic, Education

Stevens and Associates
Bernie Stevens
747 West Maple, Suite 501, Clawson
1-800-4-BERNIE

A full-service entertainment agency and event planner.

Creative Writing, Theater

Storybuilders
Helena Timmerman, Roseville
810-771-5222

Storybuilders will come into the classroom with improvisational skits to help motivate creative writing and teach students how to compose stories. If student stories are sent at least one week before Storybuilders' visit, they will bring those stories to life in light-hearted vignettes.

Music, Storytelling
The Storytellers

Robert Allison, Detroit
313-884-2780

Using state-of-the-art audio technology and ancient instruments, The Storytellers accompany their world tales with Brazilian melodies, African rhythms, Caribbean tunes, and original compositions. For all ages.

Puppets
String Puppet Theatre

Bill Siemers, Tecumseh
517-423-2414

Traditional fairytales and folktales are presented using 32-inch hand-carved marionettes with colorful costumes and hand-painted scenery. Siemers also offers science shows, and old-time medicine shows. For children of all ages.

Fitness
Tumble Bunnies Gymnastic and Dance

734-697-2352

Gymnastic and dance programs for ages 2 1/2–14.

Science
U of M Exhibit Museum

1109 Geddes Avenue, Ann Arbor
734-763-4190

Offers outreach to schools with "Journey Through Space."

Animals

Upland Hills Farm

481 Lake George Road, Oxford
248-628-1611

Farmer Webster takes the animals on the road with a wide variety of farm programs that teach children where food and fiber originate. Available March and April.

Values

"VI-PEERS"

Detroit Vipers
Palace of Auburn Hills
2 Championship Drive, Auburn Hills
248-377-0100

Representatives from the Vipers teach simple messages on teamwork, staying in school, drug and alcohol awareness, and goal setting. The 45-minute program is geared to grades K–6.

Theater

Wild Swan Theater

416 West Huron, Ann Arbor
734-995-0530

Wild Swan Theater performs children's theater for grades preschool–6 in a storytelling style using masks, theater, music, and puppets. Their productions are also accessible for and hearing- and visually-impaired children through American Sign Language interpretation and audio-description.

Performing Arts

Wolf Trap Institute for Early Learning through the Arts

(In cooperation with Michigan Association for Education of Young Children)
Todd Greenbaum, Michigan Director
248-651-9653

Wolf Trap Institute, a national non-profit organization with satellites in seven other states, trains professional performing artists to go into the classrooms to help teachers integrate the performing arts into their curriculum. Programs are geared for ages 3–5. Residencies are seven weeks or one week.

Ecology, Values

World Game Michigan Project

Upland Hills Ecological Awareness Center
2575 Indian Lake Road, Oxford
248-693-1021

Multi-media presentation involves students in a hands-on role-playing game. A giant map becomes the game board, and children role-play world leaders, developing strategies "to make the world work for 100% of humanity." For grades 4–9.

Values, Conflict Resolution

A World of Difference

Anti-Defamation League of B'nai Brith (ADL)
Southfield
248-355-3730

A diversity education program that provides training and materials for educators, students, parents, and industry and community leaders that is designed to combat racial, ethnic, and religious prejudice. The program helps participants develop skills, sensitivity, and knowledge to effectively live in our multi-cultural world. The program can be adapted to fit individual needs.

Science

Young Entomologists Society

Gary Dunn, Lansing
517-886-0630

Gary Dunn brings artifacts, collections, 3-D models, puppets, and live bugs into the classroom with a lively format that debunks insect and spider myths. Preschool–high school.

Thank You, Thank You

The artwork appearing on the cover and at the beginning of each chapter was created by the following area students:

Book cover art based on drawings by
Caitlin Tetrick (trees), Eagle Elementry School
Felicia Washington (bridge), Lessenger Middleschool
Ali Vogt (sun with glasses), The Roeper School
Trevor Toski (boat), Jayno Adams School
Meg Ernoznik (map of Michigan), Jayno Adams School
James Ciennik (balloon), Jayno Adams School

Title page:
Brenda Orozco, Parkman Elementary School

Dedication page:
Leticia Salas, Taft Elementary School

Contents:
Jason Rosenbaum, Doherty Elementary School

Preface:
Stevie Hendershot, Doherty Elementary School

Chapter 1:
Daketria Reid, Detroit, Cooper Elementary

Chapter 2:
Amanda Clark, Detroit, Parkman Elementary

Chapter 3:
Alissa Arden, Eagle Elementary

Chapter 4:
Majesty Dodson, Wyandotte, Garfield
Elementary

Chapter 5:
Jacquelene Easly, West Bloomfield, Doherty
Elementary

Chapter 6:
Shana Kirby, Detroit, Lessenger Middle
School

Chapter 7:
Brian Greiner, The Grosse Pointe Academy

Chapter 8:
Jessica Iafrate, Rochester Hills, University
Hills Elementary

Chapter 9:
Stacey Mitchell, The Roeper School

Chapter 10:
Juliann Gillespie, Waterford, Adams Jayno
Elementary

Chapter 11:
Faten Algatross, Warren, Siersma
Elementary

Chapter 12:
Kamaljit Chalal, Detroit, Burton International

Chapter 13:
Sarah Hawkins, Southgate, Allen Elementary

Chapter 14:
Zena Yaldo, Southfield, Leonhard Elementary

Chapter 15:
Yerik Garza, Detroit, Webster Elementary

Thank You, Thank You:
Amanda Kranson, Siersma Elementary
School

I'd also like to thank the following students and their art teachers for participating in the *Detroit Kids Catalog* Art Project. (Students are listed according to the school they attended in spring 1999.)

Adams Jayno Elementary, Waterford (teacher, Ann Hoydic), James Ciennick, Meg Erznoznik, Elizabeth Fogg, Juliann Gillespie, Andrew Harness, Susan Katchka, Jeffrey Kelly, Alex Land, Cody Martz, Brian Peters, Kelsey Schmidt, Kyle Tatsak, Trevor Toski, Jessica Woodruff, Kelsey Zukowski.

Allen Elementary, Southgate (teacher, Tina Doepker), Mary Bocks, Callie Bruley, Jill Burnette, Sarah Hawkins, Danny Jarbo, Stephanie Layne, Lindsay Pastor, Kaitlyn Roldan, Brittany Sheridan.

Burton International, Detroit (teacher, Janice Pou-Price), Kamiljit Chahal, Samuel George, Gabriel Harris, Jonathan Harris, Khemet McCauley.

Cooper Elementary, Detroit (teacher, Carol Steinfeldt), Kiya Barden, John Blue, Quartez Danforth, Kouther Elghazali, Daketria Reid, Austin Williams, Silvanus Willis.

Doherty Elementary, West Bloomfield (teacher, Janice Katz), Daniel Atoche, Carly Cenit, Sara Chadwick, Jaquelene Easely, Jon Garmo, Harry Hantman, Stevie Hendershot, Eslam Kersha, Alex Mishulin, Anita Odish, Vanessa Oram, David Portney, Jason Rosenbaum, Arthur Wang, Takuyuki Watanabe, Adriana Walters.

Eagle Elementary, West Bloomfield (teacher, Susan Drucker), Wesal Abdal, Alissa Arden, Allison Eckler, Amar Grewal, Hayley Imhoff, Tricia Jacobs, Zara Mogilevskaya, C.J. Opperthauser, Jessica Poota, Caitlin Tetrick, Christina Van Dyke.

Garfield Elementary, Wyandotte (teacher, Tonya Au), Kelsey Adkins, Travis Brown, Karen Buchko, Majesty Dodson, Adrienne Ferrante, George Findlay, Jessica Franks, Kathleen Hasselbach, Bobby Kaczor, Kaylee Moore, Alicia Mullins, Stephen Orr, Anthony Pearce, Cody Roberts, Leticia Salas, Thomas Turner.

The Grosse Pointe Academy, Grosse Pointe Farms (teacher, Rich Stark), Chelsea

Baumgarten, Billy Conway, Evan Feringa, Brian Greiner, Jessica Leonard, Tim Lengel, Paige Louisell, Katherine Olson, Daniel Ratliff, Liz Ridgway, James Spica, Monique Squiers, Kaitlyn Vanelslander, Alexander Wildner, Barrett Young.

Leonhard Elementary, Southfield (teacher, Joanne Brown), Aruq Asare, Alison Davis, Brittany Davis, Samantha Ann Dickow, Bianca K. Eader, Ashley Gordon, Elizabeth Harvin, Ashley Perry, Cristsandra Vance, Zena Yaldo.

Lessenger Middle School, Detroit (teacher, Robin McDaniel), Megan Benkert, DeJuan Calloway, Jessica Conley, Anthony Jeron Davis III, Shana Kirby, Jason Moore, Miguel Pardo, Christopher Soule, Robert Stonestreet, Ivan D. Tarver, Felicia Washington, Lindsey Williams.

Parkman Elementary, Detroit (teacher, Lina Wesson), Amanda Clark, Dora DeLeon, Patrick Gardner, Alicia Johnson, Jenell Morris, Brenda Orozco, Charles Smith, Brittni Taylor, Tiffany Thompson, Tareal Webster.

The Roeper School, Bloomfield Hills (teacher, Jarie Ruddy), Sharif Al-Hadidi, Allyson David, Ali Dietz, Sarah Ewing, David Golden, Jared Karlow, Lisa Lederman, Blayne Milbeck, Stacey Mitchell, Mona Nance, Kassie Parrott, Ali Vogt, Megan Wampler, Chelsea Wilmoth, Bethany Zanke.

Siersma Elementary, Warren (teacher, Bridget White), Faten Algatroos , Greg Broadwell, Mae Kasha, Amanda Kranson, Olivia Putrus, Ryan Sucaet, Devin Wilder.

University Hills Elementary, Rochester Hills (teacher, Sally Faudie), Jenna Clark, Jordan Evanson, Riley Frenak, Jessica Iafrate, Manami Inoue, Taylor Lauver, Ryan Leclerc, Sean McCauley, Lindi Nelson, Zack Reed, Alexander M. Rosenau, Mark Sandberg, Amanda Schlagel, Whitney Shyu, Scott Skrzynski.

Webster Elementary, Detroit (teacher, Goldie Martinez), Luis Chapa, Latia Davis, Jerry Fernandez, Yanalin Flores, Jessica Frierson, Yerik Garza, Janae Griggs, Justin King, Leanne Lin, Darnell Milburn, Rita Murillo, Cristina Plascencia, Sandra Tapia, Claudia Vargas, Xin Xin Yao.

Index

This index lists sites and activities, both specific and general. For a complete listing of sites by city, please see Chapter 2, A City Listing of Sites.

Michigan Lumbertowns: Lumbermen and Laborers in Saginaw, Bay City, and Muskegon, 1870–1905, by Jeremy W. Kilar, 1990

Detroit Kids Catalog: The Hometown Tourist, by Ellyce Field, 1990

Waiting for the News, by Leo Litwak, 1990 (reprint)

Detroit Perspectives, edited by Wilma Wood Henrickson, 1991

Life on the Great Lakes: A Wheelsman's Story, by Fred W. Dutton, edited by William Donohue Ellis, 1991

Copper Country Journal: The Diary of Schoolmaster Henry Hobart, 1863–1864, by Henry Hobart, edited by Philip P. Mason, 1991

John Jacob Astor: Business and Finance in the Early Republic, by John Denis Haeger, 1991

Survival and Regeneration: Detroit's American Indian Community, by Edmund J. Danziger, Jr., 1991

Steamboats and Sailors of the Great Lakes, by Mark L. Thompson, 1991

Cobb Would Have Caught It: The Golden Age of Baseball in Detroit, by Richard Bak, 1991

Michigan in Literature, by Clarence Andrews, 1992

Under the Influence of Water: Poems, Essays, and Stories, by Michael Delp, 1992

The Country Kitchen, by Della T. Lutes, 1992 (reprint)

The Making of a Mining District: Keweenaw Native Copper 1500–1870, by David J. Krause, 1992

Kids Catalog of Michigan Adventures, by Ellyce Field, 1993

Henry's Lieutenants, by Ford R. Bryan, 1993

Historic Highway Bridges of Michigan, by Charles K. Hyde, 1993

Lake Erie and Lake St. Clair Handbook, by Stanley J. Bolsenga and Charles E. Herndendorf, 1993

Queen of the Lakes, by Mark Thompson, 1994

Iron Fleet: The Great Lakes in World War II, by George J. Joachim, 1994

Turkey Stearnes and the Detroit Stars: The Negro Leagues in Detroit, 1919–1933, by Richard Bak, 1994

Pontiac and the Indian Uprising, by Howard H. Peckham, 1994 (reprint)

Charting the Inland Seas: A History of the U.S. Lake Survey, by Arthur M. Woodford, 1994 (reprint)

Ojibwa Narratives of Charles and Charlotte Kawbawgam and Jacques LePique, 1893–1895. Recorded with Notes by Homer H. Kidder, edited by Arthur P. Bourgeois, 1994, co-published with the Marquette County Historical Society

Strangers and Sojourners: A History of Michigan's Keweenaw Peninsula, by Arthur W. Thurner, 1994

Win Some, Lose Some: G. Mennen Williams and the New Democrats, by Helen Washburn Berthelot, 1995

Sarkis, by Gordon and Elizabeth Orear, 1995

The Northern Lights: Lighthouses of the Upper Great Lakes, by Charles K. Hyde, 1995 (reprint)

Kids Catalog of Michigan Adventures, second edition, by Ellyce Field, 1995

Rumrunning and the Roaring Twenties: Prohibition on the Michigan-Ontario Waterway, by Philip P. Mason, 1995

In the Wilderness with the Red Indians, by E. R. Baierlein, translated by Anita Z. Boldt, edited by Harold W. Moll, 1996

Elmwood Endures: History of a Detroit Cemetery, by Michael Franck, 1996

Master of Precision: Henry M. Leland, by Mrs. Wilfred C. Leland with Minnie Dubbs Millbrook, 1996 (reprint)

Haul-Out: New and Selected Poems, by Stephen Tudor, 1996

Kids Catalog of Michigan Adventures, third edition, by Ellyce Field, 1997

Beyond the Model T: The Other Ventures of Henry Ford, revised edition, by Ford R. Bryan, 1997

Young Henry Ford: A Picture History of the First Forty Years, by Sidney Olson, 1997 (reprint)

The Coast of Nowhere: Meditations on Rivers, Lakes and Streams, by Michael Delp, 1997

From Saginaw Valley to Tin Pan Alley: Saginaw's Contribution to American Popular Music, 1890–1955, by R. Grant Smith, 1998

The Long Winter Ends, by Newton G. Thomas, 1998 (reprint)

Bridging the River of Hatred: The Pioneering Efforts of Detroit Police Commissioner George Edwards, 1962–1963, by Mary M. Stolberg, 1998

Toast of the Town: The Life and Times of Sunnie Wilson, by Sunnie Wilson with John Cohassey, 1998

These Men Have Seen Hard Service: The First Michigan Sharpshooters in the Civil War, by Raymond J. Herek, 1998

A Place for Summer: One Hundred Years at Michigan and Trumbull, by Richard Bak, 1998

Early Midwestern Travel Narratives: An Annotated Bibliography, 1634–1850, by Robert R. Hubach, 1998 (reprint)

All-American Anarchist: Joseph A. Labadie and the Labor Movement, by Carlotta R. Anderson, 1998

Michigan in the Novel, 1816–1996: An Annotated Bibliography, by Robert Beasecker, 1998

"Time by Moments Steals Away": The 1848 Journal of Ruth Douglass, by Robert L. Root, Jr., 1998

The Detroit Tigers: A Pictorial Celebration of the Greatest Players and Moments in Tigers' History, updated edition, by William M. Anderson, 1999

Father Abraham's Children: Michigan Episodes in the Civil War, by Frank B. Woodford, 1999 (reprint)

Letter from Washington, 1863–1865, by Lois Bryan Adams, edited and with an introduction by Evelyn Leasher, 1999

Wonderful Power: The Story of Ancient Copper Working in the Lake Superior Basin, by Susan R. Martin, 1999

A Sailor's Logbook: A Season aboard Great Lakes Freighters, by Mark L. Thompson, 1999

Lakes Freighters, by Mark L. Thompson, 1999

Huron: The Seasons of a Great Lake, by Napier Shelton, 1999

Tin Stackers: The History of the Pittsburgh Steamship Company, by Al Miller, 1999

Art in Detroit Public Places, revised edition, text by Dennis Nawrocki, photographs by David Clements, 1999

Brewed in Detroit: Breweries and Beers Since 1830, by Peter H. Blum, 1999

Enterprising Images: The Goodridge Brothers, African American Photographers, 1847–1922, by John Vincent Jezierski, 2000

Detroit Kids Catalog: A Family Guide for the 21st Century, by Ellyce Field, 2000

Still not sure what to do with the kids? Call your neighborhood library for a list of free family programs, including storytelling, puppet shows, and movies. Or call the departments of parks and recreation and community education in your city. You'll find a wealth of seasonal events, workshops, classes, and sports programs listed in their brochures. Most cities also offer a variety of enrichment opportunities for children with disabilities.

I'd love to hear about your family's adventures and experiences. How has this book helped you? Have I missed any of your favorite sites? Have you found any of the information incorrect or confusing?

Your feedback will help me with the next edition of the Detroit Kids Catalog. Write to Ellyce Field, P.O. Box 250490, Franklin, Michigan, 48025-0490. Be sure to include your name, address, and phone so I can reach you for further clarification.

I frequently speak to families and newcomers on the topics "Spending Time with the Kids" and "A Guide's Guide to Michigan Sites and Activities." If your school or community group would like to book me for a program, contact me at the above post office box.

To purchase additional copies of Kids Catalog of Michigan Adventures, visit your local bookstore, or call 1-800-WSU-READ to order books from Wayne State University Press.